A Shrinking World ?

Global Unevenness and Inequality

The Shape of the World Course Team

The Open University

John Allen	Senior Lecturer in Economic Geography and Course Team Chair
James Anderson	Senior Lecturer in Geography
Robin Arkle	Graphic Designer, BBC
Melanie Bayley	Editor
Brian Beeley	Senior Lecturer in Geography
Pam Berry	Compositor, TPS
John Blunden	Reader in Geography
Chris Brook	Lecturer in Geography
Margaret Charters	Course Secretary
Allan Cochrane	Senior Lecturer in Urban Studies
Debbie Crouch	Graphic Designer
Stuart Hall	Professor of Sociology
Chris Hamnett	Professor of Urban Geography
Fiona Harris	Editor
Christina Janoszka	Course Manager
Pat Jess	Lecturer in Geography
Jack Leathem	Producer, BBC
Michele Marsh	Secretary
Doreen Massey	Professor of Geography
Anthony McGrew	Senior Lecturer in Politics
Diane Mole	Graphic Designer
Eleanor Morris	Series Producer, BBC
Ray Munns	Graphic Artist
Judith Rolph	Series Production Assistant, BBC
Philip Sarre	Senior Lecturer in Geography
Paul Smith	Media Librarian
Doreen Warwick	Discipline Secretary
Kathy Wilson	Production Assistant, BBC
Chris Wooldridge	Editor

External Assessor

Nigel Thrift	Professor of Geography, University of Bristol

Consultants

Rick Ball	Tutor Panel
Erlet Cater	Lecturer in Geography, University of Reading
Ray Hall	Senior Lecturer in Geography, University of London
Russell King	Professor of Geography, University of Sussex
Andrew Leyshon	Lecturer in Geography, University of Hull
Matthew Lockwood	Lecturer in Sociology, University of Sussex
Jenny Meegan	Tutor Panel
Richard Meegan	Senior Lecturer in Geography, University of Liverpool
Phil Pinch	Tutor Panel
Gillian Rose	Lecturer in Geography, University of Edinburgh
Steven Yearley	Professor of Sociology, University of Ulster

The Shape of the World: Explorations in Human Geography

Volume 1: Geographical Worlds
Edited by John Allen and Doreen Massey

Volume 2: A Shrinking World? Global Unevenness and Inequality
Edited by John Allen and Chris Hamnett

Volume 3: An Overcrowded World? Population, Resources and the Environment
Edited by Philip Sarre and John Blunden

Volume 4: A Place in the World? Places, Culture and Globalization
Edited by Doreen Massey and Pat Jess

Volume 5: A Global World? Re-ordering Political Space
Edited by James Anderson, Chris Brook and Allan Cochrane

A Shrinking World ?

Global Unevenness and Inequality

edited by
John Allen and Chris Hamnett

The Open University

OXFORD
UNIVERSITY PRESS

The five volumes of the series form part of the second-level Open University course D215 *The Shape of the World*. If you wish to study this or any other Open University course, details can be obtained from the Central Enquiry Service, PO Box 200, The Open University, Milton Keynes, MK7 6YZ.

For availability of the video- and audiocassette materials, contact Open University Educational Enterprises Ltd (OUEE), 12 Cofferidge Close, Stony Stratford, Milton Keynes, MK11 1BY.

OXFORD
UNIVERSITY PRESS

Great Clarendon Street, Oxford OX2 6DP

Oxford University Press is a department of the University of Oxford.
It furthers the University's objective of excellence in research, scholarship,
and education by publishing worldwide in

Oxford New York

Auckland Bangkok Bogotá Buenos Aires Calcutta
Cape Town Chennai Dar es Salaam Delhi Hong Kong Istanbul
Karachi Kuala Lumpur Madrid Melbourne Mexico City Mumbai Nairobi
São Paulo Shanghai Taipei Tokyo Toronto

Oxford is a registered trade mark of Oxford University Press
in the UK and in certain other countries

Published in the United States
by Oxford University Press Inc., New York

Published in association with The Open University

Edited, designed and typeset by The Open University

Printed and bound in Great Britain by
Butler and Tanner Ltd, Frome, Somerset

A catalogue record for this book is available from the British Library

Library of Congress Cataloging in Publication Data applied for

ISBN 0 19 874187 1 (paper)
ISBN 0 19 874186 3 (cloth)

A Shrinking World?

Global Unevenness and Inequality

Contents

Preface

A Shrinking World? Global Unevenness and Inequality is the second of five volumes in a new series of human geography teaching texts. The series, entitled *The Shape of the World: Explorations in Human Geography* is designed as an introduction to the principal themes of geographical thought: namely, those of space, place and the environment. The five volumes form the central part of an Open University course, with the same title as that of the series. Each volume, however, is free-standing and can be studied on its own or as part of a wide range of social science courses in universities and colleges.

The series is built around an exploration of many of the key issues which are shaping our world as we move into the twenty-first century and which, above all else, are geographical in character. Each volume in various ways engages with taken-for-granted notions such as those of nature, distance, movement, sustainability, the identity of places and local cultures to put together what may be referred to as the building blocks of our geographical imagination.

In fact, our understanding of the nature of the geographical imagination is one of three shared features which distinguish the five volumes as a series. In developing the contribution that geography can make to our understanding of a changing world and our place within it, each volume has something distinct to offer. A second feature of the volumes is that the majority of chapters include a number of selected readings – extracts drawn from books and articles – which relate closely to the line of argument and which are integral to the discussion as it develops. The relevant readings can be found at the end of the chapter to which they relate and are printed in two columns to distinguish them from the main teaching text. The third shared feature of the volumes is the student-orientated nature of the teaching materials. Each volume is intended as part of an interactive form of study, with activities and summaries built into the flow of the text. These features are intended to help readers to grasp, consider and retain the main ideas and arguments of each chapter. The wide margins – in which you will find highlighted the concepts that are key to the teaching – are also intended for student use, such as making notes and points for reflection.

While each book is self-contained, there are a number of references back (and a small number of references forward) to the other books in the series. For those readers who wish to use the books as an exploration in human geography, you will find the references to chapters in the other volumes printed in bold type. This is particularly relevant to the final chapters of Volumes 2–5 as they form a sequence of chapters designed to highlight the uneven character of global development today. On a related teaching point, we have sometimes referred to the group of less developed and developing countries by the term 'third world', in inverted commas to convey the difficulty of continuing to include the diverse range of countries – which embraces some rapidly industrializing nations – under this conventional category. The 'disappearance' of a second world, with the demise of the Communist bloc, also questions the usefulness of the category and, in one way, simply reaffirms the significance of the world's changing geography.

Finally, it remains only to thank those who have helped to shape this Open University course. The names of those responsible for the production of this course are given in the list of Course Team members on page *ii*. Of those, we would like to extend our thanks to a number of them in particular. It is fair to say that the course would not have had the shape that it does were it not for the breadth of intellectual scholarship provided by our external assessor, Professor Nigel Thrift. Over a two-year period, Nigel, among other activities, commented and offered constructive advice on every draft chapter discussed by the Course Team – in all, some eighty-plus drafts! The Course Team owe him a major debt. We also owe a special debt to our Tutor Panel – Rick Ball, Jenny Meegan and Phil Pinch – for their ceaseless concern that the teaching materials were precisely that: materials which actually do teach. Our editors at the Open University, Melanie Bayley and Fiona Harris, not only raised the professional standard of the series as a whole with their meticulous editing, they also became involved at an early stage in the course's life and thus were able to smooth the path of its development. Thanks also to Ray Munns for his cartographic zeal and to Paul Smith, our media librarian, who, as ever, translated our vague descriptions of this or that image into an impressive array of illustrations. The typographic design and initial cover idea were developed by Diane Mole who then relinquished the course to Debbie Crouch; their expertise has transformed our typescripts into this handsome series of volumes. The speed and accuracy with which the multiple drafts were turned round by Margaret Charters and Doreen Warwick also deserves our special thanks. Without their excellent secretarial support, the course would not be in any shape at all.

Lastly, in the collaborative style of work by which Open University courses are produced, the awesome task of co-ordinating the efforts of the Course Team and ensuring that the materials are produced to schedule, falls to that of the course manager. It is still a source of amazement to us how our course manager, Christina Janoszka, managed this task as if it were no task at all. We owe her probably more than she is aware.

John Allen
on behalf of
The Open University Course Team

Introduction

The world is shrinking – or so it seems. At the end of the twentieth century, distances are not what they used to be. True, fifty miles is still fifty miles if you pace it out, but our ability to cross such distances has altered greatly and so too has our notion of just how far is fifty miles. Places that were once thought of as far apart, distant from one another in terms of miles or kilometres, now appear accessible as if they were just beyond the next corner. Transport and communications have come a long way in the last thirty years or so. All kinds of technologies that bear little resemblance to the multicoloured jumble of plastic-coated wires that make up the modern telephone system enable us to communicate with people half-way across the globe as if they were present. Developments in air and rail transport move more people further and faster than ever before. Jumbo jets shrink the oceans and the vast land masses of the globe, whilst high-speed trains race across the landscape at a breathtaking pace. And if we choose not to travel to other parts of the world, people and places come to us in the shape of television images, foods, clothes, music and the like. The abiding impression is of a world in which everywhere is within reach and the far-off is, quite simply, no longer so.

This is the distinctive geographical moment that many take us to be living through. It is a period of accelerated change which, in some of the ways described above, is said to be making the world 'smaller'. The time taken to go back and forth between places has, in one sense, shrunk the map of the world. Our sense of space and of time have been compressed. On this view, nations and continents still look to be in about the right place on the globe, but in distance terms what is near and what is far has altered. Places that were once thought of as remote, distant in cultural terms, are now represented as familiar, as if the social distance between people and places had been crossed. In other words, the lines that connect places, that draw more and more of the globe into a web of interconnections, from faxes and satellite link-ups to long-haul tourist flights, have disrupted our sense of distance and brought people and places closer together.

To be caught up in this geographical moment is to see ourselves as part of this shrinking world. It is to feel comfortable with the common image of a globe that has become progressively smaller over time. For some, this imagery is primarily what globalization is all about: a world which is not only easier to get around, but also one characterized by closer, integrated ties and connections. Compelling as such representations are, however, we need to step back a little and explore further the nature of this moment. If the world is shrinking in distance terms, it is not necessarily shrinking for everyone in all locations. The experience of *time–space compression* is and has been a historically and geographically uneven and unequal process.

If the impression is true, for instance, as one commentator has observed, that we are now 'all in each other's backyard', then that is because some people have never left their own, as much as it is because other people possess the currency, both economic and political, to drop in on virtually anybody's 'backyard'. Without access to the world of communications or the price of an air or rail ticket, the only hustle and bustle of daily life that you will probably know about is your own.

Equally there is no straightforward relationship between travel and mobility and the lowering of social as well as spatial horizons. Travel may well involve an insight into other people's lives in their 'backyards', but it may just as easily curb understanding if, for instance, those who travel take with them their own assorted cultural baggage as a means of insulating themselves from the realities of life elsewhere. To come into contact with cultures from other parts of the world, whether it be through the lines of a satellite television link-up or through the lines of high-speed air and rail travel, is always a mediated encounter. Places are often constructed in our minds before we journey to them and such impressions may be difficult to dislodge or to modify (see **Massey, 1995**[*]). It would be wrong, therefore, to simply associate travel and movement with greater social awareness.

More broadly, there are large tracts of the globe with few lines connecting them to anywhere, only lines of communication and transport that stretch across them. Parts of Africa, for instance, are quite literally off all kinds of maps – maps of telecommunications, maps of world trade and finance, maps of global tourism and the like. Other less developed parts of the globe, within and beyond the countries of the rich, industrialized world are only tangentially tied into the global web of interconnections which sustains the image of a world that is shrinking in size.

To think about a world shrinking in this way, that is with some people and some places as part of the process and others, as it were, by-passed, also draws attention to the nature of the interconnections. The fact that only some people and places are bound together by a multiplicity of connections is one aspect of the latest wave of globalization. Another aspect that matters is *how* you are tied in. For example, there are a variety of connections which criss-cross the globe, some of which we have spoken about, such as the flows of information, media images, trade and finance, as well as the links of travel and telecommunications. Other forms of connection, such as the movement of political refugees, exiles and migrants or the flow of capital investments by transnational corporations around the globe or, indeed, the plumes of pollution that in some cases accompany them, are all part of the configuration of ties that stretch across the world. But not all ties are of the same kind. Different kinds of connections reveal different kinds of social relationships and hold different consequences for those involved.

Take, for instance, the tourists mentioned earlier who restrict their experience of other parts of the world to patterns that mesh securely with their own preconceptions. The social interactions across distances are not only limited in this case, they are also markedly unequal. The lines of tourist travel which connect, say, Europe and North America to the Caribbean islands are not of the same significance to both ends. An island such as Dominica, for example, needs tourism for its economic survival. It is vulnerable to sudden changes in demand among tourists from Europe and North America. In contrast, there is virtually no risk or indeed vulnerability attached to the travel plans of the tourists from the developed 'North' who choose to go there. The two ends of the connection are thus tied together in an unequal manner.

The same is true of political refugees and economic migrants, where the relationship of inequality is even more marked. As with tourists, they are part

[*] A reference in emboldened type denotes a chapter in another volume of the series.

and parcel of the flow of people across the globe, but unlike tourists their movement lacks a degree of choice. Political refugees from Sri Lanka, Somalia and the Sudan, for example, do not leave their own countries and enter Europe by choice. Mobility and contact with other parts of the world take on a different set of meanings in this context and draw attention to the unequal ability of groups to take charge of the process of movement. If we were to explore the different worlds of multinationals and their workforces, we would undoubtedly find a similar set of skewed abilities.

In short, there are many different kinds of social relations stretched across space and it is this network of social relationships across the globe, in all its variety and overlap, which is the concern of this book. It draws upon some of the insights explored in the first volume of the series, *Geographical Worlds*, to examine some of the connections, flows and movements, which comprise *social space*. One of the aims of this volume is to open up the issue of social space in a number of ways, not just in terms of, say, the ability of the latest in electronic highways to shrink the globe, but in ways that address the social content and implications of these changing geographies.

o   o   o   o   o

We have attempted to do this by selecting a range of topics which reveal something of the changing social relations stretched across space. As with any selection, the range of topics, from global finance, manufacturing multinationals, world cities through to the environmental consequences of much of today's global economic activity, is far from exhaustive. Each chapter, however, reveals or builds upon one or more aspect of social space, and in the final chapter those different aspects are drawn together.

In this volume we stop short of considering the impact that the networks of social relationships stretched across the globe has in particular places. This is the subject matter of Volume 4, *A Place in the World? Culture, Places and Globalization*. Likewise, the other volumes in the series pick up on geographical themes touched upon in this volume, such as environment and nature and the local character of global relations, and develop them further.

As the title of this volume – *A Shrinking World? Global Unevenness and Inequality* – indicates, the nature of the engagement with the broad idea that there has been a collapse of distance, that the world is somehow smaller today than hitherto, is one of critical reflection. In the opening chapter, 'Annihilating space: the speed-up of communications', Andrew Leyshon explores how distances have changed over time as the result of shifts in both these aspects of our lives. As he points out, the revolutions in transport and communications over the previous 150 years, but especially the last fifty years, have greatly reduced the 'friction of distance' imposed on movement and social interaction. They have also increased many people's awareness and knowledge of the world beyond their own front doors. The accelerated movement of people, products and images over space has effectively brought many places closer together. Film and television images, for example, have transformed the ways in which we make sense of the world. The world is said to be shrinking not just because it is easier to get around; it is also shrinking because, as noted earlier, we can get a sense of the world without moving very far at all.

The chapter goes on to argue that the shrinking of distance in terms of time–space has important implications for our attempts to understand and explain the world in which we live. The actions of people on the far side of the globe may now have as much, if not more, immediate influence on what happens locally as of those present. Formerly isolated and virtually self-contained places have become increasingly interdependent. And the outcome of all this, if we are to believe the work of Marshall McLuhan on the 'global village', is a disorientating shift in social organization and awareness.

Does the idea, then, that the world is shrinking mean the end of geography, where geographical location matters much less these days? On the contrary, the chapter shows that not only are some locations more important than before, but the world is shrinking in an uneven and unequal manner. Although the rise of mass transport has enabled more people to travel greater distances more often, many people are still limited in their mobility and trapped by space. The different relationship to time–space compression has tended to increase the physical and social distance between rich and poor.

This analysis is taken a step further by looking at the linkages between the financial system and time–space compression. In recent years the international money markets have experienced a remarkable compression of space and time, not least because of the evolution of money into new forms which have become progressively less material and which enable it to be moved around the world virtually instantaneously at little cost. Money has become hyper-mobile. But, rather than heralding the end of geography, these developments have encouraged the emergence of global financial centres which organize global flows and approximate, both in terms of instantaneity and disorientation, to McLuhan's view of life in the 'global village'. Although the rapid spread of new electronic technologies has helped to undermine the spatial barriers between financial markets, the lines of data and information are still interpreted by a handful of 'local' centres. It is in this sense that global processes are grounded in specific places. And, perhaps more significantly, virtually all of those lines of finance connect with places in the over-developed rather than the less developed world.

Chapter 1 concludes by drawing attention to the question of for whom is the world shrinking, highlighting the uneven and unequal character of the flows of communication and transport, and reminding us of the unequal relations of power that stretch across the globe. In so doing, it raises themes that each of the following chapters seeks to address.

In Chapter 2, 'Crossing borders: footloose multinationals?', for instance, the issues of movement, mobility and economic inequality are at the forefront of the analysis. Not that long ago multinationals aroused a mix of suspicion and awe among the politicians of host countries. The ability of such firms to open and close plants and to cross national borders with relative ease represented an alarming characteristic, above all because of the prospect of job losses. Today, the issues are more complex, with governments greatly concerned with job creation and the possibility of attracting the technology, capital and work that multinationals represent. Such firms still have the potential to move rapidly from one country to the next, but the advantages of doing so are not always so straightforward. There is a debate over how far the big multinationals and transnationals, in attempting to 'globalize' their economic activities, require an integrated presence in each of the global regions – North America, Europe and East Asia. Even if mobility is no longer the central issue, however, there are other concerns to preoccupy host countries such as the limited transfer of fundamental technologies and skills.

Another concern is the rise in the number of indirect forms of overseas involvement, such as subcontracting relationships and joint ventures. These represent a looser form of cross-border activity than direct investment in plant and machinery, and come closer to the popular conceptions of a footloose firm. Such arrangements are frequently of limited duration and infinitely more mobile than those of direct capital investment. A central consideration of the author, John Allen, in this respect is how far such recent ways of stretching the economic reach of multinationals across the globe represent a superficial or a deep-seated form of economic involvement. That such forms have the potential to reach far into the social fabric of countries, to the extent of involving sweatshops and homeworkers, is evident, and equally so for the cities of the first as well as the 'third world'. One side of the connection clearly has more to lose than the other, should the relationship be disrupted or abruptly ended.

This draws attention, once more, to the unequal relations of power stretched across the globe and to the fact, mentioned earlier, that not all interconnections are of the same significance. Some links are more important to one end of a global relationship than the other, implying a form of dependence or unequal interdependence. In this context, to talk of faxes or E-mail communications in the same breath as multinational ties is to miss the point and to gloss over the difference between interconnections across space and interdependencies. Rapidly developing countries such as South Korea, Taiwan, Singapore and Hong Kong, which in the recent past have relied heavily upon attracting foreign direct investment to boost growth and now possess their own multinationals, would not miss the point.

The economic reach of multinational firms and the big transnational corporations also figures centrally in Chapter 3, 'Controlling space: global cities'. Here Chris Hamnett looks critically at notions of control and command embedded in the spatial structures of the big global firms and considers why the centralization of key functions has occurred in a handful of 'world' or global cities such as New York or London. Drawing upon Chapter 1, if developments in transport and communication have laid the basis of networks of control around the world and created the potential for more dispersed organizational structures, why have so few places achieved dominance in recent decades? What do world cities do? And are they effective at what they do?

The core of the chapter examines the argument that world cities are distinguished by their role as centres of corporate control in the global economy. Although there is much empirical support for this thesis, it fails · nonetheless to spell out the mechanism by which world cities function as the centres of a global economy. Others have attempted to answer this question, arguing that world cities are distinguished by their concentration of advanced services which provide the necessary specialist expertise for companies engaged in complex international trade and activity. This is taken further by authors such as Sassen, who argue that global cities such as New York, Tokyo and London are distinguished by their concentration of specialist business services and by their role as financial markets, as well as the production of financial and business innovations. They are still production sites, but not for manufacturing. If anything, the concentration of bank headquarters and the offices of major accountancy, advertising, legal and other firms has increased in these locations, not diminished.

Indeed, such a concentration of social relations draws attention to the ways in which power and certain kinds of production are organized geographically. If the world is shrinking then, as argued in Chapter 1, the lines of telecommunications stretched across the globe which have brought about the convergence of places have also made it possible for more remote forms of interaction across distance to occur. Spatial proximity is not a prerequisite of effective co-ordination or the delivery of advanced services. And yet these lines of communication and control only meet at a few points on the globe. In that sense the local remains the starting-point for wider, global processes, as noted in Chapter 1.

The dynamic role played by global cities in the world economy has also produced another kind of global connection: namely that of migration. As a consequence of the growth of international services in places like New York, two rather different groups of economic migrant have been attracted – high status, skilled labour to staff the managerial and professional functions and low status, low-paid labour to meet the demand for casual and informal service work. Drawn largely from different parts of the world, these two groups occupy different social spaces within the city. In geographical terms, the global lines of migration intersect at the same point, but in this instance spatial proximity does not add up to social proximity. The two groups may be as distant or remote from one another socially as if they were at opposite ends of the Earth.

The next chapter focuses upon a rather different set of connections and flows from that of people, industry and information. In Chapter 4, 'Dirty connections: transnational pollution', Steven Yearley shows how places are also connected to one another by pollution. In recent years the flows of pollution have increased in both geographical scope and intensity, with nation-states taking a keen interest in the pollutant activities of others, especially neighbouring states. In fact, the topic of transnational pollution, particularly in relation to air pollution, gives a rather different twist to the notion of us all being in 'each other's backyard'!

As the scale of industry has grown and with it its global reach, pollution is obviously something that no one wants in their own backyard. In a shrinking world, however, trade and investment collapse distances and this, as the author points out, 'allows waste from the United States to end up in Africa'. Such examples remind us of the unequal nature of the global connections and, indeed, of more extreme cases where poorer countries import pollution from richer countries to earn foreign exchange. The export of pollution as a legitimate form of trade draws attention to the vulnerability of people in less developed countries who, to all intents and purposes, are at the wrong end of an unequal interdependency.

The chapter also goes on to point out that pollution has brought about a heightened consciousness of how interconnected and interdependent our world really is. The notion of distant places being shaped by events elsewhere has a familiar resonance in respect of environmental hazards. Through such representations as 'spaceship Earth' and attempts by various environmental pressure groups to persuade us that we are all citizens of planet Earth, the idea of the despoliation of the environment as a global concern has a strong hold. However, while some environmental problems, such as ozone depletion, are global in scope, many others are geographically uneven in their impact, often restricted to the local region. The ability to capture 'the global' for the environment is nonetheless an interesting example of how local and global spaces may combine.

Chapter 5, 'Consuming spaces: global tourism', builds upon the themes of distance and movement developed in earlier chapters and considers them in relation to past and present notions of travel. Until the twentieth century overseas travel, as the author Erlet Cater points out, was largely the prerogative of the wealthy. With the advent of mass tourism in the 1960s – as a direct consequence of rising post-war incomes and cheaper modes of travel – one of the most visible aspects of a shrinking world was precisely the movement of more people to more places on a more frequent basis. But if the rise of mass tourism led to a breaking down of spatial barriers, it also led to a greater sensitivity to the difference between places. Places that were once regarded as exotic, tropical paradises, such as Bali, Tahiti, the Seychelles and the Maldives, are now becoming part of the tourist itinerary for many affluent westerners. What was once extra-ordinary is now becoming commonplace as new destinations progressively come within reach.

As with the example of migration to the global cities of the first world, however, such sensitivities may fail to connect with the cultures of their destinations. Tourists may now be able to travel to 'exotic, distant' locations, but that does not mean to say that they become part of the local space. It is not simply what tourists bring with them that is the issue here, but rather what is constructed for them by international hotels: namely, microcosms of the familiar within the exotic location (where even the food may be 'westernized' to be acceptable, for example).What is seen in far-off places may well have become ordinary to some tourists precisely because that is what is offered to them: 'home plus'.

A further consideration of the chapter is to show how tourism may have shrunk the globe, but it has done so in a markedly uneven and unequal manner. Whereas Kenya and the Gambia are on the tourist map, other parts of Africa such as Gabon and Mali are not. Just to be on the tourist map, however, is double-edged: it involves both costs and benefits. Tourism may bring development to some countries, but the package may also include environmental degradation and the disruption of traditional ways of life. As Cater shows, Nepal is suffering the environmental impact of large numbers of trekkers and the tropical reefs in Australia, the Caribbean and elsewhere are suffering considerable damage from the sheer number of tourists. She also goes on to remind us that much of the tourist infrastructure in less developed countries is owned by overseas multinationals, with a large proportion of the revenue from the international tourist industry flowing back to the first world, along with the tourists.

Finally, Chapter 6, 'Uneven worlds', has the task of pulling together the central themes of the book and, in particular, drawing out the uneven and unequal character of global relationships. In each of the preceding chapters, a different topic has been explored to reveal something of the changing geography of social relations stretched across space. In this chapter, the multitude of ways in which people, industry, money, information and the like have been drawn into a smaller, more interdependent world through the workings of time–space compression is considered from the point of view of who is and who is not included, which places are part of the process and which are outside and, to put it bluntly, who gains and who loses.

From this, the authors go on to show how thinking about *social space* in terms of the social relationships which criss-cross the globe, also involves an understanding of the places at which the lines intersect and meet. Volume 4, as noted, picks up this theme and runs with it. In the final part of this chapter, the focus is upon the questions of social distance that arise when our notions of what is near and what is far are disrupted in the everyday worlds of such contrasting social groups as tourists and economic migrants. Here the notion of uneven worlds is highlighted through the different networks of global relations that overlap in places like global cities, yet are 'lived' in ways that remain socially distant.

○　○　○　○　○

The stress placed here upon world*s* in the plural is intentional. Thus far, we have spoken about the global in a rather loose sense, as if it implied the whole world or rather much of it. What exactly we mean by global, however, varies over time and depends on how you see yourself tied in (see **Massey, 1995**). The view of the world of the Honduran peasant will be different from that of the wealthy financier in New York which, in turn, will vary from that of a Muslim woman working 'on the line' in a semiconductor factory in a remote part of Malaysia. This is one of the ways in which it is possible to talk of many worlds. A related way is to consider some of the different representations of *globalization* which have been drawn to give some kind of shape to what is happening worldwide (see **Allen, 1995**).

Earlier, we spoke of globalization in terms of a world characterized by closer, integrated ties and connections, and one easier to get around. This conception has the basics that are common to most views of globalization, namely that more and more of the world has been drawn into a network of social relationships which transcend conventional political, economic and cultural boundaries. The first point to note here is that such a sketch tells us nothing about the different dynamics and forces that lie behind globalization, whether or not they touch everywhere uniformly, the speed at which such forces make themselves felt around the world or, indeed, the nature of the ties that are laid down between places. There is much to be coloured in and indeed no shortage of pens and stencils.

One view, which stresses the role of dominant cultural forces (usually American), represents globalization as the spread of universal cultural forms and styles across the globe. This is a world of cultural *convergence*, in which everywhere is rapidly becoming the same, from Seattle to Siena to Singapore. If the world is not attuned fully to 'global' styles, then it is only because the process is as yet incomplete and uneven; if they are not yet wearing trainers or jeans in much of Indonesia, then it is only a matter of time. Those wearing them, however, may well consider their significance in a different light from their similarly clad counterparts in New York. The symbolic meaning attached to the same garment tends to vary from place to place, drawing its purpose from the welter of meanings that make up local cultural contexts. In this sense, divergence of identity and lifestyle is part and parcel of a world marked by an increasing sameness.

Another take on globalization, this time drawn from the economic side, tends to emphasize the *integration* of the world economy, as the major players, more often than not stateless corporations, draw more and more of the globe into the networks of capitalist production and markets. On this account we are on the way to the free movement of goods, services, labour and money across national borders: that is, en route to a borderless world. Even the loudest exponents of this view acknowledge, however, that globe-spanning firms are a rare sight and that full integration is a long way off, especially in relation to labour markets.

Finally, in the political arena one conception of globalization which is gaining influence also problematizes boundaries, although here it is the conventional political boundaries of what is inside and outside the nation-state, what is within and beyond domestic affairs, which are held up for revision in an increasingly interconnected and interdependent world order. On this view, the notion that we can contain politics within the confines of clearly bounded national territories is rejected in favour of a world order based upon *overlapping* political communities which cut across nation-states.

It is not important here to dwell upon the detail of these different representations of globalization, only to note their diversity and, indeed, the fact that opinion is divided over their soundness. Even more so, perhaps, because all forms of globalization essentially refer to processes of *'western'* globalization – a series of processes with a long history that reach back to colonial and Imperial times and which has its starting-point (and often end-point) in the countries of the rich, industrialized world. From the vantage point of those on the margins of global processes in the less developed world, their forgotten geographies are only likely to figure in first world representations as appropriations, rather than common experiences.

To appear plausible, however, each of the above conceptions of globalization, or perhaps any conception, requires some notion of a world that is shrinking in size. *The reordering of distance, the overcoming of spatial barriers, the shortening of time-horizons, and the ability to link distant populations in a more immediate and intense manner, are prerequisites of global talk.* When people talk about globalization, therefore, the compression of space by time underpins their account, whether or not attention is drawn to it directly.

In this volume, it is precisely the view that the world is shrinking which is held up to question, rather than assumed as an unproblematic notion. The concepts of movement, mobility, distance and, of course, social space are central to this critical analysis. More pointedly, in this text and in the series of books which make up *The Shape of the World* it is argued that global relations have unevenness and inequality built into them. It is this way of thinking which constitutes, in small part, a geographical imagination and which also draws attention to the fact that the world is neither shrinking for everyone, nor is it of positive benefit to all those caught up in the maelstrom.

John Allen and Chris Hamnett

References

ALLEN, J. (1995) 'Global worlds' in Allen, J. and Massey, D. (eds).

ALLEN, J. and MASSEY, D. (eds) (1995) *Geographical Worlds*, London, Oxford University Press/The Open University (Volume 1 in this series).

MASSEY, D. (1995) 'Imagining the world' in Allen, J. and Massey, D. (eds).

Annihilating space?: the speed-up of communications

Chapter 1

by Andrew Leyshon

1.1 Introduction

Compared to the situation in many other countries, the level of geographical awareness and knowledge about the rest of the world possessed by people living in Britain has always been fairly high. The reasons for this are largely historical. Britain is a former imperial power and the production and acquisition of geographical knowledge played a key role in extending and maintaining an empire 'upon which the sun never set'. This description of the Empire was suitably geographical, and referred to the way in which Britain's territorial control so encompassed the globe that at any time during its daily rotation at least part of the British Empire would be in daylight. The legacies of this past run deep and wide through British society and culture, and have survived a century during which Britain's Empire has been dismantled and its economic importance in the world dramatically reduced. From the BBC's 'World Service' to the quintessentially 'English' cup of tea, the main ingredients of which (tea and sugar) were products imported from British colonies in the Indian subcontinent and the Caribbean (Massey, 1993, p. 145), the reminders of an imperial past are constantly with us.

Nevertheless, it would be entirely reasonable to expect that, as Britain's imperial reach declined, so the interest in and awareness of the world beyond Britain's shores would have declined along with it. But in fact nothing could be further from the truth. There are strong grounds for arguing that, for many, knowledge about the rest of the world has never been greater. One of the main reasons for this has been a reduction over time in the constraints of physical distance upon movement and communication.

In terms of the amount of time it takes to travel around the world, and especially in terms of how long it takes for information to be sent around it, the world is certainly a much smaller place than it was even fifty years ago. The building of a new road, the development of a faster commercial aircraft, the launch of a new communications satellite or the installation of teleconferencing facilities in a corporate headquarters are all ways in which the world can be said to be 'shrinking', as the amount of time it takes to travel over or to send information through space is reduced. These developments serve to accelerate the transportation of people, materials and ideas over space, and in so doing bring places 'closer' together. Revolutions in transport and communications technology have thus undermined the 'friction' imposed by distance upon social interaction.

The shrinking of space has important implications for our everyday conceptions of space and distance, as well as for our level of knowledge about other places. People and places that barely knew of each other's existence one hundred years ago now regularly exchange materials and information with one another. Space-shrinking technologies have enabled people to be more mobile and to have access to a far wider range of information sources than ever before – further reasons for the contemporary levels of geographical knowledge referred to earlier.

But we have to be careful here. It would be a mistake to suggest that, as the barriers to movement are overcome, people are prepared to travel greater distances or begin to communicate with ever more distant places. Long-distance migration was already an important feature of the nineteenth-century world economy, when, as we have already noted, the British Empire was indeed a global one, encircling the world. It is not so much that people are now encouraged to travel further than ever before, for the world is an enclosed space and there is a limit to how *far* people can travel. But the process of 'shrinking' has made movement over space faster, more routine, and available to more people, so that it has become a far less daunting and more common prospect than it was even one hundred years or so ago.

To illustrate this point, let us use the example of long-distance migration in general, and migration from Europe to the United States in particular. In the nineteenth century the decision to migrate from Europe to the United States would have been a truly momentous one. It was not so much the length of the journey that was the problem, although the prospect of several weeks at sea in the North Atlantic in cramped conditions was hardly an attractive one. It was more that for ordinary people the process of migration would mean they would never again see the friends and family they left behind. The cost of the journey was such that it was unlikely that they would ever be able to afford the return passage. It was also something of a leap in the dark, for the knowledge of what was awaiting them when they got there was necessarily partial, based upon what they could glean from newspaper reports or books, from the 'travellers' tales' told by those who had visited and returned, or from the frozen images provided by artists or pioneering photographers (see **Massey, 1995**). It was perhaps not surprising, then, that such a migration was accompanied by a sense of an irrevocable parting, which perhaps accounts for the emotional dockside scenes which routinely accompanied the departures of steamers en route to the United States during the nineteenth century.

Compare this to the situation facing a potential migrant to the United States today. The decision to migrate is still a very important one, but for most people it is a far less terrifying experience. For one thing, the journey is far quicker: by air, the journey from Europe to the east coast of the United States usually takes less than eight hours. For another, the real cost of the flight has fallen, which means that return visits can be undertaken more frequently. As in the nineteenth century the mail service remains an important form of communication with family and friends back home, but it is now supplemented by the telephone and a host of other instantaneous

Off to a new world: boarding a steamer bound for America, Dublin 1851

electronic media. Moreover, even those who have never been to the United States before would have a fairly good idea of what to expect. Film and television images have transformed the ways in which we make sense of the world and, as the world's leading producer of film and video entertainment, the United States serves as both the subject and the backdrop to countless numbers of movies and television drama series as well as news and documentary programmes. This means that even the first-time visitor to the US finds immediately familiar much of what they see.

The observation about the role of electronically mediated visual images is an important one, for it illustrates that the world is shrinking not just because it is now easier to move around. It is also shrinking in that we can acquire a sense of the world without moving very far at all. We can travel vicariously through the 'electronic highways' which now encircle the globe, and through them garner a level of knowledge about the rest of the world which would surpass that of even the most seasoned nineteenth-century traveller. For example, spending merely a day watching British television would expose the viewer to a wide range of representations of, and from, the rest of the world. Consider just one summer Sunday in the early 1990s. Apart from the basic fare of home-produced programmes, the four main channels offered films from the United States, France and Italy, cartoons from Russia, a documentary about Japanese automobile manufacturing, as well as live coverage of a motor race in Belgium and a football match in Italy. There were also several hours of news and current affairs programmes on offer. It is in the arena of news and current affairs that television's ability to shrink space is best illustrated. In the process of constructing a news bulletin, newsreaders and television journalists link up across vast distances with the aid of satellite communications to bring stories from the latest war-zone, intergovernmental conference or ecological disaster.

A particularly good example of the capacity of international news-gathering organizations to seemingly shrink space occurred during the Gulf War of January–February 1991. Television coverage of war is not a new phenomenon; both the Korean war and the Vietnam war were covered extensively on television. What made the Gulf War unique was that it was the first television war covered *live* and from *both* sides of the conflict (Taylor, 1992, p. 7). That this was possible was due mainly to the role played by the US news organization Cable News Network (CNN), which began to rent a military communications link from the Iraqi government during the build-up to the war in the wake of the Iraqi invasion of Kuwait in August 1990. This prescient move enabled the station to compress the time and space of the conflict to a montage of television images. For example:

While talking to its reporters, CNN was similarly transmitting live Iraqi television pictures of Saddam praying, which the reporters could not see. Then an air raid sounded in the background; silent pictures from Iraqi TV; voices from the Al-Rashid and an interlocutor in Atlanta [where CNN is based]. Then CNN cut to live pictures of President Bush entering a church at Fort Myer, Virginia, before shifting back to Iraq. It was, as the anchor pointed out, 'surreal'.

(Taylor, 1992, p. 96)

The instantaneous nature of the coverage meant that this was a war conducted simultaneously in three time-zones. It was conducted in the 'real' war time of the Middle East, but it was also fought with more than an eye to the time in Europe and the United States, with the result that military briefings were scheduled to coincide with the deadlines of European and North American media. It was for this reason that the commander of Allied forces wore a watch on each wrist – one set to local time and the other to US time. It is also worth noting that the initial attack by US and UK military planes on Baghdad took place in the early hours of the morning local time – and that this was 18.30 pm Eastern Standard Time, the beginning of the peak viewing period on US television.

The war was also prosecuted in a fashion which owed much to space-shrinking technologies. For the most part this was a war conducted at long range, made possible by supersonic fighter-bomber aircraft and remote-controlled missiles. The extraordinary imbalance in the casualties suffered by the two sets of combatants reflected the different level of access to space-shrinking weapons: the US and its Allies lost only 180 personnel, while estimates of Iraqi casualties range from at least 20,000 to at most 400,000 casualties. The scale of the losses astonished many of those who had watched the war unfold on their television screens – revealing yet another facet of the Gulf War. Representations of the war mostly flowed from extremely narrow media channels, controlled in part by the Iraqi military (in the case of CNN in Baghdad) but in the main by the US military. Hence, viewers were presented with what seemed to be for the most part a relatively antiseptic military conflict, which apparently consisted of a series of 'surgical strikes'. The screens were filled with video images taken by cameras located in the nose-cones of missiles as they accurately homed in on their military (and therefore 'legitimate') targets, the pictures breaking up and blacking out altogether at the moment of impact (Der Derrian, 1992). But the scale of the losses betrayed the fact that a great deal more destruction and death must have been meted out than television audiences were permitted to see by either the US or the Iraqi authorities.

The one-sided way in which the Gulf War was both prosecuted and represented also serves to remind us about the uneven way in which space shrinks. The US and its allies won both the real war and the media war so comprehensively because they had the superior space-shrinking military technologies. And as in military conflict, so in wider geopolitical and geo-economic struggles. From Nathan Rothschild's celebrated use of a carrier pigeon to relay the result of the battle of Waterloo back to the City of London for his considerable financial advantage, there have been numerous examples of how access to *fast information* has had beneficial economic consequences. But as the means of capturing and using this information have become more reliant upon sophisticated and expensive technologies, so the money-rich have also tended to become the information-rich. This has important consequences for uneven development in a world where information has increasingly become a commodity in its own right.

In this chapter an attempt will be made to make sense of what it means to speak of 'a shrinking world', to determine the ways in which the world can be said to be shrinking, and to ascertain for whom the world can be said to be shrinking. The remainder of the chapter is organized in four main parts. Section 1.2 looks at specific concepts which help us to make sense of a shrinking world. Section 1.3 considers the process of shrinking, by looking at the revolutions in transportation and communications technology from the nineteenth century onwards, while section 1.4 looks at some of the implications of shrinking, by considering whether or not the world in which we currently live can be described as a 'global village'. Section 1.5 considers whether the process of shrinking has brought about 'the End of Geography'. It seeks to answer this question through an analysis of the financial system. The world of money and finance is a useful object of study in this regard, for the financial system has compressed space and time in remarkable ways. The benefits of this shrinkage have been unevenly distributed, however: while the financial system has brought many places 'closer together', it has also forced some places further apart. The conclusions to the chapter are presented in section 1.6.

Activity 1   This activity seeks to illustrate the relative importance of electronic media for our images of particular places. Select a US city that you know something about but have *not* visited. Take a few minutes to jot down what you know about the following characteristics of the city:

(a) key architectural features

(b) main economic activities

(c) social conditions

(d) cultural and entertainment activities.

Now think about how you acquired the knowledge to be able to describe the city in the way you did. To what extent did information gained from film and television images inform your descriptions?

Now try performing the same exercise for a city in either South America or Asia that you have *not* visited.

Compare your descriptions and reflect on what this reveals about the way in which film and television images influence the level of geographical knowledge that you possess.

I certainly found the first part of the activity far easier than the second. I have never been to New York, but I feel that I have a fairly good sense of what the city looks like and what goes on there. I must admit that some of my knowledge of the city is drawn from written texts, for the city is an important financial centre and as such has figured in some of my work on the international financial system in recent years. However, movies such as Oliver Stone's *Wall Street*, Spike Lee's *Do the Right Thing*, and the many New York-based films of Martin Scorsese and Woody Allen are readings of the economic, social and cultural geography of New York that have been particularly influential in the 'imaginary geography' of the city constructed in my mind. How accurate this imaginary geography is I cannot judge, but it is something I will take with me should I ever visit New York.

While I can summon up similar pictures of several other US cities in this way, despite the fact that I have never visited them, I found it much more difficult to complete the activity for a city in South Asia or South America. My images of cities in such regions are fuzzy and partial. After some time, I arrived upon Hong Kong as somewhere that I felt I could describe in almost as much detail as New York. That I was able to do this reveals much about the legacies of Britain's imperial past to which I referred earlier. Hong Kong commands a fair amount of attention in the British media because of its colonial history and the furore surrounding the hand-over of the colony to the People's Republic of China in 1997. News items about other cities in

South East Asia are few and far between, as they are about cities in South America. In consequence, while I can easily place cities in these regions on the map, for some reason they seem to be relatively further away than are equally distant cities about which I have information from film and video images.

1.2 A small world? Theorizing a shrinking world

A world which is shrinking in time–space has important implications for our efforts to explain the organization and conduct of social life. Most social theory has been concerned with time, that is, to explain the evolution of societies over time. Very few social theorists have bothered themselves with matters geographical or spatial, and hardly any have sought to incorporate the notion that places are 'moving towards one another', so to speak.

Perhaps, given the implications that processes of time–space convergence have for social theory, this is not surprising, since an admission that the world *is* shrinking makes the task of theory construction even more complex than it already is. As the world shrinks, so does the ground upon which social processes are played out, making it more difficult to explicate the way in which social life unfolds (Gregory, 1994). There are a number of reasons for this, but three are particularly important:

1   The process of shrinking involves overcoming the 'friction of distance', which means that places converge on one another, as it were, as the distances between them decline in significance.

2   Whereas in the past places may have existed in a state of isolation, the process of shrinking has brought more and more places into contact with one another. Economic and social actors who are *absent* in time and space may now have as much influence upon local processes of social change as those who are *present* in time and space.

3   As the world has become smaller in time–space, so the pace of life has *accelerated*, which means that it is increasingly difficult to keep up with events, let alone incorporate them into an explanatory social theory.

These are rather terse points, so we shall now consider each of them in turn by examining three related concepts which have emerged from efforts to take the implications of a shrinking world seriously. These are: (a) time–space convergence; (b) time–space distanciation; and (c) time–space compression.

1.2.1 Shrinking the world, ...

The phrase *time–space convergence* was first employed by Donald Janelle to describe the way in which improvements in transport technologies have the effect of 'moving' places within settlement systems towards one another over time 'as the travel-time required between places decreases and distance declines in significance' (Janelle, 1969, p. 351). Janelle argued that the velocity at which settlements are moving together can be measured in terms of a 'time–space convergence rate' (1968, p. 7). He used as an example the distance between Edinburgh and London (330 miles). Measured in terms of the amount of time taken to travel between the two cities, Edinburgh and London had 'converged' in time–space at a rate of almost 30 minutes per

time–space convergence

year over a 200-year period: in 1776 it took four days or 5,760 minutes to travel between the two cities by stage-coach, but by the late 1960s it took only 180 minutes by aeroplane.

Janelle's inspiration for arguing that places should be analysed in the context of time–space was gleaned from physics:

In modern physics and philosophy, distance is no longer considered a universally valid parameter for describing the relationship between points, events or particles in space. For the physicist to describe such relationships, it is necessary that he [sic] view them in time–space and that he know their positions, their velocities and the direction in which they are moving. By velocity, he means the time-rate at which the distance between points, events or particles changes.

(Janelle, 1968, p. 5)

The message from this 'modern physics', which overthrew classical, Newtonian physics in the early twentieth century, was that it was impossible to arrive at fixed and immutable representations of space. Classical physics perceived space as absolute, which stretched to infinity in three dimensions; Einstein's theory of relativity, and the insights derived from quantum physics, suggested that space is a *necessarily* relative phenomenon, inextricably bound up with the flow of time. Einstein's proposition, that phenomena must be conceived as existing in a world of *four* inextricably linked dimensions (three of space and one of time), means that we should no longer think of time and space as separate phenomena, but instead think of *time–space*.

The importance of thinking in terms of time–space is revealed in Figure 1.1. Figure 1.1(a) is a conventional map of the Pacific Basin; Figure 1.1(b) is drawn in time–space, that is, distance is measured not in terms of absolute

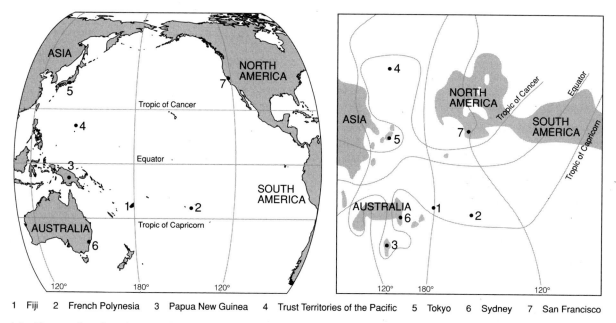

1 Fiji   2 French Polynesia   3 Papua New Guinea   4 Trust Territories of the Pacific   5 Tokyo   6 Sydney   7 San Francisco

(a) 'Conventional' projection of the Pacific basin

(b) Time–space map of the Pacific basin, based on relative time accessibility by scheduled airline in 1975

Figure 1.1 Places 'moving' together and apart: mapping time–space convergence (Source: Adapted from Haggett, 1990, Figure 3.3(C))

space, but in terms of the amount of time it takes to travel through space. When the Pacific is mapped in this way the geography of the area changes dramatically. Some places, such as Tokyo, San Francisco and Sydney, appear to 'move' towards one another. Linked to one another by a dense network of regular air and sea transport communications, the time–space distance between these places is much less than a conventional mapping of absolute space would suggest. However, notice how other places appear to become more 'distant' when mapped in this way. Poorer and less frequent communication links mean that Papua New Guinea appears to move south of Australia, while the Trust Territories of the Pacific appear to move north, apparently outside of the Pacific.

1.2.2 ... 'stretching' across it, ...

One implication of the shrinking of space is that it has served to promote the interpenetration and integration of places. In recent years some theorists have sought to make sense of this shift. One such theorist is Anthony Giddens (1990) who has sought to address the problems facing social theory because of the way in which social processes have been 'stretched' over space.

Giddens suggests that social life is made up of two main types of social interaction. The first consists of face-to-face contacts, which are entered into as people go about their daily routines in what are normally fairly tightly drawn, local areas. The second type of interaction is more 'remote', and is made possible by transport and communications systems, which permit people to interact with one another across space and time. This second form of interaction is described by Giddens as *time–space distanciation,* and is the means by which formerly separate and self-contained systems have come into contact with one another and become *interdependent.*

time–space distanciation

interdependence

The advantage of this approach is that it offers a way of thinking about social life which takes account of the fact that what goes on often owes as much to those people who are *not present* as to those who are. It also provides a way of coming to terms with similarities in social systems, as well as their variations. On the one hand, it could be argued that interaction in the form of time–space distanciation is imposing a degree of uniformity and commonality within social systems as, through contact, similar practices and ways of doing things are adopted. It is possible to illustrate this through a fairly mundane example. I write this having spent the afternoon taking my daughter to see the latest Walt Disney film, and having first stopped off at a McDonald's hamburger restaurant for a quick bite to eat. No doubt this was a pattern of behaviour being repeated not only in many other towns and cities in the United Kingdom, but in many other countries of the world as well. Disney films and McDonald's hamburgers have a global market. And yet, on the other hand, it would be wrong to assume that the way in which such global artefacts are experienced owes nothing to local contingency. In the restaurant, the accents of the people who served us and whom we sat next to were local, while many of the references in the film to popular culture would only be fully appreciated by an audience more deeply knowledgeable about American television than we are in the UK.

The advantage of seeing that social relations consist of both local face-to-face contacts *and* more remote, 'distanciated' contacts is that it enables us to think of social life as being unstable and loosely bounded. It also guards us from thinking that everywhere is becoming the same. For while time–space distanciation creates the possibilities for more uniformity, the way in which such remote social relations are experienced may vary markedly between different places.

1.2.3   … and speeding it up

Although the notion of time–space distanciation is a useful one, it does not really tell us *why* social processes should be extended over space. A way forward is to consider the concept of *time–space compression* advanced by David Harvey (1989). Harvey argues that the phenomena attributed to time–space convergence and time–space distanciation are the result of the restless expansion of capitalist relations of production on a global scale. As capitalism is an inherently competitive system, capitalists find themselves in an endless race to seek out new markets and to reduce what is known as the *turnover time of capital.* This is the amount of time it takes for money advanced to fund the cost of new production to be returned with a profit through the sale of goods and services. It has been this competitive race for new markets and the drive to reduce the turnover time of capital in the search for profit which, Harvey argues, have helped shrink the world in terms of time–space. The concept of time–space compression is an advance on the notion of time–space distanciation in that it makes explicit the cost of crossing space, and introduces an economic logic for reducing barriers to movement and communications over space. In a capitalist system time costs money; this helps to explain the inexorable *acceleration in the pace of life*, which can be seen as an endemic characteristic in the history of capitalism.

[margin: time–space compression]

[margin: turnover time of capital]

[margin: acceleration in the pace of life]

Whether or not Harvey is accurate in this assertion you will be in a better position to judge after reading the next section. But now turn to Reading A, where Harvey argues that the compression of space and time has increased markedly in recent years, leading to a feeling that the world is unfolding around us in ways that we do not understand and at a pace which is difficult to track. He links this acceleration to a change in the way in which the capitalist system is organized, from a 'Fordist' system of production to one based on what he describes as 'flexible accumulation'. Don't worry too much about these terms at the moment, except to note that the notion of flexibility is critical in this context, for it suggests that in a world characterized by time–space compression we all have to be more flexible in our ways of thinking and in our modes of behaviour.

Activity 2   Now turn to Reading A, taken from *The Condition of Postmodernity* by David Harvey, which you will find at the end of this chapter. When you have read it, return to the text below.

Note that Harvey prioritizes economic change above all else. Changes within the sphere of capitalist relations of production are seen to have profound social and cultural consequences, which in turn change the ways in which we think and live our lives. While this economism can and has been questioned, what the excerpt illustrates is the way in which the volatility and turbulence associated with a speeded-up economic world is self-reinforcing as the 'management' of volatility becomes a route to success for many economic actors.

Summary of section 1.2

o   In recent years a number of attempts have been made to come to terms with the operation of social processes not merely in time or in space but in time–space.

o   The concept of time–space convergence draws our attention to the way in which places and people in the world are constantly moving in relation to one another in time–space, and this has questioned the authority of conventional representations of space. Representations cannot be absolute; they must necessarily be relative.

o   The concept of time–space distanciation helps us to avoid seeing societies as discrete and independent. Social life is made up of two types of interaction: (a) face-to-face contacts which take place as people go about their daily routines; and (b) intermediated or 'distanciated' contacts which are made possible by the technologies of time–space convergence. As such technologies have become more efficient and available to more people, so the range and breadth of distanciated contacts have increased, which means that the nature of social life in any particular area has become more fluid, as it is influenced not only by local customs and traditions but also by those 'imported' to the area via space-shrinking technologies.

o   Time–space compression adds a propulsive element missing from both the concepts of time–space convergence and time–space distanciation. The world is seen to be shrinking as a result of the imperatives of capitalism to seek out new markets and to speed up the turnover time of capital.

1.3   The world begins to shrink

The concepts of time–space convergence, time–space distanciation and time–space compression all have a fairly recent vintage. It is interesting to speculate as to why the interest in time–space convergence developed apace from the 1960s onwards. One reason is surely the fact that the experience of time and space underwent a remarkable transformation in the period after 1945. The 1950s saw the development of the commercial jet aircraft, followed in the 1960s by an exponential increase in the number of scheduled international flights. It was also the era of large-scale highway construction in North America and Western Europe and the growth of widespread car ownership. The 1950s and 1960s also saw the general dissemination of television, which added to the stock of representations of the rest of the world. It was also a time of space explorations, the launch of the first communications satellites and of the first pictures of the Earth taken from an external viewpoint. More ominously, the 1950s and 1960s saw the Cold War between the USA and the USSR gather momentum, raising the spectre of global nuclear annihilation. In the most extreme example of time–space compression yet conceived, there was a growing awareness of living in a '30-minute world' (Janelle, 1973), this being the amount of time taken for an intercontinental nuclear missile to travel from its launch-site to its target destination on the other side of the world.

Given these examples, it would have been surprising if a concern with time–space compression did not emerge as a subject of critical enquiry. However, it would be an error to conclude from this that time–space compression or an interest in it was a product of the post-war years. Time–space compression, although not named as such, was an important concern of some nineteenth-century and early-twentieth century geographers. This much is made clear by the following comments of A. J. Herbertson, who in 1915 observed that the 'remarkable development of means of transport (of ideas as well as of men [*sic*] and materials) is sometimes said to have annihilated space and time' so that 'information and even ideas can (now) be transmitted almost instantaneously' (Herbertson, 1915, p. 151).

Indeed, the nineteenth century saw a remarkable advance in time–space compression, thanks to a wave of space-shrinking technological innovations. In the period between 1880 and 1914, conceptions of space and time were profoundly altered by emergence of the telephone, wireless telegraph, cinema, bicycle, automobile and aircraft (Kern, 1983). With this in mind, it is necessary to take a much longer-run perspective on the process of time–space convergence. It is to this task that we turn in this section.

1.3.1 The transport and communications revolutions in the nineteenth century

During the nineteenth century there occurred throughout much of the world a transformation in the perception of time and space. A series of revolutions in transport and communications technology served to bring about a shrinkage of distance, causing places to 'move' closer together. Up to the nineteenth century, transport and communications technology had been based upon the capture and utilization of tangible natural forces, such as the use of animals or the use of wind-power. For the most part, transport on land was dependent upon the horse, while at sea the sailing-ship was the fastest form of transportation. This is not to say that the speed at which people could travel over land and sea had not increased in the period leading up to the nineteenth century. Incremental changes made to the dominant forms of transport technology had brought about a gradual shrinkage of space. For example, the spread of the road network in England and Wales served significantly to increase the speed by which people could travel the length and breadth of the country (see Figure 1.2). Similarly, the construction of larger ships with more sails or rigging reduced travel times at sea. However, there were generally perceived to be upper limits on the likely speed of modes of transport which relied upon either horse- or wind-power. With one or two notable exceptions, such as semaphore and the use of carrier-pigeons, communications between people in the period leading up to the nineteenth century were also limited to the same means of transport as for carrying goods or people.

In the wake of a series of technological developments in the nineteenth century, however, it soon became possible to send messages over vast distances at great speed and to transport people from one place to another more rapidly than was possible by mere horse- or wind-power alone. The catalyst for this acceleration was the Industrial Revolution, which triggered a series of innovations that sought to harness power for the purposes of industrial production. These innovations, which used less tangible sources of natural energy than horse- or wind-power, were soon put to use for purposes of transportation. The harnessing of the kinetic power of engines and later of

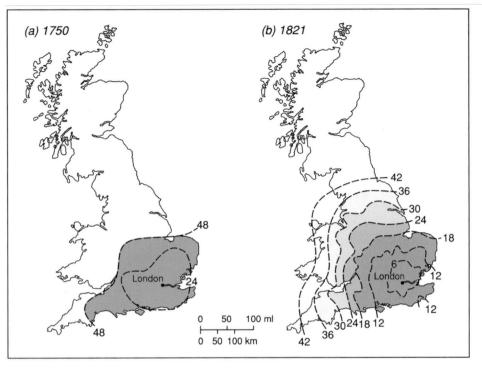

— — — — Travel times (hours from London)

Figure 1.2 *Stage-coach journey times from London in (a) 1750 and (b) 1821 (Source: Thrift, 1990, Figure 16.2)*

electricity was not only central to the advance of the Industrial Revolution but also in bringing about a *Dromocratic Revolution*: that is, a revolution in the principal means of movement, transport and communication in human society (Virilio, 1983).

Dromocratic Revolution

The development of the steam engine, fuelled by the burning of wood and coal, led directly to the development of the railways. The first true railway was opened in 1830 between Liverpool and Manchester and the railway network in Britain mushroomed thereafter. The speed at which the trains could travel led to a dramatic shrinkage in space during the nineteenth century, as the power of engines was increased and as the network of lines became more extensive (see Figure 1.3).

From the middle of the nineteenth century onwards, a growing number of writers and commentators began to refer to the way in which the increased transportation rate made possible by the railways had brought about an 'annihilation of space' by time – a phrase often attributed to Karl Marx, but which was common currency long before Marx embarked upon his analysis of the dynamics of capitalist economies. One of the reasons for this was the large numbers of people who had directly experienced the annihilation of space by time through the use of railways: in 1870 alone, 336.5 million journeys by rail were made in Britain (Thrift, 1990). The employment of the phrase by Marx was particularly appropriate, though, for it was the effort by capitalists to seek out new markets and to accelerate the turnover time of capital that was in large part causing the annihilation of space so widely remarked upon in the nineteenth century.

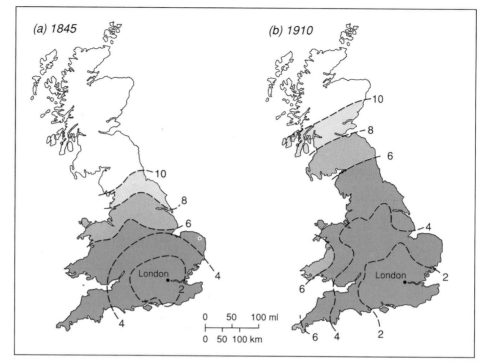

———— Travel times (hours from London)

Figure 1.3 *Railway journey times from London in (a) 1845 and (b) 1910 (Source: Thrift, 1990, Figure 16.8)*

If the railways were the main cause of time–space convergence during the nineteenth century, then the telegraph was largely responsible for bringing about time–space distanciation and time–space compression. The existence of electricity and the possibilities it offered for communication had first been recognized in the eighteenth century; it was not until 1837, however, that the first telegraph system was patented (Hall and Preston, 1988). The emergence of the telegraph at the same time as the railways was a happy coincidence, and the two proceeded to develop in lockstep with one another for much of the nineteenth century. Indeed, the railway companies were virtually the only customers for telegraph systems in its earliest years. As the railway network grew, so did the telegraph lines, so that by 1868 there were almost 22,000 miles of cables in Britain, and almost 3,400 relay stations open to the public for transmission of messages (Thrift, 1990).

It was not long before the telegraph industry went international, leading to an unprecedented level of virtually instantaneous communication across great distances. Britain began to be linked to the rest of Europe by telegraphic cables laid on the bed of the English Channel during the 1850s. In 1858, in what represented a remarkable technological achievement, a telegraph cable was laid across the 3,000 miles of the Atlantic Ocean, making instantaneous communication between North America and Europe possible for the first time. The commercial possibilities of this link between the economies of the United States and Great Britain were quickly realized as the telegraph allowed the creation of true international markets, that is, where the buy and sell prices of commodities are posted in more than one country. An important development in this regard was the creation of an active market in currencies, as foreign exchange could now be traded between the City of London and New York with ease and rapidity. Since it was the telegraph which allowed financiers in the two cities to inform one another of the rate at which they would exchange pounds for dollars and vice versa, the sterling–dollar exchange rate became known as 'Cable', and remains so today.

In line with Harvey's claim about the history of time–space compression, for the first forty years of its existence the spread of the international telegraph network had been driven mainly by commercial motives, so that 'stockbrokers, businessmen, journalists and diplomats were … the chief beneficiaries of this marvellous contrivance' (Kennedy, 1979, p. 76). However, from 1870 onwards the telegraph began to figure more strongly in the geopolitical reasoning of states. Not surprisingly, given the global spread of its imperial possessions, Britain was the first state to seek to use the possibilities of the telegraph for strategic purposes. One of the problems of holding together an empire that encircled the world was that of maintaining contact between the centre and its extremities. Despite the growth of the railways and steamships, even by the late 1860s it could still take over a month for mail to reach London from India and over two months to arrive from Australia and New Zealand. In order to speed up communications between London and the Empire, the British government sponsored the laying of thousands of miles of submarine cables in order to construct an 'all-red' telegraphic system (Kennedy, 1979). The system was described as 'all red' as it was to make contact only with land coloured red on imperial atlases, denoting membership of the British Empire. By 1900 the telegraph system had been completed, creating the world's first global communications network (see Figure 1.4), which dramatically reduced the time taken to send

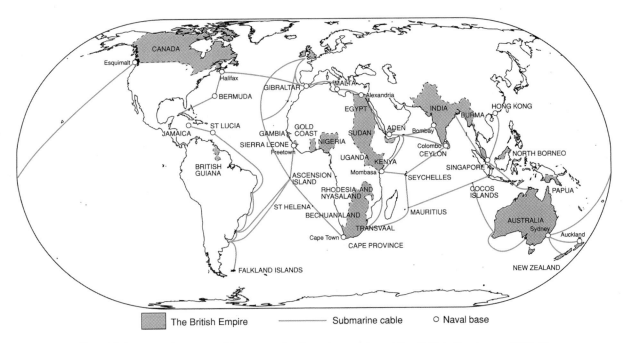

Figure 1.4 *The chief possessions, naval bases and submarine cables of the British Empire, c. 1900 (Source: Kennedy, 1988, Map 8)*

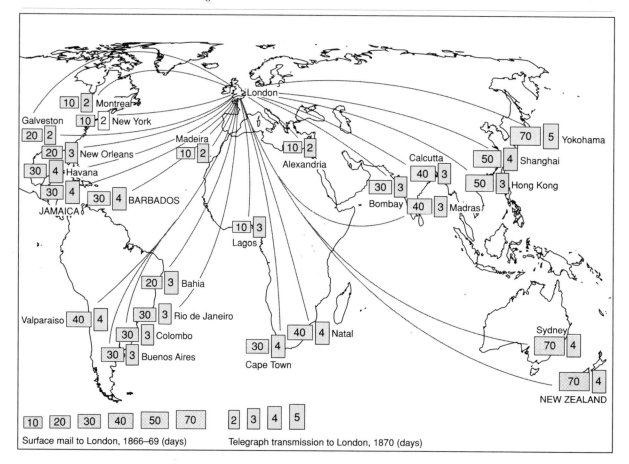

Figure 1.5 Surface mail (1866–9) and telegraphic transmission (1870) times (in days)

messages between London and even the furthest extremities of the Empire (see Figure 1.5).

If the railways had brought about an annihilation of space by time, then the development of instantaneous forms of communication created a sense of 'simultaneity' (Kern, 1983). The telegraph, and the later development of the telephone and the wireless telegraph, all created a sense of being in two places at once – the place from which the message was being transmitted and the place at which it was received. With the development of cinema towards the end of the century, the sense of simultaneity was reinforced, for it was now possible to observe events unfolding many miles away, so that viewers could feel themselves to be in two places at the same time – both in the cinema theatre and at the place where the film was shot.

The annihilation of space and the growing sense of simultaneity had widespread social, political and economic consequences. According to Stephen Kern, the response was double-edged: 'One response was the growing sense of unity among people formerly isolated by distance and lack of communication. This was not, however, unambiguous, because proximity also generated anxiety – apprehension that the neighbours were seen as getting a bit too close' (Kern, 1983, p. 88). In social terms, there was the anxiety caused by the ways in which the new means of communication were stretching social relations over space and, in so doing, disclosing information about the rest of the world to which people had previously been oblivious. With the aid of electrical news services such as Reuters, newspapers were able to provide a wider news coverage than ever before, a development which prompted one prominent British politician to remark in 1889 that, thanks to the telegraph, it was possible to find 'combined together almost at one moment ... the opinions of the whole intelligent world with respect to everything that is passing at that time on the face of the globe' (Lord Salisbury, quoted in Kern, 1983, p. 68).

It is perhaps no coincidence that in the wake of such changes a relatively new branch of medicine began to expand, focusing upon the diagnostic category of neurasthenia, or nervous exhaustion. Just as business executives today may be seen to be both utilizers and victims of space-shrinking technologies, so it was in the nineteenth century. According to the psychiatrist George Beard, author of *American Nervousness*, in 1881, 'the telegraph, railroads, and steam power have enabled businessmen to make "a hundred times" more transactions in a given period than had been possible in the eighteenth century; they intensify competition and tempo, causing an increase in the incidence of a host of problems including neurasthenia, neuralgia, nervous dyspepsia, early tooth decay, and even premature baldness' (quoted in Kern, 1983, p. 125). Contemporary analyses of mortality statistics also revealed a marked increase in the number of deaths caused by cancer, heart disease and kidney disease, which many attributed to stress caused by the accelerated pace of life brought about by the transport and communications revolutions.

These revolutions also had important political and economic consequences. Potential enemies were now much 'closer', and were to become closer still with the development of powered flight in the early twentieth century. According to the geographer and geopolitical theorist Halford Mackinder (1904), the rise of the transport revolution meant no less than an epochal change in the geographical balance of world power. During what Mackinder described as the 'Columbian Age', power rested with nations that controlled the sea, the most effective way of moving people and materials over long distances. However, the advent of a rapid means of transportation over land was causing the balance of world power to shift to land-locked states, and away from sea-based powers such as Britain. In particular, he predicted that in the 'Post-Columbian Age' the opening of Russia's transcontinental railway would consolidate its control over what he described as the 'pivot area' or heartland of the world, and would cause that state to rise to a position of global political and economic dominance. For Mackinder, the transcontinental railway meant that Russia could more effectively control and defend space, as munitions and troops could now be moved over vast distances at great speed. Moreover, it allowed Russia to exploit its vast human and environmental resources more effectively:

The Russian railways have a clear run of 6000 miles from Wirballen in the west to Vladivostoch in the east. The Russian army is as significant evidence of mobile land-power as the British army in South Africa was of sea-power ... The spaces within the Russian Empire and Mongolia are so vast, and their potentialities in population, wheat, cotton, fuel and metals so incalculably great, that it is inevitable that a vast economic world, more or less apart, will develop inaccessible to oceanic commerce.

(Mackinder, 1904, p. 434)

Mackinder would have been better advised to have looked west rather than east. For it was in the United States rather than in Russia that the annihilation of space by time and simultaneity was bringing about an economic revolution. The ability of the railway to shrink space played an important role in the rapid development of the North American economy during the nineteenth century. As the railways snaked their way westward from the urbanized eastern seaboard, so it became possible for more of the interior to be given over to commercial agriculture. The railways enabled land which was previously uncultivated and grazed only by buffalo to be used for commercial grain production and cattle-rearing, as the railways linked the Great Plains first to the ports of the Great Lakes and then to the markets of the east and even Europe (Cronon, 1992). Because of the parallel development of steam-engines for ocean-going ships, Europe was also now much closer in terms of travel-time. At the same time the city of Chicago, which grew at the heart of this agricultural economy, evolved an international market-place for commodities, thanks to the 'telegraph facilities that gathered meat prices and livestock news from every corner of the globe' (Cronon, 1992, pp. 211–12).

A particularly good illustration of the way in which the railway extended capitalist relations of production is illustrated in Reading B, which is taken from *Nature's Metropolis: Chicago and the Great West* by William Cronon (1992). Note the way in which the railroads bring a marked speed-up in the circulation of capital in the rural economy, and the way in which once isolated farmers become dependent upon other economic actors distant in time and space.

Activity 3 Now turn to Reading B, 'The coming of the railroad: economic effects in the Midwest', which you will find at the end of this chapter. While you are reading the extract, make a note of the advantages and the disadvantages accruing to the rural communities brought closer to Chicago in time–space. When you have read it, return to the text below.

What the reading reveals is the way in which the railways transformed the nature of the risks facing economic actors in rural communities. The level of short-term risk tended to decline, as farmers no longer had to tie up large amounts of capital in ventures upon which their entire future depended. Easier access to the market meant that they could turn over lower capital sums more quickly. Whereas previously farmers had to run the risk of their entire produce rotting in storage or being destroyed on the way to market, more regular contact with the market lessened the chance that such a disaster would bring complete economic ruin. However, the long-term risk for farmers increased, due largely to a marked rise in the level of competition between them. Because it became possible to enter agricultural production with less capital, which could then be turned over more quickly, the railroads encouraged more people to attempt to make a living by farming. At the same time, the railroads were forging a link between metropolitan markets and farmers all over the Midwest and beyond, which further intensified the level of competition between agricultural producers. It also meant that farmers could turn to more specialized forms of agricultural production. In the long term these developments forced down prices for agricultural commodities and ensured that the future belonged to those farmers who could produce their crops cheaply and efficiently. In other words, the coming of the railroads was the catalyst for agricultural production to be run along lines of capitalist rationality.

The railways were important in transforming the economy of the United States in another way too. They were the precursors of new types of corporate organization that illustrated to other companies how they could operate successfully *across space*. The railroad companies introduced new types of management structures that delegated responsibility to the local managers in the various operations strung out across the United States along the railway networks. This system of delegation enabled local managers to engage in day-to-day management in the absence of an overseeing authority. However, although not present, this higher managerial authority was not exactly absent either, since senior management could easily contact local management: the railroads themselves made it easier to travel rapidly from place to place, while the systematic use of the telegraph enabled the different layers of management to communicate with one another over great distances (Best, 1990). This model of 'distanciated' managerial organization was one that was widely copied. It facilitated the growth of large multi-divisional, multi-site corporations operating across the US economy, and ultimately of the multinational corporations that began to disseminate through the world economy from the late nineteenth century onwards.

The revolutions in transportation and communications thus contributed to a growth in the division of labour in industry, and to the development of *spatial divisions of labour* (Massey, 1984). First, the division of labour expanded, as a wide range of new industries and new occupations came into being associated with the design, construction and maintenance of the new technologies. At the same time, the ability of companies to engage in instantaneous communication with employees many miles away through the use of telegraphy and the telephone, as well as the greater speed of travel made possible by the railroads, encouraged many firms to separate their manufacturing and office facilities. In the middle of the nineteenth century, offices were usually located alongside factories, but at the end of the nineteenth century and the beginning of the twentieth century urban centres were increasingly given over to offices. This spatial division of labour was firmly established by the 1920s, prompting one contemporary commentator on New York to remark upon 'a territorial subdivision of functions which were formerly united in the same place', so that Fourth Avenue was 'full of establishments having names of manufacturing plants, but no fabrication in evidence' and, while New York was 'the centre of the silk industry, not a loom [was] to be found' (Haig, quoted in Dunford and Perrons, 1983, p. 306). Over time, these spatial divisions of labour would assume global proportions.

spatial divisions of labour

Summary of section 1.3

o   Advances in transport and communications technology have served to speed up the pace of life and brought progressively more areas within the orbit of capitalist relations of production.

o   The transport and communications revolutions of the nineteenth century enabled western powers such as Britain to develop a commercial empire of global dimensions, while facilitating the development of economies of continental dimensions, as in the case of the United States.

o   The processes of time–space convergence, time–space distanciation, and time–space compression gathered pace during the late nineteenth and early twentieth centuries.

1.4   Living in the 'global village'

During the twentieth century the sense that the world was shrinking became ever more pervasive. This was due to further advances in the fields of transportation and communications. The emergence of the motor vehicle was particularly important in this regard, while the invention of powered flight revolutionized conceptions of time and space, bringing places ever closer in terms of time–space. In doing so, revolutions in transport technology served to greatly extend social relations over space during the twentieth century. Social relations were also extended in ways that did not require the physical transportation of people from one place to another. Building upon the possibilities of the telegraph, telephone and the wireless radio, communications technologies have progressed at a rapid rate to create a global net which encircles the world.

Donald Janelle observed that an important outcome of the process of time–space convergence was an increase in 'human extensibility', made possible by communications technology. In other words, 'as the world shrinks, man [*sic*] expands' (Janelle, 1973, p. 11), albeit in a 'disembodied' form. While such extensibility may have certain advantages, in that it overcomes the need to engage in physical transportation in order to communicate with someone distant in time–space, it also brings with it certain disadvantages, for extensibility means that the confusions and uncertainties we all experience from time to time, in living in a world that is shrinking, rise ever closer to the surface:

Transistor radios, telephones, and television are linking most of the world's households into a global network ... Transportation and communications improvements have provided us with global information networks, and the possible combinations for interaction among nearly four billion humans are staggering. Even more staggering, however, are the perceptual lags that prevent us from adapting political, social, economic, and ecological views to the technological realities of such interaction levels.

(Abler et al., 1975, p. 4; emphasis added)

The use and understanding of a concept such as human extensibility resonate strongly with the ideas of Canadian literary critic Marshall McLuhan, whose ruminations on the social and spatial consequences of communication technologies began to be widely disseminated from the 1950s onwards. It was McLuhan who first coined the phrase 'global village', and celebrated the medium of television through the slogan 'the medium is the message'.

In *The Gutenburg Galaxy* McLuhan argued that 'electro-magnetic discoveries have recreated the simultaneous "field" in all human affairs so that the human family now exists under conditions of a "global village"' (McLuhan, 1962, p. 31). In similar vein he later went on to argue that 'our world has become compressed' and 'electrically contracted', so that 'the global is no more than a village' (McLuhan, 1964, p. 5). The phrase 'global village' has been repeated so many times since, and in so many different contexts, that it has become a cliché, devoid of its original meaning and effect. The received interpretation of the global village is that it is a metaphor for a world bound ever closer together by communications and transport technologies. However, McLuhan's use of the metaphor was more complex than that. The word 'village' was employed to convey more than just the sense of a world reduced down to village-like physical proportions.

global village

McLuhan proposed a three-fold division of history based on the dominant medium of communication – oral, writing/printing, and electric/electronic (Meyrowitz, 1985) – and was clearly influenced by the earlier investigations of Harold Innis who claimed that the rise and fall of civilizations and empires were intimately linked to changes in forms of communication media (Innis, 1950). McLuhan argued that the development of the phonetic alphabet, the written word and, in particular, the mechanical printing of written text were central in bringing about the 'de-tribalization' of human societies.

In what McLuhan describes as 'tribal society' the dominant medium of communication was the spoken word, which engendered organic, tightly knit and geographically circumscribed societies. The invention of the phonetic alphabet was to lead to the eventual overthrow of this 'society of the ear', but this was not fully accomplished until the development of the printing press. With the rapid dissemination of printed materials following the invention of printing, the rationality of written communication succeeded in opening up and 'abstracting' closed 'tribal' societies, not least by facilitating greater levels of communication between different societies through the transfer of written information, which helped extend social relations over space. In doing so,

... the typographic explosion thrust a more uniform culture into the interstices of society, and made possible the mode of social unity we know as the nation-state: it was the 'architect of nationalism', as well as the original mode of industrialism ... The print era was analysis, fragmentation, repetition, the victory of a certain type of rationality.

(Nairn, 1967, p. 6)

However, for McLuhan, the twentieth century was witness to a process which would cause as much social upheaval and change as had the spread of 'Gutenburg technology'. This crisis was founded in the new communications technologies, which were causing the rationality of the print era to 'implode', as new forms of oral communications superseded the former dominance of printed forms.

McLuhan argued that, as electronically mediated forms of communication supersede printed forms, so the dominant form of human communication becomes oral once more, as it was in the tribal villages of the past. Electronic media mean that we begin to participate in 'village-like encounters, but on a global scale. As a result of the widespread use of electronic media, everyone is involved in everyone else's business, and there is a decline in print-supported notions of delegated authority, nationalism, and linear thinking' (Meyrowitz,

1985, pp. 17–18). But in the global village confusion, uncertainty and fear are rife. The era of the global village is characterized by 'panic terrors, exactly befitting a small world of tribal drums, total interdependence, and superimposed co-existence ... Terror is the normal state of any oral society, for in it everything effects everything all the time' (McLuhan, 1962, p. 32).

McLuhan's work was undoubtedly original and made a number of prescient observations about the nature of life in a world tied together by electronic communications media. For example, consider the arena of news-gathering and dissemination. Oral forms of communication are now as, if not more, important than written forms for, as new events break and develop, we tend to find out about them first via the oral reports of television or radio newsreaders. It is becoming rare for printed news media to break important stories. This is because of the ability of electronic media to disseminate news stories 'as they happen', a process which, as we saw earlier, has been greatly facilitated by the use of satellite communications.

detraditionalization

In addition, McLuhan's observations chime with the thesis of '*detraditionalization*' which both Giddens and Harvey see as an important outcome of both time–space distanciation and time–space compression. For Giddens, the process of time–space distanciation has had the effect of 'rolling social life away from the fixities of tradition' (1990, p. 53). For Harvey, time–space compression has resulted in local social practices being overwhelmed by the power of capitalist relations of production. Thus, the electronic media of which McLuhan speaks has facilitated an increase in the number of 'distanciated' forms of social interaction, while at the same time acting as the medium by which previously remote and self-contained places have become enmeshed in an increasingly global economic system.

The ability of electronic media to 'detraditionalize' society shows no sign of abating. Indeed, the proliferation of electronic media continues to

Reporting from a war zone: journalists file a report for Sky television news from Bosnia with the aid of portable satellite telecommunications equipment

undermine many of the institutions which have traditionally held societies together. For one thing, it is estimated that half of the world's 6,000 languages will die out in the next 100 years or so, and the spread of more dominant languages via electronic media will play a major part in this (Moseley and Asher, 1994). For another, the dissemination of information made possible by electronic media has served to narrow the 'knowledge gap' between those in positions of power and authority and everybody else. This is the position taken by some communications theorists who argue that in the past, when information was mediated via the physical transportation of messages, it was far easier for those in power and authority to exercise social control by managing the flow of information in a society (Meyrowitz, 1985). Only the rich and powerful had the resources to maintain regular contact with large numbers of people distributed over large areas. For the most part, people were confined within the day-to-day routines of social life and were unable to engage in long-distance communications. It was thus difficult for people trapped in this way to challenge the interpretations and representations of events emanating from those who did control and channel the flow of information through society.

However, the rise of electrical and electronic media, from the telegraph onwards, has led to information becoming much more widely accessible, and this has served to undermine those in power and authority who owe their position to the regulation and control of flows of information. It is interesting to note that the rise of electronic media has indeed been accompanied by a decline in the esteem with which people regard certain social institutions, which were once accepted uncritically as being essential to the fabric of societies (Meyrowitz, 1985). For example, in the United Kingdom during the 1980s and 1990s a series of once taken-for-granted social institutions was undermined, ranging from the Royal Family in particular to the political system in general, and these have seen the regard in which they are held by most people plummet to new depths. Perhaps the wider availability of information made possible by the spread of electronic media has made people more critical, less deferential, and certainly less willing to assume that people in positions of power and authority are automatically deserving of respect.

But we must be careful before we go too far along the road suggested by Meyrowitz and others, who would have us believe that information and communications have flattened social hierarchies and evened out the balance of social power just because, for example, a 'telephone or computer in a ghetto tenement or in a suburban teenager's bedroom is potentially as effective as a telephone or computer in a corporate suite' (Meyrowitz, 1985, p. 170). But is it really *as* effective in the way that Meyrowitz suggests? We must beware of falling into the trap of technological determinism, that is, in believing that the existence of technologies is alone sufficient to drive social change. Merely being able to communicate with people more effectively does not necessarily by itself do much to flatten existing imbalances in social power. To extend Meyrowitz's hypothetical example, while the inner-city resident, the suburban teenager and the corporate executive may all be able to telephone a bank to ask for an interview to discuss borrowing some money, they would not all necessarily enjoy the privilege of being granted an audience with the bank manager, although it is fairly obvious who would be first in line.

Thus, even when there is equal access to communications and information technology, existing imbalances in wealth and power tend to intervene, which can sometimes deepen rather than flatten social inequalities. One of the reasons for this is that, with very few exceptions, the use of communications technologies has to be paid for. Telephones and computers have to be bought in the first place, while their use incurs costs which some people may be better able to afford than others. The same holds true for transportation technologies. This means that while the world may be shrinking, it is shrinking faster for some people than for others. While some people are moving closer together in time–space, others are moving further apart. We will examine aspects of this process of 'differential shrinking' in the next section.

Activity 4 To what extent has electronically mediated oral communication supplanted written information in your experience? Think of an average day, and attempt to classify the way in which you spend your time into the three main forms of communication identified by McLuhan:

(a) face-to-face oral communication

(b) written communication

(c) electronically mediated communication.

Most of us will engage in all three forms of communication over the course of a day, although the relative importance of each will vary markedly from time to time and from person to person. For example, the nature of my job means that I spend a disproportionate amount of my time consumed with written forms of communication, reading and writing. But I also seem to spend a great deal of my time in meetings, which depend upon face-to-face communications. To what extent is the life of an academic the exception that proves the rule of McLuhan's thesis of the importance of electronically mediated communication?

Summary of section 1.4

o The concept of the 'global village' stems from Marshall McLuhan's periodization of human history based on the predominant medium of communication – oral, writing/printing and electric/electronic.

o In the present electric/electronic age, McLuhan argues that oral forms of communication will come to supersede written and printed forms as electronic media allow people to engage in instantaneous communications with one another on a global scale.

o McLuhan's thesis can be seen as a prologue to the arguments of 'detraditionalization' that figure strongly in Giddens' concept of 'time–space distanciation' and Harvey's notion of 'time–space compression'.

1.5   The end of geography?

Many of those who have felt moved to comment on the way in which the world appears to be shrinking have rushed to the conclusion that if space is shrinking, then the subject of geography must inevitably become rather less of a concern. In 1970, in his popular commentary *Future Shock*, Alvin Toffler proclaimed 'the Demise of Geography', arguing that, thanks to transport and communications technologies, 'place ... is no longer a primary source of diversity' (quoted in Abler, 1975, p. 123). The reason for this, Toffler argued, was because flows of people and information have helped to dissolve geographical difference and distinctiveness. Almost twenty years later, in an analysis of the international finance system, Richard O'Brien made a similar but even less hopeful prognosis for geography. O'Brien heralded 'the End of Geography', which he argued referred 'to a state of economic development where geographical location no longer matters ... or matters much less than hitherto' (1991, p. 1).

In this section we will analyse the veracity of such claims. We will do so through an investigation of the world of money and finance. This is appropriate not only because the financial system was the subject of O'Brien's analysis, but also because it is a spectacular example of time–space compression.

1.5.1   A world of money and finance

In recent years there has been a dramatic acceleration in the pace of financial flows and a shrinkage of financial space. One of the reasons for this has been the evolution of money into new forms that have become progressively less material, making it easier to move money around the world at very little cost. While money still exists in the form of coinage (which has been used in human societies since around 800 BC), money can now also exist in a purely electronic form within the computer systems of banks and other financial institutions (Solomon, 1991). In consequence, the speed at which money can move around the *global financial system* has accelerated markedly in recent years. Money can now travel as electrons along telephone cables, at the speed of light as photons along fibre-optic cables, and as pulses of energy transmitted via microwave and satellite communication systems.

global financial system

Developments such as these mean that it now takes only seconds to send money from one part of the world to another. It is this 'hyper-mobility' of money which has facilitated the development of global financial markets, whereby the buy and sell prices of a wide range of financial products can be monitored by dealers and traders located in financial centres all over the world. It was this sense of financial markets all over the world collapsing into a single entity that prompted O'Brien to announce 'the End of Geography', referred to above.

The near instantaneity of the world of money and finance is driven by processes of capitalist competition and by the struggle to reduce the turnover time of capital which Harvey identified as the motor of time–space compression. For within the financial system the old adage 'time is money' is literally true. Consider the way in which financiers 'price' money. The cost of money is determined by the level of risk which a financial institution believes it exposes itself to when lending money to a borrower. The perceived level of risk is inversely related to the likelihood of the borrower repaying: the higher the risk, the more a financial institution will ask a borrower to pay or, conversely, the more likely the borrower is to repay the loan, the less the borrower will have to pay for it.

But how do financial institutions calculate risk and therefore the cost of money? In part, the cost of money is determined by the relative wealth of the person or institution wanting to borrow the money, which has an obvious influence on their ability to repay the money. The cost is also determined in part by the *length of time* that the borrower wants the money for. The longer the borrower wants the money for, the more risky it is considered to be for the lender, since over time the circumstances of the borrower may change, making it less likely that the money will be repaid. Therefore, with all other things being equal, it will be more expensive to borrow money for two years than it would be for one year, more for six months than it would be for three months, more for seven days that it would be for one day.

This link between the cost of money and time has encouraged a speed-up in the financial system, particularly as it becomes possible to make money 'work' harder by using information and communication technologies to transport money right around the world and back again in the search for investment opportunities. Not only do banks and other financial institutions bristle with the latest space-shrinking technologies, but the various markets located in the world's leading financial centres have also installed the latest electronic communications systems, to make it easier for people to buy and sell there regardless of their own location. These developments have encouraged the emergence of 'global financial trading'. Investors and speculators in the world's leading financial centres oversee vast sums of 'hot' money which they move around the world, buying and selling financial instruments in the search for trading profits. Large sums of money can be made in this way, in very narrow time horizons, which further encourage traders to take advantage of the fact that money is cheaper when borrowed for only a short period.

Although the global financial system at times appears to be nothing less than a confusing maelstrom of money, it is possible to identify two trends which are consistent with arguments being pursued in this chapter. On the one hand, s*ome places have moved closer together in relative space*. The trajectories of several national, regional and local economies have become ever more closely interconnected, held together by a dense network of financial flows and transactions. These flows have also served to bring about a greater degree of *economic homogenization* than hitherto, as traditional economic practices have been overwhelmed by a more powerful calculative rationale associated with the imperatives of global financial capital. But on the other hand, s*ome places have moved further apart in relative space*, as they have been subject to a process of financial exclusion, and this has led to a widening of economic and social space between such 'places of exclusion' and those localities which remain within the global financial system. Let us now look at both these processes in more detail.

homogenization of economic space

widening of social space

1.5.2 Money and the shrinking of space

Money has long contributed to the compression of space through time. Money serves two important functions in any economic exchange system: it acts as a medium of exchange and as a measure of value. In performing these roles, money helps to speed up processes of economic exchange, and to facilitate their extension over space. Without a medium of exchange, trade has to take the form of barter, which relies upon the mutuality of need: to obtain what I want from you, I have to have something that you want, and we have to agree that what we exchange is of equivalent value. Such exchange processes are slow and laborious, and tend for the most part to restrict the geographical extension of economic exchange. Quite simply, without money it is necessary for *both* parties to take their goods to the market.

Therefore, at one level money can be seen to be little more than a token which is inserted into the exchange process (i.e. a medium of exchange) and which acquires a value against which other items are exchanged (i.e. a measure of value). In other words, money becomes a universal equivalent, against which all other items in an exchange system are valued. It is not hard to see why the development of money enabled economic activity to expand geographically: money is portable and so eases the exchange process; only one party now needs to bring their goods to the market, the buyer just brings their money.

Money does not only have profound spatial effects upon economic activity; the development of money in its credit form enables people to move through *time*. This may seem like a rather extraordinary quality to attach to money, so let me explain. When my bank grants me an overdraft on my current account or agrees to give me a loan, they are giving me *credit*. They are giving me money that I do not currently have, but that I expect to get in due course. In the case of an overdraft, the money will be repaid (hopefully!) when my monthly salary is paid into my bank account, whereas in the case of a loan I agree to pay the money back over a longer period, in regular instalments. I pay a price for such credit (in the interest charged on the overdraft or loan), but it does allow me to use the money *now*, whereas otherwise I would have to defer that expenditure until some time in the future when I had accumulated sufficient funds on my own. The significance of the credit system in this context is that it enables people to bring their purchasing decisions *forward in time*. The advantage of the credit system in a capitalist economy is that it can help to reduce the turnover time of capital in the short term. It also helps to shrink economic space, in that it facilitates long-distance trade. Without the credit provided by the growing band of merchant banks based in the City of London, it would have been impossible for the capitalist world economy to expand in the way that it did during the eighteenth and nineteenth centuries. The banks intervened between seller and purchaser in long-distance trade deals, by providing credit notes to the sellers which could be handed in for money as soon as their goods left port; this allowed purchasers to pay for their goods only when they arrived at their destination.

Over time the financial system has evolved in ways that have accelerated the process of time–space compression. Coins composed of some form of precious metal were once the monetary base of all modern economies. Silver and gold coins were considered particularly appropriate units of exchange since they had an inherent value against which the value of other commodities in an economic system could be judged. However, while the use of this form of money was certainly an advance upon a system of barter, the use of coins presented its own barrier to the geographical extension of economic activity. Large transactions would often require large volumes of coins, which were difficult to transport from one place to another because of their weight.

This barrier was overcome by the use of paper money. In return for a deposit of money in the precious metal form, banks would issue notes which could be traded in place of coins. The notes were IOUs, which promised that the holder could reclaim the 'real money' held in the strong-boxes of the bank. As long as people were confident that the notes would be exchanged for coins when presented, the notes began to acquire their own value and to act as universal equivalents in their own right. This development also served to foster the rise of the credit economy, for banks could issue more notes than they had 'real money': as long as not all the holders of the notes came back to banks to exchange their notes for precious metal at the same time, then the economy would continue to expand. However, if borrowers and depositors did attempt to cash in their notes for real money at the same time (which tended to occur when a bank increased the supply of its bank-notes beyond a prudent multiple of its reserves of money in the form of gold or silver), then a bank would find itself in severe financial difficulties. A bank embarrassed in this way would soon be forced out of business, as the faith in the value of its bank-notes, which resided in their exchangeability with 'real money', was rapidly destroyed.

So, while the development of paper money contributed significantly to the shrinking of space, the inherent fragility of the banking system meant that this process was often fitful and liable to retreat in the face of regular financial crises, because of the periodic realization of how rapidly paper money could become worthless. In order to reduce the number of damaging financial crises caused by outbreaks of doubt about the worth of paper money, from the eighteenth century onwards governments began to think about ways in which the financial system could be regulated. The rise of the central bank, with supervisory power over the entire banking system, was a product of this interest.

Central banking is important in this context since it helps bring about a homogenization of financial space within the borders of a nation-state. By setting certain standards of prudential banking behaviour, the central bank is able to give its seal of approval to the notes issued by the 'approved' banks under its supervision. All such notes become legal tender, and equally able to act as universal equivalents. Eventually, governments were able to sever the link between paper money and precious metal, as it was the government and not the value of the metal which was seen to guarantee the value of money.

While this process of homogenization brought considerable benefits, inasmuch as it introduced a degree of confidence in money as a medium of exchange that might not otherwise exist, it also served to eradicate some beneficial local financial practices. For example, the coming of the railroads transformed the nature of financial relations in frontier areas in the United States during the nineteenth century. On the one hand, bank-notes issued by larger and more stable banks in the east came to replace those issued by smaller and more fragile banks based in the west, which was for the most part a good thing. But on the other hand, as William Cronon describes in Reading B, the incorporation of frontier areas into the wider US economy through the improvements in transport and communications links also destroyed the local credit systems which had forged close and trusting business relationships amongst local traders and merchants.

Throughout the nineteenth century a growing number of national economies were thus bound ever more tightly together through the use of a common, state-backed currency. However, before long, money began to stray beyond the confines of the borders of nation-state. Banks were some of the first economic organizations to internationalize their activities, and began to facilitate the movement of money across international borders. This led to some types of money, in particular the pound sterling and the US dollar, being used as a medium of exchange in economies thousands of miles from their country of issue. The use of sterling was commonplace throughout the world economy during the nineteenth century, while during the twentieth century, as the United States grew to economic superpower status, the demand for dollars grew alongside and at times even ahead of local currencies. Backed up by the might of the United States, the dollar was widely perceived as being more likely to hold its value than would currencies backed up by weaker states and economies.

This preference for the dollar ahead of local currencies was in fact instrumental in helping to bring about the global financial system in which we now find ourselves. In the aftermath of the Second World War, the unchallenged economic dominance of the United States ensured that the dollar became the main currency of international trade. This led to a large outflow of dollars from the United States, as US multinationals used dollars to fund new operations in Europe and Asia, which they established to take advantage of the post-war boom in the world economy. This outflow was further encouraged by banks in Europe which offered higher rates of interest on dollar deposits than could be earned in the United States; this resulted in many US residents moving their deposits from US banks to those in Europe. The rise of the 'Euromarkets' – markets for currencies held outside their country of issue – in the 1950s and 1960s was an important moment in the rise of a global financial system. It illustrated that money had a value beyond its country of issue and could be traded on an international scale. These markets have continued to grow, and are made up of a constellation of 'emigrant' money, which can now move round the world at a rapid pace, thanks to the use of fibre-optic and satellite communications systems referred to earlier. Indeed, the 'market for money' is now the largest in the world, so that the turnover in the market for currencies (the foreign exchange market) in 1993 surpassed $1,000 million *per day*.

The shrinking of financial space has also seen financial centres become much more interdependent. A good illustration of this was the stock market 'crash' of October 1987. In just a few days the value of shares traded on stock markets around the world plummeted in a remarkably parallel fashion (see Figure 1.6). Many financial products are now traded on a continuous or near continuous basis, as trading activity moves from centre to centre with the passage of the sun around the Earth: the global financial system is yet another empire upon which the sun never sets. While the 1987 crisis first broke out in New York, this was quickly passed onto Tokyo and the markets of Australia and South Asia, before being transmitted to the markets of Europe. The contagion of crisis is made possible by the fact that the main participants in global financial markets are a relatively small number of financial institutions and corporations from North America, Europe and Japan, many of which operate in the same markets in financial centres around the world. Information about market movements is therefore quickly passed on from market to market and from centre to centre (see Figure 1.7). In the light of this, it may well be that McLuhan's prediction that life in the 'global village' would be one of instantaneous interrelatedness has – in the case of the global financial market at least – already come true.

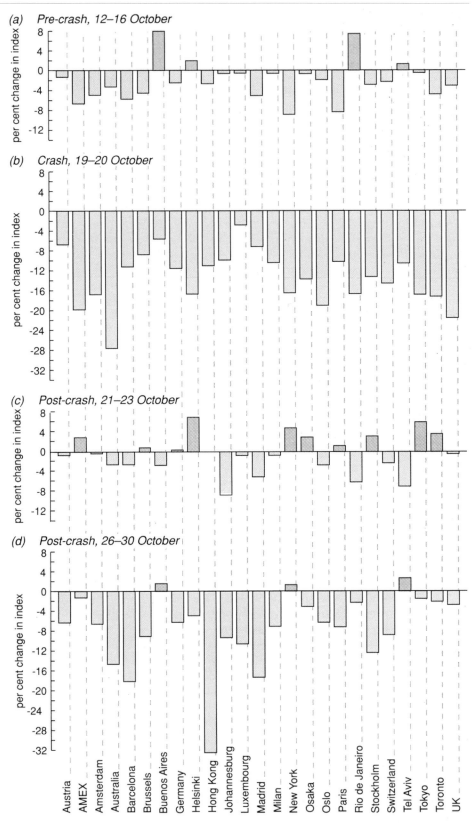

Figure 1.6 The global stock market crash of 1987: market price performance of global stock exchanges: percentage changes for four periods, 12–30 October 1987 (Source: data from International Stock Exchanges, 1988)

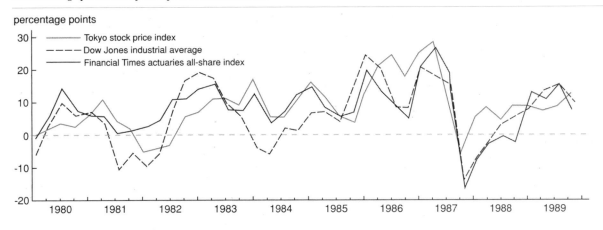

percentage points

Figure 1.7   Volatility of world stock markets* (Source: based on data from Federal Reserve Bank of New York Annual Report, 1989)

Note: *Quarterly percentage deviation from twelve-month moving average of stock prices: end-of-quarter value used in calculation of dispersion.

The global financial system has encouraged the shrinking of space in other ways too. Through the foreign exchange markets, national economies are linked together like never before. The rise and fall of currencies in relation to one another has important implications for the relative competitiveness of the products of countries, as a rise in the value of their currency makes goods relatively more expensive, while a fall makes them less so. The rise of the global financial system has also helped bring about a flattening of difference between the macroeconomic policies of many nation-states. Until the 1970s governments in Western Europe and North America were all committed to a greater or lesser extent to a form of macroeconomic policy which included a commitment to growth and full employment. But as the global financial system has grown and become more powerful, the idea of the 'Keynesian welfare state' has been in steady retreat. The reason for this is that the pursuit of growth and the push for full employment tended to be accompanied by inflation. However, there is nothing financiers and investors like less than inflation, for it erodes the value of their wealth in real terms. Therefore, as money became more mobile it was increasingly easy for investors to move their money out of inflationary states and into economies with lower rates of inflation. In response to successive episodes of 'capital flight', which more often than not were associated with sudden falls in the value of currencies in the foreign exchange market, more and more states began to adopt macroeconomic policies which placed the defeat of inflation at the top of their list of macroeconomic priorities, regardless of the implications for economic growth and levels of unemployment. In this way, the global reach of financial capital has imposed upon many economies a policy logic which comes under the banner of 'anti-inflationism'.

1.5.3   Money and the widening of space

The global financial system has not only shrunk space, it has also markedly widened the economic and social space between some people and places. We shall illustrate this with two examples.

The description of the contemporary financial system as 'global' is a contentious one. It is overwhelmingly concentrated in North America

Europe and Japan, a geography which is symbolized by the fact the world's three premier financial centres are New York, London and Tokyo. *Indeed, if anything, the space of the global financial system contracted during the 1980s.* The reason for this was a severe financial crisis which revolved around the large debts of developing countries, particularly in South America and Africa. The countries were unable to repay their debts, with the result that they were effectively excluded from the global financial system as banks refused to lend them more money, while insisting on the repayment of the debts still outstanding (Thrift and Leyshon, 1988).

The exclusion of much of the third world from the global financial system condemned many countries to a state of 'un-development', the reverse of economic development, as businesses collapsed and aid programmes faltered while levels of poverty, malnutrition and mortality spiralled (Corbridge, 1993). An analysis of some basic macroeconomic indicators reveals that during the 1980s the economies of many countries in Africa and Latin America were going backwards. For example, gross national product per capita in Brazil fell from US$2200 in 1981 to US$1640 in 1985 and from US$1200 to US$660 in Côte d'Ivorie over the same period (Corbridge, 1993, p. 61). But what did this process of un-development mean for the people in a country ravaged by debt and the associated ills of high unemployment and spiralling inflation? These are the comments of a parent in Bolivia:

Since everything is so expensive, I don't give my children breakfast any more. For lunch I give them a little rice soup. I don't buy sugar now that it has gone up. To eat, I have to make do any way I can, because the children can't get along without food. Us adults, we manage when we have to. Sometimes I say to myself, 'I'm going to give my children away to someone'. But then I think of what my parents might do to me — that's what I'm afraid of.

(quoted in George, 1988, p. 147)

For much of the 1980s the developing countries may well have been on a different planet, not just in a different hemisphere, as far as many people involved in the global financial system were concerned. *By the early 1990s the less developed countries (or LDCs) were much further away from the 'West' in terms of economic and social space than they were a decade earlier.*

It was not only people in developing countries for whom economic and social space seemed to widen rather than shrink as a result of the machinations of the global financial system. Many people living in developed countries have had a similar experience. When the global financial system turned away from the developing countries in the 1980s, it focused upon financial markets in developed countries such as the UK. This had a number of important effects. For one it was easier to borrow money, and the burgeoning credit economy helped the economy boom. However, not everyone reaped the benefits of this boom. It was based mainly in the south of Britain, and employment was concentrated within a narrow range of industries, such as financial services and high-technology industry. In the north and west, economic growth proceeded at a more pedestrian pace. The opening up of what became known as the 'north–south divide' was a geographical manifestation of a growing divergence in the economic and social structures of economies such as the UK. Many of those in work were earning large incomes and becoming progressively wealthier, but the rundown of the Keynesian welfare state in line with the anti-inflationary imperatives of the global financial system meant that those out of work became progressively worse off as state benefits were reduced or abolished altogether. Such processes help to explain the high levels of economic and social polarization which have characterized so many contemporary cities (see Chapter 3).

More recently, the financial system has begun to widen social space within some industrialized countries in a rather more direct manner. The credit-fuelled economy boom of the 1980s came crashing down in the early 1990s under the weight of unpaid debt. In response to this 'developed country debt crisis', financial services firms embarked upon a familiar strategy. As in the wake of the LDC debt crisis, financial institutions embarked upon what was described as a 'flight to quality', but which in the context of the developed countries meant a retreat to a more affluent middle-class heartland. This process is particularly important in the United States, where 'financial exclusion' has played an important role in deepening levels of uneven development within many large urban areas (Dymski and Veitch, 1992). Access to a regular supply of credit is vital to the economic development of any area. But the fact that the financial services industry is more disposed to lend money to more affluent suburban areas, and less disposed to lend to poorer inner-city areas, has caused the economic social and racial divide running through US cities to widen. Middle-class whites have joined financial capital on a flight to the metropolitan fringes, with the result that the centres of urban areas in the US have tended to become dominated by groups of poorer Blacks, Asians and Hispanics. One commentator has described this phenomenon as 'spatial apartheid', with many US cities resembling 'urban donuts'; that is, they are 'Black in the industrialized centre, lily-white on the job-rich rim' (Davis, 1992, p. 17).

Therefore, it would seem that the claims about the demise of geography made at the beginning of this section were rather overstated. The process of time–space compression does not mean that everywhere is becoming the same. Some places are, in the ways we have seen above. But at the same time, this very process of economic homogenization has the capacity to increase difference, particularly along lines of income and social class.

Summary of section 1.5

o   The financial system has facilitated the shrinking of space over a long period of time. Money is an agent of time–space compression, as is the credit system, and between them they enable economic agents to move more freely through space and to bring purchases forward in time.

o   A global financial system has developed in recent years, linked by webs of financial flows and transactions. This has facilitated some degree of interdependence and homogenization in the global economy, as the power of money has caused a logic of anti-inflationism to be installed in many economies throughout the world.

o   But at the same time, the financial system has been responsible for the widening of space. The economic gap between the developed and developing world is now much wider than it once was because of the dynamics of financial capital at a global scale, while more recently the financial system has helped to deepen levels of uneven development within industrialized countries.

1.6 Conclusions

There are a number of conclusions that we can draw from the preceding analysis. While the world has certainly been 'shrinking' over a long period of time, the speed at which the world has shrunk has gathered pace in the last 150 years or so. There is no doubt that the world will become an increasingly smaller place in the years to come. As the world contracts, so the pace of life will continue to accelerate, as it becomes easier and less expensive to move goods, people and information through space. People and places appear to be moving closer to one another through time–space convergence. Moreover, they are becoming increasingly inter-connected through time–space distanciation, and life is speeding up because of time–space compression.

However, it is important to remember that, while the world can be said to have shrunk, to have become more interdependent, and to have accelerated in an absolute sense, the relative level of shrinkage, interdependence and acceleration that people experience varies markedly from place to place and from person to person. There would appear to be a fairly strong correlation between the economic and social power of individuals and the degree to which they prosper in a world that appears to becoming ever smaller and spinning ever faster. At one extreme there are those for whom the world is now a very small place indeed, a playground of work and leisure, where nowhere is very much more than twenty-four hours away by long-haul jet. For others – the vast majority of the world's population – the world remains a very large, difficult and often terrifying place.

References

ABLER, R. (1975) 'Monoculture or miniculture? The impact of communications media or culture in space' in Abler, R. *et al.* (eds).

ABLER, R., JANELLE, D., PHILBRICK, A. and SOMMER, J. (1975) 'Introduction: the study of spatial futures', in Abler, R. *et al.* (eds).

ABLER, R. *et al.* (eds) *Human Geography in a Shrinking World*, Belmont, CA, Duxbury Press.

BEST, M. (1990) *The New Competition: Institutions of Industrial Restructuring*, Cambridge, Polity Press.

CORBRIDGE, S. (1993) *Debt and Development*, Oxford, Blackwell.

CRONON, W. (1992) *Nature's Metropolis: Chicago and the Great West*, New York, Norton.

DAVIS, M. (1992) 'Who killed LA? A political autopsy', *New Left Review*, No.197, pp. 3–28.

DER DERRIAN, J. (1992) *Antidiplomacy: Spies, Terror, Speed and War*, Cambridge, MA, Blackwell.

DUNFORD, M. and PERRONS, D. (1983) *The Arena of Capital*, London, Macmillan.

DYMSKI, G. A. and VEITCH, J. M. (1992) 'Race and the financial dynamics of urban growth: LA as Fay Wray', Working Paper 92–21, Riverside, CA, Department of Economics, University of California Riverside.

GEORGE, S. (1989) *A Fate Worse Than Debt*, Harmondsworth, Penguin Books.

GIDDENS, A. (1990) *The Consequences of Modernity*, Cambridge, Polity Press.

GREGORY, D. (1994) *Geographical Imaginations*, Oxford, Blackwell.

HAGGETT, P. (1990) *The Geographer's Art*, Oxford, Basil Blackwell.

HALL, P. and PRESTON, P. (1988) *The Carrier Wave: New Information and the Geography of Innovation, 1846-2003*, London, Unwin Hyman.

HARVEY, D. (1989) *The Condition of Postmodernity: An Enquiry into the Origins of Cultural Change*, Oxford, Blackwell.

HERBERTSON, A. J. (1915) 'Regional environment, heredity and consciousness', *The Geographical Teacher*, Vol. 8, pp. 147–53.

INNIS, H. (1950) *Empire and Communications*, Toronto, Toronto University Press.

JANELLE, D. (1968) 'Central place development in a time–space framework', *Professional Geographer*, Vol. 20, No. 1, pp. 5–10.

JANELLE, D. G. (1969) 'Spatial reorganization: a model and concept', *Annals of the Association of American Geographers*, Vol. 59, pp. 348–64.

JANELLE, D. G. (1973) 'Measuring human extensibility in a shrinking world', *The Journal of Geography*, Vol. 72, pp. 8-15.

KENNEDY, P. (1979) 'Imperial cable communications and strategy, 1870-1914' in Kennedy, P. (ed.) *The War Plans of the Great Powers, 1880–1914*, London, Allen and Unwin.

KENNEDY, P. (1988) *The Rise and Fall of the Great Powers*, London, Fontana.

KERN, S. (1983) *The Culture of Time and Space, 1880-1918*, Cambridge, MA, Harvard University Press.

KING, R. (1995) 'Migrations, globalization and place' in Massey, D. and Jess, P. (eds).

MACKINDER, H. (1904) 'The geographical pivot of history', *The Geographical Journal*, Vol. 23, pp. 421–37.

McLUHAN, M. (1962) *The Gutenburg Galaxy: The Making of Typographic Man*, London, Routledge and Kegan Paul.

McLUHAN, M. (1964) *Understanding Media: Extensions of Man*, London, Routledge and Kegan Paul.

MASSEY, D. (1984) *Spatial Divisions of Labour*, London, Macmillan.

MASSEY, D. (1993) 'Questions of locality', *Geography*, Vol. 78, Part 2, pp. 142–9.

MASSEY, D. (1995) 'Imagining the world' in Allen, J. and Massey, D. (eds) *Geographical Worlds*, London, Oxford University Press/The Open University (Volume 1 in this series).

MEYROWITZ, J. (1985) *No Sense of Place: The Impact of Electronic Media on Social Behaviour*, New York, Oxford University Press.

MOSELEY, C. and ASHER, R. E. (1994) *Atlas of the World's Language*, London, Routledge.

NAIRN, T. (1967) *Marshall McLuhan*, BFI Education Department Seminar Paper, No. 81, London.

O'BRIEN, R. (1991) *Global Financial Integration: The End of Geography*, London, Pinter.

SOLOMON, E. H. (1991) 'Today's money: image and reality' in Solomon, E. H. (ed.) *Electronic Money Flows*, Boston, Kluwer Academic Publishers, pp. 15-47.

TAYLOR, P. M. (1992) *War and the Media: Propaganda and Persuasion in the Gulf War*, Manchester, Manchester University Press.

THRIFT, N. (1990) 'Transport and communications, 1730-1914' in Dodgson, R. A. and Butlin, R. A. (eds) *An Historical Geography of England and Wales*, Second Edition, London, Academic Press, pp. 453–86.

THRIFT, N. and LEYSHON, A. (1988) '"The gambling propensity": banks, developing country debt exposures and the new international financial system', *Geoforum*, Vol. 19, No. 1, pp. 55–69.

TOFFLER, A. (1970) *Future Shock*, London, Bodley Head.

VIRILIO, P. (1983) *Pure War*, New York, Semiotext(e).

Reading A: *David Harvey, 'The concept of time–space compression'*

I want to suggest that we have been experiencing, these last two decades, an intense phase of time–space compression that has had a disorienting and disruptive impact upon political–economic practices, the balance of class power, as well as upon cultural and social life [...]

The transition to flexible accumulation was in part accomplished through the rapid deployment of new organizational forms and new technologies in production [...] Speed-up was achieved in production by organizational shifts towards vertical disintegration – sub-contracting, outsourcing etc. – that reversed the Fordist tendency towards vertical integration and produced an increasing roundaboutness in production even in the face of increasing financial centralization. Other organizational shifts – such as the 'just-in-time' delivery system that reduces stock inventories – when coupled with the new technologies of electronic control, small-batch production, etc., all reduced turnover times in many sectors of production (electronics, machine tools, automobiles, construction, clothing, etc.). For the labourers this all implied an intensification (speed-up) in labour processes and an acceleration in the de-skilling and re-skilling required to meet new labour needs [...]

Accelerating turnover time in production entails parallel accelerations in exchange and consumption. Improved systems of communication and information flow, coupled with rationalizations in techniques of distribution (packaging, inventory control, containerization, market feed-back, etc.), made it possible to circulate commodities through the market system with greater speed. Electronic banking and plastic money were some of the innovations that improved the speed of the inverse flow of money. Financial services and markets (aided by computerized trading) likewise speeded up, so as to make, as the saying has it, 'twenty-four hours a very long time' in global stock markets.

Of the many developments in the arena of consumption, two stand out as being of particular importance. The mobilization of fashion in mass (as opposed to elite) markets provided a means to accelerate the pace of consumption not only in clothing, ornament, and decoration but also across a wide swathe of life-styles and recreational activities (leisure and sporting habits, pop music styles, video and children's games, and the like). A second trend was a shift away from the consumption of goods and into the consumption of services – not only personal, business, educational, and health services, but also into entertainments, spectacles, happenings, and distractions. The 'lifetime' of such services (a visit to a museum, going to a rock concert or movie, attending lectures or health clubs), though hard to estimate, is far shorter than that of an automobile or washing machine. If there are limits to the accumulation and turnover of physical goods (even counting the famous six thousand pairs of shoes of Imelda Marcos), then it makes sense for capitalists to turn to the provision of very ephemeral services in consumption […]

Of the innumerable consequences that have flowed from this general speed-up in the turnover times of capital, I shall focus on those that have particular bearing on ways of thinking, feeling, and doing.

The first major consequence has been to accentuate volatility and ephemerality of fashions, products, production techniques, labour processes, ideas and ideologies, values and established practices. The sense that 'all that is solid melts into air' has rarely been more persuasive […]

In the realm of commodity production, the primary effect has been to emphasize the values and virtues of instantaniety (instant and fast foods, meals, and other satisfactions) and of disposability (cups, plates, cutlery, packaging, napkins, clothing, etc.). The dynamics of a 'throwaway' society, as writers like Alvin Toffler (1970) dubbed it, began to become evident during the 1960s. It meant more than just throwing away produced goods (creating a monumental waste-disposal problem), but also being able to throw away values, life-styles, stable relationships, and attachments to things, buildings, places, people, and received ways of doing and being. These were the immediate and tangible ways in which the 'accelerative thrust in the larger society' crashed up against 'the ordinary daily experience of the individual' (Toffler, 1970, p. 40). Through such mechanisms (which proved highly effective from the standpoint of accelerating the turnover of goods in consumption) individuals were forced to cope with disposability, novelty, and the prospects for instant obsolescence. 'Compared to the life in a less rapidly changing society, more situations now flow through the channel in any given interval of time – and this implies profound changes in human psychology'. This transcience, Toffler goes on to suggest, creates 'a temporariness in the structure of both public and personal value systems' which in turn provides a context for the 'crack-up of consensus' and the diversification of values within a fragmenting society. The bombardment of stimuli, simply on the commodity front, creates problems of sensory overload […]

The volatility, of course, makes it extremely difficult to engage in any long-term planning. Indeed, learning to play the volatility right is now just as important as accelerating turnover time. This means either being highly adaptable and fast-moving in response to market shifts, or masterminding the volatility. The first strategy points mainly towards short-term rather than long-term planning, and cultivating the art of taking short-term gains wherever they are to be had. This has been a notorious feature of US management in recent times. The average tenure of company executive officers has come down to five years, and companies nominally involved in production frequently seek short-term gains through mergers, acquisitions, or operations in financial and currency markets. The tension of managerial performance in such an environment is considerable, producing all kinds of side-effects, such as the so-called 'yuppie flu' (a psychological stress condition that paralyses the performance of talented people and produces long-lasting flu-like symptoms) or the frenzied life-style of financial operators whose addiction to work, long hours, and the rush of power makes them excellent candidates for a kind of schizophrenic mentality [...]

Mastering or intervening actively in the production of volatility, on the other hand, entails manipulation of taste and opinion, either through being a fashion leader or by so saturating the market with images as to shape the volatility to particular ends. This means, in either case, the construction of new sign systems and imagery [...] To begin with, advertising and media images [...] have come to play a very much more integrative role in cultural practices and now assume a much greater importance in the growth dynamics of capitalism. Advertising, moreover, is no longer built around the idea of informing or promoting in the ordinary sense, but is increasingly geared to manipulating desires and tastes through images that may or may not have anything to do with the product to be sold [...] The consumer turnover time of certain images can be very short indeed (close to that ideal of the 'twinkling of an eye' that Marx saw as optimal from the standpoint of capital circulation). Many images can also be mass-marketed instantaneously over space. Given the pressures to accelerate turnover time (and to overcome spatial barriers), the commodification of images of the most ephemeral sort would seem to be a godsend from the standpoint of capital accumulation, particularly when other paths to relieve over-accumulation seem blocked. Ephemerality and instantaneous communicability over space then become virtues to be explored and appropriated by capitalists for their own purposes.

[...]

But, as so often happens, the plunge into the maelstrom of ephemerality has provoked an explosion of opposed sentiments and tendencies. To begin with, all sorts of technical means arise to guard against future shocks. Firms sub-contract or resort to flexible hiring practices to discount the potential unemployment costs of future market shifts. Futures markets in everything, from corn and pork bellies to currencies and government debt, coupled with the 'securitization' of all kinds of temporary and floating debts, illustrate techniques for discounting the future into the present. Insurance hedges of all kinds against future volatility become much more widely available.

Deeper questions of meaning and interpretation also arise. The greater the ephemerality, the more pressing the need to discover or manufacture some kind of eternal truth that might lie therein. The religious revival that has become much stronger since the late sixties, and the search for authenticity and authority in politics (with all of its accoutrements of nationalism and localism and of admiration for those charismatic and 'protean' individuals with their Nietzschian 'will to power') are cases in point. The revival of interest in basic institutions (such as the family and community), and the search for historical roots are all signs of a search for more secure moorings and longer-lasting values in a shifting world [...]

The spatial adjustments have been no less traumatic. The satellite communications systems deployed since the early 1970s have rendered the unit cost and time of communication invariant with respect to distance. It costs the same to communicate over 500 miles as it does over 5,000 via satellite. Air freight rates on commodities have likewise come down dramatically, while containerization has reduced the cost of bulk sea and road transport. It is now possible for a large multinational corporation like Texas Instruments to operate plants with simultaneous decision-making with respect to financial, market, input costs, quality control, and labour process conditions in more than fifty different locations across the globe (Dicken, 1986, pp. 110–13). Mass television ownership coupled with satellite communication makes it possible to experience a rush of images from different spaces almost simultaneously, collapsing the world's spaces into a series of images on a television screen. The whole world can watch the Olympic Games, the World Cup, the fall of a dictator, a political summit, a deadly tragedy [...] while mass tourism, films made in spectacular locations, make a wide range of simulated or vicarious experiences of what the world contains available to many people. The image of places and spaces becomes as open to production and ephemeral use as any other.

We have, in short, witnessed another fierce round in that process of annihilation of space through time that has always lain at the centre of capitalism's dynamic.

References

DICKEN, P. (1986) *Global Shift: Industrial Change in a Turbulent World*, London, Harper and Row.

TOFFLER, A. (1970) *Future Shock*, London, Bodley Head.

Source: Harvey, 1989, pp. 284–8, 292–3

Reading B: W. Cronon, 'The coming of the railroad: economic effects in the Midwest'

The merchant's world: pre-railroad

By using speed to lower the cost of space, the new technology of rail transportation made it possible for urban markets to extend their reach not just geographically and economically but culturally as well [...] The lessons of the urban market were about newness. The merchandise one could buy was new, the way one bought it was new, the life one could live with it was new. Buying from the city meant participating in the progress of the age. It meant becoming modern.

To see how much life had changed, reflect back on what it was like to be a merchant in, say, Iowa, before Chicago extended its hinterland as far as the Mississippi River. Consider, for instance, John McDowell Burrows of Davenport [...] Burrows came to Iowa from Cincinnati in 1838 to set up shop as a grocer. His memoirs, written half a century later, supply a vivid portrait of a frontier merchant's activities, and offer a baseline against which to measure the changes emanating from Chicago and other urban markets with the extension of the railroads. Living in a thinly settled district that was linked to larger urban markets – principally St. Louis and New Orleans – mainly by water, he faced all the usual problems of a pre-rail economy. His rural customers usually had a little or no money. When they came to his store to buy merchandise, they rarely had cash to offer. Instead,

they brought with them the produce of their farms – sacks of wheat or corn, frozen hog carcasses, potatoes, onions, eggs, butter, anything that might be of value – and expected to purchase groceries, dry goods, and hardware in return. If Burrows wanted their trade, he had to be willing to take what they offered, even if he wasn't sure "what ... to do with the produce". Some merchants tried to avoid dealing in such things, but Burrows believed that they came with the territory. "I felt," he wrote, "that this country had to be settled up, and to accomplish this, some one must buy the farmers' surplus, or it would remain a wilderness."

Because his customers were so cash poor, Burrows found himself playing two roles that in the modern economy are generally quite distinct. On the one hand, he regularly purchased a full line of merchandise from wholesalers in St. Louis, Philadelphia, and elsewhere, to be marked up and sold at retail to his customers. On the other hand, he also became a produce merchant, buying a wide range of farm commodities and shipping them downriver to urban markets. Burrows handled one group of products as a seller and another as a buyer. In this way, he acquired the cash and credit he needed to purchase more merchandise and begin the cycle again. The concrete consequence of living at the bottom of a poorly developed [urban] hierarchy, in other words, was that frontier merchants could rarely afford to specialize. Instead, they had to be generalists, often operating on both sides of the market [...]

Farmers sold their crops to Burrows because they lacked the time, inclination, and money to market produce themselves. Steamboat service was infrequent and expensive, and shipping goods by flatboat often meant building the boat oneself – not cheap either, and a lot of work. Always there was the threat that shipments might be lost in a wreck, bringing financial ruin to anyone unprepared to absorb such a catastrophe. Although farmers might have valuable crops to sell, getting them to market was so difficult and expensive that it was often hard to find a buyer. And so the residents of Davenport's hinterland turned to Burrows, who made it his special business to find buyers. He and other frontier merchants had literally to *create* markets where otherwise there would have been none. Doing so was a tricky proposition that required a lot of capital and not a little luck, but there was money to be made by those who could stomach the risks.

[...]

One of a merchant's biggest problems was getting good information about supply and demand along the river. Market news moved only as quickly as a steamboat or a person on horseback, so word of someone's need for produce might take days or weeks to reach a potential seller. "We have a great demand here for Eggs," wrote a storekeeper in Illinois to a merchant in Iowa, "and hear that there are plenty of them in your place, and request you, to send us 5 or 6 Barrels of them immediately ..." (Remembering the risk in such a shipment, he also thought to add, "But you must pack them in plenty of oats, for which you may charge us".) There was good money in such a letter, but only if one could get the eggs to their would-be buyer before anyone else. All too often, the merchant went to great expense to send goods in the direction of a recent rumour, only to find the market glutted by the time they arrived. Burrows's ill-fated

shipment of potatoes to New Orleans – which brought only eight cents a bushel instead of the $2.00 he had expected – was hardly a unique occurrence [...]

But the biggest challenge of being a frontier merchant was undoubtedly the winter. The seasonal cycle that froze rivers and closed down the regional transportation system for almost half the year affected nearly every aspect of a storekeeper's business. The problem with winter was not just that customers had difficulty coming to town, or that merchants could not reach distant wholesalers to restock goods when they sold out. Much more troublesome was the freezing up of the cash economy. The only way a frontier area acquired money – whether in the form of gold, silver, or banknotes – was to send something to the outside world for which the outside world was willing to pay. Winter prevented this from happening. Worse, the greatest surge of agricultural products came to market just as the rivers were becoming dangerous to travel, which meant that a merchant who bought them would almost certainly have to store them through the winter. At the very moment when trade was about to slow nearly to a standstill and prospects for sales were at their worst, merchants had to pay out a large share of their capital to purchase the harvest from farmers in their neighbourhood. Then, for the rest of the winter, they sold merchandise on credit to those same farmers, who had spent all their cash on fall supplies and mortgage payments. Burrows's situation as the weather began to warm in 1841 was familiar to all his fellow merchants. "I found my means," he wrote, "all locked up in produce – corn, flour, pork, bacon, etc., – and that it would be necessary for me to realize on a good portion of my stock early, in order to replenish my store." Burrows's phrase captures the problem perfectly: winter *locked up* capital.

The seasonal cycling of the economy, along with the slowness of travel, meant that frontier merchants had to be prepared to handle large surges of income and expenses. Boom and bust were their normal mode of operation.

Since they made money mainly by turning over their capital as produce, cash, and merchandise, they needed a large enough means to absorb the heavy risks of such transactions. The cost of travel in time and money, and the big expense involved in laying up a stock of merchandise, meant that they could afford to make only one or two large buying trips each year. Frontier merchants journeyed for well over a month to Philadelphia and New York, guessing all the while about what their customers might be willing to buy in the next year, and then spent as much as they could afford on supplies. Because they purchased so much merchandise at once, and because they had to hold such large quantities of farm produce during the winter, they also had to devote a lot of capital just to *warehousing* their stock. Storage facilities were among their most significant costs of doing business. During a big harvest, a merchant could easily overflow his warehouse capacity [...] Burrows was known to commandeer basements and sheds all over Davenport just to hold his purchases until the river thawed.

[...]

Without credit, frontier economies would quickly have collapsed. Communities typically had so little cash that even local banks could run out of money, as happened when Davenport's banker told Burrows that the merchant's heavy produce buying had nearly broken the bank. "We are cleaned out," he announced. "We could not pay for your checks another day to save our lives." Burrows's solution was to start issuing notes on his own behalf, with a promise to redeem them for currency the next April or for merchandise in the store whenever the customer pleased. Such was the heavily leveraged world of frontier exchange. Everyone owed money to everyone else, and for much of the year the only way to sell anything at all was to do so "on time" [...]

[In] the world of money, credit, and merchandise – of capital – that existed in the upriver hinterland of St. Louis during the 1830s, 1840s, and 1850s [...] one sees concretely what it was like to live and trade within the nascent urban

hierarchy of the pre-railroad Mississippi Valley. In a landscape of scattered settlements, markets were few and far between. They sprang up wherever a merchant succeeded in linking a producer of farm crops with a seller of manufactured goods – and disappeared just as quickly. They were completely unreliable. Buyer and seller often failed to find each other. One never knew how prices might change from day to day, because there was no quick way of knowing the condition of markets in other parts of the country. Cash was always in short supply, especially during the winter months when everything – river, farms, stores, trade – froze beneath the blanket of cold. Those who could survive under these circumstances – farmers and merchants alike – needed lots of credit from anyone willing to lend it to them. Merchants had to buy their stock months in advance, hoping that they could anticipate their customers' needs because eastern visits to suppliers happened so rarely. Once purchased, goods had to be held in warehouses for months at a time, locking up capital and preventing it from earning any interest during the long winter wait. For their part, farmers paid heavily for the inefficiency of the system that brought their goods to market, and lived on credit from harvest to harvest as they tried to scrape together the funds to pay off a mortgage. It was not any easy place for anyone to earn a living.

The merchant's world: post-railroad

Such was frontier Iowa – and at one time or another every other part of the Great West – as it existed in 1854 when the Chicago & Rock Island Railroad finally pushed its way to the Illinois side of the Mississippi opposite Davenport. The immediate implications of the rails pointing back toward the eastern horizon should by now be so familiar that they barely need repeating. The railroad meant speed. It meant regular, predictable schedules. It mean year-round movement, even in winter. It meant escaping the river. It meant the East, and not the South. It meant Chicago, and not St. Louis. It meant the future.

Most people welcomed the new technology almost as a saviour, but for some it was an ill wind. Not just the merchants of St. Louis worried about what it might do to their business. Even Chicago retailers had initially been nervous that "the Railroad would ruin Chicago, because it would destroy all the team and retail trade of the city and transfer it to the country." Some storekeepers had even circulated a petition calling for limits on railroad expansion. Laughable as this idea might seem in retrospect, it was not without foundation. Chicago's retail trade *did* suffer in the immediate wake of the railroads as area farmers stopped having to make the long trips to reach Davenport. The railroad *did* eventually destroy the horse team trade. Indeed, the coming of the Chicago & Rock Island was not good news for [some merchants], for it meant the end of the way of doing business on which [they] had built their life and fortune. To understand what finally happened, one must look at the railroad yet again, this time through the eyes of those who had lived in the frontier world that preceded its coming.

By lowering the cost of travel – reducing the time spent moving through space – the railroad brought country and city closer together. It elaborated the urban hierarchy by proliferating towns and villages beneath the emerging metropolis of Chicago, but also brought the layers of that hierarchy closer together. It had once taken several days to make the round-trip between Davenport and St. Louis. Now one could reach Chicago in a little over eight hours. Moreover, one could find in that city most of the same goods that had once required a journey of many weeks for a Mississippi River merchant to purchase on the East Coast. No longer did buying trips have to be an annual affair. No longer did one have to purchase all one's stock in a single expedition that tied up most of one's capital for the rest of the year. Merchants did not have to buy such large quantities when they could travel frequently to the wholesaling center that supplied them. On the railroad, they could travel to the city once or twice a month, refilling their store shelves whenever goods sold out. This afforded the great advantage of cycling capital more quickly: instead of

tying up $10,000 in merchandise for six months or a year, one could turn over $1,000 ten times in the same period and perhaps earn just as much profit. One could carry smaller quantities of a larger variety of goods, knowing that one could replenish any popular item simply by placing an order to Chicago.

The same was true on the other side of the business for produce merchants who purchased crops from farmers. The availability of rail transport, and the existence of a reliable cash market in Chicago, meant that merchants did not have to invest nearly so much money in the warehouse facilities they had formerly needed to hold the harvest until spring. Railroad cars could serve as warehouses of a sort, and the enormous grain elevators and packing plants in Chicago also removed some storage burdens from smaller towns. Crucially, this allowed people of much more limited means to contemplate becoming merchants. Advantages that had once accrued mainly to retailers in metropolitan wholesaling centers like Chicago now became available lower down the urban hierarchy. As one Iowan reported, Chicago gave the frontier merchant "a market that can be relied upon, easily reached, and from which rapid returns are made to the seller, thus enabling him to do a large amount of business on a small capital."

With the railroad – and the access it gave to Chicago – one needed neither as much wealth nor as much credit to be as successful as Burrows had been in frontier Davenport. For Burrows, this was a disaster. Long accustomed to dominating the Davenport market, he suddenly found himself confronted with intense new competition from small dealers with much less money. The warehouse facilities that a few years before had enabled him to handle large quantities of agricultural produce now became a serious disadvantage, tying up his money while competitors without such investments could devote all their capital to buying and selling goods. "The opening of the Chicago & Rock Island Railroad," Burrows recalled, "rather bewildered me." With its arrival, produce merchants suddenly became "as thick as potato-bugs." Dealers with only a few hundred dollars to their names – without a shop, office, or warehouse – could do business right at the railroad station, filling a car with wheat, barley, oats in the morning and shipping it off by midafternoon. In pork season there was no longer any need to hire butchers or chilled warehouse space. Instead, a dealer could "place a scale on the sidewalk in some convenient place, weigh his hogs as he bought them, pile them up on the sidewalk and, in the afternoon, load them up and ship them."

The result was a striking reduction in the capital costs of doing business, for dealers under the new system "were at no expense of rent or labour." Burrows tried to respond in a variety of ways. He invested in new flour mills. He opened a sawmill. He tried to start a reaper factory. Perhaps most suggestively, he decided that "it would be necessary, in order to retain our trade, to follow the railroad", and so opened branch stores in other Iowa towns as a way of trying to become a wholesaler himself. Nothing worked. The new structural conditions created by the railroad and by Chicago's metropolitan market were simply too alien to his familiar way of doing business. The panic of 1857 put his investments under increasing pressure, and when his local bank finally went under in 1859, so did Burrows. After two of his mills burned down, he had not money left to rebuild them and was forced to abandon business altogether. The man who had once been among the most powerful and influential merchants in Davenport found himself a victim of the new economic regime.

[...]

[...I]n the post-railroad world one could buy in a small hinterland town many of the products offered in the regional metropolis of Chicago. Chicago remained a high-order market, with a wealth of goods and services that no other city west of the Appalachians could match, but the growth of its rail-based distribution network made urban goods and services more readily available to people lower down the [urban] hierarchy [...]

City and country were growing closer together. The diminishing distance separating them was measured not just in the similar products one could buy in their stores but in the information that passed between them. Crucial to the success of all the new linkages among factories, wholesalers, retailers, and final customers was the ability of each to communicate with the others. At the same time that railroads were revolutionizing transportation in the west, other new technologies and institutions were revolutionizing communication. The same telegraph that facilitated grain futures trading at the Chicago Board of Trade also enabled western storekeepers to communicate almost instantly with their suppliers. If they were willing to pay for the service, they could walk to the railroad station and send a telegram via Western Union, restocking their shelves almost as soon as an item sold out. Most of the information that sped along telegraph wires was commercial in nature: orders, instructions about payments, schedules for meetings, reports of shipments, and news about price changes. The ability to convey price information by telegraph allowed wholesalers in different parts of the country to respond to each other's competition almost instantly. "You seem to think it queer," wrote one Iowa storekeeper to a colleague in Philadelphia, "that goods should come down in Chicago as soon as they do in New York. They get the news by Telegraph in there [sic] large house 2 or 3 times a day as to the market and of course go up and down with the market [...] New York & Chicago are very closely connected in the dry good trade."

Hinterland merchants gained most of their knowledge about Chicago's markets by more traditional means, like the buying trips they all took at frequent intervals. Except when their need to telegraph was urgent, retailers placed orders with Chicago wholesalers either in person or through the regular mail. Mail service accelerated in the years following the Civil War as the post office learned how to take better advantage of railroad technology. In the late 1860s, the Chicago postmaster tried an experiment in which postal employees sorted letters while still in transit on railroad cars, reducing delays once they reached their destination. The system was so much more efficient than its predecessor that metropolitan post offices in other parts of the country adopted it was well. Rail-based mail shipments were critical in delivering Chicago newspapers to the surrounding countryside, and in making the *Tribune* and later the *Daily News* the leading regional newspapers west of the city. Their articles kept hinterland readers informed about national and regional news, while their advertisements kept merchants posted about the state of metropolitan markets.

Source: Cronon, 1992, pp. 318–22, 323, 324–7, 332–3

Crossing borders: footloose multinationals?　Chapter 2

by John Allen

2.1 Introduction

The previous chapter examined ways in which it is possible to conceive of the world as 'shrinking', not only in terms of distances crossed, but also in terms of the breaking down of spatial barriers which up to now have separated people and places. As such, it offered a critical engagement with the broad view that we are currently witnessing an intense moment of the devastation of space by time. In this chapter we explore a different angle of the 'shrinking world' thesis: namely, the idea that the places in which we live and work are tied to one another in ways that for many would have been unthinkable just a decade or two ago. On this view, the world today is not only 'smaller' in distance terms, as events and happenings in one part of the world have a more immediate impact on daily life elsewhere, it is also conceived as more *interdependent*: interdependent in the sense that the social relationships 'stretched' between places carry a series of implications which have the capacity to transform them in more than a superficial or fleeting manner.

This general thesis is examined by taking a close look at the overseas investment and cross-border activities of multinational firms. Of late, there has been increasing talk of 'footloose' multinationals, that is, of firms striding across borders switching jobs and investments almost at will. Much of this sounds like a movement towards a 'borderless' world in which work and firms criss-cross the globe at a disorientating pace, with little or no attachment to their country of origin. Before considering this highly contested economic vision, however, it is best to understand what has aroused such interest and speculation.

2.1.1 From here to there and back again

In a small office in County Kerry on the south-western tip of Ireland, a group of workers, mainly women, check liabilities and process the claims of the fifth largest insurance company in the United States. Around one-tenth of the New York Life Insurance Company's claims are flown across the Atlantic from the east coast of the States to the west coast of Ireland, where they are scrutinized and entered onto the computer at the company's office in Castleisland. The work is then returned via on-line connections to the mainframe computer at the parent company in New Jersey, whose system comes up at 3 a.m. to accommodate the Irish operation. The claims office in County Derry is one of eighteen set up by the US insurance multinational, working alongside offices in Dallas, Seattle, Los Angeles and San Francisco.

Experiencing difficulties of recruitment and retention of its trained staff in the US, the establishment of a satellite office in County Kerry, some 6,000 miles away, has enabled the insurance company to draw upon a relatively well-educated, stable pool of labour at local clerical rates. Tapping into a remote pool of low-cost labour through electronic transmission is, however, only one of the advantages that offshore data processing can deliver to an insurance multinational. Offshore office work, because it reduces costs, also enables the insurance company to undertake a more detailed scrutiny of policies and claims than would otherwise be possible, and with profitable outcomes.

Work moving across the globe in this manner has a double-sided character for those employed in the satellite offices, however. On-line connections may

Moving work across the ocean: the claims office of New York Life in County Kerry

bring work within the reach of remote pools of labour, but they may just as easily take it away. The pace at which the work moves may be shrinking economic space, but the telecommunication links themselves owe no allegiance to particular places. Although it may appear somewhat novel, there is nothing exceptional about the ability of the New York Life Insurance Company to move work across the globe in this way: Swissair flies its ticket stubs to an office in Bombay, India, to record flight information and to calculate the amount earned from and owed to other airlines; a US company uses clerical workers in South East Asia to enter court opinions into electronic databases, which are then held on mainframe computers in the US and accessed by the legal profession worldwide; and so on.

It is not only the movement of work so far and so quickly that has disrupted our geographical horizons, however. A transfer of economic ownership may have a similar effect. In the mid-1980s a steel mill not far from San Francisco in the industrial town of Pittsburg, California, won a reprieve from repeated threats of lay-offs and permanent shutdown brought about by its inability to compete against Japanese and South Korean steel-producers (Pred and Watts, 1992). The plant, which at its peak employed more than five thousand steel-workers, was rescued by an injection of funds from a foreign steel multinational, the Pohang Iron and Steel Company Ltd, the world's second largest producer of steel at the time. On the basis of a $90 million payment, the foreign multinational became the joint owner of a century-old mill and secured a future for the remaining 1,000 or so workforce. The Pohang Iron and Steel Company, however, is a South Korean multinational and the initial investment – plus a projected $350 million modernization plan for the mill – represents the largest-ever South Korean investment in the United States.

It also represents a rather unusual reversal in the direction of capital investments – from what is commonly regarded as a 'third world' or less developed nation to a first world economic power. This was given an added twist as the majority of raw steel inputs were to come from South Korean sources and the market for the finished steel enlarged from the western US states to encompass the dynamic Asian economies of the Pacific rim. In effect, what this movement amounted to was a turnaround, albeit limited, in the pattern of interdependence between South Korea and the US, with the direction of flows – of investments, inputs and outputs – reversed. And this was by no means the only impact, as the lines of connection stretched out over space held a series of consequences for the remaining workforce. To remain competitive, the company persuaded the steel-workers to accept a new contract which suspended their right to strike, reduced their holiday benefits and cut their wage levels. In broad terms, the economic fortunes of this workforce took a downturn, but in a world that, for them, had lost its familiar markings. It was evidently still a world of multinationals and global firms, but of what kind?

One thing is certain: the Pohang Iron and Steel Company's investment in the West is not a unique occurrence. A recent glance at the pages of the financial press, for instance, revealed that another South Korean multinational, Samsung, had acquired a former East German glass manufacturer as part of its strategy to expand television production facilities in Europe, that a contract electronics manufacturer based in Singapore had chosen East Kilbride near Glasgow, Scotland for its European manufacturing and research and development headquarters, and that a Thai engineering concern had made a reverse takeover of its Danish parent and at a stroke established a European presence.

At issue, therefore, in these situations is the very shape of the economic world. One of the aims of this chapter is to explore this issue through the kind of global developments which have enabled talk of 'footloose' multinationals, shrinking worlds and interdependent economies to become rather commonplace. Among the range of questions that we will address are: what is meant by the term 'global economy'? What recent changes in the flows of investment and production suggest its emergence? Are different parts of the globe locked together in a more intense fashion than before? If so, what are the likely economic and social consequences of such a development?

It is probably useful to note at the outset that this chapter is written from a standpoint which is broadly sympathetic to the view that the flows of investment and production which underpin the process of economic globalization have increased in scope and pace in recent years. It is, however, too simplistic to say that we can trace this shift to the investment activities of giant, transnational firms or that production today moves so far and so fast that it has become divorced from people and places. The global economic picture is far more complex and differentiated than that, as we shall see. As you read through the chapter, you should bear in mind that the use of the term 'economic globalization' is itself contentious and best adopted in a provisional sense. The concept represents a fallible attempt to capture something fundamental that is happening across the globe, much of which we only understand in a partial and incomplete manner (see **Allen, 1995**).

The chapter is divided into three main sections. In section 2.2 we explore the claim that there has been a shift from an international to a global economy. Central to this claim is the view that global firms are the key movers in this transition. We will consider both claims in section 2.3 through an examination of the changing nature and scope of investment and capital flows worldwide in the post-1945 period. In section 2.4 we stand back from these developments and raise the question as to whether they represent a world that is more interdependent or simply one that is more interconnected. Following that, in section 2.5, we consider the extent to which different parts of the globe are tied together by the activities of multinationals and the nature and depth of the ties involved. In particular, we look at how global firms use space and, in so doing, may reach deep into the social fabric of regional and national economies. Finally, in section 2.6, we conclude the chapter through a review of the movement and mobility of such firms.

2.2 From an international to a global economy?

At first glance, it may appear that a shift from an international to a global economy simply entails an increase in the scope of world trade and production. As more and more of the world is pulled into the networks of capitalist production, investments and markets, it follows that the scope of economic activity will also expand. Rather than merely an increase in the geographical scope of economic activity, however, the notion of a global economy implies a *qualitative shift* in the structure and organization of the economy worldwide (Dicken, 1992).

Let us be clear about what kind of claim is being pressed here. From a European standpoint, it has been possible to talk of an *international economy* since at least the seventeenth century, when trade between nations represented the major economic activity across borders. Today, international trade is still of critical significance, especially to the industrialized nations of North America, Western Europe and South East Asia who account for the bulk of cross-border trade. World trade in manufactured goods has been a mainstay of growth in the post-war period, rising more than sixteenfold since the 1950s. Recently, international trade in services has grown rapidly, especially in financial and commercial services, although its share of world trade is significantly less than that of manufacturing. Whether goods or services, however, the exchange is between economic actors embedded within national economies and it is the national economy which represents the fundamental unit of an international economy. Trade takes place between nations. Likewise, production and investment relations may be spread by multinational corporations across national boundaries, but the governing relations are those of the nation-state. In an international economy there are barriers to cross-border flows, whether they be of capital, labour, goods or services, and the maintenance of those barriers, direct and indirect, rests with the nation-state.

international economy

In contrast, a *global economy*, it is asserted, is one in which the stress is placed upon the erosion of national barriers and the movement of economic activities across national boundaries. International trade remains a significant feature of the global economy, but the key activity is the orchestration of investment flows by transnational corporations across the globe. As the major players, transnational corporations direct investment and production on a worldwide basis, with limited regard for national boundaries or any particular allegiance to a nation-state, simply a concern to secure a profitable return on their activities. Moreover, the markets that are important to them are global rather than national, albeit global markets differentiated by national and regional consumer tastes. The qualitative shift here, then, involves an interpenetration of economic activities: that is, an ever-tightening mesh of

global economy

networks which strengthens the interdependences between different parts of the globe and, in so doing, helps to undermine the ability of nation-states to manage their own economic affairs.

An integral aspect of this shift is the heightened intensity of global networks, whereby economic actions in one part of the world have a more *immediate* impact on events elsewhere. In the previous chapter, for instance, we were told how it now only takes seconds to send money from one part of the world to another. On this view, our perception of what is near and what is distant is shaken by the sheer speed of events, as 'local' developments on the far side of the world take on a more familiar feel than those happening just a few miles away. In short, our experience of space and time also undergoes a qualitative shift.

The contrast between the two types of economy has been drawn to give a sense of the broad differences. We will be considering at greater length a number of the features of both types of economy. For the moment, you should step back from an assessment of the asserted transition, bearing in mind that features of both kinds of economy are present in the current period. Few would argue, for instance, that the global economy is a well-established phenomenon; indeed, most advocates would argue that at present we are only able to discern the direction of change – and, of course, in their view it is *towards* a global economy.

Let us take a closer look at what this view entails.

2.2.1 Transnational and multinational corporations

As pointed out above, those who hold that a global economy is in the process of being made emphasize the driving role of transnational corporations in its formation. Those critical of the notion of a global economy prefer, however, to signal the ongoing transformation of multinational corporations. In their view, the notable changes in the economy worldwide are insufficient to warrant the idea of a break with an international economy.

Before elaborating upon this distinction, it is probably useful to recall that firms with operations outside of their home country have been around for some time (Dunning, 1993a). By the first half of the nineteenth century, US firms had set up branch-plants in Canada and the UK (among the latter, the best known is probably that of Samuel Colt's revolver factory, at which were made exact replicas of the US models). At the same time, European firms, especially in banking and insurance, were active in setting up operations on the other side of the Atlantic as well as further afield. Names such as Rothschild, Lazards and Baring were familiar in merchant-banking circles around the globe. Nonetheless, most foreign-based operations at that time, in one way or another, involved natural resources, rather than manufacturing or finance. The nineteenth century was an era when the likes of Dunlop and Firestone, the rubber tyre-makers, owned plantations in Liberia and Malaysia, when Standard Oil sought investments in the Americas, Europe and the Far East, and when the United Fruit Company dominated banana production in several Caribbean countries.

So, companies with international operations are hardly new, and indeed all of the firms mentioned above represent an early form of multinational enterprise.. What, then, distinguishes a multi- from a trans-national corporation?

A *multinational corporation* (MNC) by definition produces in more than one country, including its home country. Such firms therefore have *multi-country production* operations. The use of the term 'production' here is rather loose, as it can include economic activity in factories, mines or plantations as well as banks, hotels and offices. Yet although such production may take place in numerous countries, with major firms employing people of diverse nationalities across the globe, most multinationals have their headquarters and research and development functions in their country of origin and are effectively controlled from there. The retention of a home base in their country of origin is a defining characteristic of a multinational firm. Some companies, such as Royal Dutch Shell, which is jointly owned and controlled by British and Dutch interests, have split headquarters, but this is the exception rather than the rule.

multinational corporation

There is less agreement over the definition of a *transnational corporation* (TNC), however, in part because of its more recent appearance on the world stage. One characteristic that is frequently referred to, nonetheless, is the *integration* of its economic activities – research, design, purchasing, marketing, sales *and* production – at a global scale. On this view, TNCs will locate their activities, including headquarters or research and design functions, wherever is the most favourable economically. This may involve a geographical separation of functions to take advantage of what different places have to offer or an overlapping set of activities wherever they have a market presence. In either case, the headquarters-dominated model of multinational organization is no longer adequate to meet the strategy of purchasing, producing and marketing at a global level. To have a market presence in each of the major economic regions of the world requires a different form of organization, one that has shed any association it may have had with a particular country. It is in this sense that TNCs may be characterized as 'footloose', willing to locate and relocate their activities anywhere on the globe.

transnational corporation

The clearest expression of this global view is found in the work of Ohmae. In a range of books, although particularly in *The Borderless World* (1991), Ohmae sets out the kind of global economy which he considers to be taking shape. Its distinctive geography – and this is important to note – is that it centres on three '*global regions*', the US, Europe and Japan, with the latter region extending to the fast-growing economies of East Asia. This global geography has two distinctive features.

global regions

The first is the stress that he places upon how *interlinked* the economy worldwide has become since the 1960s and '70s, with the big TNCs producing, trading and networking 'inside' their major regional markets. At its simplest, this reveals that US, Japanese and European TNCs all invest in each other. There is a greater degree of interdependence between the countries of these regions, with each country said to enjoy the benefits and opportunities provided by the presence of overseas TNCs on their soil. The old zero-sum game of development, whereby one country can only advance economically at the expense of another, no longer holds. Or so it is claimed.

The second feature is the *borderless* world itself. The geography of this borderless world is the result of the daily play of economic forces, with money, information, goods, people and even companies moving across national borders with relative ease. Chapter 1 provided a qualified illustration of some of these claims, and indeed Ohmae is well aware that, in terms of movement, assets and jobs are far less mobile than, say, money and information (1991, p. 264). A more sober claim is that borders are crossed freely by the TNCs through a variety of global networks, which include partnerships, joint ventures, strategic alliances, cross-licensing agreements, and the like. These kinds of collaborative tie-ups between companies represent a form of 'going global' that divides both risks and costs although, in the longer term, competition between firms is an ever-present feature of any economy – whether global or international.

Critics of Ohmae's global view, notably those who wish to stress the international character of economic activity, take issue with the thesis of the borderless world in particular. As mentioned earlier, they question whether the play of economic forces today is really sufficiently different from movements in the nineteenth and early twentieth centuries to warrant generalization about a qualitative shift. The world economy, they argue, has been 'open' for a long time, with money and investments flowing between countries. Consider, for example, the fact that there have been surges in cross-border investments before, which have been halted by the erection of new regulatory obstacles and barriers (as happened in the 1920s and 1930s, for instance). Even the likes of national economic recessions can interrupt the flow of capital across borders. Rather than witnessing the emergence of a global economy, therefore, we are more likely to be seeing the latest in a long line of adjustments and adaptations by multinational firms as they use the advantages gained from their home base to invest overseas. Indeed, the performance of most international firms is still tied to the competitiveness of their home base and few operate in more than a handful of countries (Hirst and Thompson, 1992; Carnoy, 1993). What changes there have been – for example, the emergence of global networking between companies – may have led to a more interconnected world, but that is not the same thing as increased interdependence, a distinction we will explore later in the chapter. The degree of interpenetration of economic activities implied, as well as the economic vulnerability on all sides, is not proven.

In short, for some the notion of a global economy is an exaggeration, an idea whose time has not yet come. And yet, there is something unsettling about dismissing the idea out of hand. The very fact that there is a debate over the issue implies that the idea of a global economy has taken hold as a representation of what may be happening around us. At this point, it may be useful to consider the changing economic map of the world over the post-war period, to mull over the trends which have stimulated the debate.

2.3   Shifts in the world economy

What follows is an overview of some of the more salient, post-war changes which have provoked discussion about a global economy. As such, the picture is a partial one and, indeed, selective in the evidence presented. The main focus is on overseas investment rather than international trade, as the former has been the hallmark of recent change in the world economy, especially since the early 1980s. Broadly, we will look at the increased *diversity* of the firms which invest abroad, the shift in the geographical *direction* and *character* of their overseas investments, as well as the changing *form* of their involvement worldwide.

2.3.1   Big players and small players

Estimates vary over the actual number of firms investing abroad, although according to Dunning (1993a), there are between 17,500 and 20,000 firms engaged in *foreign direct investment* (FDI): that is, investment which takes place outside of the investing firm's home country, yet remains within the control of that company. Usually, the investment will take the form of a branch-plant or subsidiary company in another country, although not exclusively so. The investment itself may be made up of a bundle of components, including finance, technology, skills and other assets.

foreign direct investment

Of late, the number of firms investing abroad has increased rapidly, particularly from Japan and indeed from the developing countries, especially those of East and South East Asia. Interestingly, many of these firms tend to be of small and medium size, rather than the giant companies often associated with global expansion. Moreover, they tend to invest regionally, so to speak, in adjoining countries or in those nations with which they have cultural or political ties. In fact, the vast majority of firms with investments abroad are small both in size and in the number of countries they operate within. Such small firms have tended to become international by recognizing and exploiting market niches within local networks and this has certainly been the case with firms setting up overseas operations in new sectors of economic growth, such as computer services and biotechnology.

That said, what few giant companies there are – whether we call them transnationals or multinationals – are truly of size and global reach. Tables 2.1 and 2.2 offer an insight into the size of some of the world's largest corporations, as well as indicate the extent to which some are increasingly dependent upon their foreign subsidiaries for their prosperity.

Activity 1   Cast your eye down the foreign sales and assets columns in Table 2.1. The percentage figures represent the degree of dependence that each company has upon its foreign investment stake. Nestlé, the Swiss food manufacturer, for example, operates in 126 countries with a workforce of just under 200,000 and is heavily reliant upon foreign production and sales for its economic well-being. A similar degree of dependency is apparent for the Dutch electronics giant, NV Philips. With a global workforce of just over 300,000, it has an investment presence in 57 countries. Not far behind in terms of its reliance upon foreign sales is the Japanese electronics firm, Sony, at around 70 per cent exposure. Incidentally, both these electronics giants have diversified in product terms in recent years, with the sales figures reflecting activities outside of their main sphere of operations (Philips owns Motown records through its Paradour subsidiary, for instance, and Sony has a controlling stake in Columbia film studios).

Now turn to the rankings for the car and truck manufacturers and look at their varying degrees of dependence upon foreign sales. Where possible, cross-reference the sales with the percentage of assets held abroad by the car manufacturers. The higher the amount of foreign assets, the greater is the firm's involvement in production abroad.

Now do the same exercise for the large chemical firms – Du Pont, BASF, Hoechst, Bayer and ICI.

Table 2.1 Vital statistics of a selection of the world's largest industrial companies in 1989 ranked by net sales (all currency figures in millions of US dollars)

Company	Home country	Primary industry	Sales		Assets		Employment
			Global	% foreign	Global	% foreign	Global
General Motors	USA	Cars and trucks	123,212	26.9	173,297	24.1	775,000
Ford Motor	USA	Cars and trucks	96,146	33.3	160,893	19.0	366,600
Exxon	USA	Oil	86,656	82.1	83,219	55,.8	104,000
Toyota	Japan	Cars and trucks	67,659	na	620,53[1]	n.a.	96,849
International Business Machines	USA	Electronics	62,710	59.0	77,734	48.6	383,220
British Petroleum Company	UK	Oil	57,222	73.5	61,033	n.a.	119,850
KOH Nederlands Petroleum Naatscha	Netherlands	Oil	56,857	53.0	612,16[2]	56.1	134,000
General Electric Company	USA	Electrical	53,884	13.8	128,344	8.8	292,000
Hitachi	Japan	Electronics	52,093	23.4	57,445	n.a.	290,811
Daimler-Benz	Germany	Cars and trucks	51,099	61.3	46,161	n.a.	368,226
Mobil	USA	Oil	50,220	74.7	39,080	51.1	679,00
Fiat	Italy	Cars and trucks	46,297	45.9	56,862	23.5	286,294
Matsushita Electric Industrial	Japan	Electronics	44,181	43.7	577,85[3]	n.a.	198,299
Volkswagen	Germany	Cars and trucks	43,714	63.8	38,038	n.a.	257,561
Nissan Motor Company	Japan	Cars and trucks	41,548	na	422,84[3]	n.a.	n.a.
Siemens	Germany	Electrical	40,888	48.1	517,02[4]	n.a.	365,000
Shell Transport & Trading	UK	Oil	40,283	50.4	43,530	58.4	135000
Philip Morris Companies	USA	Food	39,011	28.8	38528	14.8	157,000
Nestlé	Switzerland	Food	37,675	98.1	27,767	n.a.	196,940
Du Pont (E.I.) de Nemours	USA	Chemicals	35,534	39.8	34715	2.95	145,787
Chrysler	USA	Cars and trucks	34,922	26.3	51,038	11.0	121,947
Renault	France	Cars and trucks	34,278	43.3	23,984	34.6	174,573
NV Philips	Netherlands	Electronics	33,941	93.4	33,835	n.a.	304,800
Veba	Germany	Diversified	32,915	29.3	27,703	n.a.	94,514
Texaco	USA	Oil	32,416	42.3	25,636	20.3	37,067

Notes: Foreign sales, assets and employment represent those accounted for by foreign affiliates.

[1] 30th June 1990; [2] 31st December 1988; [3] 31st March 1990; [4] 30th September 1989; n.a. = not available.

Source: Dunning 1993a; data from various sources but especially UNCTC

Table 2.1 Vital statistics of a selection of the world's largest industrial companies in 1989 ranked by net sales (all currency figures in millions of US dollars) (continued)

Company	Home country	Primary industry	Sales		Assets		Employment
			Global	% foreign	Global	% foreign	Global
BASF	Germany	Chemicals	31,851	68.1	23,496	n.a.	136,990
Toshiba	Japan	Electronics	31,924	31.6	381,34[3]	n.a.	142,000
Hoechst	Germany	Chemicals	30,701	77.2	23,040	13.8	169,295
Peugeot	France	Cars and trucks	30,050	53.5	21,032	23.8	159,100
Chevron	USA	Oil	29,253	23.7	33,884	22.6	54,826
Bayer	Germany	Chemicals	28,963	41.2	24,171	n.a.	170,200
Unilever	Netherlands	Food/ Detergents	25,761	32.8	15,163	n.a.	142,000
Imperial Chemical Industries	UK	Chemicals	25,427	77.9	21,759	37.1	133,800
NEC	Japan	Electronics	25,349	25.9	271,14[3]	n.a.	114,599
Brown, Boveri & Co	Switzerland	Electrical	25,038	n.a.	29,364	n.a.	n.a.
Asea	Sweden	Machinery	24,103	n.a.	27,464	n.a.	184,424
Procter & Gamble	USA		24,081	39.9	184,87[1]	35.3	89,000
Amoco	USA	Oil	23,966	28.5	30,430	32.7	53,653
British Telecom	UK	Utilities	23,774	n.a.	369,63[3]	n.a.	245,665
Thyssen Ag Vorm August Thyssen-Hue	Germany	Metals	22,909	48.5	154,26[4]	n.a.	133,824
Nippon Steel	Japan	Metal products	21,880	n.a.	309,18[3]	n.a.	55,863
Total-Cie Française Des Petroles	France	Oil	21,197	71.0	17,370	n.a.	35,889
Sony	Japan	Electronics	21,196	69.8	321,64[3]	n.a.	95,600
Robert Bosch	Germany	Cars and trucks	20,460	26.5	15,317	n.a.	174,742
Boeing	USA	Aerospace	20,276	na	13,278	n.a.	159,200
Occidental Petroleum	USA	Oil	20,068	6.4	20,741	10.1	53,500

Notes: Foreign sales, assets and employment represent those accounted for by foreign affiliates.

[1] 30th June 1990; [2] 31st December 1988; [3] 31st March 1990; [4] 30th September 1989; n.a. = not available.

Source: Dunning 1993a; data from various sources but especially UNCTC

Table 2.2 *Vital statistics of a selection of the world's largest service companies in 1989 ranked by employment (all currency figures in millions of US dollars)*

Company	Home country	Primary industry	Sales Global	% foreign	Assets Global	% foreign	Employment Global
Sears, Roebuck & Co	USA	Retail trading	53,794	7.7	86,972[2]	3.7	500,000
K.Mart Corporation	USA	Retail trading	29,533	3.7	13,145[4]	n.a.	365,000
McDonald's	USA	Food services	66,340	33.4	10,667	33.1	169,000
ITT	USA	Telecommunications	20,054	28.6	45,503[2]	18.2	119,000
American Express	USA	Financial services	25,047	19.4	130,855[2]	21.6	107,542
RWE Aktiengesellschaft	Germany	Utilities	25,943	19.7	32,744[5]	n.a.	97,596
National Westminster Bank	UK	Banking	28,336	40.3	224,303[2]	46.1	96,000
Trust House Forte	UK	Hotels and motels	4,023	22.1	7,135[7]	n.a.	92,900
Citicorp	USA	Banking	37,970	13.2	230,643[2]	37.8	92,000
Bougyues	France	Construction	10,468	17.1	1,1402	n.a.	64,373
Klynveld Peat Marwick Goerdler	USA	Accounting firm	3,900	42.0	n.a.	n.a.	63,700
British Airways	UK	Air transportation	9,112	77.7	7,518	n.a.	50,204
Holiday Corporation	USA	Hotels and motels	1,597	n.a.	2,139	n.a.	43,600
Thomson	Canada	Newspapers	5,003	73.3	6,954	50.7	41,600
Fluor	USA	Construction	7,446	13.0	2,476	11.1	17,876
Saatchi & Saatchi	UK	Advertising	7,428	17.5	1,860	n.a.	16,614
Interpublic Group of Companies	USA	Advertising	1,368	56.2	2,584	43.8	14,700
Sanwa Bank	Japan	Banking	28,999	n.a.	448,625[1]	n.a.	13,604
Mitsui & Co.	Japan	Wholesale trading	123,387	29.8	46,570	20.8	10,772
Mitsubishi Corp	Japan	Wholesale trading	115,139	21.9	70,012	18.4	8,005
Salomon Inc.	USA	Financial services	6,146	25.8	74,747[2]	16.3	8,000

Notes: Foreign sales, assets and employment represent those accounted for by foreign affiliates; [1] 31st March 1989; [2] 31st December 1989; [3] 31st March 1988; [4] 31st January 1989; [5] 30th June 1990; [6] 3rd February 1989; [7] 31st December 1990; n.a. = not available.

Source: Dunning, 1993a; data from UNCTC, 1991

Although the data on foreign assets are patchy (a problem in itself when trying to draw general observations), what it does show for the large car and chemical manufacturers is what a small proportion of their assets is held abroad. For the most part, they produce for export at home and invest overseas where appropriate. Among large service firms too, the extent of dependence upon foreign affiliates is, broadly speaking, not significant, although in areas such as accounting and advertising the global scope of the major firms is known to be high (UNCTC, 1988).

The figures, however, represent a static snapshot. If we focus upon trends, then, according to Dunning (1993a), the largest enterprises are becoming less and less dependent upon the economic health of their home nation. Moreover, this trend has increased significantly since the 1960s, especially among the big firms outside of the US. This observation admittedly does sit rather oddly with the fact that the vast majority of these firms – over 90 per cent – are headquartered in their home country and the best part of their productive assets are to be found there too. Borders still matter, as even Ohmae recognizes. Coca Cola, for example, is known as a US company, Toshiba as a Japanese firm, Samsung as a Korean giant, and so on.

How, then, do such contradictory tendencies mesh with the idea of a borderless world? Remember that we are talking about a direction of change, rather than any complete set of changes. For some giant firms in the motor vehicles, electronics, oil and chemical sectors, as well as perhaps in the financial and commercial service sectors, the global spread of their operations is evident. For the majority of firms engaged in foreign direct investment, however, regardless of sector, the world is still one of national economies and protected markets. The sheer *diversity* of firms engaged in overseas operations is important to note, but so too is the fact that the giant corporations wield a degree of economic power that cannot be measured in terms of their numbers. In that sense, they are *structurally* rather than numerically significant.

2.3.2 First world and the rest

Alongside an increase in the number of firms investing abroad, the investment flows themselves have grown rapidly in the post-war period. The 1960s saw a rapid growth of foreign direct investment flows, followed by a steady increase up to the early 1980s. World recession and the international debt crisis took its toll on investment flows in the first half of the 1980s, although by the end of the decade they had risen fourfold. What was significant, however, was not so much the rate of growth of foreign direct investment as the *altered geography of the flows*. There are a number of trends that lie behind a rather complex geography.

First of all, more countries became overseas investors: that is, they were the source of foreign direct investment. Figure 2.1 gives you an idea of some of the broad shifts involved. Up to the 1980s around half of the outward investment flows was accounted for by US firms. By the end of the 1980s, however, Japanese firms had come from a remarkably low base to become, like the US, a major source of overseas investment. As before, the UK continued to be a significant source of foreign direct investment, although it was joined in the 1980s by Germany, France, Canada and the Netherlands. Interestingly, by the late 1980s Western Europe as a whole had become the world's largest source of overseas investment.

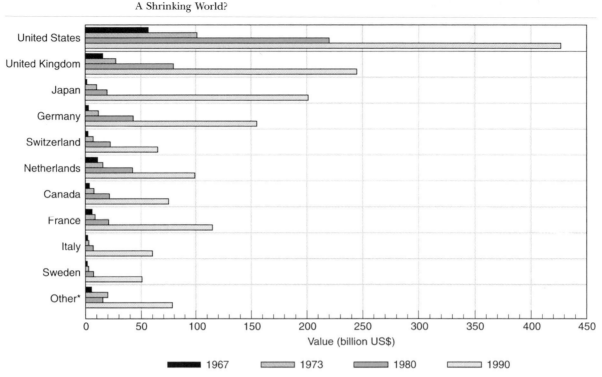

(a) By value (billions of US dollars)

Figure 2.1 Stocks of outward foreign direct investment, by major home country, 1967–1990 (Source: based on data from Dunning, 1993b, Table 11.1)

Notes: *Australia, Austria, Belgium, Denmark, Finland, Greece, Ireland, New Zealand, Norway, Portugal, South Africa, Spain

Second, with the exception of Japan, most of these countries were investing in one another. Western Europe played host to much US investment in the latter half of the 1980s. At the same time, the UK, followed by the Netherlands, France and Germany, were major investors in the US. Significantly, around half of Japan's dramatic burst in foreign investment went to the US. Indeed, as can be seen from Figure 2.2, the major shift in investment flows was away from the developing countries, in particular Latin America, and much of it has been towards the US. With the continuing recession in the developed economies in the early 1990s, however, this concentration of investment in the three 'global regions' has fallen somewhat, but not sufficiently to detract from the overall pattern (UNCTAD, 1993).

Third, although the share of worldwide investment in the developing countries continued to fall over the 1980s, the exception was a select group of East and South East Asian countries, namely Singapore, Hong Kong, Malaysia, South Korea, Thailand and Taiwan, which became a major target for foreign investors throughout the 1980s. Over the same decade, however, investment by overseas firms in the *whole* of Africa dropped to just over two per cent of world FDI, and in sub-Saharan Africa it is negligible (UNCTAD, 1992). What is not revealed by these figures, however, is the opening up of Eastern Europe to overseas investment. Although difficult to read, there are signs of increased investments in Poland, Hungary, the Czech and Slovak Republics and, of course, what was East Germany (undertaken largely by firms in western Germany and thus not strictly FDI) (UNCTAD, 1993).

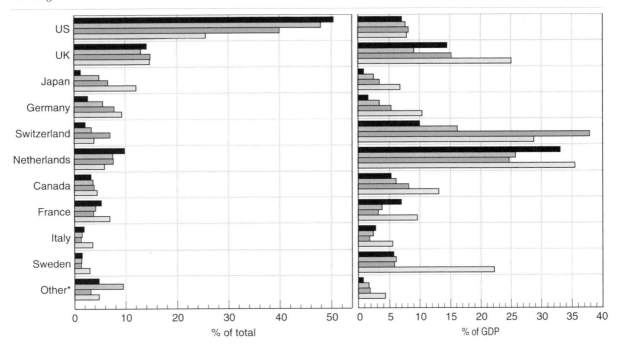

Figure 2.1 cont. (b) As percentage of total   *(c) As percentage of Gross Domestic Product*

Drawing these different trends together reveals a stark, uneven geographical pattern. The bulk of overseas investment by multinational firms is now more concentrated than ever in the industrialized world, with three-quarters of the outward investment stemming from just five countries – the US, Japan, UK, Germany and France. But that is not all. The industrialized world is also the major *destination* of these investment flows. The first world countries are increasingly investing among themselves, with little interest for much else besides the growing economies of East Asia and Eastern Europe.

Is this, then, an indication of greater interdependence between first world economies? How far is Ohmae's claim that transnational firms now operate 'inside' each of the three major economic regions of the world reflected in the changing geography of investment flows? It is difficult to say with any degree of confidence as, in addition to producing and selling in each other's markets, we would also need to know the extent to which such firms are engaged in research and development activities, as well as, perhaps, reproducing some of their headquarters functions. What is discernible from the pattern of flows and also what we know about the extent of the activities of most multinationals, however, is their limited geographical reach. Most multinationals, especially manufacturing multinationals, concentrate their investments in their own 'global region' first, in other rich regions second. Figure 2.3 provides a sense of the accumulated stocks and flows involved and their magnitude.

We will have to wait a while, though, before we can assess the degree of interdependence taking shape. One thing that we do know, however, is that manufacturing firms are not representative of the companies involved in the latest wave of internationalization: namely, the sectoral shift in foreign investment from manufacturing to services.

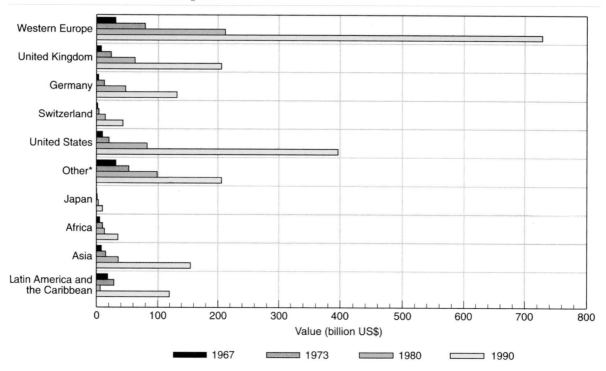

(a) By value (billions of US dollars)

Figure 2.2 Stocks of inward foreign direct investment, by major host countries, 1967–1990 (Source: based on data from Dunning, 1993b, Table 11.2)

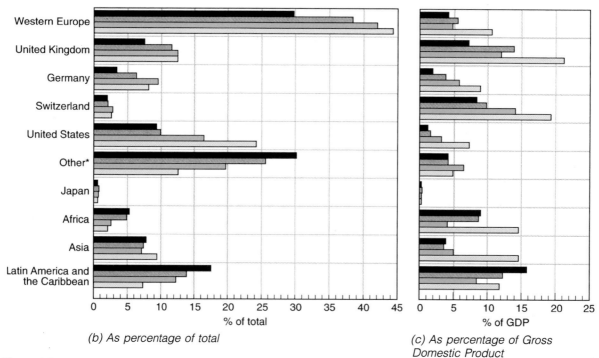

(b) As percentage of total

(c) As percentage of Gross Domestic Product

Figure 2.2 cont.

Notes: *Other developed = Australia, Canada, Japan, New Zealand, South Africa, Sub-Saharan Africa, Algeria, Egypt, Tunisia, Morocco

Figure 2.3 Intra-global region foreign direct investment, 1990 (billions of dollars) (Source: UNCTAD, 1993, Figure II.2)

Notes: The European Economic Area includes the European Union (EU) and the European Free Trade Association, excluding Iceland and Liechtenstein. North America includes the United States and Canada.

Dollar figures show estimated values of stock of Foreign Direct Investment based on data on inward and outward investment from North America and the EEA. (Intra-North American investment and intra-EEA investment have been netted out.) Percentages show average annual growth rates for stocks (1980–90) and flows (1985–91).

2.3.3   From manufacturing to services

It is only relatively recently that services have become a extensive site of foreign direct investment. Back in the nineteenth century the great majority of the early multinationals, as noted previously, were involved in resource extraction and the production of foodstuffs. Moreover, much of this investment was in what was to become the third world, reflecting a pattern of old colonial ties between developed and underdeveloped countries. All of this was to change in the post-war period. Multinational investment in raw materials continued, but it was soon outstripped by investment in manufacturing

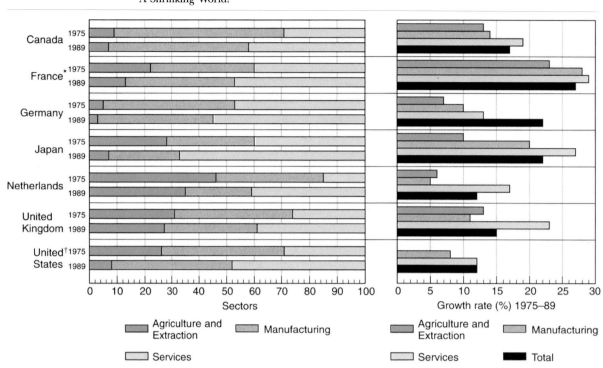

Figure 2.4 *Sectoral composition of the stock of outward foreign direct investment of major home countries (percentage share and compound annual growth rate 1975–1989) (Source: based on Dunning, 1993b, Table 11.3)*

Notes: * Based on cumulative flows of direct investment from 1972.

† The vertically integrated petroleum industry is included in the extractive sector in 1975. In 1990, only the extractive portion of the industry is included, with processing included in the manufacturing sector and marketing and distribution in the service sector.

production. Most of this investment was directed towards the industrialized economies, to serve markets directly rather than indirectly through exports from home. It thus gave the manufacturing multinationals a market presence in the wealthiest nations. With the shift in direct investment to services in the 1980s, the concentration of flows within the developed world intensified.

Figure 2.4 gives you an indication of the sectoral shifts that have taken place in the major industrialized nations of late. In each case, with the exception of France, the proportion of investment in manufacturing fell, while services took a greater share. Japan, in particular, experienced a dramatic shift in the size of its overseas service investment, much of it in banking, insurance and property. By the end of the 1980s foreign direct investment in services accounted for around forty per cent of the world's stock of overseas investment and about half of the annual flows. Fewer restrictions on foreign investment in services within the developed economies, the liberalization of the major financial markets, and the fact that services account for an ever-increasing proportion of the output of the industrialized nations, have led to the share of overseas service investment rising sharply in recent years.

Within this upward trend, the major overseas investments have been in banking, finance, insurance, trading and a range of commercial services, especially advertising, accountancy and legal services. Less significant in terms of volume, although equally revealing in terms of the rate of change, has been investment in what are commonly held to be 'local' domestic services, such as cleaning, catering and security. The internationalization of these routine services, alongside the more technologically sophisticated services of modern finance or telecommunications, is indicative of the range of economic activities orchestrated by global firms today. It is also indicative of a different kind of economic geography.

In the first place, the spatial structure of the service industries tends to differ from that of manufacturing. Unlike manufactured goods, only a restricted number of services are tradeable over space. For most services, whether it be the professions of accountancy or law, or whether it be the mass production of fast food or tourism, the consumption of that service is less easily divorced from its production. Put another way, both the producer and the consumer have to be physically present and thus foreign direct investment, rather than export, is the only way to deliver an international service. These service corporations are necessarily stretched out over space, with their spatial reach often emanating from the global cities (discussed in Chapter 3). As Sassen (1991) and others have pointed out, the key production sites of these services, especially those of finance and commerce, as well as many of the headquarters of global firms, are to be found in the major global cities. They are not only sites of production, however, they are also major sites of consumption, acting as beacons for overseas investment in services in the developed world.

Secondly, the integration of economic activities within international service firms involves a different geography. Without going into detail, many of the skills and technologies in use within service firms are of the 'soft' variety: that is, they consist of the 'know-how' associated with the delivery of a particular service, the accumulated expertise that, for example, an insurance analyst draws upon in the measurement of risk. Unlike much manufacturing, however, these skills and technologies tend to form part of an overseas investment package. They are inseparable from the delivery of a service and thus tend to be located within the host country, rather than in the central offices of a distant parent company. We will return to the full implications of this in the next section.

Finally, there is the internationalization of the financial markets themselves and of the institutions which play them (Thrift, 1988). This refers to the speed-up of capital movements, not in the shape of the plants and factories of the giant corporations supposedly uprooting themselves at a moment's notice when profitability falls, but to a different kind of 'footloose' capital: namely, currency, shares, bonds, and money generally. As the previous chapter noted, it is perhaps this kind of economic activity, where money slips across national borders at the touch of an electronic button, which has given rise to the more colourful claims about the arrival of a borderless world economy.

The growth in the share of overseas service investment, however, does raise a series of questions about the so-called interpenetration of economic activities, in particular ones that are not answered by pointing to an increased acceleration of financial flows across the globe. If the spatial structure of the giant service firms entails a producer presence as well as perhaps an integration of skills, technology and investment, then the process of deepening that is associated with globalization may owe more to the sectoral shift in the make-up of foreign direct investment, than to the activities of the giant manufacturing corporations or to the extraordinary pace of monetary flows.

2.3.4 Direct and indirect overseas involvement

A final consideration is the changing *form* of foreign involvement practised by global firms. It is readily assumed that the ownership of plant, factories or subsidiaries abroad is the best indicator of where these firms are involved globally, with the scale of overseas investment providing a measure of their economic significance. The 1980s, however, witnessed a proliferation in forms of international involvement other than direct investment abroad.

Dicken (1992) among others has drawn attention to the growing importance of two forms of collaboration between firms in different parts of the world. *strategic alliance* One is the formation of international *strategic alliances* whereby firms enter into agreements with one another over, say, the development of costly new technologies or the use of sales and distribution networks already in place within a particular market. The US-based telecommunications giant, AT&T, for example, recently linked up with the Japanese electronics multinational, NEC, to jointly develop the next generation of semiconductors. IBM, Toshiba and Siemens have formed an alliance to ensure that they, too, are not left behind in the semiconductor race. Glaxo, the UK pharmaceuticals company, has internationalized a number of its activities, although not in a manner that has led simply to a replication of facilities at each location. On entering the Japanese health market, rather than attempt to build up its own sales and service network, it linked up with Japanese partners, exchanged drugs with them, and concentrated its sales efforts in Europe where it already had an established network. It is a similar story among the major players in the car industry, telecommunications, defence, aerospace and a host of others. In this way, companies may realize global aims that they could not have achieved by their own efforts, or at least not without loss to their overall competitiveness.

international subcontracting Another form of collaboration that has increased significantly in recent years is *international subcontracting*. This refers to an arrangement whereby firms contract out a specific piece of work to an overseas company. It is regarded as one of the most *in*direct ways in which international firms may involve themselves in the economies of countries other than their own. One of the best-known examples is that of Nike, the US sports footwear producer, which has developed a variety of subcontracting relationships, mainly with firms in South East Asia (see Box 2.1). The advantage of such arrangements to an incoming multinational are many and varied, and include among other things the possibility of passing on the economic risks of supplying a particular good or service, the flexibility of changing subcontractors or varying the amount of work purchased, and the ability to concentrate upon their core activities.

In practice the interrelationships between firms, large or small, global or local, are labyrinthine. Tie-ups between manufacturing companies in various industries take the form of joint ventures involving an investment stake, cross-licensing agreements involving patent rights on a particular piece of technology, as well as the strategic alliances and subcontract relationships mentioned above. They may involve one product or many, part of a production process, an aspect of design or research, marketing or distribution arrangements, and be of limited life.

Take a look at the tie-ups shown in Figure 2.5 between the major vehicle manufacturers in the US, Europe and Japan. Drawn in the mid-1980s, the diagram is already out of date. Nonetheless, the widespread adoption of such collaborative forms does rather complicate our sense of just where the boundaries of a firm begin and where they end.

Box 2.1 Nike's subcontracting system

'The figure below shows the chronology of the changing geography by country of assembly plants producing Nike shoes. Most of the international ties Nike created were on a contract basis. The company did, however, purchase its own factories in countries other than the United States; for example, in the United Kingdom and [the Republic of Ireland]. The wholly-owned production facilities, however, are no longer part of Nike's network of producers. The relatively rapid relocation of production between countries illustrates how Nike's subcontracting system has allowed the company to quickly disassociate itself from factories that failed to meet standards of performance set by Nike or where price changes rendered a product uncompetitive. Despite Nike's history of changing producers, the company maintains very close and persistent ties with a core group of affiliated factories and regular relations with some other manufacturers.'

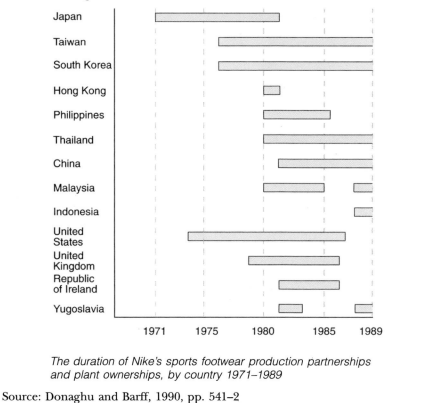

The duration of Nike's sports footwear production partnerships and plant ownerships, by country 1971–1989

Source: Donaghu and Barff, 1990, pp. 541–2

Among international service firms, too, many of the above forms of collaboration are present, plus a few specific to certain industries. Within hotels, fast food and retailing, for example, franchising or management contracts are frequently drawn up between companies. McDonald's, the fast-food chain, is probably one of the best-known firms engaged in franchise agreements, laying down detailed requirements to the franchisee on how to cook and sell their hamburgers. Within international accountancy, the major firms are little more than a loose-knit collection of partnerships, with the likes of an Arthur Anderson or a Price Waterhouse bearing little resemblance to the centralized operations of most manufacturing multinationals.

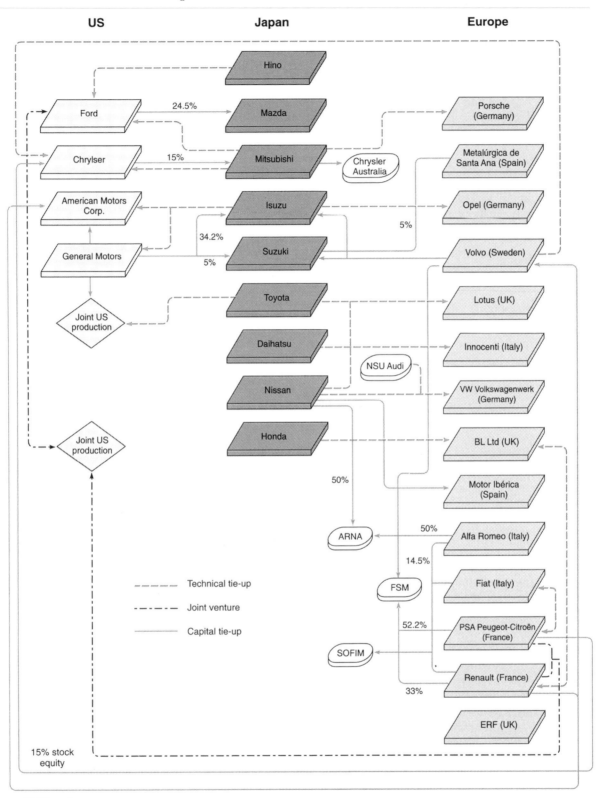

US   **Japan**   **Europe**

Figure 2.5 *Car tie-ups (Source: Best, 1990, p. 261, based on Ohmae, 1985, p. 134)*

Summary of section 2.3

What, then, do these trends tell us about the emergence of a global economy. At best, we can say the following from the trends that we have observed.

o   International firms come in all shapes and sizes, from the small multinationals in computer software to the giant transnationals in cars and chemicals. If pushed to generalize about 17,000-odd firms, it is that many remain tied to their home countries and that most reach out little further than their own 'global region'.

o   International firms are more diverse in their geographical origin than hitherto, although those based in first world countries are more inclined to invest in one another and less likely to invest outside of the developed world, unless it is East Asia or Eastern Europe.

o   The rise in the share of overseas services involvement, stimulated by falling regulatory barriers, and freer domestic and international capital markets, may entail a more integrated presence abroad, given the nature of most service production.

o   The increase in indirect forms of overseas involvement – joint ventures, subcontracting relationships and the like – represents a more diffuse form of cross-border activity than traditional investments. In one sense, such ties are a recognition of the geographical limitations of a firm's direct 'global reach'.

What is less clear from all this, however, is the degree of interdependence implied by such shifts. Do they lead to a tenuous form of connection between firms and places or to ties that imply a greater degree of interdependence?

2.4   An interconnected or an interdependent world?

So far, we have used the terms 'interconnected' and 'interdependent' in a rather loose fashion. At a general level, the idea that today places and people across the world are more interdependent simply implies that the links between them are perhaps drawn more tightly or experienced more immediately than before. Thus the fact that clerical work, in the form of data processing, is transmitted half-way across the world by satellite to be inputted by labour at a fraction of the cost from whence the data came is merely an indication of these new times. Of course, there is some truth in this broad interpretation, but here I want to draw a sharper distinction between the kinds of links that criss-cross the globe.

Think of it this way. If the different parts of the world economy are more *interconnected* today, this may refer to the fact that people's lives in the far distant corners of the world are now affected by recent advances in telecommunications, or transport, or by the arrival of multinationals wishing to market a particular global brand of soap, foodstuff, or whatever. It may also imply that all kinds of people from a variety of cultures and places are able to tune in to world music on their radio. The lines of connection in

interconnection

these instances refer to the increased *scope* and *pace* of global events and actions. People are sensitive to the fact that their world appears to be shrinking, or at least those people who are not passed by may be aware of this effect. The sensitivity in this instance may be the product of the immediacy of the connections, as in the case of faxes and high speed data transmissions, or the product of a heightened response to, say, the latest advertising campaign run by a global agency such as Saatchi and Saatchi.

interdependence If, however, the lines stretched out over space, and the social relations that they embody, bind the economic fortunes of places, then some form of *interdependence* is at work. It may be an *unequal* form of interdependence, where, for example, a multinational firm based in one country takes advantage of low-cost labour in another; or it may be a form of *mutual* dependence where, say, transnational firms forge alliances with their major competitors in different parts of the world, or where a global firm reconcentrates its activities in each of its major geographical markets. In either case, one or both ends of the line are tied in in a fundamental way. The lines of interdependence in such cases may refer to a *deepening* or interpenetration of economic activities. The awareness of global connections here involves more than a receptiveness to change in the wider world, however; it involves a knowledge that local economic fortunes are tied to wider events and decisions – as, for example, the steel-workers in Pittsburg, California found out in a more graphic way after Pohang bought into 'their' company. The social relations stretched over space are also relations of mutual vulnerability which, in this instance, are of an unequal nature.

What is new, if anything, about this state of affairs? It is easy to forget, for example, that those people who lived under imperial rule in Europe's former colonies or who were on the receiving end of unequal trading relationships experienced at first hand a form of unequal interdependence. And in many cases this can be traced to the actions of the early multinationals we spoke about in Section 2.1. The depth of relationships laid down by global firms is not a recent attribute therefore. What has happened of late, it is argued, is the accelerated pace *coupled with* the greater depth of global relations (Thrift, 1988). It is not simply an increase in the number and scope of cross-border movements that is at issue, therefore, it is also the immediacy *and* depth at which their impact is experienced. This is the qualitative shift in the structure and organization of the world economy that is said to have occurred and that was referred to earlier.

Activity 2 Bearing this distinction in mind, what kind of ties do the following social relationships 'stretched' across space represent to you? Is each one an example of an interconnected or an interdependent world? Jot down your first thoughts on each in turn before you read on.

o   Swissair transfers its revenue accounting operation to Bombay, India.

o   An Asian electronics firm sets up its European headquarters and research and development facilities in Scotland.

o   Swissair faxes its revised flight times to a variety of global destinations.

o   A US firm shifts its vacuum-cleaner production from Dijon, France to Glasgow, Scotland to reduce its labour costs.

o   An Australian-based multinational conducts a meeting with executives in Europe through video-conferencing facilities.

If your response was similar to mine, some of the examples are more difficult to place with any certainty than others. To my mind, the shift in vacuum-cleaner production from France to Scotland involves the re-working of an established pattern of unequal interdependence on the basis of the labour costs involved. The Swissair transfer of its accounting operation involves a similar shift. The Asian electronics firm, however, is probably involved in a situation of mutual dependence where both sides are vulnerable to external events. The link-up between places provided by fax machines and video-conferencing facilities are perhaps easier to identify as examples of global interconnections.

Our task would have been made easier if more detailed information on some of the cases had been presented, but in practice for many of the geographical ties drawn between places, the distinction between a set of interconnections and a set of interdependencies is not a hard and fast one. While all interdependencies are interconnections, the reverse does not apply. The distinction is primarily an analytical one, a necessary simplification whose value is that it draws attention to the straightforward fact that *not all links circling the globe are of the same kind or hold similar sets of consequences*. Some economic relationships stretched out over space involve relationships of inequality or entail mutual vulnerability, whereas other relationships between places are superficial in their impact. In the following section, we look at two aspects of the global reach of international firms and consider the nature and depth of the ties involved.

2.5   Why reach across borders?

Firms reach across borders for a variety of reasons, although for the sake of simplicity we can, in the first instance, narrow it down to two considerations: *markets* and *production*. Both elements have been present throughout this chapter, yet neither has been a central focus thus far.

Much overseas investment in the post-war period has taken place simply because firms wish to gain access to new markets, and in some cases to control those markets or at least to shape them through their direct presence. Some national economies are more 'closed' than others, because of the erection of tariff barriers or the imposition of trade restrictions by national governments, and direct investment in a country offers a way around such barriers – for both manufacturing and service investments. Thus, the need to gain a market share in various countries is the reason to reach across borders in this instance.

Equally significant today, however, is for firms to invest abroad, not with a view to serve the 'local' market in which their production is based, but to re-export for sale in the global market. If you wear trainers, take a quick look at the label inside. It is quite likely that it will reveal something of the latest geography of footwear production. A similar investigation of a range of electronics goods, such as radios and pocket calculators, or the latest battery-operated toys, would provide you with a map of today's low-cost locations around the world. Here the reason to seek locations abroad is the advantage to be gained by cheaper or more efficient production. The outcome of this type of investment is a 'global factory', so to speak.

Investment abroad to serve the global market, or for that matter a range of differentiated national markets, is not restricted to routine, low-cost operations, however. The attraction of a specific location may well be its pool of talented researchers or highly skilled technicians. Multinationals seek out different kinds of labour according to what they produce, how they produce it, and the intensity of the competition in the markets they serve. As more and more products are made nearer their point of sale, in some cases because of the need for local design and marketing, there may be pressure on firms to integrate the full range of their activities in a number of markets across the globe. We spoke of this earlier, for example, in respect of companies in the pharmaceuticals, electronics, telecommunications and car industries.

location factor   Thus, there will be a variety of *location factors* influencing the overseas investment pattern of firms, with different firms and industries arriving at specific trade-offs to meet their particular needs at any one time. Whatever the reason to invest abroad, however, the *nature* and the *depth* of the ties formed by companies across the globe is open to various interpretations.

2.5.1 Off to market

The view that companies are internationalizing themselves along the whole chain of their activities, rather than simply at the production end, is one close to Ohmae's position. To hold this view, however, it is not necessary to argue that such companies will have shed all association with their home country. Rather, it is to argue that they now have a more *integrated* presence in each of the world's important regional markets, namely North America, Europe and East Asia. An integrated presence in this context may be translated as the transnationalization of research and development activities, as well as production, sales and distribution. It may also include the decentralization of head office functions, although the stress is placed upon bringing together research and development *and* production *within* local markets.

The justification for this geographical shift runs something like this. With advances in technology and communications in the post-war period, those firms that were able to split their production processes relocated their repetitive, standardized functions to wherever in the world was considered to be the most efficient or cheapest. This led ultimately to the 'global factory' scenario mentioned earlier. Meanwhile, most of the critical activities – those of research, design and development – as well as the strategic capacity to switch investments from one place to another, remained in the home country of the parent. The factory units attracted such labels as 'runaway' or 'screwdriver' plants, because of their vulnerable, assembly-type nature. And the whole process was referred to as the 'new international division of labour' (Fröbel, Heinrichs and Kreye, 1980). Much of the labour-intensive production, primarily in the textiles and clothing industry and electronics, re-located to what was then thought of as the third world, in particular to Latin America and East and South East Asia.

From the 1980s on, though, a different set of economic and organizational arrangements was said to be taking shape. The setting for this shift, however, was the industrialized first world, not the third world, and the drive was market competition, rather than the relative costs of labour between countries. Even the main industries involved are different, apart that is from electronics.

In this setting what was highlighted were the advantages to be gained by firms *concentrating* their activities in the heartlands of the developed world, rather than *dividing* them geographically across the world. An economic edge was to be gained through firms innovating 'inside' their main markets, bringing out new products at a quicker pace and anticipating market opportunities among their customer base. Above all, it was necessary to keep abreast of the competition in each of the major markets. At issue, therefore, was the ability of global companies to adapt to a fast-changing economic environment in the markets themselves. Organizationally, this increased the pressure upon them to become embedded locally, albeit on a global basis. The outcome, we are told, is that companies are internationalizing themselves from the sales and production functions upwards along the chain (Best, 1990).

Howells (1990) has drawn attention, for example, to the nature and scale of research activities globally within the pharmaceuticals and chemicals industries, and elsewhere he has shown how the internationalization of research and development is also occurring in the electronics, telecommunications, computer and car industries (Howells and Wood, 1993). Highly concentrated within the wealthy, industrialized nations, especially the United States, research activity has nonetheless moved overseas from the home country of the big corporations. There is now said to be a greater tie-up between the research establishments of a global firm, as well as a closer integration with what is produced and sold in the major markets. The development of Glaxo's research network since the 1960s, set out in Figure 2.6, provides an illuminating example of both the internationalization of their R&D activities *and* its restriction geographically to the rich, first world markets. What is interesting to reflect upon is that, despite the setting up of new centres, a common pattern among big multinationals like Glaxo is to retain existing research locations. In other words, the research activities of such firms exhibit a *locational inertia*.

locational inertia

Howells also notes the increased demand and competition for skilled scientific and technical labour within the industrialized nations. As such skills become more critical to an information-intense economy, a worldwide shortage has led multinationals to seek this kind of labour wherever they can find it. India, for example, has one of the largest pools of scientific and technical expertise in the world and it is available at a cost that is significantly lower than in the US. Texas Instruments, the US electronics giant, for example, employ Indian consultants to develop software which is then beamed to the US and elsewhere via the Indian government's satellite communication system (Mitter and Pearson, 1992).

The rise of international research and development networks, based in part on a dispersed pool of scientific talent, does not necessarily entail real *depth* at the local level, however. As Howells notes, the big firms may be integrating research and production at the local level, but the economic benefits of local innovation do not automatically reside with the local economy. The benefits that arise from secondary and support research units may well find their way to other parts of the firm's research network. After all, not all parts of a corporate global network are on an equal footing. And, indeed, it is this recognition which has led others to remain sceptical about the nature and depth of the ties laid down by the so-called fully integrated global firms.

The scepticism usually takes the following form. Firms may well have orchestrated their research and production in new ways, co-ordinating

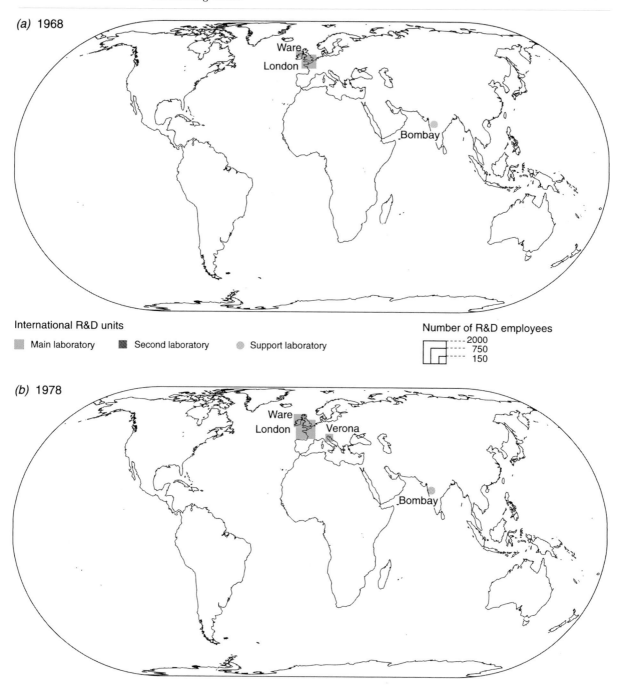

Figure 2.6 Development of Glaxo's global R&D network (Source: Howells, 1990, Figures 2–5)

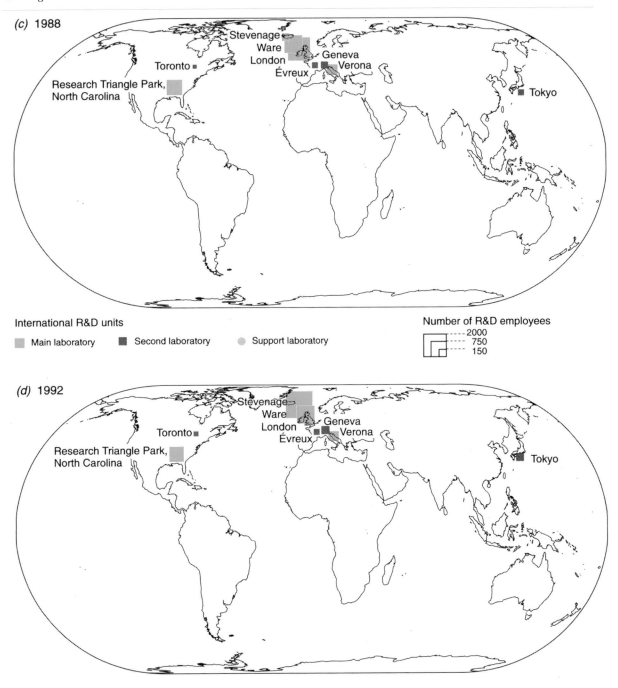

(c) 1988

Stevenage
Ware
London
Évreux
Geneva
Verona
Toronto
Research Triangle Park,
North Carolina
Tokyo

International R&D units

Main laboratory   Second laboratory   Support laboratory

Number of R&D employees
2000
750
150

(d) 1992

Stevenage
Ware
London
Évreux
Geneva
Verona
Toronto
Research Triangle Park,
North Carolina
Tokyo

research centres in market locations, but they still retain the 'core' or fundamental technologies at home. In other words, those technologies that create the real wealth, that is those operations which give value to something by transforming it, rarely move beyond the borders of the parent country. Scotland, for example, puts together and exports nearly half of all the computers and accessory equipment that go out from the UK. The industry is, however, dominated by foreign-owned firms, much of it from the US and Japan. Of concern to many is that, despite some indication of increased research activities and greater investment in more sophisticated automation technologies, transfer of the 'real' technologies and the know-how of design and development has not taken place (Turok, 1993). At root, the big electronics firms are still home-based national concerns and there are distinctive roles performed at the centre of these corporations: namely, the development of fundamental technologies, the provision of finance and the allocation of production and investment to the various sites abroad.

In part, the scepticism may be a reflection of the differences of opinion over what it means to 'globalize' economic activities. Hitachi, another of Japan's electronics giants, for example, intends to open four 'research and development centres' in Europe and the US: one in Cambridge, another in Dublin and the remaining two in Detroit and San Francisco. While it is acknowledged that it is feasible to manage research units across the oceans, it is decidedly tricky to integrate design, development and production across such vast distances. Even given advanced communications, it is exceptional even for the big firms to integrate their thinking and practice on the design and development of new products across borders. There *is* adaptation of existing designs to local markets and also design to meet the peculiarities of different local markets, but there are few instances of *truly* global design and development.

The notion of research and development 'inside' markets is further complicated if we consider what this actually means to a giant service multinational in, for example, the financial or advertising sectors. There are, of course, 'hard' technologies embodied in the information and communications equipment that these firms use, but there are also 'soft' technologies as mentioned earlier. These 'soft' technologies – the accumulated know-how and expertise associated with the putting together of a financial 'deal' or advertising product – are honed and developed in the market-place; they are not centralized in the parent company and flown out to subsidiaries. These types of service markets are ill-defined and ever-changing and they are part and parcel of the development of these 'soft' technologies; indeed the very design of the product occurs at the point of production, so to speak – that is, at the market.

A fuller presence for many service multinationals, therefore, is one that has been shaped by what they do. If they look like miniature versions of their parents, that is because they reproduce an integrated range of skills, technologies and routine work wherever they go in the world. Perhaps the real issues here though are, first, how embedded are these service replicas in their local markets, and, second, is their free-standing presence little more than an indication of how loose-knit these giant service organizations really are? If the latter is the case, then we are merely talking about new lines of connection rather than of interdependence. Not all service industries are of the type discussed here, however, as we shall discover shortly.

2.5.2   Seeking labour

Even though the likes of a Nissan or a Canon may be attempting to globally integrate their activities centred on the world's largest markets, labour is still a location factor for these big production industries. International companies wishing to be 'inside' the wealthy market economies of Europe, North America and Japan, will think carefully about the *kind of labour* they seek and where *within* the markets it is to be found. To the high-volume, mass-production industries like cars and consumer electronics, the cost of labour will be a key factor, but this will include a whole host of considerations which are only indirectly related to the level of wages and salaries.

In the first place, there are the costs of employing people associated with health care, pension schemes and redundancy packages. These costs vary from country to country, with the tab for the costs being picked up by different agencies and social groups and with different legislative practices governing their regulation. The countries with a workplace culture of 'hire and fire', for example, may attract certain multinationals precisely because it is easier and cheaper to close a factory than elsewhere, say in Europe. Critics of the UK's increasingly insecure workplace culture in the 1990s have not been slow to point this out.

A further consideration would be the extent to which labour is organized or unionized in different locations. Some multinationals, for instance, seek non-union or single-union agreements at 'greenfield sites', that is, new plants in new locations, such as Nissan's car factory in the north-east of England or Toyota's car plant in Derbyshire. Some companies may actively seek a location which has no past history of industrial activity or legacy of industrial relations. In such cases, they may also seek a workforce that has had little or no experience of an industrial atmosphere. The increasing proportion of women employed in the branch-plants of global firms, both in the developed *and* less developed economies, has often been accounted for in these terms.

Another critical concern to an incoming multinational is the productivity of labour. Costs are directly related to output, and an overall assessment of a workforce's potential may well be concluded in favour of those who combine low costs and high output. This, however, is likely to be more important to firms which employ labour intensively, rather than to more automated or technologically sophisticated companies – even when they belong to the same industry. Some commentators, for instance, have suggested that global firms entering Europe's markets may well opt to serve them from low-technology operations in the former communist countries of Eastern Europe, rather than from more sophisticated manufacturing plants in high-cost, Western European locations at the heart of the market. If this were to happen, and we have seen that the signs are there, then, arguably, it would reproduce a variant of the 'global factories' that sprang up in the third world in the early post-war period: a case, perhaps, of third world conditions moving closer to the centre of Europe.

Seeking labour *close* to the markets of the wealthy industrialized world on the grounds of cost, however, has perhaps more similarities today to labour sought by western multinationals in the less developed world than is readily acknowledged.

In the first place, there is a greater *diversity* of trends in the kind of labour sought by overseas firms in both developed and less developed worlds. True the 'global factories' set up by western MNCs in Latin America and in South East Asia in the 1960s did seek explicitly to make use of a mass of unskilled workers, mainly women. This kind of routine assembly-work continued in these regions throughout the 1970s and 1980s with other countries in these parts of the world, such as Malaysia, Indonesia and Thailand, joining the first wave of countries targeted by western multinationals – namely, Hong Kong, Singapore, South Korea and Taiwan. And over the same period a number of Caribbean countries joined the ranks of Mexico and Brazil. But things have not stood still in these regions.

In Singapore, for example, women still comprise a significant proportion of the multinational workforce, but this is no longer the low-skilled, labour-intensive operation that it once was (Pearson, 1992). In the late 1970s the Singapore government, faced with a changing technological environment and skills base in its overseas electronics industry, attempted to upgrade its operations. With a small population and tight labour markets, the government actually sought to keep women in the labour market through a range of educational, training and childcare policies. In consequence, women now occupy positions in the workforce that cover the whole spectrum of skills, including managerial and professional work. In contrast, in South Korea, where a technological upgrading has also occurred in the industrial base, women still occupy the low-wage, low-skilled jobs and continue to draw their economic identity from the home, not the workplace (Phongpaichit, 1988).

A second similarity in the use of labour by global firms in the developed and less developed economies is the use of international subcontracting to reach low-skilled, low-cost labour. In third world locations the use of sweatshops or homeworkers to perform some of the routine production tasks that help to fashion global products has been a constant feature of the post-war period. Much of this work is performed by women, young and old, and often outside the boundaries of the formal, waged economy (Portes, Castells and Benton, 1989). In this way, global firms reach deep into the social fabric of third world countries, connecting sweatshops and impoverished households to the world economy (see Box 2.2).

In like manner, however, such firms now reach into the depths of first world, global cities. The flow of migrants from less developed countries to the big cities of the industrialized world, many with few skills and little money, provides a ready source of informal or sweated labour for global firms (discussed further in the following chapter). This, then, is not simply the case of western firms sending global factories to the third world; it is also about such firms bringing back third world working conditions to the first world.

In fact, what all this points to is the increasingly blurred character of global firms and the indirect ways in which they reach out and connect with different parts of the world. A graphic example of this is the expanding offshore data processing industry referred to in the introduction. In most cases it involves a set of subcontractual relationships between firms where the *work* of a multinational may move across the ocean – seeking out suitable labour – yet not involve any *direct investment* on the part of the multinational.

Before you read an extract from an article by Pearson and Mitter (1993) on the rise of the offshore data-processing industry, you should note that this activity represents one side of a growing export industry that sells

---

Box 2.2 Subcontracting links in Mexico City

Subcontracting chains

	Chain A		Chain B		Chain C	
	No. of workers	Description	No. of workers	Description	No. of workers	Description
Level 1	3,000	Electrical appliances	2,500	Cosmetics	2,500	Electrical outlets
Level 2	350	Radio and TV antennae and microphones	50	Plastic injection	20	Parts for Level 1
Level 3	6	Electronic coils and assembling	Fluctuat-ing number	Homework: plastic polishing		No homework in this chain
Level 4	Fluctuat-ing number	Homework: tasks as in Level 3				No homework in this chain

'[This table] contains three typical subcontracting chains of four, three and two levels that range from multinational capital to homework. In Chain A, production is subcontracted from a large multinational to increasingly smaller firms. The last level is homework, in this case distributed from a workshop operating illegally in the basement of the owner's home. The multinational firm at the top draws from a list of three hundred regular and fifteen hundred occasional subcontractors and sends out 70 per cent of its production.

The firm at Level 2 represents Mexican capital. It employs 350 workers and subcontracts out 5 per cent of its production – mostly to units such as that at Level 3, a sweatshop that operates illegally in the basement of the owner's residence and employs six young workers (15–17 years of age) and a fluctuating number of homeworkers. Employment at the last two levels is occasional and follows the patterns of work associated with the informal sector. Workers at Level 3 are paid a minimum wage without fringe benefits, and homeworkers receive an average wage equivalent to one-third of the minimum ...

In Chain B, the cosmetics firm at the top is also a multinational, which contracts out the production of plastic containers to firms at Level 2. The specific firm referred to at that level employs an average of fifty workers but shows wide fluctuation in employment according to the number of orders coming in. Such fluctuation is due not only to variations in economic activity in the subcontracting industries (cosmetics and pharmaceuticals) but also to a high degree of competition among subcontractors to attract orders from the larger firms.

Chain C is one of the few in which homework has been eliminated. At the time of fieldwork, the small unit of twenty workers (all women) operating at Level 2 was managed by the only woman encountered in that position. The enterprise was an underground workshop whose employees assembled electrical components on the patio of the woman's house. Although some homework had been distributed to women in the past, the woman reported that her home operation allowed her a greater degree of control over production.'

Source: Beneria, 1989, pp. 177–8

information technology services. The high status side, which involves the export of software and computing services, is dominated by men; the low-status computerization of data processing is overwhelmingly undertaken by women.

Activity 3 Now turn to Reading A, 'Offshore data processing', by Pearson and Mitter, which you will find at the end of this chapter. As you read the extract, you should bear in mind the double-sided character of offshore data work mentioned in the introduction: namely the potential for the technology to move work away from, as well as bring it to, distant pools of labour. In your view, how mobile is this kind of work? Is it really as 'footloose' as it appears to be at first glance?

Clearly there is the potential for the technology to shift work around the globe, but electronic transmission technology is an expensive business, often involving dedicated equipment. Firms investing in such equipment will need to recoup their investment rather than switch work at will. Where the appropriate infrastructure is provided by the host country, the competitiveness of the offshore operation will be a major factor in attracting and retaining contract work. What matters most, however, is likely to be the political and institutional stability of the offshore locations, especially if the data involved are in any way sensitive or confidential. The women employed in the Caribbean 'data factories', however, are likely to be fully aware of the precariousness of their position should the work move elsewhere for whatever reasons. In that sense, they are at the vulnerable end of an interdependent set of relationships that stretches across much of the globe.

2.5.3 'Third world' investors

In talking about vulnerable labour in the less developed countries, there is of course always the risk of conveying the impression that the 'third world' is *only* a location for the types of routine, low-skilled labour sought by western multinationals. Much subcontracting work of this nature does take place in less developed countries, as indicated earlier. It takes place in first world cities too, as also noted. But there is more happening in the 'third world' than simply the provision of low-cost labour for the West. In the example of the Pohang Iron and Steel Company, the South Korean multinational, we have already seen a different face of the so-called third world. Indeed, the increasing amount of foreign investment by firms based in South Korea, Taiwan, China, Singapore, Hong Kong, India and certain Latin American countries challenges the persistent representation of the third world as an identifiable, common group of countries (see **Allen, 1995**).

Most of the overseas investments by multinationals in the less developed countries are small in comparison with their counterparts in the developed world and, like their counterparts, tend to cluster in their neighbourhood region. Of late, however, there has been a perceptible shift, especially by Taiwanese and South Korean multinationals, to invest in the industrialized nations, in particular the United States. To gain a clearer picture of the nature and diversity of foreign investments from the less developed world, you should now turn to Reading B.

Hyundai – the largest of the South Korean car-makers and one of the world's leading producers of vehicles. A 'third world' MNC?

Activity 4 The extract from an article by Sanjaya Lall, entitled 'The rise of multinationals from the third world', provides an historical sketch of global activity in a range of Asian and Latin American countries. As you read through the extract, jot down the different sectors of economic activity associated with particular countries. The case of India is of especial interest, so be sure to note it. Also, think about which part of the less developed world is absent from the coverage, and why.

On the final point above, it is the vast continent of Africa which is missing from the analysis. Sub-Saharan Africa is virtually off the multinational map (or rather the tables of worldwide foreign direct investment). In terms of the types of investment undertaken by different countries, it is interesting to note the way in which firms have used a home-base advantage to enter foreign markets. Thus Singapore and Hong Kong's overseas investments include a significant proportion of service activities, South Korea has invested heavily in trading and natural resource-based heavy industries, and so forth.

India's investments are spread more widely, although what is interesting about India (alluded to earlier in the Texas Instruments example) is a different form of overseas activity: namely, the provision of consultancy and various technical 'know-how' services to the West. The provision of these services to overseas customers does not take place in India, however, but on site at the client's premises. On the basis of a fixed-term contract, Indian consultants work directly at the western plant, usually for US-owned companies, at Indian wages plus a living allowance. This form of subcontracting, where the person rather than the work moves, is known in India as 'body shopping' (Mitter and Pearson, 1992).

The major reason for overseas involvement in the first world by the less developed nations, however, is to broaden market outlets and to strengthen their global position through the acquisition of productive assets and control. It would be premature, nonetheless, to draw any conclusions as to the depth of the ties involved or to their long-standing nature.

Summary of section 2.5

o   Some transnational firms, especially in pharmaceuticals, chemicals, electronics and telecommunications, are internationalizing themselves from sales and production upwards. How far such 'fully integrated' firms are embedded locally in design and development terms is uncertain, however. Integration may be of a shallow nature, with few relationships of depth laid down outside the home country.

o   Subcontractual relationships between western multinationals and those who produce something for them, whether the workforce is located close to the markets of the first world *or* based in the third world to serve wider markets, have extended the reach of global firms into new pools of vulnerable labour. Such workers are part of a series of unequal interdependencies.

o   Not all multinationals or giant firms are first world based or 'western'. The developing economies are the source of a number of firms expanding their investments in the rich, industrialized nations. The world economy today is cross-cut in ways that make simple generalizations about the less developed nations inappropriate.

2.6   Conclusion: in what sense footloose?

In the introduction to this chapter, we spoke of 'footloose' multinationals in terms of their ability to move investments and jobs across borders with little or no attachment to a national home base. The implication here is that such firms are more ready to review their locational options should an insufficient return on their investment be realized. In other words, such firms are much quicker to open and close branch-plants or subsidiaries: that is, the whole process of economic investment over space is speeded up. Whether it is possible to assert that such firms are the mainstay of an emergent global economy, however, is difficult to sustain for a number of reasons.

In the first place, while investment finance may be volatile and easily moved around the world, investment in plant and equipment is relatively immobile and, as we have seen, restricted in scope to the 'global regions' of North America, Europe and Japan. Having said that, more recent ways of 'stretching' the economic reach of multinationals around the globe, such as alliances, subcontracting relationships and other such networks, do offer potentially looser and more mobile connections between places; we saw this in the case of Nike, the US sports shoe manufacturer, for example. Such companies, however, are not the giant monoliths which are assumed to trample across borders with a single, strategic intent passed down from a central HQ. The increase in the extent of indirect forms of overseas involvement draws attention to the variety of relationships set up by global firms and the shift towards looser organizational structures.

The notion of 'footloose' firms also suggests a shallowness in the ties laid down. Yet in some manufacturing industries, as we have seen, there is greater rather than less integration of the activities of global firms within the main regional markets. What this represents in terms of commitment and control is far from clear, however. Much the same could be said about the increasing number of service multinationals seeking out new markets and locations. The issue of depth is also something that is assumed to be absent from subcontractual relationships, although it is perhaps useful to note that of Nike's associations, for example, whilst some were brief, other links have been close and long term, in particular those with Taiwan and South Korea (see Box 2.1). Again, however, it would be wrong to slip into easy generalizations, especially as soaring wage costs in South Korea are currently undermining their once-booming footwear industry.

In this context, it is perhaps of greater significance to consider the *forms* of interdependence laid down by global firms from a range of industries, including those based in the less developed economies. If there has been a qualitative shift in the global economy, then it is both the pace *and* the depth at which interdependent relationships are lived to which we should now look.

References

ALLEN, J. (1995) 'Global worlds' in Allen, J. and Massey, D. (eds) *Geographical Worlds*, London, Oxford University Press/The Open University (Volume 1 in this series).

BENERIA, L. (1989) 'Subcontracting and employment dynamics in Mexico City' in Portes, A., Castells, M. and Benton, L. (eds).

BEST, M. H. (1990) *The New Competition: Institutions of Industrial Restructuring*, Cambridge, Polity Press.

CARNOY, M. (1993) 'Multinationals in a changing world economy: whither the nation-state?' in Carnoy, M., Castells, M., Cohen, S. S. and Cardoso, E. H. (eds) *The New Global Economy in the Information Age*, University Park, PA, The Pennsylvania State University Press.

DICKEN, P. (1992) *Global Shift: The Internationalization of Economic Activity*, 2nd edition, London, Paul Chapman.

DONAGHU, M. T. and BARFF, R. (1990) 'Nike just did it: international subcontracting, flexibility and athletic footwear production', *Regional Studies*, Vol. 24, No. 6, pp. 537–52.

DUNNING, J. H. (1993a) *Multinational Enterprises and the Global Economy*, Wokingham, Addison-Wesley.

DUNNING, J. H. (1993b) *The Globalization of Business*, London, Routledge.

FRÖBEL, F., HEINRICHS, J. and KREYE, O. (1980) *The New International Division of Labour*, Cambridge, Cambridge University Press.

HIRST, P. and THOMPSON, G. (1992) 'The problem of "globalization": international economic relations, national economic management and the formation of trading blocs', *Economy and Society*, Vol. 21, No. 4, pp. 357–96.

HOWELLS, J. (1990) 'The internationalization of R & D and the development of global research networks', *Regional Studies*, Vol. 24, No. 6, pp. 495–512.

HOWELLS, J. and WOOD, M. (1993) *The Globalization of Production and Technology*, London and New York, Belhaven Press.

LALL, S. (1983) 'The rise of multinationals from the third world', *Third World Quarterly*, Vol. 5, No. 3, pp. 618–26.

MITTER, S. and PEARSON, R. (1992) 'Global information processing: the emergence of software services and data entry jobs in selected developing countries', *Sectoral Activities Programme, Working Paper 51*, Geneva, International Labour Office.

OHMAE, K. (1985) *Triad Power: The Coming Shape of Global Competition*, New York, The Free Press.

OHMAE, K. (1991) *The Borderless World: Power and Strategy in the Interlinked Economy*, London, Fontana.

PEARSON, R. (1992) 'Gender issues in industrialization' in Hewitt, R., Johnson, H. and Wield, D. (eds) *Industrialization and Development*, London, Oxford University Press.

PEARSON, R. and MITTER, S. (1993) 'Employment and working conditions of low-skilled information-processing workers in less developed countries', *International Labour Review*, Vol. 132, No. 1, pp. 49–64.

PHONGPAICHIT, P. (1988) 'Two roads to the factory industrialization strategies and women's employment in South East Asia' in Agarwal, B. (ed.) *Structures of Patriarchy: The State, The Community and The Household*, London, Zed Press.

PORTES, A., CASTELLS, M. and BENTON, L. A. (eds) (1989) *The Informal Economy: Studies in Advanced and Less Developed Countries*, Baltimore, MD, and London, The Johns Hopkins University Press.

PRED, A. and WATTS, M. J. (1992) *Reworking Modernity: Capitalisms and Symbolic Discontent*, New Brunswick, NJ, Rutgers University Press.

SASSEN, S. (1991) *The Global City: New York, London, Tokyo*, Princeton, NJ, Princeton University Press.

THRIFT, N. (1988) 'The geography of international economic disorder' in Massey, D. and Allen, J. (eds) *Uneven Re-Development: Cities and Regions in Transition*, London, Hodder and Stoughton/The Open University.

TUROK, I. (1993) 'Inward investment and local linkages: how deeply embedded is "Silicon Glen"?', *Regional Studies*, Vol. 27, No. 5, pp. 401–17.

UNITED NATIONS CENTRE ON TRANSNATIONAL CORPORATIONS (1988) *Transnational Corporations in World Development: Trends and Prospects*, New York, United Nations.

UNITED NATIONS CONFERENCE ON TRADE AND DEVELOPMENT (1991) *World Services Directory*, New York, United Nations.

UNITED NATIONS CONFERENCE ON TRADE AND DEVELOPMENT (1992) *World Investment Report: Transnational Corporations as Engines of Growth*, New York, United Nations.

UNITED NATIONS CONFERENCE ON TRADE AND DEVELOPMENT (1993) *World Investment Report: Transnational Corporations and Integrated International Production*, New York, United Nations.

The increased use of computer technology in less developed countries (LDCs) has led to the emergence of a new group of white-collar employees specializing in information-processing work. They perform a wide range of tasks, from simple data entry or word processing to high-powered software programming or system specification. In spite of their growing numbers, little hard information is available on their employment characteristics or working conditions. In the past two or three years software programming has received some attention but the low-skilled end of the jobs spectrum has been largely neglected.

[...]

The use of computers in clerical and related occupations is not confined to a single or specific type of organization or enterprise in LDC economies. It extends, if unevenly, through all sectors and all types and sizes of workplace. With increasing frequency this sort of work is being undertaken specifically for export, through the international subcontracting of data-entry and routine data-processing work. This is generally referred to as 'offshore' data entry.

The international decentralization of data-entry activity arises out of the convergence and application of two technological developments: the automation and computerization of office and clerical work, and the growth of sophisticated telecommunications systems with flexible bulk data-transfer capacities. Some international relocation of tasks associated with mainframe computer processing, such as card punching, was already taking place in Jamaica and elsewhere in the early 1970s. Internationalization, in the form of offshore data entry, accelerated in the 1980s with the development of personal computer systems and electronic links to mainframe systems.

Many analysts expect the potential of on-line transmission via enhanced telecommunications to lead to further relocation of data-entry and other work offshore. However, the introduction of such systems has not been as rapid as some analysts predicted.

The principal location of such activities has been in the Caribbean, mainly in Barbados and Jamaica and, more recently, in the Dominican Republic, with a handful of facilities in smaller Caribbean islands such as St. Lucia, St Christopher-Nevis and St Vincent. Other facilities are known to operate in China, India, Ireland, the Republic of Korea, the Philippines and Singapore. One of the largest and earliest foreign-owned companies operating in the Caribbean is Caribbean Data Services, a subsidiary of American Airlines, which operates data-entry shops in Barbados and the Dominican Republic. American Airlines set up the Barbados facility in 1984 in order to process corporate data at a lower cost than was possible in Oklahoma. Its fully owned subsidiary now also undertakes subcontracted data-entry work for other clients from North America and the Caribbean. Although there are several US-owned companies with data-entry subsidiaries in the Caribbean, this is not the only form of corporate activity in the region. In Jamaica and Barbados there are also a number of joint venture companies, as well as locally owned independent enterprises working on a subcontracting basis for North American clients.

US companies also have fully owned subsidiaries in a number of Asian countries, some of them being primarily responsible for servicing their regional offices in Australia; however, an increasing number of European enterprises, from both the private and public sectors, have begun to subcontract routine word processing and also data entry and record keeping to offshore facilities in the Republic of Korea, the Philippines and Singapore.

Most of the foreign-owned subsidiaries in the Caribbean and elsewhere are located in Free Trade Zones; this is the case, for example, in the Dominican Republic, Jamaica, Mexico and the Philippines. Incentives available to foreign-owned data-entry firms in Jamaica's Montego Bay Free Zone include low-cost premises, tax benefits and the right to repatriate all profits and dividends to their home countries.

The volume of employment in offshore data-entry operations is difficult to estimate and no comprehensive information source exists. On the basis of published studies and other references the authors estimate employment at up to 5,000 within the Caribbean, with a possible 3,000 elsewhere in the world. Future technological developments are likely to make it a growth area for female employment, especially in the context of expanding Free Trade Zones and export-oriented industrialization. Such employment could also spread to the well-educated workforce in eastern Europe.

Likely impact of technological innovations on offshore data-entry work

To date offshore data entry has primarily involved the physical outshipping by air freight or courier of hard copy in the form of paper documents, magnetic tapes, cards, diskettes and audio recordings. Data are entered electronically onto diskettes and magnetic tapes, which are then shipped back to North America (in the case of Caribbean operations) for storage, printing on paper or direct input into computers for analysis. In some instances where data are entered from hard copy that has been physically transported to the offshore processing site, they are transmitted back electronically using digitalized data-switching telecommunications systems. International electronic transmission depends on the existence of earth stations allowing satellite transmission or connection with submarine cables. It also depends on domestic access to such systems. This, in turn, is governed not just by the physical existence of equipment but also by regulations governing access to it, particularly for data transmission systems which operate in parallel with a country's standard telecommunications system.

It is likely that the electronic transmission of digitalized data will increase, following recent investment in dedicated international telecommunications systems in the Caribbean Basin and elsewhere. A major new facility, which came on stream in 1989, is the Jamaican Digiport at Montego Bay, which was established for the specific purpose of promoting offshore teleworking – both data entry and other activities – on the island. Such developments will make offshore sites more competitive than decentralized locations within the industrialized countries, since the turn-round time for many data-entry jobs can be cut significantly – from three days or more to under 36 hours.

An additional technological possibility is the two-way transmission of digitalized copy and data. This could cut turn-round time to within the 15 hours required for handling current financial data. Two-way electronic transmission also depends on the extension of appropriate telecommunications facilities. The development of optical scanning technology, which can read paper copy and convert it into a transmittable digitalized form, may also facilitate two-way transmission. On the other hand it could eliminate the need for manual data entry by programming digitalized data directly into the format required by the end user. However, while this technology is said to be advancing rapidly, it remains relatively expensive and is not yet feasible for the large-volume, low-value data sets which form the bulk of most offshore data-entry operations.

As the infrastructure for electronic transmission between industrialized countries and offshore sites is extended, the competitiveness of offshore data entry will be improved dramatically, possibly leading to an exponential growth in international relocation in the 1990s. Some analysts argue that technological innovations will ultimately remove the demand for cheap labour for data-entry work. This view, however, is balanced by the fact that the use of offshore operations reduces the cost of data entry by a factor of two or more. Offshore working not only cuts the cost of current data-entry operations but makes possible the conversion of a whole series of records and information to machine-readable forms which would not be undertaken in the absence of this cheap option.

Competition from peripheral regions of Europe

Offshore data entry in LDCs consists, typically, of high-volume activities such as processing airline ticket data, retail coupon promotions, credit ratings, or population censuses. Offshore processing of financial or other time-sensitive data has been limited, to date, because of difficulties in electronic transmission. It is therefore interesting that, in the past three years, a number of US financial institutions, both banks and insurance companies, have established data-entry facilities in the Republic of Ireland. These operations differ from the subcontracted or subsidiary-based high-volume activities which have been sent offshore to the Caribbean and Asian locations described above. They constitute a type of offshore activity which is intermediate between routine data entry and software exports. The Irish workers, overwhelmingly women, are linked via on-line connections to the mainframe computers of the parent companies in the United States.

New York Life Insurance Company, which established a satellite office in Castleisland, County Kerry, in 1988 to carry out most of the corporation's claims processing, is thought to be among the first to export 'intelligent' office work, as opposed to 'mindless' data entry. Relocating to a lower-wage economy on the periphery of industrialized Europe enabled it to employ educated staff (at local clerical rates) who, by checking the company's liabilities under detailed and complex insurance policies, have reduced the money paid out to claimants by up to 10 per cent.

The internationalization of 'intelligent office work' is still in its early stages. It is estimated that total employment in such offshore data-processing activities remains small in absolute terms, probably not more than a couple of thousand worldwide. However, given the predicted demographic trends in the OECD countries and probable future shortages of cognitive skills, it is important to consider the potential of LDCs as sites for intelligent as well as repetitive and low-skilled data-entry and data-processing work. Insufficient research has been carried out on the precise functions performed by offshore data-processing facilities in different LDC locations to rule out the possibility that some portion of offshore work may in fact already entail more than direct data copying and entering. The types of work carried out under the rubric of 'data entry' in Jamaica suggest that the range of activities may be wider than previously thought.

[...]

Working conditions

Many studies have been made of the working conditions, employment status, relative wages and health and safety of data-entry and data-processing personnel in industrialized countries, but little reliable information is available on these aspects of employment for the same categories of workers in LDCs.

While electronic homeworking is not nearly as widespread in economically developed countries as is sometimes believed, it exists and is growing; in LDCs it is still unknown. Indeed, in some ways the relocation of data-entry activity offshore may be seen as offering employers an alternative to homeworking or distance working within industrialized countries, rather than an extension of it. Relocation of IT office work has as its prime objective the reduction of wage costs; since wage costs in LDCs are lower than those in industrialized countries, decentralization in the form of homeworking is not necessary in order to achieve planned cost savings. Moreover, it is most unlikely that the homes of average office workers in most LDCs could offer the necessary infrastructure: adequate office space; connection via a modem to the company's computer system; the possibility of periodic physical contact with the contracting employer; and reliable supplies of electricity to maintain the operation of the terminal and to ensure the safety of the data being converted.

There are some similarities between the working conditions of offshore data workers and those of electronic distance workers (teleworkers) in industrialized countries. This is particularly true of the insecurity of their contractual and earnings situation. In Jamaica it is frequently the case that workers are hired only after a lengthy period of selection and training, during which they are paid a training allowance whilst actually processing data for commercial contracts. Once a proper offer of employment is made, remuneration is dependent as much on reaching (variable and non-negotiable) productivity targets as on a fixed weekly or monthly wage. The basic wage is rarely more than half of the stated average earnings, with productivity-related piece rates accounting for the remainder. It is also quite common for workers to be laid off without pay, or to receive only the minimum payment, when there is insufficient work to occupy the whole workforce.

In spite of the precariousness of employment contracts and low basic wage rates, total remuneration for offshore data-entry clerks often compares well with earnings in other local employment (this was found to be the case in Jamaica, for instance, vis-à-vis manufacturing employment). An American-owned data-processing company in the Philippines advertised to potential clients that wages were pegged to the US dollar and were adjusted to compensate for any devaluation of the local currency. Minimum wage rates cited were compared not with industrial but with white-collar and professional wages. Even so, in comparison with prevailing rates in the developed countries, the cost advantage for employers is very clear. The OTA study (1985) estimated that wage costs in the early 1980s (calculated on the basis of hourly wage rates) were between six and 12 times higher in the United States than in third world offshore locations. A more recent source estimates that the wages of Filipino keyboard operators in 1989 were one-fifth of those of equivalent employees in the US-based companies, indicating that – at least in some locations – the gap may be narrowing as demand for efficient data-entry operators increases. However, there are no systematic data allowing a reliable comparison of wage rates, and no comparative data on total labour costs including non-wage employee costs.

The situation regarding data-entry employees' rights to organize in labour unions is also unclear. Employment in Free Trade Zones often precludes the right to organize, as is the case in the manufacturing sectors of Malaysia and the Republic of Korea (though not, it should be said, of Jamaica. Mexico or the Philippines). However, it was clear that in Jamaica there was no unionization among data-entry workers; in both Jamaica and Barbados keyboard operators were encouraged to think of themselves as white-collar employees, apparently in an attempt to pre-empt the development of militancy characteristic of organized industrial workers. Management styles were often based on notions of responsibility for the employees' welfare, highlighting caring rather than conflictual relationships between workers and management. In the Philippines managers stressed the benefits granted to their employees, including bonuses, medical care and profit-sharing plans, while confirming these employees' non-union status.

[…]

Conclusion

The rise of computer-based white-collar work offers the developing world opportunities for the upgrading of human capital in technical skills where shortages, on a global level, have been predicted for the year 2000 and beyond. On the other hand, growing evidence concerning low wages, precarious employment and health hazards warrants serious concern. The implications of the 'non-bargaining status' of a large section of information-processing workers and of an insignificant rate of unionization among data-entry workers deserve special attention.

Reference

Office of Technology Assessment (1985) *Automation of America's Offices, 1985–2000*, Washington, DC, OTA

Source: Pearson and Mitter, 1993, pp. 49, 54–8, 59–61, 64

Introduction: the background

The internationalization of economic activity has taken many new and dynamic forms in recent years, of which perhaps the most dynamic and least expected has been the emergence of multinationals from less developed countries. Not that the phenomenon is particularly new. The first recorded instance of a third world multinational investing abroad dates back to 1890, when an Argentine textile manufacturer, Alpargatas, set up an affiliate in Uruguay, and followed it up in 1907 with a similar plant in Brazil. But Argentina is a very unusual case in many ways. At the turn of the century it was the most highly industrialized of the LDCs. Waves of immigrants from Europe who were skilled technicians and entrepreneurs had given it a diverse and sophisticated industrial base. By the time the Great Depression struck, three giant firms, Alpargatas in textiles, Siam di Tella in mechanical engineering, and Bunge y Born in grain trading, finance and miscellaneous manufacturing activities, were already well established in several Latin American countries.

But these are unusual cases from an unusual country. They did not herald the growth of Argentine industry as a leading force in third world industrialization or multinationalization. In the past quarter-century, the pace of Argentina's economic growth faltered for numerous political and economic reasons. It has now become a relatively stagnant (if technologically advanced) industrial and trading nation in the community of 'newly industrializing countries'. Of its early multinationals, Alpargatas has been reduced to a tiny shareholder in its major affiliate in Brazil, Siam di Tella has gone into government ownership because of sustained losses, and Bunge y Born has effectively shifted out of Argentina to its major base in Brazil (where it controls over 50 firms with total sales of over $1.5 billion). These multinationals have not really been 'multinational corporations' in the normal sense of the term, with the parent company supplying technology and skills to its affiliates, making strategic decisions and exercising corporate control, for many decades now. After the initial injection of capital and know-how, the different branches have gone their different ways. And, given the prolonged crisis in their original home country, the affiliates have tended to grow faster and larger than their parents. The participation this entails thus resembles a portfolio rather than a direct foreign investment.

These cases apart, the real growth of third world direct investments started in the 1960s and gained momentum in the 1970s. By now a larger number of developing countries – between 30 and 50 – can claim to have at least some companies which have direct investments abroad. It is difficult to quantify the total amounts of investment involved with any accuracy, because many countries do not collect data on their overseas direct investments. In any case, many such investments are undertaken without the knowledge of the authorities, in order to bypass foreign exchange and other regulations. And, for countries which do keep records of foreign investments, it is impossible to separate out direct investments by national companies from those made by affiliates of foreign firms or by 'expatriate' firms (for instance, British firms headquartered in Hong Kong). Needless to say, I exclude portfolio-type investments by oil-rich developing countries, even when these involve buying shares in manufacturing firms abroad, from the category of 'third world MNCs'.

Despite these problems in assessing the value of foreign investments by third world enterprises, a number of studies in recent years enable us to identify which countries are the leading exporters of private capital and what their areas of specialization are.

The largest investor in the third world is Hong Kong, with over $2 billion worth of equity held abroad (including some in the People's Republic of China). A substantial proportion of this is, however, accounted for by British 'expatriate' firms such as Jardine Matheson, which have investments all over the world in a variety of manufacturing, real estate, trading, banking and other activities. However, indigenous Chinese enterprises are also very aggressive investors abroad – a very rough estimate (by Professor Edward Chen of the University of Hong Kong) puts their foreign capital stake at $600-800 million.[1]

This estimate makes Hong Kong a slightly smaller indigenous investor than Brazil, whose overseas capital stock (excluding banking) was estimated at over £1 billion in 1980.[1] There are interesting differences between these countries which I will touch on later, but one worth noting now is that a major part of Brazilian overseas investment is accounted for by the giant state-owned enterprise, Petrobras. Hong Kong overseas investment, by contrast, is entirely by private enterprises, and by enterprises which are not very large even by third world standards.

A capital exporting developing country which is almost as important as Brazil is Singapore – though its investments are highly concentrated in contiguous Malaysia (of which it was historically part). As with Hong Kong, it is relatively small Chinese entrepreneurs who account for its indigenous multinationals. However, Singaporean enterprises are less dynamic in the international field than their Hong Kong counterparts, in terms of the amount, spread and diversity of activity. This may be somewhat surprising at first sight. Singaporean industry is generally more skill-based, high technology and capital-intensive than Hong Kong's, and so may be expected to have a relatively greater foreign presence. However, over three-quarters of Singapore's industrial output, and over 90 per cent of its manufactured exports, come from foreign-controlled enterprises, as compared to under one-quarter for Hong Kong. The weaker position of indigenous enterprise in Singapore thus undoubtedly reflects itself in its lower international profiles vis-à-vis Hong Kong.

There is, then, a whole group of middle-income countries which have foreign investments of around $50–100 million each – South Korea, Taiwan, Argentina (excluding its early investments), Mexico and Venezuela. Thus, the group of NICs (newly industrializing countries) are all involved in international production, and they lead the third world in this activity. Smaller and less industrialized countries in Latin America and Asia are also foreign investors, but their activity is more sporadic and less firmly grounded in domestic industrial expertise.

A country which is a relatively large foreign investor but does not fit into the broad pattern of high per capital income associated with overseas investment is India. With income levels far lower than the NICs, India now has foreign equity of over $100 million. Even more surprisingly, India's direct investment overseas has far surpassed the inflow of new foreign capital in the 1970s – certainly not a pattern common to developing countries. There are other features of interest in India's overseas investment which will be remarked on later.

To sum up this introduction, therefore, we note that the emergence of third world multinationals is a real and growing phenomenon. It encompasses a large range of countries, but is spearheaded by the NICs (and India). The amounts involved are still small; probably the entire stock of third world direct foreign equity (excluding portfolio investments by oil-rich countries) is not more than $10 billion. The great bulk of this investment is directed to other developing countries, though a few investments in manufacturing (and several in distribution, banking, and hotels) have been made in the developed world. This geographical distribution is entirely to be expected. Third world enterprises do not have the wherewithal to compete with developed country firms on their home ground. What is of interest, however, is that they do compete with them in other developing countries. […]

The nature of industrial MNCs from developing countries

Much has been written recently about the specific advantages that third world firms may have in investing abroad and competing both with local firms and the host countries and with affiliates of MNCs from the developed countries. As this discussion has really focused on manufacturing investments, we also confine ourselves to this. Before reviewing the current state of knowledge, however, we should form some idea of the pattern of third world foreign investments.

There are marked differences between the major third world capital exporting countries, as far as the share of manufacturing in total investment is concerned, and, also, in the sorts of manufacturing industries in which different countries reveal their strengths.

Thus, over 95 per cent of Brazil's overseas capital is invested in oil exploration, construction and agricultural activities. About 70 per cent of Korean foreign investment is in trading and natural resources based activities. About half of Argentine investment is in non-manufacturing. A significant but unknown proportion of Hong Kong and Singapore investments is in the service sectors. And about 5 per cent of Indian foreign investments is in hotels, banks, insurance and trading ventures.

In terms of manufacturing industry alone, the major third world investors are Hong Kong, Singapore, India and Argentina. The other NICs such as South Korea, Taiwan, Brazil and Mexico have relatively few manufacturing investments overseas. The first two and Hong Kong have started to follow the early Japanese pattern of resource-scarce economies investing abroad in the development of natural resources. Brazil's absence in the field of industrial investments is very unexpected, since it is by far the most individualized LDC – the explanation may be partly in the locational advantage of producing in Brazil, and partly in the dominant role of foreign MNCs in most advanced industries.

The four leading third world industrial investors show quite different patterns of manufacturing activity abroad. The differences arise both in the nature of activity undertaken as well as the extent of indigenous embodied (capital goods) and disembodied (know-how, managerial skills, marketing and so on) technologies

involved in overseas ventures. They reflect the size of the capital exporting economy, the diversity of its industrial base (in particular, the development of the capital goods sector) and its level of indigenous technological development.

Hong Kong invests abroad mainly in the simpler of its major export products – textiles, garments, plastic goods and simple consumer electronics. Those of its export products demanding more intensive use of skills and marketing – toys, fashion garments, watches, and the like – do not figure largely in its overseas investments. Essentially, the overseas affiliates transfer the production of relatively standardized products with well-diffused technologies. These face increasingly severe competition from new entrants into world trade and industry, which enjoy the advantage of lower labour and land costs. Thus, Hong Kong enterprises are forced to locate in those very countries in order to take advantage of lower production costs. This shift is further encouraged by protectionist policies in Hong Kong's major markets, which allocate quotas for textiles and garments by country – once the home quota is filled, exports can only take place by producing in other countries with unfilled quotas (and less competitive local manufacturers). Products which require greater design, marketing and entrepreneurial skills are kept in Hong Kong because these skills are more difficult to transfer abroad, and also because protectionist and competitive pressure are relatively less on these products.

Hong Kong's direct investments are unusual in that they tend to be export-oriented rather than import-substituting, and they contain relatively little embodied technology from the home country. Hong Kong investors source their equipment worldwide (for second-hand as well as new machines), and have very limited capabilities to design and manufacture capital goods at home. Though some minor modifications are often made to machines sent to overseas affiliates, the basic production technology is imported. The technological contribution of Hong Kong investors is thus that of efficient production engineering (know-how), rather than basic equipment or plant design and manufacture (know-why). Since this is unlikely to provide a special competitive edge in international markets, their monopolistic advantages must lie elsewhere, in good management and intimate knowledge of export markets.

Much less is known about Singapore multinationals. In terms of their marketing strategy they seem to be very different from their Hong Kong counterparts. They specialize in import-substituting or ethnic (Chinese) products. Despite even greater cost pressures than Hong Kong, major export activities have not been transferred abroad by local firms. The overwhelming significance of developed country MNCs in Singapore's industry has meant that higher wages and rentals have led to rapid upgrading of local manufacturing activities, with older, more labour-intensive products being phased out and transferred to cheaper locations by these MNCs rather than local ones.

In technological terms, Singapore's foreign investors are similar to those from Hong Kong. Singapore is into 'heavier' and technologically more advanced industry than Hong Kong, but it does not have a diverse capital goods base to serve local manufacturing industry. Its foreign investors rely, in consequence, on imported technology and essentially complement it with their entrepreneurial and managerial skills. The ethnic factor gives them a strong additional advantage in countries where the local Chinese community is well entrenched in commerce and distribution.

Argentina's manufacturing investments are firmly rooted in local technology and capital goods, and the products are directed mainly at import substitution in the host country markets. Given Argentina's strong base in food products and engineering, the majority of its overseas activities are in these two sectors, supplemented by an unusually active and dynamic (but not truly innovative) indigenous pharmaceutical industry.

Indian manufacturing MNCs are rather similar to those of Argentina, in terms of the high indigenous technological content and the main emphasis on import-substitution in the host economies. There are, however, noteworthy differences also. Indian investments are spread over a much broader spectrum of activity than those of Argentina. Indeed, they are the most diverse in terms of the range of technologies spanned in the whole third world. The largest sector is textiles and yarn, accounting for a quarter of total capital held abroad. This is followed by papers and pulp, engineering of various types, food-processing, and chemicals. In these broad categories, there are individual investments which are unexpected if one believes that third world MNCs are confined to labour-intensive, small-scale, low-technology activities. The largest pulp and paper mill in less-developed Africa is an Indian venture; Indian firms are assembling their trucks in Malaysia and jeeps in Greece; one firm makes precision tools for the electronics industry, mainly for export, in Singapore, while another manufactures mini computers there; two of the newest rayon plants in Indonesia have Indian participation; Malaysia's largest integrated palm-oil fractionation facility is controlled by an Indian firm, as is Thailand's sophisticated carbon black plant; an Indian public sector firm has taken a share in a machine-tool manufacturing venture in Nigeria; and so on.

Indian industrial investors abroad are required to contribute their equity in the form of plant and equipment from India. This ensures that the manufacturing technology used (or a major part of it) has been transferred from India. Most of the technologies have, of course, been imported by India in the first place but over time they have been assimilated and adopted to Indian conditions, and occasionally changed in significant ways to perform better in those conditions than developed country technologies.

India is also engaged in other forms of overseas activity which involve the transfer of its technology but which do not entail direct investment. It has exported over $2 billion worth of industrial turnkey projects, about $125 million of consultancy services (about half of which are directly for manufacturing activity), and a large number of low-value services for management, trouble-shooting, know-how and various technical matters. In fact, it appears that, as far as manufacturing industry goes, India is the largest exporter of technology in the third world.

This surprises most observers. Although it is well known that India has a major industrial sector, it is also regarded as having the worst growth and export performance in the group of NICs. In the two decades when the other new industrializers recorded high rates of growth and rapidly expanded their share of world industrial trade, India has had a variable but generally poor rate of growth and steadily lost its share of world markets. A number of studies have shown that Indian industry is, broadly speaking, highly protected, high cost, and technologically obsolete; few plants reap proper economies of scale; there is little attention paid to product quality and marketing in the consumer goods sector; and there is little evidence of major technological innovation. Indian firms remain highly inward-looking and resistant to any attempt at genuine liberalization of the economy.

The fact that India is simultaneously able to export more technology than richer, more export-oriented and more efficient NICs raises something of a paradox. The explanations are complex and need much further research. However, I believe they lie partly in the nature of the highly interventionist and inward-looking nature of the policy regime which has itself led to poor overall economic performance, and partly in the nature of the technical effort which has been undertaken in India. The import-substitution regime has spawned a highly diverse capital goods industry, parts of which have developed basic design capability and in a few cases (where scale economies are not crippling), are competitive abroad. The government has severely restricted the entry of foreign MNCs and controlled the inflow of technology via licensing, so forcing local firms to develop their own technological base. At the same time, excessive regulation at home has forced firms to look for diversification abroad. Diversification by exporting has been difficult because of high cost inputs at home, small scales

of production, infrastructural failures, and technological lags. Thus, technology exports and direct investment have appeared as a logical means of escape.

Technological lags have not prevented the sale of Indian technologies overseas because many other developing countries deliberately opt for somewhat older and simpler technologies. In many process industries, technological lags take the form of smaller-sized plants rather than very different products or processes; here the competitive disadvantage of Indian firms in the third world markets is minimal or non-existent. Of course, this leaves out a large number of modern industrial technologies where Indian firms are uncompetitive.

There are, therefore, interesting differences between developing countries in the nature of their foreign investment which can be traced to the nature of the economy and home government policies. Small open economies basically export production know-how and efficient management and marketing. Larger, more closed economies export some basic technology and capital goods as well as production know-how, but their technologies may be somewhat outdated and their marketing skills relatively less developed. There are also several cases where third world MNCs provide technologies practically identical with that provided by developed countries.

[…]

A final note on a new form of overseas investment by some NICs which is also expected to grow in the future: the taking of equity shares in some high technology firms in developed countries in order to obtain direct access to their technology. Hong Kong, Taiwan and Korea have already undertaken investments of this sort. It is not yet known how effective they have been in transferring the basic technology to their home countries, but in principle there is no reason why small, specialized producers (without strong international interests) in the developed countries should resist the offer of equity participation from the NICs. Even large firms, facing financial difficulties in the current recession, may look to the new giant corporations in the NICs for cooperation. Of course, given the nature of the innovation process, the newest and most valuable technologies may not be given even to equity shareholders who might become strong rivals.

Note

1 These findings are part of the IRM project on third world multinationals (Institute for Research and Information on Multinationals, Paris).

Source: Lall, 1983, pp. 618–24, 626

Controlling space: global cities

by Chris Hamnett

Chapter 3

3.1 Introduction

Chapter 1 conveyed a sense of the world in which, in the modern era, more people and places have been drawn together through a wide variety of transport and communication links, financial ties and media flows. Other kinds of connections raised in the previous chapter, such as those laid down by multinational firms – investment outlays in plant and machinery, looser subcontractual relationships and, of course, trade – add to this global configuration. What was equally apparent from the preceding chapters, however, was that this configuration of ties, although global in scope, was extremely uneven in respect of the parts of the world drawn in. This was true of its geography, with large expanses of the globe remaining unconnected, and also evident in terms of those people who live and work outside the broad web of capitalist ways of organizing production and exchange. Indeed, much of what we have considered so far has been centred on the countries of the developed world.

The key word here is *centred*, because the networks of social relationships stretched out across the globe are not confined to the developed world. They stretch well beyond it, albeit in a geographically uneven manner. Such relationships, however, whether they are inscribed in the electronic flows of money across the globe or in the decision of a multinational to switch its contract to produce footwear from one Asian country to another, are usually traceable to a first world location. Not all relationships by any means, but if we were to look at where the majority of the connections and ties overlap and intersect, the locations are likely to be cities in one of the three global regions – North America, Europe and East Asia.

These points of intersection have been designated *global* or *world cities* and, although far from a new description, the term draws its contemporary meaning from their position as sites of power and strategic control within the global economy. London, Paris, New York, Los Angeles and Tokyo are among those that are frequently referred to as global or world cities in the present world order – although which cities are included and which are excluded varies somewhat according to the characteristics of power and control emphasized. Indeed one of the aims of this chapter is to consider why some cities are referred to as 'global cities' and others are not. At one level, as already indicated, it is simply because the flows of people, information, money, images and so on converge on certain locations. But, as intimated above, there have been larger claims than that made of global cities.

The chapter is divided into four main sections. The following section looks at what is said to be different about world, as opposed to, say, 'big' cities with large populations and many activities happening within them. It also looks at the broad thinking which lies behind the claim that a new type of city, a global city, has appeared. Following that, section 3.3 critically examines the different conceptions that have been put forward to justify this contention. Section 3.4 briefly explores the question of why, given the kind of space-shrinking technologies discussed in Chapter 1, the lines of communication and control should appear to meet in just a handful of first world cities. Finally, section 3.5 looks at another kind of flow which converges on global cities: that of people seeking the kinds of work and economic lifestyles that such places promise, yet deliver only to a privileged few.

Before that, however, we need to know what it is that is distinctive about world or global cities that merits their suggested importance.

3.2   What are world cities?

One of the first people to attempt to define *world cities* was Peter Hall in his influential book *The World Cities* (1966), which started from the premise that 'there are certain great cities, in which a disproportionate share of the world's most important business is conducted' (p. 7). It is useful to set out Hall's views on the characteristics of world cities at some length and worth reading carefully:

world cities

> By what characteristics do we distinguish world cities from other great centres of population and wealth? In the first place, they are usually the major centres of political power. They are the seats of the most powerful national governments and sometimes of international authorities too; of government agencies of all kinds. Round these gather a host of institutions, whose main business is with government: the big professional organizations, the trades unions, the employers' federations, the headquarters of major industrial concerns.
>
> These cities are the national centres not merely of government but also of trade. Characteristically they are great ports, which distribute goods to all parts of their countries, and in return receive goods for export to the other nations of the world. Within each country, roads and railways focus on the metropolitan city. The world cities are the sites of the great international airports ... Traditionally, the world cities are the leading banking and finance centres of the countries in which they stand. Here are housed the central banks, the headquarters of the trading banks, the offices of the big insurance organizations and a whole series of specialised financial and insurance agencies.
>
> Government and trade were invariably the original *raisons d'être* of the world cities. But these places early became the centres where professional talents of all kinds congregated. Each of the world cities has its great hospitals, its distinct medical quarter, its legal profession gathered around the national courts of justice. Students and teachers are drawn to the world cities; they commonly contain great universities, as well as a host of specialized institutions for teaching and research in the sciences, the technologies and the arts. The great national libraries and museums are here. Inevitably, world

London: a world city

cities have become the places where information is gathered and disseminated: the book publishers are found here; so are the publishers of newspapers and periodicals, and with them their journalists and regular contributors. In this century also the world cities have become headquarters of the great national radio and television networks.

(Hall, 1966, pp. 7–8)

Activity 1 List the key characteristics of world cities as identified by Hall. Does he see any characteristics as more fundamental than others? Think about which cities you know that might come into this category using this definition.

Hall's characterization of world cities is certainly a comprehensive one. In his view, world cities are characterized by a wide range of important national and international functions – cultural, governmental, economic, financial, educational, retailing and judicial. It is this range of functions which distinguishes them from other cities. Note, for example, that world cities are not distinguished by population size alone. A city of nearly 12 million for instance, such as Calcutta, would not fall within Hall's characterization. Significantly, he accords primacy to the governmental and political role of world cities, together with their economic and financial role. He also makes considerable play of their role as centres of education and professional skills, culture and information. Written in the mid-1960s, however, it could be said this account adds up to little more than a very comprehensive list of major urban functions. But there is more to it than that.

Hall does state that world cities are 'usually the *major centres* of political power' and 'the seats of the *most powerful* national governments' and that 'there are certain great cities in which a disproportionate part of the world's *most important* business is conducted' (p. 7). Read in this way, Hall is clearly pointing towards a definition of world cities as centres of global power and influence. Such a definition would, for instance, exclude cities, however large or populous, which have a merely national or regional importance. Thus, area or population size per se, as already noted, are not defining characteristics of world cities and Frankfurt (with the Bundesbank) is arguably more a world city than Cairo or Calcutta which are ten times larger. In terms of this definition, a world-city status cannot be attributed to a large national city such as Stockholm or Oslo, because they do not have any major international influence or importance. Nor would Birmingham or Glasgow rank as world cities, however important they may be within the UK. On this definition the only city which would qualify for world-city status in the UK is London. It is the home of one of the world's most important stock markets, a world centre of insurance (Lloyds), of ship chartering (The Baltic Exchange, Lloyds Register), of world finance (the City of London) and a major centre for corporate headquarters, as well as an important international centre for commercial services such as law, advertising, accountancy, management consultancy, commercial property agencies and the like.

London, New York and Tokyo are clearly sites at which many lines of global interconnection meet and intersect today. But their importance as cities is hardly a novel or new insight. So what makes a city 'global' today?

3.2.1 What's new about global cities?

A small number of major cities have long played a key role at the centre of the world's economic, trading and political systems: ancient Rome, Renaissance Florence and Venice, seventeenth- and eighteenth-century Amsterdam. In the nineteenth century and early twentieth centuries as the loci of industrial capitalism, London, Paris and Berlin were the centres of their respective empires, controlling half the globe between them. As Charles Booth (1901) observed of London at the turn of the century:

It is not only an unrivalled national emporium and world market, but it is also the Mother-city of the Kingdom and of the Empire. London is the centre, moreover, not only of the Imperial Government and the Judiciary, but also of banking and finance, both national and international. It is in London that the agents-general in the great colonies, as well as the chief business agencies, and official commercial representatives of foreign countries are found, their presence illuminating the fact that it is the recognized national centre, not only of government, but of trade ... Everything can be bought in London and therefore everyone comes to buy ... London is as much an emporium for raw materials coming from all over the world as for finished products.

(quoted in Stedman Jones, 1971, p. 161)

But the identity of these cities, their roles and functions have changed over time and we can legitimately ask the question as to what, if anything, is new about the current international order and the role of what are termed world or global cities within it.

A number of reasons have been offered. The first should be familiar from Chapter 2 and involves the scale and intensity of globalization in the modern world and the key role played by transnational companies. Thus, Friedmann and Wolff (1982) have argued that although 'the concept of a world economy articulated through urban structures is as old as the ancient empires', the present situation is very different because the world economy is far more integrated and interdependent than in previous eras:

Even imperial London, ruling over an empire 'where the sun never sets', controlled only portions of the world. The present transnational system of the space economy, on the other hand, is in principle unlimited ...

The world economy is no longer defined by the imperial reach of a Rome, a Venice or even a London, but by a linked set of markets and production units organized and controlled by transnational capital. World cities are a material manifestation of this control ... Without them, the world-spanning system of economic relations would be unthinkable.

(Friedmann and Wolff, 1982, pp. 311–12)

The second – related – reason, put forward by Sassen (1991) and others, is that the global reach of the world economy now necessitates a need for centralized control and co-ordination on a scale not previously necessary. Somewhat paradoxically, the greater the internationalization of production, sales and marketing of goods and services by companies, the greater the degree of centralized control and co-ordination required. We return to this point in section 3.4.

A third reason put forward is that there has been a marked shift in the structure of many national economies. As one mode of economic organization and production gave way to another, so the role, importance and dominance of particular cities have changed. Up until the Industrial Revolution, for example, the great majority of towns and cities had very small populations and served a relatively small local area; they were primarily market towns and cathedral cities. The Industrial Revolution changed this picture dramatically. Cities in England such as Manchester, Birmingham, Glasgow, Liverpool, Leeds and Bradford grew with enormous rapidity. These cities served a much wider area and exported their products worldwide, having a global reach and influence in particular industries. With the more recent shift away from manufacturing towards services and the rise of finance capital, a small number of rather different cities can now be said to have a truly global reach and influence.

A fourth reason is the advent of transport and telecommunications technologies which, as Chapter 1 showed, have lowered spatial barriers and made the world a much smaller place for people and information to get around. Together these reasons make up an interrelated argument concerning the role of world or global cities in co-ordinating the contemporary global economy and financial system. These four reasons frame the rest of the chapter.

Before you move on, you may find it helpful to work through the following activity as a way of consolidating your thinking about what does and what does not constitute world-city status.

Activity 2   Table 3.1 shows a list of the world's largest cities – those projected to have more than 10 million people by the year 2000. Which of them would you include as world cities at present and why? Are there any cities which are not on the list that you think might merit world-city status?

At first sight only four of the cities listed in Table 3.1 – London, Los Angeles, New York and Tokyo – would probably count as world cities, primarily on the basis of their global economic and financial dominance. São Paulo, Shanghai and Bombay (to name but some of the others) are all very large and important within their own countries or regions, but few of them would count as world cities in the sense that they have a major global role or influence or comprise key sites of global economic interconnection. Moscow might have counted as the political capital of one of the two superpowers prior to 1990, but its economic dominance was largely limited to Eastern Europe. The only potential contenders among the other cities might be Beijing because of its role as capital of the largest, and arguably most rapidly industrializing, nation in the world. Shanghai may also become globally important by the turn of the century. Other smaller world cities not on the list would include Paris, San Francisco and possibly Singapore, Hong Kong, Sydney and Frankfurt. World-city status is not a permanent attribute, however, and the rapid economic growth of some South East Asian countries, notably Malaysia and South Korea could put cities such as Kuala Lumpur and Seoul on the world-city map in a decade or two.

Table 3.1 *Megacities projected to be greater than 10 million by the year 2000*

City	Population (million)		Area (km^2)
	1990	2000	
Bangkok	7.16	10.26	1,565
Beijing	9.4	11.47	16,800
Bombay	11.13	15.43	603
Buenos Aires	11.58	13.05	7,000
Cairo	9.08	11.77	214
Calcutta	11.83	15.94	1,295
Delhi	8.62	12.77	*591
Jakarta	9.42	13.23	590
Karachi	7.67	11.57	**3,530
London	10.57	10.79	1,579
Los Angeles	10.47	10.91	16,600
Manila	8.40	11.48	636
Mexico City	19.37	24.44	2,500
Moscow	9.39	10.11	994
New York	15.65	16.10	3,585
Rio de Janeiro	11.12	13.00	6,500
São Paulo	18.42	23.60	8,000
Seoul	11.33	12.97	1,650
Shanghai	13.3	14.69	6,300
Tokyo	20.52	21.32	2,162

Note: * 1981; ** 1982. (Dacca, Lagos, Osaka, Tehran and South Africa's PWV complex have been omitted from the study.)

Source: Simon, 1993, Table 3; data from UNEP/WHO, 1992

Summary of section 3.2

o   World cities are distinguished by their degree of global reach, influence and power. They are not distinguished by size per se. Although world cities are generally large cities, not all large cities are world cities.

o   The influence and power of global cities may be economic and financial, cultural and political or a mixture of all three. But capital-city status is not a guarantee of world-city status.

3.3   Global cities as networks of co-ordination, control and global expertise

We now have a background sense of why a new type of city may have appeared. We have as yet little sense of what such important cities do, however, or indeed whether they are effective at what they do. In order to shed more light on this, we shall now consider three influential interpretations of the role of world or global cities which have been advanced from the early 1980s. It is important to note at the outset that each of them places a different stress on the role of world cities in the organization of the global economy. Whereas Friedmann and Wolff stress the key role of transnational corporate headquarters, Cohen stresses the role of commercial and financial services for multinational companies and Sassen stresses the key role of global cities as production sites for the services which effectively control the world economy.

3.3.1   ... as command centres for transnational firms

The world-city thesis was first put forward by Friedmann and Wolff (1982). Their argument is largely economic in character and rests on the key role of transnational firms in the remaking of the post-war international capitalist economy. Such firms are said to be no longer attached to a home country and are able to cross borders with relative ease to suit their own interests. More importantly, the world economy is now seen to be organized through, and controlled by, transnational corporations in a small number of key urban locations:

The specific mode of their integration with this system gives rise to an urban hierarchy of influence and control. At the apex of this hierarchy are found a small number of massive urban regions that we shall call world cities. Tightly interconnected with each other through decision-making and finance, they constitute a worldwide system of control over production and market expansion. Examples... include such metropolises as Tokyo, Los Angeles, San Francisco, Miami, New York, London, Paris, Randstadt, Frankfurt, Zurich, Cairo, Bangkok, Singapore, Hong Kong, Mexico City and São Paulo.

(Friedmann and Wolff, 1982, p. 310)

As with Hall's view, population size is not the determining characteristic of these world cities, but rather the extent and the ways in which the urban areas are integrated within the global system of economic relations. They identify two aspects. The first is the form and strength of the city's *integration* into the global economy: that is, the extent to which it serves as a *headquarters location* for transnational corporations, its importance as a producer of commodities for world markets, or its strength as a world market. Secondly they identify 'the *spatial dominance* assigned by capital to the city': that is, whether a city's financial and/or market control is primarily global in scope, or whether it is regional or national. Their account thus relates only to the capitalist world and specifically excludes China and the countries of the former USSR and its ex-satellites.

Friedmann and Wolff argue that these criteria of 'world system integration' must be looked at from a historical perspective and that urban roles in the world system are not permanently fixed. Thus, while they accept that there is

headquarters location

spatial dominance

a degree of historical continuity between the world economy of the past and that of today, they argue that the present situation is very different, primarily as a result of the global nature of the modern world economy, which is defined by an interlinked set of markets and production units organized and controlled by transnational capital. Importantly, they see world cities as a *manifestation* of this control, with the major cities in the world city system falling into an *urban hierarchy*, divided into those cities in the western capitalist core countries and those in the semi-periphery. Figure 3.1 sets out the hierarchy. It is interesting to note that only two primary world cities – São Paulo and Singapore – fall outside of the core (both of which are said to articulate their own 'regional' economy).

urban hierarchy

Friedmann and Wolff's account, although interesting, can be criticized in a number of ways. First, their argument places undue reliance on an international capitalist system dominated by transnational companies. As we have seen from Chapter 2, however, such a conception is problematic. Second, it accords capital a very deterministic role. Recall their second criterion for world-city status which is 'the spatial dominance assigned by capital to the city'. World cities, in their view, are seen merely as a manifestation of the dominant role of transnational capital.

While their argument can be seen as somewhat functionalist (that is, a view in which world cities *function* only to serve the needs of global capital), perhaps more problematic is the fact that Friedmann's list of world cities includes Bangkok, Mexico City and Caracas. While there is no doubt that they are important cities in their own right, it is questionable, as we shall see, whether they are major sites of global corporate control or whether they play a key role in the co-ordination of the global economy. At worst, it could be

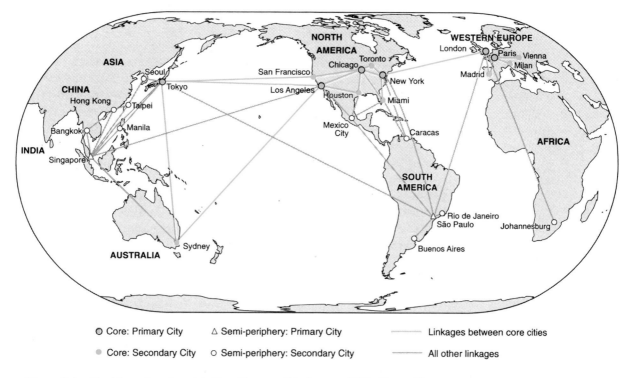

Figure 3.1   *The hierarchy of world cities (Source: Friedmann, 1986, Figure 1)*

111

said that Friedmann and Wolff have taken a list of major cities around the world and simply designated them as world cities.

A major weakness of their thesis is that they do not spell out the nature of the *mechanisms* by which world cities are said to control the world economy. They suggest that without them the idea of an integrated world economy is difficult to comprehend, but they do not say why. The heart of their thesis is that world cities function as headquarters locations for multinational corporations. They refer to the ability of such places to serve as banking and financial centres and administrative headquarters, but these are really no more than assertions. They provide no evidence of the concentration of corporate headquarters, financial and banking functions in world cities, nor do they spell out precisely *why* this concentration is necessary for the control of the world system. While corporate headquarters may be concentrated in the world cities, this does not explain *why* they are concentrated there.

Activity 3 How does Friedmann's view of world cities as centres of transnational corporate control measure up to empirical evidence? Table 3.2 shows the headquarters locations of the world's 500 largest multinational firms (excluding banks). Compare it to Friedmann's classification. You should note when comparing it that Osaka is almost part of Greater Tokyo and that Essen is part of the Ruhr area of Germany.

Table 3.2 Headquarters location of the world's largest transnational firms, 1984

		Metropolitan area population (000s)	Number of firms
1	New York, US	17,082	59
2	London, UK	11,100	37
3	Tokyo, Japan	26,200	34
4	Paris, France	9,650	26
5	Chicago, US	7,865	18
6	Essen, Germany	5,050	18
7	Osaka, Japan	15,900	15
8	Los Angeles, US	10,519	14
9	Houston, TX, US	3,109	11
10	Pittsburgh, PA, US	2,171	10
11	Hamburg, Germany	2,250	10
12	Dallas, TX, US	3,232	9
13	St Louis, MO, US	2,228	8
14	Detroit, MI, US	4,315	7
15	Toronto, Canada	2,998	7
16	Frankfurt, Germany	1,880	7
17	Minneapolis, MN, US	2,041	7
18	San Francisco, US	4,920	6
19	Rome, Italy	3,115	6
20	Stockholm, Sweden	1,402	6
21	Turin, Italy	1,191	5

Notes: Banks are excluded. Size is in terms of sales. The population figures are Ranally Metropolitan Areas (RMAs), which include outlying urbanized areas (e.g. suburban towns) around the city giving the area its name.

Source: Feagin and Smith, 1987, Table 1.1

Table 3.2 Headquarters location of the world's largest transnational firms, 1984(continued)

		Metropolitan area population (000s)	Number of firms
22	Hartford, CT, US	1,020	5
23	Fairfield, CT, US	100	5
24	Seoul, South Korea	6,889	4
25	Atlanta, GA, US	2,196	4
26	Montreal, Canada	2,828	3
27	Stuttgart, Germany	1,835	3
28	Cologne, Germany	1,810	3
29	Cleveland, OH, US	2,174	3
30	Milan, Italy	3,775	3
31	Basle, Switzerland	580	3
32	Eindhoven, Netherlands	374	3
33	Midland, MI, US	100	3
34	Genoa, Italy	830	2
35	Zurich, Switzerland	780	2
36	Akron, OH, US	606	2
37	Winston-Salem, NC, US	291	2
38	Peoria, IL, US	320	2
39	Ashland, KY, US	100	2
40	Wilmington, DE, US	100	2
41	Bethlehem, PA, US	100	2
42	Southfield, MI, US	100	2
43	Moline, IL, US	100	2
44	Philadelphia, PA, US	5,254	2
45	Johannesburg, South Africa	3,650	2
46	Madrid, Spain	4,515	2
47	Melbourne, Australia	2,722	2
48	Munich, Germany	1,955	2
49	San Diego, CA, US	1,788	2
50	Cincinnati, OH, US	1,481	2
51	Rotterdam, Netherlands	1,090	2

Notes: Banks are excluded. Size is in terms of sales. The population figures are Ranally Metropolitan Areas (RMAs), which include outlying urbanized areas (e.g. suburban towns) around the city giving the area its name.

Source: Feagin and Smith, 1987, Table 1.1(continued)

Clearly a disproportionate number of the world's largest companies had their headquarters in New York, London, Tokyo and Paris in 1984: 203 of them were based in the top eight cities and 297 were based in the top twenty cities. This suggests that on an empirical level there is a concentration of headquarters in major cities, and evidence on the location of Britain's top 500 companies shows that about half of them are based in London. Feagin and Smith note:

The New York metropolitan area is the headquarters capital of the core cities, capturing 59 of the top 500 transnational firms, including 18 of the top 100. London and Tokyo are at roughly the same level in the 1980s, both now house the headquarters of more than 30 of the top transnationals. Somewhat less important are Paris, Chicago, Essen, Osaka and Los Angeles with 14–26 each of the top 500 companies, followed by an industrial grouping including Houston, Pittsburgh and Hamburg. All cities with five or more of the top 500 companies are in the United States, Great Britain, France, Germany, Italy, Canada, Sweden and Japan. More countries are included when we examine cities with 2–4 of the top 500 firms. These include Australia, Belgium, the Netherlands, and the first 'third world' country, South Korea ... When cities with only one large transnational firm are examined, we find many more countries represented, including a scattering of firms in underdeveloped countries from Brazil to India.

(Feagin and Smith, 1987, pp. 7–8)

But although a large number of major companies are located in the top 20 cities, this does not *necessitate* a head office location in a world city. Philips, for example, is based in Eindhoven in the south of the Netherlands, and Ford and General Motors are based in Detroit, not New York or Los Angeles. In fact, as Table 3.2 shows, some of the world's 500 biggest corporations are headquartered in some unlikely places. Several are based in very small American cities (for example, Moline, Illinois and Wilmington, Delaware).

3.3.2   ... as a concentration of corporate services

An attempt to explain *why* the majority of large transnational (and many large national) companies are headquartered in global cities was made by Cohen (1981) who stresses the importance of these cities as centres of corporate services. Cohen argues that, with the rise of the new international division of labour and the development of multinational corporations, the operations of such firms are now spread out across the globe. This requires more information about potential markets and greater control over investment and production, distribution and sales worldwide. While many day-to-day decisions are delegated to local managers it is necessary to maintain a greater degree of central control and co-ordination over worldwide operations to ensure continuing success in developing new products and markets.

Cohen places considerable stress on the changing structure of major companies, in particular their widening geographical spread, and the growing complexity of the international business environment, both of which require a greater need for, and reliance on, sophisticated or specialist commercial services such as law and accountancy firms, management consultants and the like. Such firms have grown rapidly in size and importance in the last thirty years, and they are overwhelmingly concentrated in the major world cities. He argues that, while these services have provided support for business operations in the past, they have now become sources of information and intelligence which are of crucial significance to the global running of companies. Cohen also argues that similar changes have occurred in corporate dealings with governments and other regulatory bodies, and that big law firms now play a major role in dealing with political and legal issues across the globe and that this has significant implications for the corporation as a whole. As a consequence of these demands, there has tended to be a concentration among these commercial services into a smaller number of larger firms which are overwhelmingly based in a small number of major cities. Thus key business services have become more concentrated at the top of the urban hierarchy.

There is no doubt that worldwide operations do require more sophisticated financial, legal and accountancy inputs than purely national operations, and the concentration of advanced business services in the major cities suggests this is where the market for such services is greatest. Indeed international distribution of US advertising agencies, the European and Asian offices of major US law firms and international accounting firms are almost all in the major world cities (Moss, 1987), a fact which lends support to Cohen's argument. Cohen also stresses that as the position of a handful of new global cities has been reinforced, so the rest of the urban hierarchy has also been reshuffled into a series of key international regional centres with several previously important industrial centres losing out in the process. This is particularly true of some of the older industrial cities of Europe and North America which have fallen in importance as manufacturing industry has closed down or moved abroad. Manchester, Liverpool and Glasgow, Pittsburgh and Baltimore, for instance, are no longer as important as they once were.

Cohen's analysis, with its focus on the concentration of commercial services in global cities and the role they play for major companies, could be said to take us further than Friedmann and Wolff's analysis, in that he provides a clearer and more developed view of the mechanisms whereby concentration of business services in world cities helps to co-ordinate and control the global economy.

3.3.3 ... as production sites for global control

As Chapter 1 pointed out, vast sums of money and capital now flow around the world at the touch of a computer keyboard, aided by the developments in electronic data transmission such as satellites and fibre-optic cables. The lines of finance, however, are at their most dense in the new global cities and one of the leading proponents of such cities in international financial control and co-ordination has been Saskia Sassen. Unlike Friedmann and Cohen, she sees global cities, not primarily as centres of corporate control, but as centres of commercial services, financial markets and the production of financial innovations. Thus in her book *The Global City*, Sassen argues that:

> ... a combination of spatial dispersal and global integration has created a new strategic role for major cities. Beyond their long history as centres for international trade and banking, these cities now function as centres in four new ways: first, as highly concentrated command points in the organization of the world economy; second, as key locations for finance and specialized service firms, which have replaced manufacturing as the leading economic sectors; third, as sites of production, including the production of innovations, in these leading industries; and fourth, as markets for the products and innovations produced.
>
> *(Sassen, 1991, p. 3)*

She goes on to argue that as a result of these changes in the functioning of major cities, a new type of city has arisen. This is the global rather than the world city, of which London, New York and Tokyo are the key representatives. While Sassen agrees with Friedmann that *global cities* function as command points for the global economy she differs considerably in the

global cities

115

emphasis she gives to financial and commercial service production and innovations.

Her focus is not upon the power of the large multinationals to co-ordinate and control the global economy, but rather upon the *practice* of global control. By this, she means the production of those services – financial and commercial – which actually do the controlling and managing across the vast corporate networks. It is in this sense that global cities *produce* things: they are sites of production for services and financial products which co-ordinate global economic activity.

What are the consequences of these developments for the urban pattern? Sassen argues, like Cohen, that while a few major cities have become production sites for the practice of global control, a large number of other cities have lost their role as manufacturing centres as a result of decentralization and closure.

Activity 4 At this point you should look at Reading A, the extract from Sassen's (1991) book, *The Global City*. As you read, you should bear in mind *four* key questions:

(a) Why do global cities now have a new strategic role in the world?

(b) How does the position of these cities in the world economy differ from that which cities have historically held as centres of banking and trade?

(c) What are the consequences of the rise of global cities for the rest of the urban hierarchy?

(d) Why are producer services and finance strongly concentrated in these cities?

Sassen also discusses the implications of various changes for the social structure of global cities, and this aspect will be taken up again in section 3.5.

As you will realize, Sassen makes some very strong claims for the role of global cities. Perhaps the most important of these is her view that it is only through an understanding of why the key structures of the world economy are to be found in certain cities that we can start to fathom the nature of the contemporary global economy. She rejects Friedmann's view that global cities are simply the outcome of a global economic machine and argues instead that the territorial dispersal of modern economic activity creates a *need* for greater central control and co-ordination. This stress on 'need' goes far beyond Friedmann's argument and she attempts to explain why particular commercial and financial functions are concentrated in global cities rather than being located at random. She is quite explicit about this, asserting that, whereas new developments in telecommunications might seem to point to greater dispersal of economic control and management, the reverse is actually the case. As transnationals spread their economic reach further and further afield, connecting deep into the social fabric of distant economies, for example through the use of homeworkers and casualized labour, so the concentration of key functions in a few locations has increased.

What is particularly novel about Sassen's analysis, however, as noted earlier, is the stress she gives to global cities as production sites for financial and business services. In focusing on the production of business services and financial innovations, she explicitly seeks to turn attention away from the power of large corporations over governments and economies, arguing that this is insufficient to explain what actually contributes a *capability* for global control.

This is a radical thesis which goes further than that of Friedmann. Essentially, Sassen is arguing that, although global corporate control capability is important, it does not alone explain the concentration of financial and business services in global cities. She argues that a focus on transnational banks would be equally misleading in that the real growth has taken place outside the banks during the 1980s. Sassen breaks free of theories that see large companies as the motive power of global cities, and argues that in an increasingly globalized world there is a requirement for specialist service production sites. Thus, if Sassen is correct, the trend towards headquarters decentralization from major cities could continue without significantly threatening their economic viability. Unlike Friedmann, and Cohen to a lesser extent, Sassen does not see corporate headquarters as essential for global cities.

Indeed, she argues that the real need for concentration is not between **agglomeration** corporations and specialists but in fact between specialists themselves. On this view, in today's global economy, legal firms, accountancy practices and management consultancies, amongst others, no longer need a face-to-face relationship with their customers, yet to remain globally competitive each of these specialist services needs to be close to other kinds of commercial or business expertise. Because such key inputs to a global control capability often come as a kind of 'package' to a large client firm, it requires that each participant knows and understands the contribution of others and how they fit together. If true, then this gives a new twist to the concept of *agglomeration*, whereby the links between various activities in these cities are constituted for global rather than local reasons. As such, it is precisely because such services reach out across space, that they are able to be found in only a handful of sites.

Sassen's work therefore, does not simply reflect a shift in emphasis from corporate headquarters to financial and business services; rather it reflects a major shift in the economic base and rationale of global cities themselves – away from transnational corporations and towards advanced service products. Whereas, in the 1950s and 1960s such activities existed to service the needs of large corporations based in these cities, they now have a global importance in their own right as key industries.

Sassen's thesis seems persuasive, although others such as Thrift (1993) have their doubts. In his view, Sassen's account fails to show why such service agglomerations are necessary in today's shrinking world. Above all, it glosses over the need to be able to read and interpret what is going on in the economic world 'out there'. Places such as Wall Street or the City of London, for example, are not simply aggregations of people and institutions who carry out specialist tasks; they are nodes of information and experience, alive with messages and social contacts. This dense clustering of people and information in a small area is crucial to the functioning of such places. As Walter Wriston, the ex-Chairman of Citibank, famously put it: 'Information about money has become almost as important as money itself.' What Thrift is pointing to here is the importance of a concentration of social relationships in a few global cities, despite the compression of global space by time. It is to this last point that we now turn.

Summary of section 3.3

o   A number of arguments have been put forward regarding the key role of world or global cities in the international economy. Friedmann stressed the role of world cities as centres of control and co-ordination by transnational corporations. Yet, although there is evidence of much headquarter concentration in such cities, Friedmann failed to explain *why* such companies should locate there.

o   Cohen took the argument further by stressing the growing corporate need for sophisticated business services which tend to be concentrated in such cities.

o   Sassen, however, takes the argument a stage further by arguing that advanced business services have become important in their own right, as the inputs to a capability for global control. Global cities are centres of corporate control, but, more importantly, they are now production sites for services and financial innovations at a global level.

3.4   So near, yet so far away

spatial dispersal

As Chapter 1 argued, many of us now live in a 'shrinking world' in which the time and cost of movement and communications between places have fallen dramatically in recent decades. As a result, places have been brought closer together, in terms of travel time or communications costs, though not, of course, in terms of absolute distance. But the compression of space by time poses an interesting paradox for global cities. If time–space convergence brings places closer together and enables greater global connectivity, why are global centres of command and control really necessary? Surely, operations can be conducted as quickly and efficiently from Mobile, Alabama or Luton, as they can be from New York or London? If the nineteenth century was an Age of Great Cities, brought about in part as a consequence of the limitations of transport and communications and the friction of distance, surely the development of high-speed transport and communications in the twentieth century allows *spatial dispersal* to take place on a scale hitherto unknown. As Melvin Webber (1968) graphically suggested, it may now be possible to locate your business on a mountain-top and yet keep intimate contact with business or other associates in real time. There are a number of reasons, however, why this vision has not materialized.

First, as Chapter 1 pointed out, some places are much better 'connected' than others. Global cities run on information, and information and information-processing are highly centralized. Rather than reducing the need for central cities, they reinforce their existing dominance. In modern equity and foreign exchange dealing, every second counts. To be a few hours – or even minutes – late is to be out of the game. Thus, the existing major financial centres have an inbuilt advantage which they can build on as long as they continue to invest in the latest information-processing and telecommunications technologies to help them stay at the forefront of competition. According to Moss (1987), Manhattan alone had twice the telephone-switching capacity of the average nation, more computers than Brazil, and more word processors than all of Europe combined. This dominance may have weakened in recent years but the point of the example remains.

The second argument, noted earlier and cited by Sassen, is that it is precisely because of a decentralization of activity which advanced telecommunications systems have permitted, that there is a need for greater central control and co-ordination. In this view, the dispersal of some activities and the centralization of control are two sides of the same coin. As it has become increasingly easier for firms to disperse their economic activities across the globe, with more and more places brought within reach, so the need for co-ordination and central control has increased. Whether such co-ordination is effective or not is a different matter; for it may simply be that greater complexity and awareness of the differences between locations across the globe has pushed big corporations to try to keep their increasingly 'blurred empires' under control.

The third reason advanced for the continued importance of global cities is the changing importance of place. In Chapter 1, Andrew Leyshon referred to the global financial system as another kind of empire upon which the sun never sets. The significance of continuous, twenty-four-hour trading in this context has therefore heightened rather than diminished the significance of those locations which, in one sense, 'drive' the flows of finance from one global city to the next.

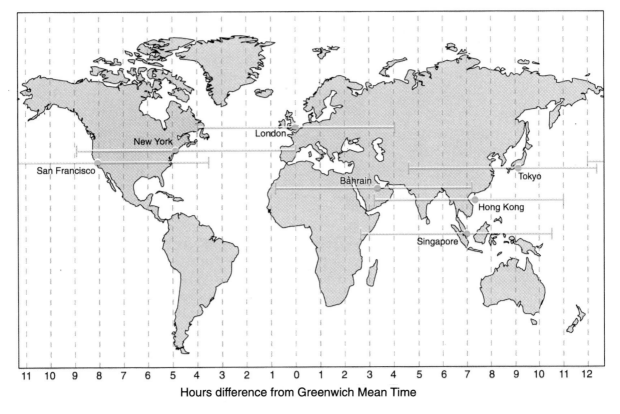

Figure 3.2 *Trading hours of the major financial centres (Source: Warf, 1989, Figure 5)*

Activity 5 Chapter 1 referred to places on the global map of finance becoming further apart, parts of Africa and Latin America in particular becoming more distant from the 'West'. Figure 3.2 gives you an idea of the overlap in the time–horizons for a number of financial centres. In your view which cities or parts of the world are moving closer and which are moving apart in terms of finance? You may find it useful to skim sections 1.5.2 and 1.5.3 of Chapter 1 before you start this activity.

centres of interpretation

spatial proximity

The final reason for the lack of spatial dispersal is the one noted at the end of the last section, namely that global cities are not just centres of information-processing and control; they are also *centres of interpretation*: that is, they possess 'institutional thickness' (Amin and Thrift, 1992). By this, they mean that the likes of Tokyo or New York have a key role in the creation and maintenance of a specific culture, a set of contacts, and a body of carefully built-up knowledge and expertise which cannot be electronically duplicated. Put simply, a thin film of electrons will not, and cannot, replace the need for the geographical concentration of knowledge and expertise which are embodied in global cities. There is a need for *spatial proximity*. If correct, then there is a degree of locational inertia in global cities which cannot be replaced or built up overnight.

Global cities are not about to disappear, therefore. Telecommunications have intensified, not eliminated, the historic role of certain cities as centres of specialist knowledge, information and power. Although developments in transport and communications technologies have led to the spatial dispersal of certain economic activities, the need for proximity and centrality for key functions is still a powerful cement. Such functions provide a new logic for agglomeration in a handful of global cities.

Global cities as centres of interpretation

3.5   Converging on the city: global lines of migration

The latest wave of globalization to hit the world economy has not only meant an increase in flows of goods and services and information. It has also been associated with an increase in the flows of labour between countries. There is a growing degree of global labour market interdependence. Moreover, these flows are not random. Given most people's desire to better themselves economically, the majority of the flows are from the less developed, low-wage economies, to the more developed, high-wage economies of North America, Western Europe and East Asia. And, within these economies, the flows of migrants are predominantly to the major cities where the concentration of job opportunities is greatest. This is also the case with the major labour flows within the third world, from poor rural areas to the major cities such as Mexico City, São Paulo, Rio de Janeiro, Bangkok, Cairo and Lagos.

Flows of migrants to big cities, of course, are not new. London's massive population growth from 1 million in 1801 to 6.5 million in 1901 was primarily the result of mass migration, as was the growth of other major industrial cities in the nineteenth century. North American and Australian cities were largely populated by European migrants in the nineteenth and early twentieth centuries. The United States also saw major migrant flows from the poor, black, rural south to the northern industrial cities from the 1950s onwards. These flows radically changed the ethnic and racial composition of major US cities, post-war; as the Italians, the Irish, the Poles and others moved out of the inner-city areas, their places were taken by black migrants from the southern states and, more recently, by Hispanics, Asians and other overseas migrants.

There has also been a major shift in the composition of migrant flows into the cities of north-western Europe. As the economies of these countries expanded rapidly in the 1950s, '60s and early '70s, growing labour shortages led to migrants being attracted from southern Europe and the ex-colonies. Thus, in the UK there were flows of migrants from the Caribbean, India, Pakistan and Bangladesh and in France from Algeria, Morocco and central Africa; in the Netherlands they came from Turkey, Morocco and the ex-colonies of Surinam and Indonesia; in Germany and Switzerland the flows of what were termed *Gastarbeiter* or 'guest-workers' were largely from Turkey, Yugoslavia, Italy, Greece and other southern European countries. Many Italians moved from the 'Mezzogiorno' to Turin, Milan and northern Europe to take up jobs in catering, hotels and cleaning. More recently, as economic development has proceeded apace, Italy has ceased to be a source of migrant labour and has, instead, become a destination for migrants from north Africa, Yugoslavia and elsewhere (Pugliese, 1993). In Germany the bulk of the migrant flow is now made up of refugees from Eastern Europe and the former Yugoslavia.

The main point to note about these flows, however, alongside the change in migrant composition, is the fact that the great majority of migrants, as indicated, head for the big cities. The next reading gives an idea of the flows of migration involved and their social impact in relation to New York and London.

Activity 6 You should now turn to Reading B, 'Migration, minorities and world cities' by Cross and Waldinger. As you read, note the contrasts between New York and London in terms of:

(a) The changing ethnic composition in the two locations.

(b) The lines of migration – where people are coming from and the historical ties involved.

(c) Any form of economic migration not considered, and why.

One thing that struck me about the lines of migration, especially in the case of London, was the colonial ties involved, whereas for New York it was a mix of historical ties, ranging from past economic connections to geopolitical ties. Although far from clear-cut, there is a sense of the ties of the past reversing this direction of flow, from the 'rest' to the 'West'.

On the last point, there is one group of workers who would not fall under the rubric of 'minorities' and that is the flow of highly qualified and highly paid professional and managerial workers. This phenomenon has two aspects. First, within nations, there is a constant migration of younger, educated people to cities such as London, New York and Paris because of the concentration of specialist jobs and career opportunities they offer. Such cities are a Mecca for the highly skilled and ambitious in business, media and the professions. The role of global cities as centres of economic and financial co-ordination means that their job and income structures are skewed; they are the major concentrations of wealth and centres of conspicuous consumption. Thus, Fielding (1992) terms the South East of England an *escalator region* where occupational and class mobility are much higher than in other regions.

escalator region

Secondly, there is now a high level of skilled international migration linked to the growing degree of global economic interdependence between the three global regions. A good deal of this takes place within major firms and between global cities as skilled personnel are sent to other branches of the company, either to acquire experience or to run specific operations. The flows between New York, London, Los Angeles, Paris and Tokyo now amount to several tens of thousands of people a year. In this context, it is interesting to note that Tokyo is included, whereas for those converging on world cities from the third world, mainly those with fewer skills, Tokyo is not a major destination (leaving aside the fact of illegal immigration).

3.5.1 Social polarization

Section 3.3 discussed the changes in the economic role and structure of global cities and we have just looked at the migration flows to these cities. Here the implications of these changes for the social structure of world cities are examined. Two distinct processes seem to be at work.

First, as noted, the concentration of advanced service firms and key cultural functions in global cities has led to an influx of highly qualified and highly paid professional and managerial workers to staff these jobs. Not only do global cities attract many of the most highly qualified people from within their own countries and beyond, they also attract many of the global rich who come to live in Paris, London, New York or Los Angeles. Global cities are where money is made and spent in large quantities. They are centres of wealth production and conspicuous consumption.

The second process is altogether different. By no means all the jobs created in world cities are of a high status kind. There are also many low-paid service jobs in restaurants, cleaning and personal services – waiters, maids, security guards and the like – and by no means all the jobs in banks, corporations and law firms are highly paid; there are also many low-paid clerical jobs. Also, because global cities attract a large number of low-skilled migrants from the third world, they tend to have a large, low-wage population. As a result, the gap between rich and poor also tends to be greatest in global cities.

It would be wrong to suggest that these conditions are totally new. Because of their role as focal points of the worldwide economy, large cities have long had concentrations of wealth and wealthy people. This was true of medieval Florence and Venice, of seventeenth- and eighteenth-century Amsterdam and nineteenth-century London. They have also had large numbers of poor people. There was a massive gap in eighteenth- and nineteenth-century London and Paris between the well-to-do and their townhouses, carriages and servants and the vast army of the labouring poor (Stedman Jones, 1971; Harvey, 1985).

But, while these massive inequalities apparently disappeared or weakened over much of the post-war period, they seem to have surfaced once again in New York and London. Some have argued that there is a process of *social polarization* occurring in global cities, that the middle of the social structure is being eroded and that the numbers of rich and poor are growing, as is the size of the gap between them. This polarization thesis has been developed by Sassen (1991), who argues that the changes in social structure are a direct result of the changes in the economic base. In the extract from her book, *The Global City*, which you read earlier, you will have noted that she argues that the changing structure of economic activity in global cities, particularly the rapid growth of services and the decline of manufacturing industry, has 'brought about changes in the organization of work, reflected in a shift in the job supply and polarization in the income distribution and occupational distribution of workers' (from Reading A). She argues that three changes are particularly important. First, the decline of manufacturing industry which is associated with the loss of relatively well-paid, skilled manual jobs. Second, the growth of service-sector jobs is split into a highly skilled and highly paid group of professionals and managers and a low-skilled and low-paid stratum of maids, porters, cooks and cleaners, often in insecure, part-time jobs. Many of these jobs are required to service the growing high-income group. And thirdly, she points to the existence of an expanded, 'down-graded' manufacturing sector, often organized through 'sweat-shops' and homeworking. Taken collectively, these trends have led to what she refers to as a new class alignment in global cities.

Activity 7 It may be useful at this point to re-read Reading A from 'The fourth and final theme ...', to review the kind of shifts which are said to be involved.

The polarization thesis is a persuasive one and it is supported by many contemporary writers who have pointed to the yawning gulf between rich and poor in some global cities. Writing in the *Observer*, Neal Ascherson (1986) argued that:

Under the surface of London, there are strange tremors. Something is rising to the surface ... That something is middle-class money. London is ceasing to

social polarization

Divided cities: the gulf between rich and poor?

be a city with a large, organized factory proletariat and is reverting towards a capital in which a huge, under-employed proletariat works to service a wealthy minority. London is slipping backwards in time and becoming a plebeian city. This is more like Paris in the nineteenth century than the working-class London of 40 years ago.

Tom Wolfe's novel *The Bonfire of the Vanities* focused on the different worlds of the highly paid financial traders and poor ghetto blacks in New York in the 1980s. They may live in the same city but they inhabit different social spaces. This chasm was also captured by Jonathan Raban in his book *Hunting Mr Heartbreak*. His graphic depiction of the lives of the 'air people' and the 'street people' in New York, and the social distance between them, makes compelling reading. Raban argues that modern Manhattan is now polarized into two distinct worlds: that of the 'street people' – the poor, the homeless and the hungry – who live, literally, on the streets; and the wealthy, upper middle-class professionals and managers or 'air people' who live in high-rise apartment buildings with security staff to keep out undesirables. The air people are, Raban suggests, generally terrified of the streets and the street people, who are seen as the focus of crime, violence, poverty and despair. A similar kind of thesis is to be found in Mike Davis's account of 'Fortress LA' which you should now read.

Activity 8 Now turn to Reading C, 'Fortress LA' by Mike Davis. Although similar to Raban's stress on a divided city, how does it differ from his account of Manhattan?

You may have noticed a number of differences, but perhaps the most obvious one is that instead of the vertical segregation of the rich into high-rise apartment buildings, as in Manhattan, the rich in Los Angeles are insulating themselves from the poor and ethnic minorities geographically – with, of course, a little help from the erection of high-security, walled enclaves patrolled by security guards and plastered with 'armed response' signs. Interestingly, Davis also argues that the traditional public spaces of Los Angeles are rapidly disappearing as they are effectively declared 'off limits' to minorities and the poor.

Although it is only possible to gain a broad impression of social division from such sources, if the rich have become richer and the poor become relatively poorer during the 1980s in New York, London and Los Angeles, it does not follow that there has been an absolute increase in the numbers of those at both the top and bottom of the occupational and income hierarchy. In other words, there are not necessarily now more rich people and poor people, just a widening of the gap between them. Although it may be true for New York and Los Angeles, and, indeed, for many large third world cities, the evidence for London and some other European cities is less convincing. In London, for example, the trend seems to be towards *professionalization*, rather than polarization, with an overall increase in the number of professional and managerial jobs and a fall in the number of jobs at the bottom end of the occupational ladder (Hamnett, 1994). Of course, it is possible that those working in low-paid, low-skilled service jobs are outside the *formal* employment structure and therefore would not be identified in the official trends, but in London – in comparison to say New York – the scale of informal work is certainly smaller (Gordon and Sassen, 1992).

professionalization

Summary of section 3.5

o Migration has long been a characteristic of world cities. Migration is both national and international in origin, and it takes two main forms: highly skilled and highly paid managers and professionals to staff the companies, banks and business services; and low-skilled, low-paid migrants, increasingly from the third world.

o The flows of migrants are changing the ethnic composition of world cities very rapidly. Labour migration to world cities is a key part of increasing global integration and interdependence. The migrants often occupy very different economic positions in the urban social structure. In many respects they live a different set of global relations.

3.6   Conclusion

One of the assumptions of this chapter is that there are places at which many of the lines of communication, control and command which go around the globe overlap and intersect. These points of intersection are referred to as global or world cities precisely because it is from such *local* points that *global* processes are said to take their starting-point. In fact, the developments in transport and telecommunications technologies which have effectively shrunk space, as it were, have laid the basis for such possible sites and are now inseparable from their representation as global cities.

Such cities, it should be noted, are characterized not simply by a wide range of social functions, nor by population size alone. It is the concentration of certain kinds of economic and social flows, rather than the concentration of a range of political, economic or cultural functions which are said to be a prerequisite of global cities. To be precise, it is the fact that such cities co-ordinate and control the global flows of information, money and investment – whether directly through corporate hierarchies or indirectly through a generalized control capability – which distinguish them from other cities, past and present.

In the past, cities of varying size have been at the apex of worldwide flows of communication, transport and the like, but it is the magnitude, speed and nature of the networks of social interaction which meet in New York, Tokyo, London and Paris, and to an extent Frankfurt, which set such cities aside. Conversely, cities with a density of activities today, such as Mexico City, São Paulo or Jakarta would not fall under the global city hallmark because they fall outside the most significant economic and cultural flows.

In referring to *global* cities, in this context, however, we need to reflect upon how much of the globe's ties and interconnections they actually do co-ordinate. From one point of view, as centres of interpretation they may well be sites of specialist knowledge, information and power, but how far the whirl of the financial markets or the complexity of global economic shifts is actually 'controlled' in global cities is decidedly unclear. The power to make sense of what is happening globally is not the same as the power to make it happen or prevent something from happening locally.

Even if a weaker sense of co-ordination were more accurate, however, there is still a *particular* geography to the networks of social interaction. As noted in the chapter introduction, such networks are centred in the main global regions and they reach out in an uneven and unequal manner across the world. Strikingly, however, some of the places missed out are locations from which the poorer peoples of the world have moved towards the global sites, precisely because they hold out the promise of a better way of life. In a shrinking world, global relations do not simply flow one-way, from the first world out; they go in both directions, even though they may well meet in the same global city.

References

AMIN, A. and THRIFT, N. (1992) 'Neo-Marshallian nodes in global networks', *International Journal of Urban and Regional Research*, Vol. 16, No. 4, pp. 571–87.

ASCHERSON, N. (1986) 'London's new class: the great cash in', *Observer*, September.

BOOTH, C. (1901) *The Life and Labour of the People of London* (1902 edn. pub. 1970, New York, Kelley).

COHEN, R. (1981) 'The new international division of labour: multinational corporations and urban hierarchy' in Dear, M. and Scott, A. J. (eds) *Urbanization and Urban Planning in Capitalist Society*, London, Methuen.

CROSS, M. and WALDINGER, R. (1992) 'Migrants, minorities, and the ethnic division of labour' in Fainstein, S., Gordon, I. and Harloe, M. (eds).

DAVIS, M. (1990) *City of Quartz: Excavating the Future in Los Angeles*, London, Verso (Vintage edn, 1992).

FAINSTEIN, S., GORDON, I. and HARLOE, M. (eds) (1992) *Divided Cities: New York and London in the Contemporary World*, Oxford, Blackwell.

FEAGIN, J. and SMITH, M. P. (1987) 'Cities and the New International Division of Labour: an overview' in Smith, M. P. and Feagin, J. (eds) *The Capitalist City: Global Restructuring and Community Politics*, Oxford, Blackwell.

FIELDING, A. (1992) 'Migration and social mobility: the South East as an escalator region', *Regional Studies*, Vol. 26, No. 1, pp. 1–15.

FRIEDMANN, J. (1986) 'The world city hypothesis', *Development and Change*, Vol. 17, No. 1, pp. 69–84.

FRIEDMANN, J. and WOLFF, G. (1982) 'World city formation: an agenda for research and action', *International Journal of Urban and Regional Research*, Vol. 6, pp. 309–43.

GORDON, I. and SASSEN, S. (1992) 'Restructuring the urban labor markets' in Fainstein, S., Gordon, I. and Harloe, M. (eds).

HALL, P. (1966) *The World Cities*, London, Weidenfeld and Nicolson.

HAMNETT, C. (1994) 'Social polarisation in global cities: theory and evidence' *Urban Studies*, Vol. 31, No. 3, pp. 401–24.

HARVEY, D. (1985) *Consciousness and the Urban Experience*, Oxford, Blackwell.

MOSS, M. (1987) 'Telecommunications, world cities and urban policy', *Urban Studies*, Vol. 24, No. 4, pp. 534–46.

PUGLIESE, E. (1993) 'Restructuring of the labour market and the role of third world migrations in Europe', *Environment and Planning D: Society and Space*, Vol. 11, No. 5, pp. 513–22.

RABAN, J. (1990) *Hunting Mr Heartbreak*, London, Collins Harvill (new edn, Picador, 1994).

SASSEN, S. (1991) *The Global City: New York, London, Tokyo*, Princeton, NJ, Princeton University Press.

SIMON, D. (1993) 'The world city hypothesis: reflecions from the periphery', Centre for Developing Areas Research Paper No. 7, Royal Holloway, University of London.

STEDMAN JONES, G. (1971) *Outcast London: A Study in the Relationship between Classes in Victorian Society*, London, Oxford University Press.

THRIFT, N. (1993) 'An urban impasse?' (Review article), *Theory, Culture and Society*, Vol. 10, No. 4, pp. 229–38.

UNEP/WHO (1992) *Urban Air Pollution in Megacities of the World*, Oxford, Blackwell.

WARF, B. (1989) 'Telecommunications and the globalization of financial services, *Professional Geographer*, Vol. 41, No. 3, pp. 257–71.

WEBBER, M. M. (1968) 'The post-city age', *Daedalus*, Vol. 97, No. 4, pp. 1091–110.

WOLFE, T. (1987) *The Bonfire of the Vanities*, New York, Farrar, Strauss and Giroux.

For centuries, the world economy has shaped the life of cities [...] Beginning in the 1960s, the organization of economic activity entered a period of pronounced transformation. The changes were expressed in the altered structure of the world economy, and also assumed forms specific to particular places. Certain of these changes are by now familiar: the dismantling of once-powerful industrial centres in the United States, the United Kingdom, and more recently in Japan; the accelerated industrialization of several third world countries; the rapid internationalization of the financial industry into a worldwide network of transactions. Each of these changes altered the relation of cities to the international economy.

In the decades after World War II, there was an international regime based on United States dominance in the world economy and the rules for global trade contained in the 1945 Bretton Woods agreement. By the early 1970s, the conditions supporting that regime were disintegrating. The breakdown created a void into which stepped, perhaps in a last burst of national dominance, the large US transnational industrial firms and banks. In this period of transition, the management of the international economic order was to an inordinate extent run from the headquarters of these firms. By the early 1980s, however, the large US transnational banks faced the massive third world debt crisis, and US industrial firms experienced sharp market share losses from foreign competition. Yet the international economy did not simply break into fragments. The geography and composition of the global economy changed so as to produce a complex duality: a spatially dispersed, yet globally integrated organization of economic activity.

The point of departure for the present study is that the combination of spatial dispersal and global integration has created a new strategic role for major cities. Beyond their long history as centres for international trade and banking, these cities now function in four new ways: first, as highly concentrated command points in the organization of the world economy; second, as key locations for finance and for specialized service firms, which have replaced manufacturing as the leading economic sectors; third, as sites of production, including the production of innovations, in these leading industries; and fourth, as markets for the products and innovations produced. These changes in the functioning of cities have had a massive impact upon both international economic activity and urban form: cities concentrate control over vast resources, while finance and specialized service industries have restructured the urban social and economic order. Thus a new type of city has appeared. It is the global city. Leading examples now are New York, London, and Tokyo [...]

As I shall show, these three cities have undergone massive and *parallel* changes in their economic base, spatial organization and social structure. But this parallel development is a puzzle. How could cities with as diverse a history, culture, politics, and economy as New York, London, and Tokyo experience similar transformations concentrated in so brief a period of time? [...] To understand the puzzle of parallel change in diverse cities requires not simply a point-by-point comparison of New York, London, and Tokyo, but a situating of these cities in a set of global processes. In order to understand why major cities with different histories and cultures have undergone parallel economic and social changes, we need to examine transformations in the world economy. Yet the term *global city* may be reductive and misleading if it suggests that cities are mere outcomes of a global economic machine. They are specific places whose spaces, internal dynamics, and social structure matter; indeed, we may be able to understand the global order only by analysing why key structures of the world economy are *necessarily* situated in cities.

How does the position of these cities in the world economy today differ from that which they have historically held as centres of banking and trade? When

Max Weber analysed the medieval cities woven together in the Hanseatic League, he conceived their trade as the exchange of surplus production; it was his view that a medieval city could withdraw from external trade and continue to support itself, albeit on a reduced scale. The modern molecule of global cities is nothing like the trade among self-sufficient places in the Hanseatic League, as Weber understood it. The first thesis advanced [...] is that the territorial dispersal of current economic activity creates a need for expanded central control and management. In other words, while in principle the territorial decentralization of economic activity in recent years could have been accompanied by a corresponding decentralization in ownership and hence in the appropriation of profits, there has been little movement in that direction. Though large firms have increased their subcontracting to smaller firms, and many national firms in the newly industrializing countries have grown rapidly, this form of growth is ultimately part of a chain. Even industrial homeworkers in remote rural areas are now part of that chain. The transnational corporations continue to control much of the end product and to reap the profits associated with selling in the world market. The internationalization and expansion of the financial industry has brought growth to a large number of smaller financial markets, a growth which has fed the expansion of the global industry. But top-level control and management of the industry has become concentrated in a few leading financial centres, notably New York, London, and Tokyo. These account for a disproportionate share of all financial transactions and one that has grown rapidly since the early 1980s. The fundamental dynamic posited here is that the more globalized the economy becomes, the higher the agglomeration of central functions in a relatively few sites, that is, the global cities.

The extremely high densities evident in the business districts of these cities are one spatial expression of this logic. The widely accepted notion that density and agglomeration will become obsolete because global telecommunications advances allow for maximum population and resource dispersal is poorly conceived. It is, I argue, precisely because of the territorial dispersal facilitated by telecommunication that agglomeration of certain centralizing activities has sharply increased. This is not a mere continuation of old patterns of agglomeration; there is a new logic for concentration. In Weberian terms, there is a new system of 'co-ordination', one which focuses on the development of specific geographic control sites in the international economic order.

A second major theme [...] concerns the impact of this type of economic growth on the economic order within these cities. It is necessary to go beyond the Weberian notion of coordination and Bell's (1973) notion of the post-industrial society to understand this new urban order. Bell, like Weber, assumes that the further society evolves from nineteenth-century industrial capitalism, the more the apex of the social order is involved in pure managerial process, with the content of what is to be managed becoming of secondary importance. Global cities, however, are not only nodal points for the co-ordination of processes (Friedmann, 1986); they are also particular sites of production. They are sites for (a) the production of specialized services needed by complex organizations for running a spatially dispersed network of factories, offices, and service outlets; and (b) the production of financial innovations and the making of markets, both central to the internationalization and expansion of the financial industry. To understand the structure of a global city, we have to understand it as a place where certain kinds of work can get done, which is to say that we have to get beyond the dichotomy between manufacturing and services. The 'things' a global city makes are services and financial goods.

It is true that high-level business services, from accounting to economic consulting, are not usually analysed as a production process. Such services are usually seen as a type of output derived from high-level technical knowledge. I [...] challenge this view. Moreover, using new scholarship on producer services, I [...] examine the extent to which a key trait of global cities is that they are the most *advanced* production sites for creating these services.

A second way this analysis goes beyond the existing literature on cities concerns the financial industry [in that it looks at] how the character of a global city is shaped by the emerging organization of the financial industry. The accelerated production of innovations and the new importance of a large number of relatively small financial institutions led to a renewed or expanded role for the market-place in the financial industry in the decade of the 1980s. The market-place has assumed new strategic and routine economic functions, in comparison to the prior phase, when the large transnational banks dominated the national and international financial market. Insofar as financial 'products' can be used internationally, the market has reappeared in a new form in the global economy. New York, London, and Tokyo play roles as production sites for financial innovations and centralized market-places for these 'products'.

A key dynamic running through these various activities and organizing my analysis of the place of global cities in the world economy is their capability for producing global control. By focusing on the production of services and financial innovations, I am seeking to displace the focus of attention from the familiar issues of the power of large corporations over governments and economies, or supracorporate concentration of power through interlocking directorates or organizations, such as the IMF. I want to focus on an aspect that has received less attention, which could be referred to as the *practice* of global control: the work of producing and reproducing the organization and management of a global production system and a global market-place for finance. My focus is not on power, but on production: the production of those inputs that constitute the capability for global control and the infrastructure of jobs involved in this production.

The power of large corporations is insufficient to explain the capability for global control. Obviously, governments also face an increasingly complex environment in which highly sophisticated machineries of centralized management and control are necessary. Moreover, the high level of specialization and the growing demand for these specialized inputs have created the conditions for a freestanding industry. Now small firms can buy components of global capability, such as management consulting or international legal advice. And so can firms and governments anywhere in the world. While the large corporation is undoubtedly a key agent inducing the development of this capability and is a prime beneficiary, it is not the sole user.

Equally misleading would be an exclusive focus on transnational banks. Up to the end of the 1982 third world debt crisis, the large transnational banks dominated the financial markets in terms of both volume and the nature of firm transactions. After 1982, this dominance was increasingly challenged by other financial institutions and the innovations they produced. This led to a transformation in the leading components of the financial industry, a proliferation of financial institutions, and the rapid internationalization of financial markets rather than just a few banks. The incorporation of a multiplicity of markets all over the world into a global system fed the growth of the industry after the 1982 debt crisis, while also creating new forms of concentration in a few leading financial centres. Hence, in the case of the financial industry, a focus on the large transnational banks would exclude precisely those sectors of the industry where much of the new growth and production of innovations has occurred; it would leave out an examination of the wide range of activities, firms, and markets that constitute the financial industry in the 1980s.

Thus, there are a number of reasons to focus a study on market-places and production sites rather than on the large corporations and banks. Most scholarship on the internationalization of the economy has already focused on the large corporations and transnational banks. To continue to focus on the corporations and banks would mean to limit attention to their formal power, rather than examining the wide array of economic activities, many outside the corporation, needed to produce and reproduce that power. And, in the case of finance, a focus on the large transnational banks would leave out precisely that institutional sector of the industry where the key components of the new growth have been invented and put into circulation. Finally, exclusive focus on corporations and banks leaves out a number of issues about the social, economic, and spatial impact of these activities on the cities that contain them. [...]

A third major theme [...] concerns the consequences of these developments for the national urban system in each of these countries and for the relationship of the global city to its nation-state. While a few major cities are the sites of production for the new global control capability, a large number of other major cities have lost their role as leading export centres for industrial manufacturing, as a result of the decentralization of this form of production. Cities such as Detroit, Liverpool, Manchester, and now increasingly Nagoya and Osaka have been affected by the decentralization of their key industries at the domestic and international levels. According to the first hypothesis presented above, this same process has contributed to the growth of service industries that produce the specialized inputs to run global production processes and global markets for inputs and outputs. These industries – international legal and accounting services, management consulting, financial services – are heavily concentrated in cities such as New York, London, and Tokyo. We need to know how this growth alters the relations between the global cities and what were once the leading industrial centres in their nations. Does globalization bring about a triangulation so that New York, for example, now plays a role in the fortunes of Detroit that it did not play when that city was home to one of the leading industries,

auto manufacturing? Or, in the case of Japan, we need to ask, for example, if there is a connection between the increasing shift of production out of Toyota City (Nagoya) to offshore locations (Thailand, South Korea, and the United States) and the development for the first time of a new headquarters for Toyota in Tokyo.

Similarly, there is a question about the relation between such major cities as Chicago, Osaka, and Manchester, once leading industrial centres in the world, and global markets generally. Both Chicago and Osaka were and continue to be important financial centers on the basis of their manufacturing industries. We would want to know if they have lost ground, relatively, in these functions as a result of their decline in the global industrial market, or instead have undergone parallel transformation toward strengthening of service functions. Chicago, for example, was at the heart of a massive agro-industrial complex, a vast regional economy. How has the decline of that regional economic system affected Chicago?

In all these questions, it is a matter of understanding what growth embedded in the international system of producer services and finance has entailed for different levels in the national urban hierarchy. The broader trends – decentralization of plants, offices, and service outlets, along with the expansion of central functions as a consequence of the need to manage such decentralized organization of firms – may well have created conditions contributing to the growth of regional subcentres, minor versions of what New York, London, and Tokyo do on a global and national scale. The extent to which the developments posited for New York, London, and Tokyo are also replicated, perhaps in less accentuated form, in smaller cities, at lower levels of the urban hierarchy, is an open, but important, question.

[...]

The fourth and final theme [...] concerns the impact of these new forms and conditions of growth on the social order of the global city. There is a vast body of literature on the impact of a dynamic, high-growth manufacturing sector in the highly developed countries, which shows that it raised wages, reduced inequality, and contributed to the formation of a middle class. Much less is known about the sociology of a service economy. Daniel Bell's (1973) *The Coming of Post-Industrial Society* posits that such an economy will result in growth in the number of highly educated workers and a more rational relation of workers to issues of social equity. One could argue that any city representing a post-industrial economy would surely be like the leading sectors of New York, London, and increasingly Tokyo.

I [...] examine to what extent the new structure of economic activity has brought about changes in the organization of work, reflected in a shift in the job supply and polarization in the income distribution and occupational distribution of workers. Major growth industries show a greater incidence of jobs at the high- and low-paying ends of the scale than do the older industries now in decline. Almost half the jobs in the producer services are lower-income jobs, and half are in the two highest earnings classes. In contrast, a large share of manufacturing workers were in the middle-earnings jobs during the post-war period of high growth in these industries in the United States and United Kingdom.

Two other developments in global cities have also contributed to economic polarization. One is the vast supply of low-wage jobs required by high-income gentrification in both its residential and commercial settings. The increase in the numbers of expensive restaurants, luxury housing, luxury hotels, gourmet shops, boutiques, French hand laundries, and special cleaners that ornament the new urban landscape illustrates this trend. Furthermore, there is a continuing need for low-wage industrial services, even in such sectors as finance and specialized services. A second development that has reached significant proportions is what I call the downgrading of the manufacturing sector, a process in which the share of unionized shops declines and wages deteriorate while sweatshops and industrial homework proliferate. This process includes the downgrading of jobs within existing industries and the job supply patterns of some of the new industries, notably electronics assembly. It is worth noting that the growth of a downgraded manufacturing sector has been strongest in cities such as New York and London.

The expansion of low-wage jobs as a function of *growth* trends implies a reorganization of the capital–labour relation. To see this, it is important to distinguish the characteristics of jobs from their sectoral location, since highly dynamic, technologically advanced growth sectors may well contain low-wage dead-end jobs. Furthermore, the distinction between sectoral characteristics and sectoral growth patterns is crucial: backward sectors, such as downgraded manufacturing or low-wage service occupations, can be part of major growth trends in a highly developed economy. It is often assumed that backward sectors express decline trends. Similarly, there is a tendency to assume that advanced sectors, such as finance, have mostly good, white-collar jobs. In fact, they contain a good number of low-paying jobs from cleaner to stock clerk.

[... Here] I must sketch the reasons why producer services and finance have grown so rapidly since the 1970s and why they are so highly concentrated in cities such as New York, London, and Tokyo. The familiar explanation is that the decade of the 1980s was but a part of a larger economic trend, the shift to services. And the simple explanation of their high concentration in major cities is that this is because of the need for face-to-face communication in the services community. While correct, these clichés are incomplete.

We need to understand first how modern technology has not ended nineteenth-century forms of work; rather, technology has shifted a number of activities that were once part of manufacturing into the domain of services. The transfer of skills from workers to machines once epitomized by the assembly line has a present-day version in the transfer of a variety of activities from the shop floor into computers, with their attendant technical and professional personnel. Also, functional specialization within early factories finds a contemporary counterpart in today's pronounced fragmentation of the work process spatially and organizationally. This has been called the 'global assembly line', the production and assembly of goods from factories and depots throughout the world, wherever labour costs and economies of scale make an international division of labour cost-effective. It is, however, this very 'global assembly line' that creates the need for increased centralization and complexity of management, control, and planning. The development of the modern corporation and its massive participation in world markets and foreign countries has made planning, internal administration, product development, and research increasingly important and complex. Diversification of product lines, mergers, and transnationalization of economic activities all require highly specialized skills in top-level management (Chandler, 1977). These have also 'increased the dependence of the corporation on producer services, which in turn has fostered growth and development of higher levels of expertise among producer service firms' (Stanback and Noyelle, 1982, p. 15). What were once support resources for major corporations have become crucial inputs in corporate decision-making. A firm with a multiplicity of geographically dispersed manufacturing plants contributes to the development of new types of planning in production and distribution surrounding the firm.

The growth of international banks and the more recent diversification of the financial industry have also expanded the demand for highly specialized service inputs. In the 1960s and 1970s, there was considerable geographic dispersal in the banking industry, with many regional centres and offshore locations mostly involved in fairly traditional banking. The diversification and internationalization of finance over the last decade resulted in a strong trend toward concentrating the 'management' of the global industry and the production of financial innovations

in a more limited number of major locations. This dynamic is not unlike that of multi-site manufacturing or service firms.

Major trends toward the development of multi-site manufacturing, service, and banking have created an expanded demand for a wide range of specialized service activities to manage and control global networks of factories, service outlets, and branch offices. While to some extent these activities can be carried out in-house, a large share of them cannot. High levels of specialization, the possibility of externalizing the production of some of these services, and the growing demand by large and small firms and by governments are all conditions that have both resulted from and made possible the development of a market for freestanding service firms that produce components for what I refer to as global control capability.

The growth of advanced services for firms, here referred to as producer services, along with their particular characteristics of production, helps to explain the centralization of management and servicing functions that has fuelled the economic boom of the early and mid-1980s in New York, London, and Tokyo. The face-to-face explanation needs to be refined in several ways. Advanced services are mostly producer services; unlike other types of services, they are not dependent on proximity to the consumers served. Rather, such specialized firms benefit from and need to locate close to other firms who produce key inputs or whose proximity makes possible joint production of certain service offerings. The accounting firm can service its clients at a distance but the nature of its service depends on proximity to other specialists, from lawyers to programmers. Major corporate transactions today typically require simultaneous participation of several specialized firms providing legal, accounting, financial, public relations, management consulting, and other such services. Moreover, concentration arises out of the needs and expectations of the high-income workers employed in these firms. They are attracted to the amenities and lifestyles that large urban centres can offer and are likely to live in central areas rather than in suburbs.

References

BELL, D. (1973) *The Coming of Post-Industrial Society: A Venture in Social Forecasting*, New York, Basic Books.

CHANDLER, A. (1977) *The Visible Hand: The Manager in American Business*, Cambridge, MA, Harvard University Press.

FRIEDMANN, J. (1986) 'The world city hypothesis', *Development and Change*, Vol. 17, pp. 69–84.

STANBACK, T. M., Jr, and NOYELLE, T. J. (1982) *Cities in Transition: Changing Job Structures in Atlanta, Denver, Buffalo, Phoenix, Columbus (Ohio), Nashville, Charlotte*, Totowa, NJ, Allanheld, Osmun.

Source: Sassen, 1991, pp. 3–12

Reading B: Malcolm Cross and Roger Waldinger, 'Migrants, minorities and world cities'

Immigration has been a constant in London as in New York. But in the past several decades the flows of people converging on these world cities have changed in dramatic and important ways. Both cities have gained a substantial non-European-origin population base: New York, first through the internal migration of African-Americans and Puerto Ricans, and, subsequently, through foreign immigration from the third world; London, through the influx of workers recruited from England's former colonies.

That both cities should be transformed by long-distance migration is testimony to their changing relationship to the world economy. As the cities' economies have become increasingly international in focus, movements of population have paralleled the movement of capital and goods [...]

New York

The demographic transformation of New York can be divided into two phases. The first, which began with the end of the Second World War and lasted to the end of the 1960s, involved the exodus of the city's white population and the massive immigration of displaced black agricultural workers from the south and of Puerto Ricans uprooted by that island's modernization. The second phase, beginning in the 1970s, marked by initial population decline, led to a shift in migration flows in and out of the city. While white New Yorkers accelerated their departure to greener pastures in the suburbs and beyond, native black and

Puerto Rican migration to New York withered. Instead of moving to New York, native blacks and Puerto Ricans joined the outward flow.

While New York no longer retained its native population, it once again became a Mecca for the new immigrants arriving after the liberalization of US immigration laws in 1965. The arrival of the new immigrants is the driving force of demographic and ethnic change in New York – today and for the foreseeable future. We first briefly describe the characteristics of the new immigration to the United States, then focus on those immigrants moving to New York.

The new immigration began with the passage of the Hart–Cellar Act in 1965, which abolished the old country-of-origins quotas, affirmed family connections as the principal basis for admission to permanent residence in the United States, and increased the total numbers of immigrants to be admitted to the country (Reimers, 1985). Despite a number of changes, this system has essentially remained in place to this day. The major, entirely unanticipated consequence of the Hart–Cellar Act was a dramatic increase in immigration from Asia, which has become the largest regional source of legal immigrants. While arrivals from Europe have fallen off sharply over the past 20 years, immigration from the Caribbean and Latin America has also been on the upswing. The size of the legal immigration flow has also increased.

Between 1966 and 1970 an average of about 374,000 newcomers entered the country each year; between 1982 and 1986, by contrast, annual inflows averaged approximately 574,000.

In addition to the legal immigrant flow have come substantial numbers of undocumented immigrants – people who either cross the borders illegally, or enter the US legally but extend their residence beyond their legally permitted stay. Just how many undocumented immigrants have been living in the United States has been a matter of controversy for over two decades. However, there is now a consensus among experts that the number of illegal immigrants lies within the three to four million range.

As in the past, the new immigrants have overwhelmingly settled in cities and no city has captured as large a share of the new immigrant population as New York. Between 1966 and 1979 New York absorbed over 1 million legal immigrants; the 1980 Census recorded 1.67 million foreign-born New Yorkers, of whom 928,000 had arrived after 1965. Data gaps, due to the virtual collapse of record-keeping procedures in the Immigration and Naturalization Service, afflict the record for 1980 and 1981, but the figures available for the years since 1982 indicate a steadily rising immigrant flow.

As in the country at large, an indeterminate number of undocumented or illegal immigrants can be added to the legal immigrant population base. In 1980 the Census counted 210,000 undocumented immigrants in the New York standard metropolitan statistical area (SMSA) (Passel, 1985). If the city's share of the New York SMSA's undocumented population is the same as its share of the new immigrant population overall, this would produce a total of 188,000 undocumented immigrants counted in the 1980 Census. Some undocumented immigrants were undoubtedly missed in the Census counts: but it seems implausible, given the immigrants' characteristics, and, in particular, their high level of employment, that the undercount for

the undocumented could exceed the 20 per cent undercount for black males – the group most severely missed in Census enumerations (Passel et al., 1982). Even if the undocumented were undercounted by half, the undocumented population would barely total 380,000.

New York differs from other principal immigrant-receiving areas in several important respects, as data for metropolitan areas from the 1980 Census shows. First, leading immigrant-receiving areas vary in the diversity of their new immigrant populations. Of the five main receiving areas, three are dominated by a single origin group: Mexicans in Los Angeles and Chicago and Cubans in Miami comprise, 47, 32, and 59 per cent respectively of 1965–80 immigrants in those areas. By contrast, San Francisco is diverse, with the largest group, Filipinos, making up 19 per cent of the new immigrant population. New York's new immigrants are even more heterogeneous, with no group accounting for more than 10 per cent of the newcomers.

Second, those groups that dominate the other major immigrant entrepôts have a greatly reduced profile in New York. There were barely 7,000 Mexican residents living in New York City as of 1980; Filipinos and Cubans were more numerous but still comprised only 2 per cent and 2.5 per cent respectively of the 1965–80 newcomers residing in New York. In New York the most important source countries have been the Dominican Republic, followed by Colombia and Ecuador, with substantial numbers from the rest of the Caribbean. Less than 2 per cent of the Asian immigrants resident in New York as of 1980 were from Vietnam; almost a third were from China; Indians, Koreans, and Filipinos accounted for 10 per cent each.

Immigration patterns since 1980 have been remarkably stable. Newcomers from the Caribbean are the largest single component, accounting for about 40 per cent of the annual inflow, with Dominicans consistently the largest single national grouping. Close to 25 per cent of the post-1980 immigrants have come from Asia, with China providing the most numerous, but by no means dominant, contingent of Asian newcomers.

The consequence of immigration has been to both accelerate and transform the post-war pattern of demographic change. Although small samples make intercensual population estimates subject to error, consistent findings from different surveys using differing sample bases provide strong grounds for the following generalizations.

o First, New York's population decline decisively turned around during the 1980s. In 1987 the city had 245,000 more people than it did in 1980. Furthermore, almost all of the population gained by the New York region was concentrated in New York City, representing a dramatic reversal of a more than 50-year-old trend.

o Second, despite net population gains, the white, non-Hispanic share of the city's population continued to decline. Although it seems likely that the economic boom of the 1980s may have reduced the imbalance between out- and in-migration flows, this change was too modest to offset the impact of low birth rates and high mortality rates. Hence, the white share of the population appears to have fallen just below the 50 per cent mark.

o Third, the immigrant presence has continued to be strongly felt, more so than at any time since the 1920s. Not only has the foreign-born proportion of adult New Yorkers increased since 1980, but the immigrant population has shifted decisively to newcomers who arrived after the liberalization of the immigration laws. Today's most common source area, the Caribbean, is itself extraordinarily variegated, culturally, linguistically, and ethnically. And the three most important Caribbean source countries, the Dominican Republic, Jamaica, and Haiti, each represent distinct cultural systems.

Consequently the 'minority' population, now the numerical majority, is far more diverse than before. High rates of immigration have made Hispanics, rather than blacks, the larger of New York's minority groups, while also diminishing the relative weight of Puerto Ricans among this expanding Hispanic population. And large foreign inflows from Asia have produced high rates of growth for this group as well, albeit on a relatively small population base.

[...]

Thus, New York is now a 'majority minority' city, but one that is most unlike the other large, older cities of the United States. The impact of immigration is what makes the import of New York's transition to 'majority minority' status different. In contrast to Chicago or Detroit, New York's minority population is extraordinarily heterogeneous. That diversity makes it unlikely that the dichotomy inherent in the 'minority/majority' distinction will capture much of the variation in economic position, political orientation, and social integration that actually characterized 'minority' New Yorkers.

London

Just as in New York, migrants from abroad have also converged on Greater London. Though the size of the London-bound migration stream has been considerable, the numbers have never approached the levels reached in New York. Consequently London's ethnic demography has changed more gradually than New York's and persons who could claim recent migrant origin account for a smaller proportion of its population.

Post-war migration to Great Britain is often considered a seamless process, but in fact it falls into two distinct phases. The first resembles the internal migration from the rural south of the United States to its manufacturing heartlands. This phase involved movement from the colonial 'south' in the Caribbean to the 'mother country' of Britain in response to demands for unskilled labour power that arose in the years after 1945. Approximately 1.1 million people from the West Indian territories made this journey to British cities in search of work. This process was all but complete by [the time of] the Commonwealth Immigration Act in 1962.

A second phase, much more characteristic of migrant labour flows into the rest of northern Europe, started in the late 1950s and ran on until 1973. Whereas migrants to Germany or France mainly came from the European periphery (e.g. Turkey or Yugoslavia), these migrant workers to Britain came from the Indian subcontinent to work in the manufacturing industries of the South East, Midlands, and North of England. In 1974 this population was supplemented by a sizeable influx of Ugandan Asians who were fleeing the repression of Idi Amin.

The total size of the populations which result from these processes of migration is notoriously difficult to estimate. The British Census did not include an 'ethnic' question until 1991, leaving researchers no recourse but to make estimates based on increasingly erroneous projections from birthplace data. Insofar as a consensus exists among analysts, most estimates suggest a population of visible minorities numbering approximately 3.5 million, most of whom come from Commonwealth (or former Commonwealth) countries (Smith, 1989). National surveys provide results that fan within reasonably close range of this estimate, but also point to the distinctive age structure of the minority population. Thus, it is estimated that 7.5 per cent of the total population of Great Britain under 16 could be classified as 'ethnic minority', 4.6 per cent of those of working age, and only 0.8 per cent of those of retirement age (Department of Employment, 1988). These figures imply a steady increase in the proportion of the total population that is ethnic minority, even without future immigration.

Whatever the national origins of the migrants, economic considerations provided the main motivation for the move to Great Britain in the first place. As a result, these populations mainly live in the main industrial centres. Angus Stuart (1989) calculates, using the Longitudinal Sample from the 1971 and 1981 Censuses, that 60 per cent of Asians and nearly three-quarters of Afro-Caribbeans are found in the four main conurbations. This concentration makes the geographic distribution of the minority population very different from

that of whites. Of the 'white' population who are of working age and economically active, 11.5 per cent live in Greater London and 9.2 per cent in the traditional industrial heartland of the West Midlands. By contrast 46 per cent of ethnic minorities live in Greater London and 15 per cent in the West Midlands. Workers of recent migrant origin are approximately six times as likely as others to live in these two industrial centres (Department of Employment, 1988).

We have very little reliable evidence on whether this pattern has changed much in recent years but differential processes of out-migration and a differential age-structure, with its consequent effects on fertility, would suggest further concentration. Data from the Census, however, suggests that in 1981 the pattern of internal migration for Afro-Caribbeans was rather different from the two main Asian groups and the majority of the population. Afro-Caribbeans are less likely to migrate internally, whereas all Asian groups have an internal migration rate over the 1971–81 decade approximately the same as that of the majority population.

Within Greater London ethnic minorities constitute a higher proportion of the total population than in the country as a whole. According to the official estimate, ethnic minorities make up 14 per cent of Greater London's residents; this population is divided almost equally into those of Asian origin, those of African/Caribbean ancestry, and a mixed group composed of many others. At first sight the concentration of minorities in London is far less pronounced than in New York. But this disparity is partially an effect of differences in city demarcations. The ethnic minority population fans into two categories: an archetypal 'inner-city' sector and one that is located near zones of recent suburban growth. Estimates for 1996, for example, show that 14 boroughs in Greater London will by then have ethnic minority populations of approximately 20 per cent or more. Generally Afro-Caribbeans dominate in the inner-city boroughs (Hackney, Hammersmith, Haringey, Islington, Lambeth, Lewisham, Southwark, and Wandsworth) whereas

South Asians cluster in the outer boroughs (Brent, Ealing, Hounslow, and Waltham Forest). Two boroughs, the adjacent inner boroughs of Tower Hamlets and Newham, which lie to the east of the City of London, do not conform to this pattern: here South Asians (mostly Bengalis) outnumber Afro-Caribbeans by two to one. In addition, substantial numbers of Afro-Caribbeans live in the north-western borough of Brent, although in quite separate parts of the borough from the majority Asian population [...]

A corollary of this pattern is that a far higher proportion of London's Afro-Caribbean population is physically located in the 'inner city'. Two-thirds of this group reside in the 14 boroughs that make up the inner area, compared with one-third of London's Asians.

As in New York, the effects of labour market change in Greater London interact with the extent of broader population change. Twenty-two per cent of the whites living in Greater London in 1971 were living outside the area in 1981 – a rate of out-migration that was almost three times the rate of ethnic minorities. But out-migration rates varied considerably among ethnic minority groups as well, with those of Indian origin twice as likely to migrate out of Greater London as Afro-Caribbeans.

[...]

This review suggests two major generalizations about the incorporation of postwar migrants from the 'New Commonwealth' into Greater London. First, the populations are not proportionately as large as in New York, although they are certainly larger than the figures in the previous section suggest. Underestimation is partly the result of under-enumeration and partly the consequence of an inadequate statistical base that precludes the possibility of estimating the smaller minority communities (e.g. Chinese, Arabs, etc.). These other groups probably add another third to the proportion of visible minorities in the city as a whole.

Second, the two largest groups (those from the Caribbean and from South Asia) settled in different parts of the city,

although the latter grouping is itself divided into an 'inner city' (largely Bengali) population and a much larger 'outer city' segment (mainly Hindu, Sikh, and Muslim). The differential distribution of ethnic minorities is not simply true in settlement terms but also dynamically; that is, over time the differences are widening as London comes to have two main areas of ethnic minority concentration.

[...]

Conclusion

[... Thus, the ethnic make-up of London and New York is very different from what it was three or four decades ago.] Most striking is the disparity in the flows of immigrants to the two cities. In New York, as we have noted, the trend has been continuously upward for a 25-year period. Immigration on this scale has linked New York-based ethnic communities, with their established niches in the housing and labour markets, to sending areas around the world. With such networks in place, immigration becomes a self-feeding and self-sustaining process. In the absence of new and unexpected legal barriers to immigration it is difficult to imagine the circumstances that would diminish the immigrant stream. London is also a magnet for immigrants, notwithstanding many attempts to restrict entrance, especially to newcomers from the third world. Indeed, Great Britain, like most other European countries, has seen an increase in foreign immigration over the past few years. But the scale of immigration to London will remain much smaller than in New York. Consequently the ethnic issue agenda is shifting from matters associated with the arrival and settlement of foreign populations to those related to the concerns of a second generation of settlers.

References

DEPARTMENT OF EMPLOYMENT (1988) 'Ethnic origins and the labour market', *Employment Gazette*, March, pp. 164–77.

PASSEL, J. (1985) 'Estimates of undocumented aliens in the 1980 Census for SMSAs', Memorandum to Roger Herriott, US Bureau of the Census.

PASSEL, J., SIEGEL, J. and ROBINSON, J. (1982) 'Coverage of the national population by age, sex and race in the 1980 Census: preliminary estimates by demographic analysis', Current Population Reports, Series P-23, No. 115, Washington, DC, US Government Printing Office.

REIMERS, D. (1985) *Still the Golden Door*, New York, Columbia University Press.

SMITH, A. (1989) 'Gentrification and the spatial constitution of the state: the restructuring of London's Docklands', *Antipode*, Vol. 21, No. 3, pp. 232–60.

STUART, A. (1989) *The Social and Geographical Mobility of South Asians and Caribbeans in Middle Age and Later Working Life*, LS Working Paper No. 61, London, City University.

Source: Cross and Waldinger, 1992, pp. 151, 152–6, 157–61, 172

Reading C: Mike Davis, 'Fortress LA'

The carefully manicured lawns of Los Angeles' Westside sprout forests of ominous little signs warning: 'Armed Response!' Even richer neighbourhoods in the canyons and hillsides isolate themselves behind walls guarded by gun-toting private police and state-of-the-art electronic surveillance. Downtown, a publicly-subsidized 'urban renaissance' has raised the nation's largest corporate citadel, segregated from the poor neighbourhoods around it by a monumental architectural glacis. In Hollywood, celebrity architect Frank Gehry, renowned for his 'humanism', apotheosizes the siege look in a library designed to resemble a foreign-legion fort. In the Westlake district and the San Fernando Valley the Los Angeles Police barricade streets and seal off poor neighbourhoods as part of their 'war on drugs'. In Watts, developer Alexander Haagen demonstrates his strategy for recolonizing inner-city retail markets: a panoptican shopping mall surrounded by staked metal fences and a substation of the LAPD in a central surveillance tower. Finally on the horizon of the next millennium an ex-chief of police crusades an anti-crime giant eye – a geo-synchronous law enforcement satellite – while other cops discreetly tend versions of 'Garden Plot', a hoary but still viable 1960s plan for a law-and-order armageddon.

Welcome to post-liberal Los Angeles, where the defence of luxury lifestyles is translated into a proliferation of new repressions in space and movement, undergirded by the ubiquitous 'armed response'. This obsession with physical security systems, and, collaterally with the architectural policing of social boundaries, has become a zeitgeist of urban restructuring, a master narrative in the emerging built environment of the 1990s. Yet contemporary urban theory, whether debating the role of electronic technologies in precipitating 'post-modern space', or discussing the dispersion of urban functions across poly-centered metropolitan 'galaxies', has been strangely silent about the militarization of city life so grimly visible at the street level. Hollywood's pop apocalypses and pulp science fiction have been more realistic, and politically perceptive, in representing the programmed hardening of the urban surface in the wake of the social polarizations of the Reagan era. Images of carceral inner cities (*Escape from New York, Running Man*), high-tech police death squads (*Blade Runner*), sentient buildings (*Die Hard*), urban bantustans (*They Live!*), Vietnam-like street wars (*Colors*), and so on, only extrapolate from actually existing trends.

Such dystopian visions grasp the extent to which today's pharaonic scales of residential and commercial security supplant residual hopes for urban reform and social integration. The dire predictions of Richard Nixon's 1969 National Commission on the Causes and Prevention of Violence have been tragically fulfilled: we live in 'fortress cities' brutally divided between 'fortified cells' of affluent society and 'places of terror' where the police battle the criminalized poor. The 'Second Civil War' that began in the long hot summers of the 1960s has been institutionalized into the very structure of urban space.

The old liberal paradigm of social control, attempting to balance repression with reform, has long been superseded by a rhetoric of social warfare that calculates the interests of the urban poor and the middle classes as a zero-sum game. In cities like Los Angeles, on the bad edge of post-modernity, one observes an unprecedented tendency to merge urban design architecture and the police apparatus into a single, comprehensive security effort.

This epochal coalescence has far-reaching consequences for the social relations of the built environment. In the first place the market provision of 'security' generates its own paranoid demand. 'Security' becomes a positional good defined by income access to private 'protective services' and membership in some hardened residential enclave or restricted suburb. As a prestige symbol – and sometimes as the decisive borderline between the merely well-off and the 'truly rich' – security has less to do with personal safety than with the degree of personal insulation, in residential, work, consumption and travel environments, from 'unsavory' groups and individuals, even crowds in general. Secondly, as William Whyte has observed of social intercourse in New York, 'fear proves itself'. The social perception of threat becomes a function of the security mobilization itself, not crime rates. Where there is an actual rising arc of street violence, as in South-central Los Angeles or downtown Washington, DC, most of the carnage is self-contained within ethnic or class boundaries. Yet white middle-class imagination, absent from any first-hand knowledge of inner-city conditions, magnifies the perceived threat through a demonological lens. Surveys show that Milwaukee suburbanites are just as worried about violent crime as inner-city Washingtonians, despite a twenty-fold difference in relative levels of mayhem. The media, whose function in this arena is to bury and obscure the daily economic violence of the city, ceaselessly throw up spectres of criminal underclasses and psychotic stalkers. Sensationalized accounts of killer youth gangs high on crack and shrilly racist evocations of marauding Willie Hortons foment the moral panics that reinforce and justify urban apartheid.

Moreover, the neo-military syntax of contemporary architecture insinuates violence and conjures imaginary dangers. In many instances the semiotics of so-called 'defensible space' are just about as subtle as a swaggering white cop. Today's upscale, pseudo-public spaces – sumptuary malls, office centres, culture acropolises, and so on – are full of invisible signs warning off the underclass 'Other'. Although architectural critics are usually oblivious to how the built environment contributes to segregation, pariah groups – whether poor Latino families, young Black men, or elderly homeless white females – read the meaning immediately.

The destruction of public space

The universal and ineluctable consequence of this crusade to secure the city is the destruction of accessible public space. The contemporary opprobrium attached to the term 'street person' is in itself a harrowing index of the devaluation of public spaces. To reduce contact with untouchables, urban redevelopment has converted once vital pedestrian streets into traffic sewers and transformed public parks into temporary receptacles for the homeless and wretched. The American city, as many critics have recognized, is being systematically turned inside out – or, rather, outside in. The valorized spaces of the new megastructures and super-malls are concentrated in the centre, street frontage is denuded, public activity is sorted into strictly functional compartments, and circulation is internalized in corridors under the gaze of private police.

The privatization of the architectural public realm, moreover, is shadowed by parallel restructurings of electronic space, as heavily policed, pay-access 'information orders', elite data-bases and subscription cable services appropriate parts of the invisible agora. Both processes, of course, mirror the deregulation of the economy and the recession of non-market entitlements. The decline of urban liberalism has been accompanied by the death of what might be called the 'Olmstedian vision' of public space.

[...]

In Los Angeles, once-upon-a-time a demi-paradise of free beaches, luxurious parks, and 'cruising strips', genuinely democratic space is all but extinct. The Oz-like archipelago of Westside pleasure domes – a continuum of tony malls, art centres and gourmet strips – is reciprocally dependent upon the social imprisonment of the third-world service proletariat who live in increasingly repressive ghettoes and barrios. In a city of several million yearning immigrants, public amenities are radically shrinking, parks are becoming derelict and beaches more segregated, libraries and playgrounds are closing, youth congregations of ordinary kinds are banned, and the streets are becoming more desolate and dangerous.

Unsurprisingly, as in other American cities, municipal policy has taken its lead from the security offensive and the middle-class demand for increased spatial and social insulation. De facto disinvestment in traditional public space and recreation has supported the shift of fiscal resources to corporate-defined redevelopment priorities. A pliant city government – in this case ironically professing to represent a bi-racial coalition of liberal whites and Blacks – has collaborated in the massive privatization of public space and the subsidization of new, racist enclaves (benignly described as 'urban villages'). Yet most current, giddy discussions of the 'post-modern' scene in Los Angeles neglect entirely these overbearing aspects of counter-urbanization and counter-insurgency. A triumphal gloss – 'urban renaissance', 'city of the future', and so on – is laid over the brutalization of inner-city neighbourhood and the increasing South Africanization of its spatial relations. Even as the walls have come down in Eastern Europe, they are being erected all over Los Angeles.

[...]

From Rentacop to *Robocop*

The security-driven logic of urban enclavization finds its most popular expression in the frenetic efforts of Los Angeles' affluent neighbourhoods to insulate home values and lifestyles [...] New luxury developments outside the city limits have often become fortress cities, complete with encompassing walls, restricted entry points with guard posts, overlapping private and public police services, and even privatized roadways. It is simply impossible for ordinary citizens to invade the 'cities' of Hidden Hills, Bradbury, Rancho Mirage or Rolling Hills without an invitation from a resident. Indeed Bradbury, with nine hundred residents and ten miles of gated private roads, is so security-obsessed that its three city officials do not return telephone calls from the press, since 'each time an article appeared ... it drew attention to the city and the number of burglaries increased'. For its part, Hidden Hills, a Norman Rockwell painting behind high-security walls, has been bitterly divided over compliance with a Superior Court order to build forty-eight units of seniors' housing outside its gates. At meetings of the city's all-powerful homeowners' association (whose membership includes Frankie Avalon, Neil Diamond and Bob Eubanks) opponents of compliance have argued that the old folks' apartments 'will attract gangs and dope' (*sic*) (*Daily News*, 1 November 1987).

Meanwhile traditional luxury enclaves like Beverly Hills and San Marino are increasingly restricting access to their public facilities using baroque layers of regulations to build invisible walls. San Marino, which may be the richest, and is reputedly the most Republican (85 per cent), city in the country, now closes its parks on weekends to exclude Latino and Asian families from adjacent communities. One plan under discussion would reopen the parks on Saturdays only to those with proof of residence. Other upscale neighbourhoods in Los Angeles have minted a similar residential privilege by obtaining ordinances to restrict parking to local homeowners. Predictably, such preferential parking regulations proliferate exclusively in neighbourhoods with three-car garages.

Residential areas with enough clout are thus able to privatize local public space, partitioning themselves from the rest of the metropolis, even imposing a variant of neighbourhood passport control on outsiders. The next step, of course, is to ape incorporated enclaves like Rolling

Hills or Hidden Hills by building literal walls. Since its construction in the late 1940s Park La Brea has been a bit of Lower Manhattan *chutzpah* moored to Wilshire Boulevard: a 176-acre maze of medium-rent townhouses and tower apartments, occupied by an urbane mix of singles, retirees and families. Now, as part of a strategy of gentrification, its owners, Forest City Enterprises, have decided to enclose the entire community in security fencing, cutting off to pedestrians one of the most vital public spaces along the 'Miracle Mile'. As a spokeswoman for the owners observed, 'it's a trend in general to have enclosed communities' (*Times*, 25 July 1989). In the once wide-open tractlands of the San Fernando Valley, where there were virtually no walled-off communities a decade ago, the 'trend' has assumed the frenzied dimensions of a residential arms race as ordinary suburbanites demand the kind of social insulation once enjoyed only by the rich. Brian Weinstock, a leading Valley contractor, boasts of more than one hundred newly gated neighbourhoods, with an insatiable demand for more security. 'The first question out of their [the buyers'] mouths is whether there is a gated community. The demand is there on a 3-to-1 basis for a gated community than not living in a gated community' (*Times*, 8 October 1989).

The social control advantages of 'gatehood' have also attracted the attention of landlords in denser, lower-income areas. Apartment owners in the Sepulveda barrio of the Valley have rallied behind a police programme, launched in October 1989, to barricade their streets as a deterrent to drug buyers and other undesirables. The LAPD wants the City Council's permission to permanently seal off the neighbourhood and restrict entry to residents, while the owners finance a guard station or 'checkpoint charlie'. While the Council contemplates the permanency of the experiment, the LAPD, supported by local homeowners, has continued to barricade other urban 'war zones' including part of the Pico-Union district, a Mid-Wilshire neighbourhood, and an entire square mile around Jefferson High School in the Central–Vernon area. In face of

complaints from younger residents about the 'Berlin Wall' quality of the neighbourhood quarantines, Police Chief Gates reassured journalists that 'we're not here to occupy the territory. This isn't Panama. It's the city of Los Angeles and we're going to be here in a lawful manner' (*Times*, 15 November 1989).

Meanwhile the very rich are yearning for high-tech castles. Where gates and walls alone will not suffice, as in the case of Beverly Hills or Bel-Air homeowners, the house itself is redesigned to incorporate sophisticated, sometimes far-fetched, security functions. An overriding but discreet goal of the current 'mansionizing' mania on the Westside of Los Angeles – for instance, tearing down $3 million houses to build $30 million mansions – is the search for 'absolute security'. Residential architects are borrowing design secrets from overseas embassies and military command posts. One of the features most in demand is the 'terrorist-proof security room' concealed in the houseplan and accessed by sliding panels and secret doors. Merv Griffith and his fellow mansionizers are hardening their palaces like missile silos.

But contemporary residential security in Los Angeles – whether in the fortified mansion or the average suburban bunker – depends upon the voracious consumption of private security services. Through their local homeowners' associations, virtually every affluent neighbourhood from the Palisades to Silverlake contracts its own private policing; hence the thousands of lawns displaying the little 'armed response' warnings. The classifieds in a recent Sunday edition of the Los Angeles *Times* contained nearly a hundred ads for guards and patrolmen, mostly from firms specializing in residential protection. Within Los Angeles County, the security services industry has tripled its sales and workforce (from 24,000 to 75,000) over the last decade [...] Anyone who has tried to take a stroll at dusk through a strange neighbourhood patrolled by armed security guards and signposted with death threats quickly realizes how merely notional, if not utterly obsolete, is the old idea of the 'freedom of the city'.

Source: Davis, 1992, pp. 223–8, 244–50

Dirty connections: transnational pollution

Chapter 4

by Steven Yearley

4.1 Introduction

In the late 1980s many people in Europe began to worry in an unprecedented way about the ozone-depleting chemicals (chlorofluorocarbons or CFCs) which were to be found in the majority of aerosols. Through the awareness-raising activities of groups such as Friends of the Earth (see Figure 4.1) and through the response of the media, the public came to accept that whenever they sprayed deodorants or many polishes and spray foams, polluting chemical gases escaped into the atmosphere. These gases are dangerous because they encourage the breakdown of the Earth's protective ozone layer – a stratum of the atmosphere in which naturally occurring molecules of the gas ozone (a gas which filters out harmful ultra-violet radiation) are particularly numerous.

The striking thing about this form of pollution was that the geographical connection between the release of the pollutant and the damage it caused was extremely remote. CFCs sprayed in Edinburgh were not likely to affect the ozone layer over the city, nor indeed over London or even the United Kingdom. The CFCs were carried by winds and only gradually worked their

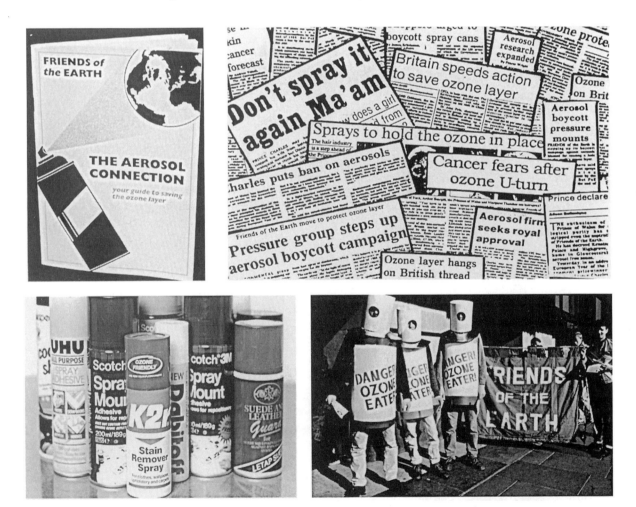

Figure 4.1

way into the upper atmosphere. The most extreme loss of ozone in fact occurs over the two poles, the more so at the Antarctic, where presumably there is less call for deodorant. So, pollution emitted in the UK or Japan or Brazil could end up causing a problem across the other side of the globe.

People had long got used to the idea that private citizens or companies could pollute their local environment, with loud noise, smelly industry or whatever. But here was a startling example which showed that modern substances and modern technology (CFCs were developed in the middle of the twentieth century) could cause pollution on a global scale. Such pollution shrinks the world, allowing us to despoil the environment of our 'neighbours', thousands of kilometres away on the planet.

This case is also striking because the danger is insidious and sinister. Before the scare, the authorities and the few people who had heard of CFCs were complacent, since CFCs themselves are harmless to human beings and animals, and because none of us ever sees the ozone layer. Yet the ultraviolet radiation which enters through the 'holes' (actually regions of *ozone depletion*, not holes in a literal sense) in that layer can promote skin cancers, one of the dread diseases in the industrialized countries. CFCs changed from being harmless, beneficial molecules into an invisible cancer-provoking menace.

ozone depletion

Spray-cans disrupting the atmosphere is not the only form of pollution that shrinks the world, however; US trash can do much the same.

Kassa Island lies just off the coast of Guinea, a former French colony in the west of Africa, a little north of the Equator. In 1988, the thirtieth anniversary of the country's independence, it was discovered that a large quantity (the Guinean authorities estimated around 15,000 tonnes) of incinerator ash from Philadelphia had been dumped on the island. According to the US Environmental Protection Agency, the ash from such incinerators includes dangerous materials such as heavy metals (the general term for various toxic metals such as cadmium) and poisonous organic compounds known as dioxins. The people of North America are increasingly aware of the potential dangers from such materials and do not wish to have them disposed of in their own locality. Hence they had been exported over five thousand kilometres to Guinea and, just to make sure that local people did not object too much, they were re-described as 'building materials' (*The Independent*, 17 June 1988, p. 8). Of course, this ash could be used in the construction business, but it is safe to assume that it would not be a popular building material. To add to the international flavour of the incident, the material was transported in a Norwegian-owned ship. Following the discovery of the true nature of the ash, the Guinean authorities arrested the Norwegian Consul. Norway subsequently undertook to remove the waste.

In this second case, too, it is clear that people are capable of polluting the other side of the globe. But in this instance it is international trade rather than the international dispersion of molecules which links the world. From these two examples we can see that, first, certain modern pollutants can contaminate the global environment while, second, the transnational nature of modern trade allows, even encourages, the waste from industrialized regions and countries to pollute every region of the world.

In this chapter we will examine the way in which pollution simultaneously *illustrates* and *is caused by* the shrinking of the world. Section 4.2 sets out the broad ways in which transnational pollution, despite its selective impact, has been represented as a global issue, one that has brought about a collective sense of the hazards that appear to face us all. Following that, in section 4.3, the various types of pollution are reviewed. At the same time we see how the different kinds of pollution can have uneven and unequal impacts, impacts that are shaped by global interconnections. This examination is taken a step further in section 4.4 through a consideration of the pollution spread around the globe by 'dirty industries': that is, industries based primarily in the developed countries of the 'North', yet with a spread of investments and trading links worldwide. Invariably, it is the less developed countries and those seeking to develop who bear the brunt of the first world's 'dirty' investments, as well as those of 'dirty' trade. Finally, in section 4.5, the shrinking world of environmental protest and governance is briefly considered.

Before that, however, we look at how the experience of pollution makes the world a small, highly interconnected place.

4.2   How pollution shrinks the world

The cases of ozone-depleting pollution and the international voyages undertaken by North American incinerator rubbish symbolize in a striking way the theme of this chapter, that the world's growing environmental problems are connecting the lives of people in very different societies. And while individuals can try to minimize the impact on their own lives, it is ultimately impossible to hide oneself away from these phenomena altogether. No humans and virtually no plants or animals are exempted from these problems. That's not to say that all forms of pollution are now global in scale. They are not. Much pollution is still local or restricted to a region. Furthermore, the impact of any given pollutant is liable to be modified by the details of the local geology and geography. But, as we shall see, pollution has increased markedly in the last quarter of a century and continues to intensify. As trade and manufacture grow more international in their organization, local pollution problems are repeated and reproduced the world over, thereby becoming a global phenomenon. Also, more and more of present-day pollution has an international impact, so that in the closing years of the twentieth century no-one is immune from all of it.

But while the experience of *suffering* from pollution is nowadays almost universal, the rest of the story displays far greater inequalities. Some of the world's people contribute far more to the causes of pollution than do others – and of course wild animals and plants which suffer from pollution create practically none (though see Box 4.1 about defining pollution). Moreover, of the people causing pollution, some derive more personal benefit from each unit of pollution caused than do others: for example, Europeans typically create more pollution than Africans because more of them can afford cars, washing-machines, goods with masses of packaging and so on. In other words, the wealthier society tends also to be the more polluting society. But, for every kilometre they drive, car-drivers in the former Soviet Union countries are likely to cause more pollution than their Western European counterparts because their cars are dirtier and less efficient. So, though wealth and pollution generation are usually connected, they are not completely bound to each other.

Finally, as we shall see (and as we saw with Kassa Island), some people cause pollution deliberately: they dump substances into the environment because it saves them money or trouble. Other polluters have little practical choice about what they do, while there are some people who have pollution dumped on them, without even gaining the benefit of the processes which caused it in the first place.

Overall, then, while pollution is a very widespread experience, its sources are far less uniformly spread, and sometimes those who cause it and benefit from it are rich and powerful enough to try to limit its impact on themselves by imposing it on others. The experience of pollution demonstrates our international interconnectedness but it also reveals that the connections are highly unequal.

Nevertheless, the experience of pollution and the growing concern with environmental issues more generally have lent support to the idea that social organization is becoming globalized. Environmental writers and campaigners have put a great deal of effort into getting people, as the saying goes, to 'think global'. This image of a global identity has been built up through the use of terms such as 'spaceship Earth', through the much-used pictures of the globe suspended in space and through a string of conferences and seminars focusing on 'global' themes, culminating in the 'Earth Summit' in Rio de Janeiro in 1992. Environmental issues sound even more significant if they are described as global environmental issues.

As we have seen with the issue of ozone depletion, some pollution problems can legitimately be presented as global by their very nature. It is in virtually everyone's interest to oppose such forms of pollution. And this is the message that some environmentalists try to convey by stressing that we are all cosmonauts on our global spaceship. A sense of global identity is supposed to promote the idea that we face environmental hazards *together*. Yet many other 'global' forms of pollution have global effects because they are dispersed through trade and the spread of industrialization, not because they are inherently global. It would be wrong, therefore, to assume that responses to pollution problems are globally harmonious. There may be some common threats, but other pollution problems result from people in one part of the globe displacing their problems onto other parts. Furthermore, certain kinds of pollution are diminishing in the prosperous North (because of tighter regulations or because of technological advances), even while they are on the increase in the developing world because of the growth of industrialization. Different parts of the globe may thus be experiencing markedly different pollution trends, at least with regard to certain types of pollution.

According to Robertson (1992), 'Globalization as a concept refers both to the compression of the world and the intensification of consciousness of the world as a whole' (p. 8). *Transnational pollution* exemplifies both these trends. First of all, pollution arises from, and contributes to, the world getting smaller, as it were. Trade compresses the world and allows waste from the United States to end up in Africa; air pollution obliges nations to worry about what their neighbours are doing about their emissions. The world is a smaller place than once it was and other people's pollution crowds in on us. Consequently, and this is Robertson's main point, pollution intensifies consciousness of our global interconnectedness. It leads us to worry about global pollutants such as ozone-depleting CFCs *and* has encouraged environmentalists to try to foster a new identity for people as citizens of planet (spaceship) Earth.

transnational pollution

Friends of the Earth

Friends of the Earth's 'globe' logo

Activity 1 Robertson claims that we are becoming more conscious of 'the world as a whole'. Printed in the margin is the globe logo used until recently by Friends of the Earth, an image of the world as a whole. Why are environmentalists attracted to using the globe as an image? What does this symbolism do for them?

Environmentalists are keen to suggest that their concerns are – or should be – everyone's concerns and that all the people of globe are in crucial respects all in the same boat. But for us to assess the global significance of pollution and its causes, we need to examine the kinds of pollution hazards which are important today and to look at the geography of their international distribution. Those issues are covered in the next section. There is also the related question about how exactly 'pollution' is defined. For the time being I shall work with an implicit notion of pollution, returning to the question of definitions in Box 4.1 at the end of the next section. Some of you may wish to look ahead to that box while reading the next section.

4.3   Forms of pollution and their global reach

To gain a sense of how significant a phenomenon international pollution is and to be able to assess whether and why it is increasing, contributing to the shrinking of the world, we need to have a way of classifying types of pollution. The most convenient method of classification focuses on the *medium in which the pollution ends up*, whether that is the air, water or land, although – as we shall see – this classification is far from 'watertight'.

media of pollution

4.3.1   Land pollution

Beginning with the last of these, we can take a brief look at each medium in turn. Land tends to be polluted either because humans have buried things in it or carried out messy operations on it. In Britain, for example, the places where chemical factories or town-gas production works have been located, especially when they have been there for decades, are typically heavily contaminated. Worse still, records of land contamination may not have been kept. This issue was in the news in the early 1990s because environmental campaigners were pressing the UK government to publish a register of contaminated sites (Friends of the Earth, 1992). The authorities resisted this demand, arguing that only very few sites were actually dangerous to human health and that public disclosure of information about the other 'contaminated' sites would cause unnecessary anxiety and result in property-owners seeing the value of their land and buildings decline dramatically. While increased regulation in recent years has meant that some forms of land contamination in the developed countries are declining, the worldwide growth of manufacturing and chemical industries dictates that overall the problem is on the increase. With the spread of industrialization, a primarily local problem – the contamination of the factory site and adjacent area – is being replicated across the globe.

Land is also polluted when waste is dumped in quarries, gravel pits, drained lakes or specially dug holes. Landfill, as this waste disposal method is known, is still the commonest disposal technique in the United Kingdom; the refuse tipped there varies from packaging from shops and builders' rubble, through mixed domestic waste (a mix of paper, metals, glass, plastics as well as organic waste) to industrial wastes, which may include highly toxic and corrosive material. Until recently, dangerous wastes were deliberately 'diluted' with ordinary refuse, a practice which was made to sound more scientific by being labelled 'co-disposal'. As world industrial production continues to rise and as trade brings manufactured and packaged goods to more and more consumers, these waste disposal practices are spreading throughout the globe. Pollution from landfill is now causing environmental problems in industrializing countries such as Taiwan, Mexico and Brazil. In the countries of the developed North, the dumping of material is now supposedly regulated, though the presence of suspect private operators in the market still gives cause for alarm. But even if regulators were to control tightly the substances entering dumps, there would still be considerable problems since rainwater seeping into these sites can wash out chemicals which can then be transported into water supplies. Natural decay of organic matter in the dumps also gives rise to methane gas which can ignite or cause explosions.

The problems of methane gas production and of water leaching indicate that pollution incidents in the three media – land, water and air – are not really distinct. These connections are acknowledged in recent UK and European legislation which promotes the idea of integrated pollution control; in other words, it aims to stop people overcoming their solid waste problems by, for example, burning their refuse, only to give rise to air pollution. Legislation achieves this by giving one agency the responsibility for granting licences for (and inspecting) all types of pollution at a given factory or dump. Previously, different agencies were responsible for land, air and water pollution, so that the overall performance of polluters was not monitored.

4.3.2 Water pollution

Turning to the second medium, water pollution also has many causes. Rivers have long been used to transport filth away from towns and sadly this process has intensified in the last century. Rivers have been contaminated in three main ways. First, human sewage has been expelled into rivers; this problem is magnified around towns and large cities because of the sheer density of human populations. In underdeveloped countries, city populations have grown at extremely high rates adding vastly to water pollution and often overwhelming sewage treatment facilities. Poor countries can afford little expenditure on such infrastructural items – a situation which has tended to worsen in the last decade for reasons which are dealt with later in this chapter. But urban folk have not been the only culprits. There has been repeated river pollution from farms, both effluent from animal husbandry (slurry from animal wastes and the highly polluting effluent from silage-making) and the accumulated contamination from chemicals spread on the fields. Fertilizers, for instance, are dissolved by rainwater and enter water-courses; there they fertilize the growth of microscopic plants (algae and the like) which use up oxygen and exclude sunlight, reducing overall water quality. These problems have increased at a global level, too, as more land has been brought into intensive cultivation, either to trade or to feed growing populations, and as the spread of agribusiness has meant that fertilizer and pesticide use in the underdeveloped world has accelerated. The 1993 GATT settlement, which is designed to promote unrestricted international trade, will encourage intensive cultivation in underdeveloped countries and will thus add to the pressures for worldwide agrochemical use.

Finally, industrial wastes have also been dumped into rivers. Industry took advantage of the nineteenth-century sewerage systems to dispose of waste from factories; consequently a good deal of industrial waste can be disposed of free or very cheaply through the sewers. Factories also experience spills, when materials inadvertently (or so it is said) overflow into watercourses. When these episodes are put down to accidents, companies are rarely punished. Environmental campaigners are convinced that spills by one company are frequently used by neighbouring firms as an opportunity to dump their wastes too.

The story with sea pollution is essentially similar though the extent of deliberate dumping of hazardous wastes has been even greater:

Many coastal towns around the UK simply discharge untreated sewage down pipes into the sea while, in other cases, the waste is treated but the resulting sludge is taken out by boats (colloquially known as 'bovril boats') and dumped offshore. Some waste is incinerated at sea before being dumped. Nuclear waste used to be sealed in metal or concrete containers and dropped into deep areas of the sea.

(Yearley, 1992, pp. 34–5)

The sea-dumping of nuclear waste has already been halted (though not renounced entirely) by western nations and, by a European Union agreement, other marine pollution will be reduced by 1998. However, this applies only to the EU. In October 1993 Russia dumped nuclear waste from scrapped nuclear submarines into the sea off Japan and indicated it might have to do so again unless rapid progress was made with new processing plant (*The Independent*, 22 October 1993, p. 6). Elsewhere in the world, growing cities and expanding industry mean that marine pollution is on the increase.

The seas are also subject to pollution when boats, especially oil-tankers, are wrecked. In the last thirty years there has been a series of huge and distressing oil spills, including the *Exxon Valdez* in Alaska in 1989 and the *Braer* wreck on Shetland in 1993.

Yet, surprisingly enough, oil spills from wrecked ships are not the major cause of oil pollution at sea. The United Nations Environment Programme … reckons that 500,000 tonnes of the 1.6 million annually discharged into the sea by shipping is released accidentally; the remainder is non-accidental in origin and results from regular discharge by ships of contaminated ballast water and water used for flushing out tanks. [Yet according to] the US National Academy of Sciences … [m]ore oil enters the oceans from automobile exhausts, and from oil-changes in city garages that are then dumped down the drain, than from any other source.

(Elsworth, 1990, p. 240)

In other words, while a series of large oil spills has dominated media coverage and popular awareness of marine pollution, most oil pollution derives from myriad small discharges. These are so extensive that the world's oceans are now thoroughly contaminated; traces of oil can be found in sea-water the world over. Since nearly all the seas are linked, they unfortunately serve as a means for spreading pollution internationally.

Here again we see that pollution has a two-fold shrinking effect. First, industrial and agricultural sources of pollution are spreading across the world as western methods of production are introduced, though ironically this is happening even as the North is cleaning up its own act. Second, the oceans and many large rivers which flow internationally act as media for the transnational distribution of pollution.

4.3.3 Air pollution

The third medium into which effluents and contamination can be discharged is the air. In the industrialized world people have been familiar with air pollution for many years and the chronically poor air quality in London in the middle years of the twentieth century has become legendary. At present, our air is polluted in a variety of ways but the chief culprits are soot and gases produced by the burning of fuels for heating or power generation, the exhausts from motor vehicles and emissions from factory chimneys and incinerators. Given that we all have to breathe the air and that it cannot be filtered before use, air pollution is probably the most pervasive environmental problem – although some entrepreneurs have tried to come up with a privatized solution, so that, for example, Japanese commuters have been offered the opportunity to buy 'gulps' of clean air on the way to the office.

Some dangerous and polluting gases are formed in very large quantities. For example, the acid gas sulphur dioxide (known by its chemical symbol SO_2) is formed from the inevitable impurities in fuels when coal or oil is burnt in power-stations or in people's homes, in fires and boilers. It is bad for people because, in the long term, it can attack the lungs and because it aggravates asthma as well as bronchial and other respiratory problems. It is also bad for the environment in general because its acidity encourages the destruction of many building stones and because it can attack trees and acidify rivers,

Spared the expense of buying their own clean air, Tokyo traffic control police refresh themselves by inhaling oxygen on their return to headquarters after duty

spoiling conditions for fish and aquatic life. Other acidic gases – various oxides of nitrogen (collectively referred to as NO_x) – are produced from power-stations and cars; they too irritate lung tissue and contribute to atmospheric acidity. Both these types of gas are formed by the millions of tonnes each year: in Britain alone the amounts of SO_2 and NO_x discharged at the end of the 1980s were approximately 3.5 and 2.5 million tonnes per year respectively (Friends of the Earth, 1990, p. 3). Being produced by motor traffic and by homes, as well as by industry, these gases are highly pervasive. Acid rain is caused when they are transported in the atmosphere and then washed down by rain, snow and so on. Since these gases are released in such large quantities and since they are discharged from tall stacks as well as by ground-level cars, they can be carried over large distances (hundreds of kilometres) by prevailing winds. In this way one country's emissions can end up polluting a neighbour's air, as has happened with British acid gases blown to Scandinavia and with US acid pollution which has ended up in Canada.

At present, policy measures are being implemented to reduce acid emissions in most countries of the developed North. For example, in the late 1980s the countries of the (then) European Community negotiated a joint agreement to cut emissions from power-stations and other large plant; in the UK this is largely being achieved by substituting gas for dirtier coal. But the production of acid pollution is still increasing on a worldwide scale as industrialization proceeds and the low-cost UK 'solution' of using cheap-to-build gas-fired power stations clearly cannot be adopted the world over; there is simply not enough natural gas for industry in China, India, Latin America and the former Soviet Union. In any case, coal is a cheaper fuel, even if clean coal-fired power stations are costly.

Other forms of air pollution are less pervasive but can be equally alarming. With SO_2 and NO_x, we at least know what the culprits are. But in other cases of air pollution it is far harder to establish the exact identities of waste gases. Thus, emissions from various factories, chemical plants and incinerators may contain 'cocktails' of gases, some of which are harmful in themselves and others which may be hazardous in combination. So far this form of air pollution has received less attention than the acid gases because acid rain is a comparatively well-understood problem suffered by large numbers of people; it has been relatively easy to mount campaigns around this theme and to interest politicians and policy-makers. To date, circumstances have tended not to promote so much public and political interest in the other types of air pollution.

Finally, there are two very important air pollution problems which are highly general. The first was described at the very start of this chapter – the pollution which is depleting the ozone layer. While CFCs in aerosols are the most well-publicized problem here, it is important to realize that CFCs are also used in refrigerators, freezers and similar heat-regulating appliances and as gases for blowing foams (such as the bubble-filled plastics used for lightweight containers and for insulating material). Other chemically related compounds can exhibit similar 'ozone-eating' characteristics, including the smothering gases in certain kinds of fire extinguishers (halons) and the solvents in common use in such products as typing-correction fluids. As pointed out earlier, these ozone-destroying chemicals demonstrate the hazards of transnational pollution terrifyingly well, since they tend to have their chemical impact thousands of kilometres away from the place where they were released (climatic factors concentrate their activity around the poles) and because they allow solar radiation to harm people, animals and plant-life across the other side of the planet. These chemicals exert their effects for decades. They are globally inescapable.

The final example to be discussed here is equally well known and just as global. It is the problem of *global warming* or the enhanced greenhouse effect. Despite the fluctuations of the seasons and even despite the occasional growth of massive ice sheets covering the northernmost and southernmost lands, the average temperature on Earth has remained very stable for the last million years (Ross, 1991, p. 85). From the hottest to the coldest periods, the overall average temperature change has been around 5° Celsius. When one considers that this is less than the temperature change common in a house or in one's garden in just a day, this long-term stability seems remarkable.

global warming

The Earth's warmth is largely due to the radiation arriving from the sun. This heats the surface of the Earth and the moon alike. But the Earth is conspicuously warmer than the moon (by about 33 degrees on average) and this difference is attributable to the greenhouse properties of the atmosphere (Ross, 1991, p. 77). In a rough way, we can say that the atmosphere acts like the panes of glass in a greenhouse, letting radiation in but slowing down its escape. With no atmosphere, the moon experiences no greenhouse warming.

Some gases in the atmosphere are better at performing this insulating role than others. For example, nitrogen – the gas which is much the commonest in the atmosphere – is a poor insulator. By contrast, methane and carbon dioxide are effective insulators. The more insulators there are, the warmer the Earth's surface and the immediate surrounding atmosphere would tend to become. The current anxiety is that since the insulating gases are present in the atmosphere in extremely low concentrations, human activities which cause more of these gases (the burning of fuels to produce carbon dioxide or decay from waste tips and leaks from gas fields leading to increases in methane) could alter the temperature balance. Relatively small quantities of greenhouse gases could raise the global temperature to unprecedented levels, taking it outside of the temperature band within which the Earth has been confined since prehistoric times. However, since it is extremely difficult to work out how quickly these greenhouse gases will build up in the atmosphere and extraordinarily hard to calculate what their detailed effect on the climate will be, there is still plenty of scope for disagreements over the global consequences of this type of pollution.

This is an unusual form of pollution since we are not worried about the toxic nature of the gases; indeed both methane and carbon dioxide are natural ingredients of the atmosphere and would not be directly harmful unless their concentrations were multiplied many times over. We are not worried about breathing them in or about immediate health effects. Rather, we are worried about a long-term consequence of the gases' release: the concern is that global warming would be extremely disruptive, possibly catastrophic. For example, climatic conditions would be likely to become more extreme with more hurricanes, storms and floods. Also, a rise in world temperatures would lead to expanding deserts, to probable loss of wildlife as temperature bands on the Earth's surface shifted (forests, for example, cannot easily 'migrate'), a corresponding disruption to agriculture and food supply and, because the overall temperature is rising, a melting of ice-sheets and an expansion of the water in the seas. Resulting changes in sea-levels would lead to flooding, particularly of low-lying countries without sea defences and of port cities which, by their very nature, are seldom far above current sea-level.

This form of pollution stands out not just because of the unusual threat it poses, but because it is almost thoroughly global. Because of air currents, the CO_2 produced in one place can affect the temperature virtually anywhere on the globe. Unlike a waste dump or a chemicals spill, the threat is not localized, but very highly dispersed. Furthermore, the uncertainty about the exact impact of global warming means that no country or group can be sure of the impact on them. A little warming might produce benefits for a few areas, with warmer summers and milder winters in Canada, for example. But the difficulties of climate prediction mean that no-one knows with any degree of certainty what the impact in their area will be, though flood-prone countries such as the Netherlands and Bangladesh must see themselves as in the front line of likely victims.

Finally, in this section it should be emphasized that both these major global air pollution problems have intensified in recent years. In particular, carbon dioxide emissions are virtually bound to rise as industrialization proceeds so that global totals are likely to increase whatever the countries of the North do and, so far, their progress on limiting greenhouse gas emissions has been meagre. These two examples both indicate that international policy solutions are needed if global pollution problems are to be tackled. But these examples also indicate that, even with the most 'global' problems, the global consequences are not uniform. For one thing, geography plays a key part. Ozone depletion, as we have seen, is worst at the poles while global warming appears most terrifying at sea-level. Secondly, as we have suggested, wealth plays a large role too: the Dutch need fear less than Bangladeshis. Even the most global environmental threats have socially and geographically unequal impacts.

Activity 2 Quickly draw up a table listing examples of land, water and air pollution. Is it possible to see which type is more global in its impacts? Bear in mind that some forms of pollution can be global in themselves while others become global by being repeated the world over in numerous locations.

4.3.4 Cross-media pollution: from Chernobyl to polluted diets

Although an overview of the three media into which pollution can enter would appear to be exhaustive, there are in fact significant types of pollution which fall outside this classification.

Radiation

The first of these would be radiation, the collective term for particles and energy released by radioactive materials. Radiation itself cannot really be called an aspect of land, water or air, yet it can contaminate all three. Since the discovery of radioactivity at the end of the last century, radioactive materials have been used more and more – predominantly but by no means exclusively in the North. These materials have been employed in nuclear weapons, in nuclear power, in X-raying and other diagnostic techniques, in radiation treatment and in numerous other uses. As is well known, radioactive materials are potentially very harmful. High doses of radiation can kill by attacking the central nervous system or bone marrow; radiation can also promote cancers and genetic defects and cause other, more diffuse, ill-health. The threat from radioactive material is greatly increased if the material is ingested, for example by eating contaminated food or by breathing in minute dust-borne radioactive particles.

Pollution of this kind is alarming both because of the invisible yet frightening threat it poses and because the danger is hard to guard against: gamma radiation can penetrate buildings while alpha radiation-emitting substances can occur in the air we breathe or in food and water. The pollution risk is generally higher around nuclear installations but it can be much more widely spread; the fact that the naturally occurring radioactive gas radon is released from certain rocks (some granites, for example) means that communities living in affected areas can also suffer intense risks. As the explosion at the Chernobyl nuclear power plant in the Ukraine in 1986 showed, the risk of contamination from nuclear accidents extends across nations and continents. Similarly, pollution from nuclear testing has been spread around the atmosphere for decades. As the map of the spread of radio-active clouds from Chernobyl shows, a Soviet problem quickly became a pan-European threat (see Figure 4.2). The explosion compressed the European environment in a matter of hours though, again, the vagaries of climate and geography meant that the effects were felt unevenly: the soil

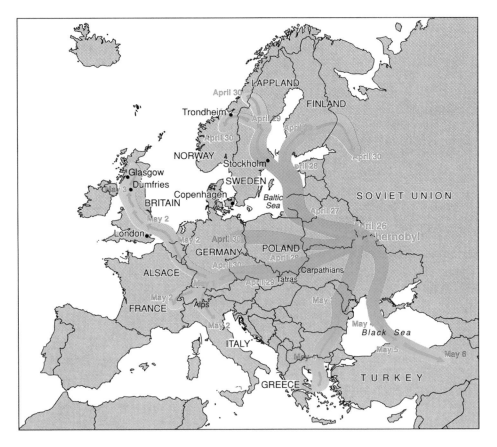

Figure 4.2 A cloud over Europe: a map of the progress of the Chernobyl plume (Source: Gould, 1990, Figure 1)

character and farming practices in Cumbria and North Wales meant that livestock have been contaminated for years; elsewhere in the United Kingdom the most obvious impacts passed in weeks.

Much of the world's uranium is mined in countries of the South, often from low-grade ores. This means that there is a vast residue of mine 'tailings' left behind, waste material which inevitably has some radioactive contamination; dust and small particles from the tailings can also be dispersed by winds or swept along by nearby rivers, thus spreading the pollution around a locality. In this way the production of fuel for French, Swedish, British or Russian nuclear power gives rise to radioactive pollutants elsewhere on the globe. Furthermore, after the energy has been generated the nuclear industry is left with contaminated waste which the citizens of Northern countries have shown themselves increasingly reluctant to have disposed of near to them; consequently Northern countries have been trying to find other geographical outlets for it. Also, as the industry has fallen out of public favour in the North, nuclear entrepreneurs have 'globalized' and nuclear power-stations have been sold to countries of the South and to the formerly communist countries of Eastern Europe. New installations arising from these promotional activities will produce their own waste disposal problems within the next few years.

Lastly, it is often said – and quite correctly – that there is a level of naturally occurring 'background' radiation. Life on Earth has evolved to withstand some radiation. But the sheer growth of human interest in radioactive materials in the last hundred years has effectively increased that 'natural' level. By mining and grinding radioactive ores, for example, we add to the background levels. This too can be seen to be part of international – indeed literally global – pollution.

Food pollution

A second type of pollution which defies ready classification is the pollution of foodstuffs. This is not so much the pollution of water or the other media, as it is of organisms themselves. A graphic example is provided by the case of the cattle disease, bovine spongiform encephalopathy (BSE). Otherwise known as 'mad cow disease', BSE is a disease of the cow's central nervous system which was first identified in 1985. It is believed to be closely related to the degenerative disease, scrapie, which has been found in sheep for at least two hundred years. The key point is that the cattle disease is believed to have originated when scrapie-infected sheep meat was used to make a high-protein cattle feed. Cattle became contaminated by consuming a food which was far removed from their normal diet – many would say it was extremely unnatural. The danger which commentators now fear is that the disease, having leaped from one species to another through ingestion, could pass to beef-eating humans. Since the BSE scare first became publicized at the end of the 1980s, measures have been taken to stop cows being fed such material and to stop possibly infected cattle material (their brains and spinal cord essentially) from entering the human food chain; miscellaneous cow-meat pieces were formerly used in meat pies, burgers and other convenience foods.

Although this example stands out as particularly alarming, it is not the only example of food pollution. Great public anxiety was stimulated in the USA in 1989 around a chemical known as Alar, a plant growth regulator used on apples and other fruit. Evidence suggested, though there was doubt about how definitive the evidence was, that Alar could cause cancer, especially in children. The possibility that agricultural chemicals can enter the water supply has already been mentioned; since insecticides are designed to kill certain animals there is clearly a danger that they will harm broader communities of creatures. Early work on long-lasting pest-control chemicals in fact indicated that they could accumulate biologically through the food chain. A hawk which ate many birds each of which had in turn eaten thousands of contaminated insects could receive a lethal dose of such toxins. But the Alar case was different. This was not a roundabout threat caused by pollution of the environment, but the danger of directly ingesting a reputedly deadly substance which had been deliberately spread on foodcrops. Since agrochemicals are now manufactured for a world market and extensively traded internationally, food pollution too must now be regarded as a global risk.

There is one final twist to this type of pollution threat. Since the prosperous North imports much exotic fruit (mangoes, passion-fruit, even strawberries) as well as meat and vegetables from the South, the environmentally aware Northern citizen has to worry about agricultural practices not only at home but in the countries where these crops are grown. The chemicals in use on the farms of the North can for the most part be regulated, but it is far harder to regulate the South where Northern inspection agencies cannot oversee the actions of growers, whether they are indigenous farmers or the workers on the plantations of Northern transnational firms. As we shall see later on in this chapter, Susan George speaks of this kind of feedback from practices in the South as the 'boomerang' phenomenon, since we may find that hazardous material exported to the South returns to us on our food.

We are, as the saying has it, what we eat. We build our bodies out of the molecules we put into them as food. Ingestion is thus a very direct way in which people can suffer from pollution and it too is an international issue since agricultural production is itself a highly international business.

Genetic pollution

A third and increasingly important alternative form of pollution can be referred to as genetic pollution. By that I mean that it is a contamination of natural genetic resources. Three quick examples will illustrate what is at stake here. First, consider the case of ornamental ducks. Down the years people have taken colourful ducks from their native areas and brought them to ponds and gardens from where – inevitably – they escape. There is currently a case where introduced American, escapee drakes are arriving early on the Spanish nesting-sites of a closely related European duck and striking up relationships with all the females before the same-species males have begun to swing into action. The genetic stock is in danger of unplanned change which would not have arisen but for human intervention in the ducks' lives. A similar example concerns farmed salmon. Such salmon have not faced natural selection to ensure that they are good survivors; indeed they have been selected by humans for quite different attributes, such as rapid weight gain and tolerance of overcrowding. When they escape, which they may do in relatively large numbers, they interbreed with river salmon, upsetting natural selection. The qualities of the natural salmon, qualities which have ensured their survival, may thus be lost.

The final example of genetic pollution is the starkest; this deals with genetically engineered organisms. There is currently great commercial pressure for the development of genetic engineering, the technology which allows the molecular building-blocks of life to be manipulated and 'customized'. For example, it may be possible to take the genetic elements which stimulate disease resistance in certain plants and introduce those elements into foodcrops, so that the need for pesticides is reduced. Plants, viruses, bacteria or animals which have been treated in this way are referred to as *genetically modified organisms* (GMOs). The companies producing these GMOs clearly want to be allowed to sell them widely, including in the 'third world' in order to boost agricultural productivity; this means that they will move beyond the exhaustive control that can be exercised in laboratory conditions. Engineered viruses will move around with the creatures they occupy; engineered bacteria cannot be closely contained. There will inevitably be some risk of genetic pollution, a risk spread throughout the world by the reach of agricultural transnational corporations. And in this case it will be pollution by genetic material unprecedented in nature.

genetically modified organisms

Before concluding this section it is worth reminding ourselves that, while pollution problems are very serious, they are not the only environmental problems facing the globe. The other major threat is that we may run out of resources, particularly energy resources and water (see **Blunden, 1995a, b**). The two issues are linked in that, as mineral resources become scarcer and poorer quality seams are mined, the degree of pollution tends to rise. Nonetheless the two issues are distinct. We also face problems of species extinction across the globe. And while these extinctions may sometimes come about because of pollution, more often the threat is simply habitat loss: humans chop down the trees or tarmac over the land where certain species live.

In this chapter a broad interpretation of pollution has been adopted and this has allowed us to see the connection between pollution and other problematic themes such as biotechnology. Still, it is important to stress that pollution is not the only environmental threat, nor even the only transnational one.

Summary of section 4.3

o On a worldwide scale, pollution problems are increasing, both in scale (for example, as more areas industrialize or as more electricity is generated) and in terms of new forms of pollution (such as genetic pollution by GMOs).

o Not all forms of pollution are increasing. Several pollutants are being successfully regulated in the North (notably acid gases) – though the North's reductions are usually offset by increases elsewhere as industries re-locate or start up in the developing world – and some (notably CFCs) are being tackled internationally.

o Some forms of pollution are inherently global (greenhouse gas pollution, for example), while most other 'global' problems are rendered global by the effects of international trade and the spread of industrialization.

158

o Because of differences of geography, wealth and social organization, the impacts of global problems are not uniform the world over. Even the most thoroughly global problems, such as 'greenhouse' warming, will affect different regions to varying degrees and their impacts can usually be managed more easily in wealthier societies. Global problems have uneven consequences.

o The processes by which pollution is spread are diverse. It can be spread by wind or ocean currents, by deliberate export, through chemicals sprayed on a field, by a decision to re-locate a factory or by the release of a bacterium.

Box 4.1 Why is pollution so hard to define?

Having discussed the many forms of pollution in the modern world and having examined their global reach, it is helpful to consider one obvious-looking question: the question of what we mean by pollution. At an everyday level this is not usually a controversial or especially complex issue; most people would share ideas about what substances are polluting. But it is a problem in the following three ways.

It is often hard to decide exactly which substances should be viewed as pollutants. While it might initially seem tempting to suggest that all pollution must stem from non-natural substances, a definition based on that idea would not stand up. Human and domestic animal sewage is perfectly natural but in many societies it causes a pollution problem. Equally, cows naturally discharge methane gas. As cow numbers have increased, this has come to make a considerable contribution to the greenhouse effect, so much so that New Zealand scientists have apparently introduced anti-flatulence tablets for the nation's cattle (*The Guardian*, 3 June 1993, p. 12). The principal greenhouse gases are all naturally present in the atmosphere. And other natural phenomena, notably volcanic eruptions, produce toxic and environmentally damaging gases which, when produced by human processes, are regarded as pollutants. As we have seen, radon gas can cause a radiation hazard in people's homes. Conversely, some substances which would not occur in nature unless they had been produced by people (such as rare and highly reactive metals) break down or re-combine into naturally occurring substances and are thus not necessarily a pollution problem. The complementary argument is also heard, to the effect that other human-made substances, such as some plastics, are so inert that they pose no threat of contamination to the natural world, though they make it untidy and can disturb animal and plant life.

In fact, what these examples make clear is that different groups or individuals can offer differing representations of the 'natural' and the 'unnatural'. Methane-discharging cattle can be presented as natural because cows stem from natural ancestors or as unnatural because they only exist in such numbers on account of human (mostly western) diets. The 'natural-ness' of a substance cannot really be used to decide whether it is a pollutant or not since there is so much room for disagreement about what is natural.

continued overleaf

Box 4.1 continued

Second, some substances are very subtle pollutants and it is hard to know whether they are hazardous or not. Often, complex scientific investigations are needed to try to determine whether substances are dangerous and these scientific tests may be inconclusive or controversial. The membership of the category 'pollutants' is thus not cut-and-dried. For example, it took many years before scientists realized how CFCs could be a dangerous form of pollution and years more to work out how serious the threat was.

Finally, in case this whole question about defining a pollutant seems 'academic', it is important to remember that the difficulties mentioned above will lead to problems with the legal definition of pollutants. And this matters in a practical way because polluters and those accused of pollution will often try to use the law to protect themselves from attack and prosecution. Unless societies have procedures for identifying what substances count as pollution, it is impossible to outlaw or regulate them. This was a problem in the West African countries targeted by waste exporters; in many cases the trade was initially legal precisely because the receiving countries – having no experience of certain toxic industrial chemicals – had no laws regulating their disposal.

The following is a commonly used and helpful definition of pollution, given at the 1972 United Nations Conference on the Human Environment. Though it relates specifically to the seas, it is a useful starting-point:

Pollution means the introduction by human beings, directly or indirectly, of substances or energy into the oceans resulting in harm to living resources, hazards to human health, hindrance to marine activities including fishing, impairment of quality for use of sea-water and reduction of amenities

(cited in Smith, 1991, p. 56)

More recently, in his study of pollution control policies, Weale has defined pollution as:

The introduction into the environment of substances or emissions that either damage, or carry the risk of damaging, human health or well-being, the built environment or the natural environment. There is no implication in this definition that the substances involved stem purely from human sources ... The assumption is simply that emissions or substances introduced into the environment in quantities or concentrations greater than those that can be coped with by the cleansing and recycling capacity of nature constitute pollution.

(Weale, 1992, p. 3)

Helpful though such definitions are, it is clear that they are not in agreement with each other (for example, about tracing pollution to human actions). Nor do they solve all the practical problems since elements of the definition, such as 'damage to human well-being' or amounts greater than can be absorbed by the 'recycling capacity of nature' are themselves open to conflicting interpretations. Different cultures may disagree about what is essential to human well-being while scientists are likely to disagree about the exact recycling capacity of nature. The definitions help us to become clearer about what we mean by pollution but they do not tell us precisely, once-and-for-all, what it is. Furthermore, pressure groups, industries and governments spend a lot of energy trying to re-draw the precise boundaries around 'pollution' in ways which favour their objectives, so we cannot even assume that the definition is static.

4.4   Economic activity and pollution

Although in the preceding sections we have examined the chief types of pollution and have noted their international but uneven spread, we have not yet asked what determines where and whether they are produced, and in what quantities and combinations. A simple, yet still quite informative, answer to this question is that the types and extent of pollution are influenced by developments in economic activity. The vast majority of pollution arises from economic activities themselves, from power generation, from the operation of chemical plants, from mining operations, from travelling to and from work and from agricultural enterprises.

Of course, pollution is not limited to modern industrialized societies. Manufacture and mining have always been able to generate contamination. But three things set the modern economy apart.

Firstly, there is its scale. Modern societies are enormously more productive than their predecessors so that they generate far more pollution. These societies also trade and operate internationally to an unprecedented degree, so pollution can be dispersed along with the goods.

The second factor is the nature of modern production. It is only for the last hundred years or so that industries have been producing numerous innovative substances which are not directly derived from organic materials. It is only in this century, for example, that people have introduced radioactive materials for medical, military and energy-generation purposes. Only in this century have humans produced vast quantities of plastics and other carbon-based materials which are foreign to the natural world. These first two points amount to a re-statement of the lessons drawn from the examples with which this chapter started: namely, that certain modern pollutants can contaminate the global environment, while the transnational nature of modern trade allows the waste from industrialized regions and countries to pollute every region of the world.

The third factor has to do with the way that pricing works in a free-market economy. The free market is supposed to lead to the optimum use of goods and services because prices respond to demand and availability. As things become scarce, demand for each one intensifies and so the price rises, giving customers an incentive to search for an alternative. But certain things escape this price mechanism. Until relatively recently, industries would use the environment as a cost-free waste-disposal facility. Unwanted gases were simply discharged into the atmosphere, while waste fluids were pumped into the sewers, the river or the sea. Because use of the environment was free, there was no incentive to try to minimize your firm's effluents or your firm's impact on the environment. Even if a small investment would have allowed you to reduce your waste gases by 90 per cent, there was no financial incentive to do so. Rather the opposite. The firm that performed the clean-up would have its profits reduced while its competitors saw theirs maintained. Only altruistic 'mugs' would pay their own money for an improvement which benefited the general good but did not help their own business; they could even risk going out of business since their dirtier competitors would be able to undercut the cleaner firm's prices. When a firm's actions result in a load or cost being borne outside the firm itself (in this case they are borne by the environment), economists refer to this as imposing *negative externalities*.

negative externalities

To make this point about externalities is not to imply that industrial pollution is unique to capitalist, free-market systems. On average, state socialist countries had a worse record of pollution, particularly when one bears in mind the low levels of productivity they achieved. Their emphasis on production targets gave them a different kind of reason for disregarding the pollution they caused. Rather, the point is that the free-market system, which is now the dominant global model, provides a systematic incentive to firms to lower their costs by causing pollution. Firms which operate in a country with lax pollution control legislation will – all other things (such as wage costs and so on) being equal – enjoy higher profits than those operating in a cleaner environment. The 'logic' of the market thus inclines companies to pollute.

Activity 3 Take the example of a chemical company which releases harmful substances into a river. Who might end up bearing the costs of this pollution and why? Would it be possible to cover these costs by making the company pay in some way, such as through additional taxes or by charging for a 'pollution permit'?

Now turn to Reading A by Jacobs at the end of the chapter. Does his analysis of the problems caused by negative externalities and of the potential for getting the polluters to meet the 'costs' coincide with your response to the action?

For the reasons Jacobs gives, pollution has come to be seen as the inevitable consequence of economic development, particularly in the underdeveloped world. It is almost as though environmental degradation is the 'cost' to be paid for growing material wealth. For example, according to an article by Stott in the development journal *Links*, Brazilian delegates at the 1972 UN Conference on the Human Environment proclaimed that it was 'their country's "turn" to industrialize, and assured multinational corporations that it was alright [*sic*] to send this pollution down to Brazil so long as they sent the industries and the jobs that went with it' (1984, p. 28). Politicians and business people in the developing world have often been willing to bear (or – at least – allow their people and employees to bear) the negative consequences of development in return for an increase in wealth. This willingness to tolerate pollution has interacted with the strategy of Northern firms to ensure that the negative externalities of modern industry have been spread around the globe, as we shall see in the next section.

4.4.1   Where dirty industries end up

There has always been controversy over the location of industry because of the effluent it produces. In the nineteenth century aristocrats and large landowners in Britain complained that emissions from the soap and allied chemicals businesses were poisoning their livestock (less thought was given to workers' health). Planning laws have since been tightened to ensure that consideration is given to the consequences of location. But another factor has worked in the contrary direction. Industry has spelled jobs and the prospect of wealth. Accordingly, there has generally been an *environmental trade-off* – a trade-off between wanting the benefits that industry brings and wishing to avoid the associated pollution. Many working-class communities have simply had to put up with high levels of pollution in order to keep jobs in the local economy. It was not that the businesses couldn't be cleaner, it was that rather than pay the costs of cleaning up, they would have located elsewhere.

environmental trade-off

The trade-off of jobs for pollution can even be self-perpetuating. For example, the presence of the British nuclear industry in Cumbria around Sellafield has meant that it is easier to site successive developments in the same location than to persuade other communities to accept the nuclear industry. Following community opposition at a series of sites outside Cumbria being considered for their suitability for nuclear waste disposal, in 1987 the British government cancelled these investigations. By the early 1990s the revised plan was to dispose of the waste beneath the Sellafield complex. Successive investments come because of the proven acceptance of the nuclear industry, an industry which other communities regard (rightly or wrongly) as intolerably polluting.

This problem of trade-offs has been internationalized in two ways. First the effluent has itself been dispersed internationally. As the scale of industry has grown, there have been more wastes and these have led, for example, to the pollution of large rivers such as the Rhine and Danube which pass through many countries, bearing Swiss wastes to the Netherlands or Austrian wastes to Hungary and Rumania. Similarly, air pollution has been 'handled' by building higher chimneys. Firms have tended not to reduce the production of pollutants so much as to try to spread them more thinly. Pumping them higher into the air reduced local contamination but meant that they landed over a wider area and further away, leading to pollution of neighbouring territories.

The second path of internationalization relates to the discussion of multinational firms in Chapter 2 and concerns the re-location of industry away from the developed countries of the North to areas desperate for jobs, investment and economic development. In the most well-known examples, from the 1970s US companies started moving away from the pioneering domestic environmental legislation to less developed countries in the South with laxer laws, sometimes referred to as *pollution havens*.

pollution havens

There is a push and pull effect here. The push is the urge to escape tightening regulations which would mean increased costs or limitations on productivity: for example, new laws which demand cleaner emissions to the atmosphere or which impose charges on the dumping of wastes into sewers drive up production costs. Firms also face tougher planning controls on the development of new plant. If these companies can find overseas locations which are keen to get investment and with less demanding laws, they are able to make the same products more cheaply. On the face of it, this urge to escape regulation looks morally dubious. If a substance is harmful in the USA or France, then one can only suppose that it is harmful elsewhere too. In other words, by re-locating, these firms are imposing risks on the host country which are deemed unacceptable in their home state. Firms often seek to rationalize this decision by arguing that the new regulations are unnecessarily tight; they tend to imply that they are the victims of a form of environmental hysteria. Also, they tend to argue that in the less developed world poverty is more harmful than pollution so that the receiving population stands to make an overall gain in quality of life. In some cases firms re-locate not so much to escape regulations as to avoid protest and the delays which accompany public inquiries. For example, whatever the actual facts about the dangers of waste incinerators (and these 'facts' are fiercely disputed at present), no western community is keen to take the risk of having an incinerator cited near it. Firms which want to build such a facility know they will face prolonged protest and legal challenges. It can be this prospect rather than the laws themselves which incline them to look overseas.

The complementary pull comes from the governments and development authorities of countries eager for investment. Stott (1984) cites the example of a brochure designed to persuade companies to locate in an industrial complex in Trinidad: the text informs companies that, '*In the absence* of legislation dealing with the discharge of effluents and other forms of pollution', intending investors have to convince the development authorities that the environmental impact of the proposed factory has been properly assessed (p. 30; emphasis added). In other words, at the time the country itself had no legislation covering the discharge of likely pollution and the only obligation on incoming firms was to convince the economic development agency that an assessment had been made of the environmental impact of the development. Given that this agency's job was to stimulate investment, one can only assume that they would have been sympathetic to investors' claims about the cleanliness of their operations.

Through the 1970s and 1980s more and more attention was focused on these reasons for re-location and on the possibility that dirty industry from the North was spreading pollution around the globe (Ives, 1985). An authoritative summary of these views is provided in the reading from Michalowski and Kramer's overview of international corporate crime.

Activity 4 You should now turn to Reading B, 'Transnational corporate crime'. As you read, make a list of the different reasons why environmental risks in the less developed countries are likely to be increased by the actions of transnational corporations.

As well as providing an account of the dangers exported to the underdeveloped world by TNCs in the North, Michalowski and Kramer indicate two important points. First, they highlight the dispute that has arisen over 'whether pollution control costs actually play a significant role in location decisions'. In other words, there are many economic factors which incline Northern companies to move to the underdeveloped world, including cheaper labour, fewer legal benefits and rights for employees, more lenient tax laws and direct financial inducements such as subsidies for building factories. Where the avoidance of pollution control costs comes in, any hierarchy of benefits is hard to specify. Leonard (1988) carried out a comparative study of this issue which concluded that the story varied greatly from one industrial sector to another. In some businesses, such as basic mineral processing, environmental protection measures are very costly; in others, such as pulp and paper production, they are more or less easily affordable.

Activity 5 You will find a summary of Leonard's findings in Reading C, to which you should now turn. Note that from his study it appears that the less developed countries are most likely to attract ailing dirty industries, not the 'sunrise' industries they might prefer to have.

All the same, and this is Michalowski and Kramer's second point, even if it is some factor other than the avoidance of pollution control costs which directs TNCs to the less developed countries, once located there they 'remain legally free to expose the water, air, soil and bodies of workers to hazardous substances at rates higher than those allowed in their home countries' (1987, p. 37). Even if they did not move to the developing world in order to pollute, companies may be tempted to pollute once they get there. To install pollution abatement equipment which is not required by law would only cut into their profits.

4.4.2 Where wastes turn up

It is clear that the less developed countries of the South can face environmental damage if dirty industries re-locate there. Given the low standards of environmental control which often prevail, local firms are also likely to pollute. But, as the example of Kassa Island vividly shows, the South can sometimes end up with the pollution without even the benefit of hosting the industrial processes which cause it. Some countries are so poor, so in need of earnings of foreign currencies (to pay for necessary imports and so on) and so lacking in resources (a problem often compounded by the over-exploitation of ecological resources such as forests which exhausts any riches the country may originally have had) that they will consider any trade that is likely to generate an income.

In the 1980s, as citizens of the rich, Northern countries became more aware of environmental threats, there was a growing problem of hazardous waste disposal. Such wastes were either very expensive to dispose of because the authorities insisted on special treatment or impossible to dispose of because no community would tolerate having the waste dumped near their town. Local politicians tended to side with the outraged citizens of their constituency so it became difficult for governments to impose a solution in the face of parliamentary protest. The obvious answer was to export the wastes to countries which were so desperate for income that they would overlook the risks. Such pollution export deals were easier when the receiving country had a non-democratic government. They were easier still when the recipients were misled about the nature of the wastes or when local officials were offered bribes.

The double standards in this trade are, however, immediately apparent and disclosures in the late 1980s led to protests in the receiving countries and in the North. Through bodies such as the Organization of African Unity, the receiving countries (many of which, like Guinea, were in West Africa) were able to co-operate in pushing up standards and in 1989 the United Nations Environment Programme agreed an international convention concerning trade in waste. The European Community subsequently developed complementary policies for its member-states. Such measures may have halted the worst excesses of the trade but they did not stop it entirely. The North can still off-load a part of its disposal problems on to the South and, as with any UN agreement, there are always countries which refuse to be signatories and through which wastes can still be traded.

Two further factors have led to the perpetuation of this trade. The first – ironically enough – is the continuing rise in environmental standards within the industrialized, Northern countries. For example, Germany has recently introduced demanding regulations on recycling. Picking through waste to sort and recycle the various components is labour-intensive work and can only be made economically attractive if it is subsidized or if wage-rates are very low. Consequently, an attractive approach to recycling policy is to collect the waste of wealthy people and send it to poor countries with low wage-rates. This makes some sort of economic sense, but an 'incidental' benefit, of course, is that it helps to solve one's waste disposal problems. Better still – at least for those doing the exporting – the North is no longer 'dumping' waste on the South but providing the South with environmentally-sound employment opportunities!

The second factor is rather more complicated and demands a subsection to itself.

4.4.3   International debt and transnational pollution

Countries seeking to develop industrially usually suffer from a lack of capital. They want modern factories, for example, but before the factories ever generate any profit the countries will need to make a large investment. As we have seen, one way to overcome this problem is to attract foreign investors by making one's country a cheap or convenient place in which to set up business. An alternative approach is to try to obtain loans or grants – often in the form of aid – to assist with the initial investment costs. In the 1970s the sources of such loans were revolutionized when Northern commercial banks began to seek new business in the developing world. Banks are obviously in the business of making loans and living off the profits from the interest. For big western banks, such as the Midland and Lloyds, lending to developing countries was appealing for three reasons. First, this was a relatively neglected market so there was initially little competition in the granting of loans. Second, certain developing countries' economies – for example, those of Mexico and Brazil – were expected to grow quickly thus yielding a good return on the loan. Third, there was a belief that countries were a special, low-risk sort of borrower; unlike individuals or even companies who might default on loans, countries would always be there: as Lever and Huhne (1985, p. 53) expressed it, people believed that 'Countries simply could not go bankrupt'.

The banks, notably US ones, lent enthusiastically and loans accumulated so that by the 1980s several South American countries had debts of around $100 billion and the total indebtedness of the less developed world came close to $1,000 billion. And, effectively, these big debtors *did* start to go bankrupt. In their eagerness to lend, the banks had backed some very poor investments. Very little of it generated enough profits to pay the interest on the loans, though the banks still demanded their repayments. In the worst cases, countries were having to use all their export earnings just to service their debts and their populations were therefore not benefiting at all from trade or from the loans.

Through the 1980s this complex and distressing story unfolded. Three consequences are of particular importance to the present discussion. The first and pivotal consequence was the growing importance of two international financial bodies, the World Bank and the International Monetary Fund. As the commercial banks fretted over the extent of their bad debts and the indebted countries tried to work out a strategy for survival, these two bodies assumed a powerful advisory and brokerage role. Although they are both international agencies, they are dominated by Northern representatives (who, they would say, put up most of the money) and their priority was to safeguard the international monetary system and only secondarily to assist debtor nations.

The second and third consequences followed from the strategy advocated by the World Bank and IMF. Their view was that debtor countries should try to meet repayments by increasing their export earnings. They should thus do more to attract investment even if that meant accepting dirty industry or building incinerators to deal with the wastes of the industrialized North. By the early 1990s this had re-invigorated the business of international waste-handling, a business which had seemed set to vanish just two or three years earlier. The recent spread of the international waste trade is captured in Figure 4.3.

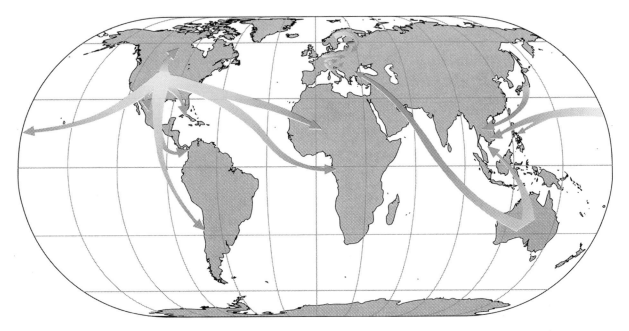

Figure 4.3 International waste trade (Source: adapted from The Guardian, *14 February 1992, p. 29)*

These financial institutions' advice thus made pollution of the developing world more likely. Their focus on increasing earnings was to be coupled with decreases in government spending, a policy which hit expenditure on such government tasks as maintaining sewerage systems, pollution monitoring and abatement measures. At the same time as pollution was likely to be on the increase, spending on pollution control was reduced.

In February 1992 an internal memo (which the bank later claimed was meant ironically) from Lawrence Summers, chief economist and vice-president of the World Bank, was leaked; it stated:

Just between you and me, shouldn't the World Bank be encouraging more *migration of the dirty industries to the LDCs [least developed countries]? I can think of three reasons:*

1   *The measurement of the costs of health-impairing pollution depends on the forgone earnings from increased morbidity and mortality. From this point of view a given amount of health-impairing pollution should be done in the country with the lowest cost, which will be the country with the lowest wages. I think the economic logic behind dumping a load of toxic waste in the lowest-wage country is impeccable and we should face up to that.*

2　*The costs of pollution are likely to be non-linear as the initial increments of pollution probably have very low cost. I've always thought that under-populated countries in Africa are vastly* under-*polluted; their air quality is probably vastly inefficiently low [sic] compared to Los Angeles or Mexico City. Only the lamentable facts that so much pollution is generated by non-tradable industries (transport, electrical generation) and that the unit transport costs of solid waste are so high prevent world-welfare-enhancing trade in air pollution and waste.*

3　*The demand for a clean environment for aesthetic and health reasons is likely to have very high income-elasticity. The concern over an agent that causes a one-in-a-million change in the odds of prostate cancer is obviously going to be much higher in a country where people survive to get prostate cancer than in a country where under-5 mortality is 200 per 1,000. Also, much of the concern over industrial atmospheric discharge is about visibility-impairing particulates. These discharges may have very little direct health impact. Clearly trade in goods that embody aesthetic pollution concerns could be welfare-enhancing. While production is mobile the consumption of pretty air is non-tradable.*

The problem with the arguments against all of these proposals for more pollution in LDCs (intrinsic rights to certain goods, moral reasons, social concerns, lack of adequate markets, etc.) could be turned around and used more or less effectively against every Bank proposal for liberalisation.

(The Guardian, 14 February 1992, p. 29)

Whether it was meant ironically or not, this passage makes clear why the free-market responses to the problem of debt would tend to encourage international pollution and (as his final paragraph makes clear) why environment protection measures tend to run counter to the World Bank's policies for economic liberalization.

Summers' account also neglects to mention ways in which environmental problems in the poorer countries can rebound on populations in the North. As described earlier, agricultural pollution in the South, for example, can have repercussions for consumers in the North. Ironically, these trends can be encouraged by Southern countries' response to their debt problems – a
debt boomerang　situation which George has dubbed the *debt boomerang*.

Activity 6　The next reading from George's work on the 'debt boomerang' presents a case study of these free-market solutions in action. Your should now turn to Reading D. It concerns the use of maquiladora zones in Mexico, which are essentially custom-free areas with limited environmental regulation.

What George makes particularly clear towards the end of this passage is that the environmental problems arising from countries' responses to debt are not confined to those countries; there is a boomerang effect. Their neighbours have to suffer the air pollution from Mexican factories, the sewage from Mexican industrial areas and the contaminated foodstuffs from Mexican agriculture. For the USA, the most important source of loans to the less developed countries, there is certainly an irony: the environmental costs of Mexico's debt are rebounding on US citizens too. Some commentators fear that these problems in Mexico will intensify as a result of increasing trade arising from the North American Free Trade Agreement (NAFTA), which reduces trade barriers in Mexico, the USA and Canada.

This river, next to a chemical plant on Mexico's border with the US, is polluted not only with visible refuse but with dissolved toxic wastes, not so readily apparent

Summary of section 4.4

Drawing together this section on the numerous and overlapping links between economic activity and pollution, it is worth re-stating three points.

o   First, though it may seem a little obvious, it is important to recognize that the overwhelming majority of pollution arises from economic activity. Therefore, the ways in which countries' economies are organized inevitably have a strong influence on the types and amount of pollution which are caused.

o   Second, many of today's large firms and industries are globally mobile. They think carefully about where to locate themselves, from where to draw their materials and where to dump their wastes. Environmental considerations play a significant part in these deliberations. Though the importance of this factor varies from one type of industry to another, firms can be drawn to set up plants in pollution 'havens' where pollution control is meagre. They also have a strong economic incentive to take advantage of weak pollution control laws in a country or region even if that wasn't the firm's reason for locating there. Additionally, they have a pressing economic interest in disposing of their wastes as economically as possible. All three of these considerations (concerning location, the exploitation of weak laws, and the search for cheap waste disposal) tend to encourage the global yet unequal spread of pollution.

o   Third, the fact that many less developed countries have been led to become heavily indebted means that they are in urgent need of investment and may be inclined to accept environmentally dubious contracts, whether for 'dirty' manufacturing operations or for waste disposal. It may appear that these countries act as a 'sink' for pollution, but such is the potential of some forms of pollution to spread internationally that the North's polluting practices can sometimes boomerang back on itself. Shifting pollution to the other side of the globe does not necessarily free you from its effects.

4.5   The shrinking world of environmental response

So far, we have been examining evidence that pollution in the modern world demonstrates, as well as contributes to, the shrinking of the world. In other words, this chapter has presented arguments for accepting that, objectively considered, pollution truly does shrink the world. However, people's beliefs don't always correspond with the assessments of outside commentators. Accordingly it is important to ask whether the citizens of the world are coming to accept that international pollution is a problem for them.

Both in the early 1970s and more recently, a leading stimulus to environmental awareness and protest in the industrialized North has been growing evidence about pollution and its possible health effects; people were also concerned about the loss of unspoilt countryside and about dangers to wildlife. In the underdeveloped world, by contrast, a major additional stimulus to environmental protest has been the awareness of double standards. Campaigners, working people and some politicians in the less developed countries of the South have been incensed that their countries are being made to bear risks which the rich North will no longer accept. The international trade in waste has been a particularly powerful stimulus to this way of thinking, since in these cases the underdeveloped world gets all the risks without any of the benefits of the industrial process which generated the waste in the first place (apart, that is, from a small waste-handling fee) (see Yearley, 1994, pp. 164–5).

For their part, leading environmental *non-governmental organizations* (NGOs) in the North such as Friends of the Earth and Greenpeace (both of which have national bodies, as well as international co-ordinating groups on which developing countries are represented) have also responded strongly to these double standards. This has come about for three reasons. First, they realize that some pollution is inherently transnational. To shift ozone-depleting chemicals or marine pollution to the developing world does nothing to reduce the problems about which they have campaigned. Thus, campaigning about policies in the developing world is a logical extension of their current work. Secondly, because of the boomerang effects, the countries in which such groups attract most of their support – Germany, the UK, the USA – are not insulated from developing world problems such as food contamination or air pollution. It makes no sense to protest about these problems within their home countries yet to ignore the problems in their trading partners. Thirdly, environmental organizations have realized that they are in danger of practising double standards too. They can hardly campaign for improvement in environmental conditions in the North if that is only achieved by inflicting environmental damage on the less developed world (for example, by protesting about incinerators in the UK but ignoring their construction in Central America). These organizations have faced some internal tension over this question since their supporters want to see progress at home in return for their financial and other donations. But, increasingly, these leading organizations are moving onto an international level of campaigning and, according to McCormick's research, it is precisely groups which concentrated on international issues that have grown most successfully in the last decade (1991, pp. 153–4).

non-governmental organizations

Increasingly, protest is being co-ordinated in two ways. Groups in the less developed world are joining with Northern NGOs to document and oppose the double standards of commercial companies and the destructive policies of international monetary organizations. Northern NGOs play their part by lobbying these international bodies and by pressing their home governments to raise standards in their deals with the less developed world. Second, environmental NGOs are realizing that their agendas overlap with those of development NGOs such as Oxfam and Action Aid (Yearley, 1992, pp. 182–3). They appreciate that solutions to the world's pollution problems cannot be made to last unless these solutions simultaneously meet the needs of the world's poorest people – people who might be tempted or obliged to exchange environmental quality for a small increase in income or for work in dirty industry. The joint expertise of environmentalists and development specialists is needed before these solutions can be worked out.

4.5.1 Regulating transnational pollution

So far we have looked mostly at two sets of actors – companies and commercial banks which have often been held responsible for aggravating pollution problems, and campaign groups which have tried to publicize and counteract these problems. Here, we turn briefly to a third set of influential actors – policy-makers (for more detail see **Yearley, 1995**).

In a study of the politics of pollution control, Weale (1992) has argued that there have been two waves of policy responses to environmental problems. In the first wave in the 1970s, governments established environment departments which had responsibility for protecting the natural environment. Well-meaning and far-sighted though some of these bodies were, their problem was that they existed alongside other departments whose business often resulted in adding to pollution. Agriculture ministries strove to increase food yields by encouraging the use of chemical fertilizers; transport ministries favoured road construction; and ministries of energy commonly encouraged nuclear power or the development of polluting fossil-fuel-powered generating stations.

The second wave, which is still gaining momentum, should see the introduction of environmental considerations into the business of all ministries, including the Treasury or finance ministry. For example, governments may move towards high rates of taxation on polluting substances, thus partially addressing the problem about externalities described above. 'Second-wave' policies will also be developed in open acknowledgement of the fact that international collaboration is needed to respond to transnational pollution problems. These issues are summarized in the reading from Weale, to which you should now turn.

Activity 7 As you work your way through Reading E, 'The new politics of pollution', try to pull out any significant differences between the 'old' and the 'new' politics of pollution. What do these differences tell us about the way in which pollution intensifies the relationships between nations?

The 1980s and early 1990s saw a number of successful intergovernmental agreements. European Community members agreed steep reductions in emissions of acidic gases; a successful international agreement on certain ozone-depleting chemicals was introduced; and some advances were made in combating marine pollution in the North Sea and the Mediterranean. Governments appeared to be responding to the demands of a world shrunk by pollution. On the other hand, even despite the Earth Summit in Brazil in 1992, no real progress was made on countering global warming. Countries failed to agree a method for stopping the amount of atmospheric-warming pollution increasing from year to year. There is no prospect of an agreement on *actually reducing* the worldwide amount of this pollution.

sustainable development

In principle, thanks to a UN agreement at the Rio Summit, countries are committed to devising plans for moving to *sustainable development* – that is, they are supposed to offer plans for socio-economic development which can continue indefinitely without exhausting the world's resources or overburdening the ability of natural systems to cope with pollution. But none of the world's leading economic powers (and therefore major polluters) has made any real advance in this direction yet. They are still exhausting the resources of the Earth and, as we have seen, polluting the globe in a variety of ways. Governments are coming to recognize the truth of pollution. But there is little sign of them devising appropriate policy responses in the hardest areas, most notably over global warming.

4.6   Conclusion

Modern pollution is shrinking the world and giving citizens, governments and corporations a heightened consciousness that there are real global ties and, maybe, a global identity for the occupants of spaceship Earth. In this chapter we have reviewed how pollution ties the lifestyles and policies of people in one part of the globe to the quality of life of their global neighbours. We have seen also how trade, investment and international finance join with wind and air currents and other natural processes in determining the distribution of pollution across the globe. These global ties continue to be intensified.

Yet while pollution illustrates global interconnectedness and offers the possibility for people to embrace a global identity, it also indicates that – in fact – global relations are characterized by exploitation and inequality. The geographical spread of pollution is highly uneven, with pollution problems in danger of increasing faster in the less developed world than in the North. While soil geography and wind currents play a part in shaping the spread of pollution, the principal influence comes from socio-economic forces, the investment decisions of national and multinational companies, the policies of banks and the politics of international relations. Waste dumping continues, the world's oceans become annually more polluted, and pollution reductions in the developed North are more than offset by the consequences of industrialization in the underdeveloped world. The image of a fragile globe on which we all depend has not yet reversed our tendency to pollute that globe. Pollution shrinks the world and reveals that shrinking to us, and yet we still lack the political and policy responses demanded by a shrunken and polluted globe.

References

BLUNDEN, J. (1995a) 'Sustainable resources?' in Sarre, P. and Blunden, J. (eds).

BLUNDEN, J. (1995b) 'Trade globally, pollute locally' in Sarre, P. and Blunden, J. (eds).

ELSWORTH, S. (1990) *A Dictionary of the Environment*, London, Paladin.

FRIENDS OF THE EARTH (1990) *How Green is Britain?*, London, Hutchinson.

FRIENDS OF THE EARTH (1992) *A Survey of Gassing Landfill Sites in England and Wales*, London, Friends of the Earth.

GEORGE, S. (1992) *The Debt Boomerang: How Third World Debt Harms Us All*, London, Pluto Press with the Transnational Institute.

GOULD, P. (1990) *Fire in the Rain: The Democratic Consequences of Chernobyl*, Cambridge, Polity Press.

IVES, J. H. (1985) *The Export of Hazard*, London, Routledge and Kegan Paul.

JACOBS, M. (1991) *The Green Economy*, London, Pluto Press.

LEONARD, H. J. (1988) *Pollution and the Struggle for the World Product: Multinational Corporations, Environment and International Comparative Advantage*, Cambridge, Cambridge University Press.

LEVER, H. and HUHNE, C. (1985) *Debt and Danger: The World Financial Crisis*, Harmondsworth, Penguin.

McCORMICK, J. (1991) *British Politics and the Environment*, London, Earthscan.

MICHALOWSKI, R. J. and KRAMER, R. C. (1987) 'The space between laws: the problem of corporate crime in a transnational context', *Social Problems*, Vol. 34, No. 1, pp. 34–53.

ROBERTSON, R. (1992) *Globalization: Social Theory and Global Culture*, London, Sage.

ROSS, S. (1991) 'Atmospheres and climatic change' in Smith, P. M. and Warr, K. (eds).

SARRE, P and BLUNDEN, J. (eds) (1995) *An Overcrowded World? Population, Resources and the Environment*, London, Oxford University Press/The Open University (Volume 3 in this series).

SMITH, P. M. and WARR, K. (eds) (1991) *Global Environmental Issues*, London, Hodder & Stoughton/The Open University.

SMITH, S. (1991) 'The oceans' in Smith, P. M. and Warr, K. (eds).

STOTT, M. (1984) 'Industrial pollution' *Links*, 19, pp. 28–30.

WEALE, A. (1992) *The New Politics of Pollution*, Manchester, Manchester University Press.

YEARLEY, S. (1992) *The Green Case*, London, Routledge.

YEARLEY, S. (1994) 'Social movements and environmental change' in Redclift, M. and Benton, T. (eds) *Social Theory and the Global Environment*, London, Routledge.

YEARLEY, S. (1995) 'The transnational politics of the environment' in Anderson, J., Brook, C. and Cochrane, A. (eds) *A Global World? Re-ordering Political Space*, London, Oxford University Press/The Open University (Volume 5 in this series).

Reading A: *Michael Jacobs, 'Environmental costs'* _____

Most environmental problems come into the category of 'negative externalities'. They represent the costs of production and consumption decisions which are not borne by the agents involved in the transaction.

Take a simple case of pollution. If a chemicals factory releases effluent into a river, the fish catch in the estuary further downstream may fall. Two things may then happen. Either the income of the fishing industry will be reduced, or the authorities may be forced to spend money cleaning the water. Meanwhile, the chemicals firm will price its products on the basis of the costs it bears in making them: rent, material inputs, labour and so on. These 'private' costs will not include the cost of releasing the effluent, since this is not paid by the firm. The result is that the consumers of the chemicals will effectively pay less than the full ('social') cost of making them, while the fisheries workers or taxpayers are forced to bear the difference. The pollution is thus an externality of the agents involved in its generation (the chemicals firm and its consumers); it is a cost falling on third parties.

Since it does not pay the cost itself, the chemicals firm actually has an economic incentive to pollute. It is cheaper to pollute the river than it is to clean up the effluent before it leaves the factory. So long as this is the case, and the firm is not legally prevented from doing so, rational economic behaviour suggests that, for the firm, polluting is the right action. In this sense, pollution is not an accident, but a deliberately chosen occurrence.

External costs can be both monetary and non-monetary. In some cases, as in the example of the authorities cleaning up the estuary, expenditure is actually incurred by another agent. In others, such as in the fishing industry's reduced income, money may be lost rather than spent. Sometimes harm may be done which cannot be valued in financial terms.

For example, one of the external costs of motor transport is the dirtying of buildings from exhaust emissions. These costs are borne by the owners of the buildings, who have to spend more on cleaning than they otherwise would. Such costs can be estimated in money terms whether or not the cleaning is actually done. But another type of cost is borne by children whose brains are damaged by

atmospheric lead. This cost cannot be given a monetary figure, because people's lives are not amenable to financial calculation. Though it might be possible to add up the costs of hospital treatment, the employment of remedial teachers, and so on, this will not reflect the real cost to the child. It is non-monetary.

Many environmental costs have both monetary and non-monetary components. When a new motorway bulldozes a stretch of countryside, the loss in value of nearby houses can be calculated, but the loss in pleasure, and the worth of all the animals and plants destroyed, cannot. The importance of non-monetary externalities lies in the fact that, unlike monetary costs, they cannot generally be 'paid for' by the participants in the original causal transaction. Vehicle owners can be taxed to give a rebate to landlords; homeowners near the new motorway can be compensated. But no financial transfer will compensate the brain-damaged child.

An important feature of external costs is that they increase in the process of industrial modernization. As population rises, particularly in cities, more people are affected by pollution. There are fewer places where wastes can be deposited without harm. Moreover, as pollution and resource use rise, their impact is likely to be cumulatively greater. Each emission or unit of resource extracted adds to previous ones. In this sense external costs can form a vicious spiral, each one worsening the effects of the next.

Source: Jacobs, 1991, pp. 27–8

Reading B: Raymond J. Michalowski and Ronald C. Kramer, 'Transnational corporate crime'

Over the last quarter century, foreign investment by TNCs has expanded dramatically. In the 20 years from 1960 to 1980, the revenues of TNCs grew tenfold – from 199 billion dollars to 2,155 billion dollars – with US-based corporations accounting for 50 per cent of this growth [...] This internationalization of corporate activity necessitates an expansion of corporate

crime research beyond its dominant focus on offences by corporations in their home countries.

While, on a dollar basis, foreign investment in developed nations exceeds that in developing nations, it is transnational investments *in developing nations* that pose the greatest likelihood of injurious corporate activity, and which raise the most perplexing problems for the definition and study of corporate crime. There are several reasons for this.

First, the most significant change in patterns of foreign investment since the Second World War has been the increased location of TNC industrial facilities in developing nations. Three-fourths of all US companies with sales over 100 million dollars had manufacturing facilities in other countries by 1975. By 1977, developing nations had surpassed developed ones in dollar value as locations for manufacturing by US industries. Reimportation of overseas assembly by US companies increased five-fold between 1969 and 1983, and in the textiles and electronics industries more than half of all current sales by US corporations are now assembled abroad. As TNCs export their industrial operations to developing nations, many of the hazards of industrial production and the associated possibilities for corporate crime are relocated from developed to developing countries. Moreover, as the fatal poisoning of over 2,000 residents of Bhopal, India dramatized, the settlement patterns, population density and limited disaster preparedness of developing nations means that, when problems do occur, the human and environmental costs are likely to be greater than those resulting from similar incidents in developed countries.

Second, the growth in consumer exports to the third world, as well as the increased local production of consumer goods by TNCs in developing nations, has generated significant consumer safety issues. Differences in marketing practices of TNCs in home versus host nations, variations in the provision of information by TNCs regarding product hazards, and variations in cultural practices regarding product usage have led to unnecessary injury, illness, and death for third world consumers of TNC products.

Finally, in comparison to developed nations, developing nations frequently have fewer legal controls over workplace, environmental and consumer hazards of industrial production. Therefore, the potential for corporations to behave in socially-injurious ways in developing

nations is greater. For these reasons the growing internationalization of business points to developing nations as a significant emerging arena for injurious corporate activity.

[...]

In some instances TNCs have located and/or relocated high-pollution industries in less developed countries in order to escape the pollution control costs imposed by environmental protection laws in their home nation. Blake and Walters (1976, p. 159) have suggested that TNCs 'will be very sensitive to disparities among various [national] pollution control standards which affect production costs and competitiveness in international trade' as a means of expanding or protecting profit margins. This sensitivity reflects the fact that pollution control costs in the United States are higher than in most other countries. Robert Strauss, President Carter's chief trade negotiator, warned in 1978 of a developing 'pattern of flight' as US companies are drawn to developing nations with less costly pollution control laws [...] In some cases entire industries involving highly toxic substances such as asbestos, arsenic, mercury, and benzidene dyes have been exported to rapidly developing nations such as Korea, Mexico, Brazil, India and Ireland. Even computer and electronics assembly, once thought to be 'clean' industries, often expose the environments of developing nations to a wide range of toxic substances that are more closely regulated in the United States.

There has been some disagreement over whether pollution control costs actually play a significant role in location decisions. However, the debate over the relative importance of pollution regulations for location decisions speaks only to the question of corporate motivation, not the consequence of corporate behaviour. Even if they are not actively seeking 'pollution havens', in many developing nations TNCs remain legally free to expose the water, air, soil and bodies of workers to hazardous substances at rates higher than those allowed in their home countries.

In addition to the problem of pollutants produced by TNCs operating in host countries, hazardous waste produced *in developed countries* has begun to find its way into developing nations. Some TNCs have sought to avoid the costs of mandated controls on hazardous waste storage in their home nation by transporting waste to countries which have few or no legal controls on hazardous waste disposal. In these cases, the TNCs involved are clearly acting to circumvent laws in their home nations rather than simply being passive beneficiaries of the difference in laws between home and host nations.

Reference

BLAKE, D. H. and WALTERS, R. S. (1976) *The Politics of Global Economic Relations*, Englewood Cliffs, NJ, Prentice Hall.

Source: Michalowski and Kramer, 1987, pp. 35–38

Reading C: *H. Jeffrey Leonard, 'Responses to environmental regulation'* _____

Despite the predictions of industrial flight, the evidence in the mid-1980s reveals that there are only a relatively small number of American industries whose international location patterns have been significantly affected by environmental regulations in the United States. A recent in-depth study of the particular industries most susceptible to industrial flight, conducted by the author, concludes that they tend to fall into three categories.

First, manufacturers of some highly toxic, dangerous, or carcinogenic products have not yet developed safer substitutes or adapted their technologies to meet environmental, workplace, health, and consumer standards in the United States. For these few industries, pollution and workplace-health standards have led to declining production in the United States and increasing production overseas. Strict regulation and growing public awareness of the dangers of hazardous and toxic substances [have] disrupted or halted production in the United States of asbestos, arsenic trioxide, benzidine-based dyes, certain pesticides, and a few other known carcinogenic chemicals.

Second, stricter American environmental regulations have contributed to the international dispersion of some basic mineral-processing industries, such as copper, zinc, and lead processing. This trend is enhanced by other factors, such as the changing availability of raw materials, other nations' requirements that minerals be processed in the country where they are mined, and various economic factors including low prices, high interest rates, and recessions.

Finally, environmental regulations may have increased, at least slightly, the trend toward worldwide purchasing of 'intermediate' organic chemicals – that is, organic chemicals needed for the manufacture of other chemical products. This shift is partly attributable to stricter pollution control laws, but more significantly to workplace health regulations. Although whole industries have not fled the United States, some large American chemical companies have increasingly gone abroad to produce or purchase intermediates needed for chemical production in the United States.

But [my] study emphasizes that these are exceptions to the norm. Most individual industries have responded to environmental regulations with technological innovations, changes in production processes or raw materials, more efficient process controls, and other adaptations that in the United States have proved more economical and less drastic than flight abroad. Even when these adaptations have not reduced regulatory burdens, the environmental problems have generally not been substantial enough to offset more traditional factors – market considerations, transportation, availability of raw materials, labour costs, political stability – that determine how most firms select overseas locations for branch-plant construction.

[...]

A most important point emphasized by the study is [that] there are no instances of industrial flight from the United States in industries where domestic demand is expanding and US producers enjoy technological superiority. Polyvinyl chloride and acrylonitrile are two notable examples of industries in which intense environmental regulatory pressures and adverse publicity in the 1970s did not prompt significant movements by US producers to other countries. This is true even though both are produced by major chemical firms with worldwide operations and even though other locational factors such as availability of raw materials and transportation costs have not severely hampered industry mobility. Ultimately, rapid expansion of domestic demand for these two chemicals and the concomitant incentives to invest in new technological developments have given these industries large cushions to help weather the onslaught of new regulations and public concern.

Thus, the study concludes that long-term domestic demand and technological outlook are significant variables affecting the way an industry responds to intense regulatory pressures and public concern. If demand is forecast to remain strong in spite of environmental problems and if technological gains appear possible through the application of research-and-development resources, flight is unlikely to occur. On the other hand, if demand is static or declining and no significant technological breakthroughs can be envisioned to reduce workplace-health, pollution, and other environment-related hazards, chances are greater that in its waning stages the industry will produce and source more and more abroad.

Source: Leonard, 1988, pp. 111–14

Reading D: Susan George, 'The debt boomerang'

Like many other debtors, Mexico exports raw materials and foodstuffs but it has also made a great effort to encourage export manufactures and has given every incentive to entice foreign firms to set up shop within its borders. This policy has been successful: today, just across the border from the United States, nearly 1800 factories employing half a million workers have been built. Most are North American, but the Germans and the Japanese have begun to install plants as well, and other countries are testing the waters. This is the *maquiladora* zone, for so-called 'in-bond' production which encourages cross-border sharing of production with almost no customs restrictions in either direction.

There are few environmental regulations in this zone either, and virtually none that Mexico can now afford to enforce. Ann Bourland, whose job with the Mexican state of Sonora is to help attract foreign companies, says that 'the red tape and the expense' of American environmental law is a powerful motivation for firms to come to Mexico:

In order to stay in the United States, a lot of these companies would have to invest in very expensive equipment to treat these chemicals and solvents and wastes. I've had a couple of companies come down solely for that reason.

The *maquiladora* area is now such an ecological disaster zone that the US embassy in Mexico has estimated it would cost $9 billion to clean up the border environment.

Even in the unlikely event of such an investment, the area would probably not stay clean for long. New companies, creating more pollution, would soon follow and the older ones would have scant reason to change their behaviour. Besides the lack of environmental standards, they have another powerful incentive for settling in the *maquiladora* zone. The International Monetary Fund, following the dictates of the export-led growth model, and on grounds of making Mexican exports more competitive, has demanded so many devaluations of the Mexican peso that workers are now paid below-subsistence wages. For example, in February 1990, a 48-hour week at the La Reynosa Zenith television plant netted workers the equivalent of US$26.16 at the then going dollar–peso exchange rate – just under 55 cents an hour. Testimony from workers like these stresses their exposure to dangerous chemicals and fumes, lack of protective clothing or other safeguards and serious health problems directly related to workplace conditions.

These companies, if they think about it, must be glad of Mexico's debt burden which helps to keep their own operating restrictions at a minimum and wages at rock-bottom, thus ensuring them millions of dollars in savings and much higher profits than they could obtain in their home countries. US trade unions are understandably less pleased with this situation since [tens of thousands of American workers have lost their jobs to lower-paid Mexican workers.]

Since about three-quarters of Mexico's debt is owed to US banks, the financial Establishment is also doubtless grateful for the debt management policies applied by the Fund and a compliant Mexican government, allowing the accumulation of a transferable surplus in dollars.

For ordinary people, however, crowded and unsanitary living conditions, social degradation and rampant environmental destruction have combined to make the *maquiladora* zone a reasonable facsimile of hell on earth. United States immigration policies can keep at least some of the social problems at bay, but ecological havoc recognizes no boundaries, as is becoming increasingly clear in the US states bordering on Mexico.

Tijuana, just the other side of the California border from San Diego, has grown from a sleepy, middle-sized town to a city of more than one million inhabitants, with an annual employment growth rate of 7 per cent. The combined metropolitan area of Tijuana–San Diego has swelled to 3.5 million people. More people means more sewage. Already, discharge of untreated sewage from Tijuana into the Pacific Ocean has forced the closure of California beaches on several occasions. In the coming decade, existing facilities are likely to be completely swamped whereas the area will have to deal with 140 million gallons (about 560 million litres) of raw sewage daily. Since there seems no hope of sufficient investment in treatment plants, much of this untreated waste will doubtless find its way to the Pacific as well.

Water sources vital to both sides of the border are dwindling and becoming [unusably salty]. Sixty million yearly border crossings in cars, trucks and buses foul the atmosphere. The *maquiladoras* themselves generate huge quantities of toxic wastes, many of which end up in California via the New River which flows northward. The Salton Sea, California's largest lake, in the Imperial Valley 'contains 100 industrial chemicals traceable to factories in Mexico', whereas the New River itself 'contains every disease known in the Western Hemisphere' according to a US Environmental Protection Agency official quoted in the *San Francisco Examiner.*

US states separated from Mexico by the Rio Grande are doing no better. Juarez, on the Texas border, has undergone the same chaotic growth as Tijuana and there is no sewage treatment system for its growing population, so waste used in the plants goes into a canal that is used for irrigating crops. Thus the risks from bacterial and industrial contaminants may be to the workers in the fields and consumers in both Mexico and the United States who eat foods grown in these areas. Falco Lake in Texas receives so much waste from Nuevo Laredo (Mexico) that it has become 'one of the largest sewage ponds in the United States' according to a Texas official. The same person notes that, 'As *maquiladoras* increase in number and production, we will get toxic waste in the river [Rio Grande] which we can't treat out and which is detrimental to the human system.' Not surprisingly, studies of 33 US counties that take their drinking water from the Rio Grande have already shown significantly higher rates of liver and bladder cancer than the US national average.

Land, sea and air are polluted by the activities and the waste products of 1800 *maquiladora* plants. Authorities in both countries are confronted with insoluble public health problems and millions of Mexican and US citizens are threatened with their consequences. The stage is now set for a major human and environmental disaster. Toxic substances, dangerous chemicals and flammable materials are trucked daily back and

forth across the border or left lying about on factory property without proper storage facilities. The whole border region is a Bhopal waiting to happen.

Source: George, 1992, pp. 25–7

By the late 1980s it had become clear that the shortcomings involved in the environmental policy strategies of the 1970s left many problems of pollution unresolved or growing worse. Trends on key environmental indicators suggested a widespread increase in pollution and an associated deterioration in the quality of the environment. For example, emissions of nitrogen oxides, which contribute to photochemical smog and acid rain, increased by an average of 12 per cent in OECD countries between 1970 and 1987, with some countries, for example Canada, the Netherlands, Norway and Portugal recording very large percentage increases.

[...]

Trends were not all negative, of course, between 1970 and 1990. The issue of sulphur dioxide emissions had been kept on the international policy agenda by the Scandinavian countries throughout the period, and partly as a result of this pressure and partly because of changes in the character of production technologies emissions of sulphur dioxide from OECD countries fell by 25 per cent between 1970 and the end of the 1980s. More importantly, perhaps, the link between sulphur dioxide emissions and GDP has been broken, so that trends in sulphur dioxide emissions in Canada, the US, Japan, France, Germany, Italy and the United Kingdom are now negatively correlated with trends in GDP [...] Moreover, behind many pollution problems there lies the inefficient use of energy, so that it is striking that energy intensity, or the use of energy resources per unit of GNP, has declined in most OECD countries between 1970 and 1990 and has only recorded rises in Spain, Portugal and Turkey as a result of their efforts to industrialize. This does not mean that

rich countries are necessarily using less energy per capita, but it does mean that energy use is not rising at the same rate as GDP. There is no reason to assume an automatic and unbreakable link between economic growth and increased energy consumption.

Despite these positive environmental trends, there was a widespread feeling by the end of the 1980s that the problems of pollution were growing more serious and that existing policy strategies failed adequately to deal with them. In 1988 and 1989 the Harris polling organization surveyed public opinion and leadership attitudes around the world. The survey encompassed fifteen countries in all parts of the globe and it found that in all but one country, Saudi Arabia, most of those surveyed thought that the environment had become worse in the previous decade. The Dutch National Environmental Policy Plan caught the prevailing mood when it claimed that current environmental problems pose risks not only to public health and the survival of many plant and animal species, but also to the functions of the environment that are essential for good social and economic development.

This sense of policy failure rested upon several observations concerning the results of previous policy approaches. Despite the establishment of regimes of environmental protection at both national and international level in the 1970s, new and potentially serious problems had emerged in the 1980s. Nitrate pollution, ozone depletion and global climate change were new, largely unanticipated, issues that existing policy process seemed unable to deal with. Moreover, the selective attention built into existing approaches meant that certain problems, most obviously soil contamination, had simply been ignored in the earlier policy strategies. As scientific instrumentation improved and environmental knowledge grew, so awareness of the scale and seriousness of problems increased.

This awareness was also accompanied by an increased understanding about the sources and consequences of pollution. The origins of pollution came to be seen not simply as a by-product of economic activity but also as something that reflected the policy priorities of the state, most notably in terms of economic support given to farmers and the encouragement given to road transport. Other policy sectors, outside of the designated area of the environment ministry or its equivalents, were thus seen to be pursuing policies that had environmental implications that could be of more importance than the policies of the environment ministry. If the sources were various, the consequences were widespread. The international scale of pollution problems posed hitherto unheard of challenges to the organization of the international system, premised as it was on the assumption of the sovereignty of nation-states [...] The economic consequences of permitting continued pollution also became apparent. A tolerance for pollution because of the costs of reduction was now being seen not as a way of successfully avoiding costs, but as a device by which costs were shifted across space, as with the UK's contribution to acid rain in Scandinavia, or across time, as with the contamination of groundwater that would prevent future generations from using certain sources. [...]

The net effect of these trends, it can be argued, was to intensify some of the distinctive characteristics of pollution control as an issue of public policy, and to change the structure of political processes that dealt with the problem of pollution. The policy response of the 1970s both by its decisions and by its non-decisions, had to give way to the new politics that emerged in the 1980s. As these processes took place they began to unravel the key assumptions of the 1970s' reform strategies, of which one central element was the belief that environmental policy stood in a simple trade-off relation with economic growth and development. According to the conventional wisdom of the 1970s, the pursuit of environmental policy involved a zero-sum game between the protection of the environment and a reduction in the costs of economic production: more of one necessarily means less of the other. The sharing of this assumption meant that less attention was necessarily given to creating and nurturing policy institutions whose task it was to find positive-sum solutions to policy problems, by which both environmental protection and economic prosperity could be secured.

[...]

Throughout it was implicit in the conventional wisdom that the administrative apparatus of the nation-state was the appropriate way to deal with the central problems of pollution. The European Economic Community treaty had not included provision for environmental regulation in its original version, and the Commission therefore found in the early 1970s that it had to establish its legal competence in the field by stressing the implications for international trade of environmental standards. Outside the framework of the EC, certain issues were dealt with by international treaty, but these clearly rested upon the assumption that independent nation-states should be sovereign so that their freedom of action could only be limited by their own voluntary agreement. The notion that the main processes of pollution control might take a cross-boundary form that would create international patterns of mutual interdependence had to await the emergence of acid rain, ozone depletion and global climate change.

The persistence and intensification of old pollution problems and the growth of new issues provided the occasion for a new politics of pollution to emerge in the 1980s. The new politics reflected the new scale of problems, including their international dimensions, new patterns of interaction within the relevant policy communities and, ultimately, new intellectual and ideological conceptions of the policy issues.

Source: Weale, 1992, pp. 23, 25–7, 28

Consuming spaces: global tourism

Chapter 5

by Erlet Cater

5.1 Far and near

Picture a scene at the turn of the century. The location is the Stepping Stones river-crossing in Dovedale, in what is now the Peak National Park: a tranquil setting as a small group of Victorian gentlefolk pick their way gingerly across the stones. Almost a century later, the same scene on a Bank Holiday weekend. Visitors approach the crossing from the two opposite banks, the mix of people is evident in terms of age, socio-economic background and family structure, mothers or fathers struggle with buggies and young children in tow. As many as two thousand people an hour now use the Stepping Stones on a busy Sunday in summer. They arrive from both the area immediately surrounding the Park, which has 16 million population within an hour's travelling time, as well as from further afield. Dovedale now receives 2 million visitors a year; the Peak National Park, as the most visited park in Europe, receives a staggering total of 22 million visitors a year (Anfield, 1993).

Another scene: London Croydon Airport, Saturday 6th October 1934. An Imperial Airways service is about to leave for Bangkok with eleven privileged passengers on board. It will arrive there eight days later, having landed at Paris, Brindisi, Athens, Alexandria, Cairo, Gaza, Baghdad, Basra, Sharjah, Karachi, Jodhpur, Delhi, Cawnpore, Allahabad, Calcutta and Rangoon en route. Each of the wealthy passengers will have spent £279 for their ticket, the equivalent of around £7800 at today's prices. Sixty years later to the day, the BA 009, one of the airline's latest long-range 747–400s, leaves London Heathrow Airport at 22.25, arriving in Bangkok 10 hours later, having flown direct. It carries a full load of 386 passengers, a large proportion of whom are flying on the first leg of a trip to Australia to 'Visit Friends and Relatives' (known as VFR traffic). The maximum full economy fare to Bangkok would have been £622; it is possible to purchase a special return fare to Australia for under £800.

Both of these examples are graphic illustrations of the shrinking of space in time–distance and cost–distance terms, enabling much larger numbers to travel, whether domestically or internationally, for business or for leisure. There has also been a very evident change in the social and economic backgrounds of such tourists: contrast the Victorian élite with day-trippers from Manchester, the colonial élite with the VFR passengers.

This chapter will examine how tourism has been an important force in a shrinking world. Not only in terms of greater distances travelled in shorter times, but also in making the unfamiliar more familiar, tourism has helped to change our notions of what is 'near' and what is 'far'. This compression of space by time has meant not only that far more people travel further to more destinations, but that different cultures have been brought together and juxtaposed, although not always to their mutual benefit. Writers such as Urry (1990) talk of the democratization of domestic and international travel over time. It will become evident, however, as we examine the organization of international tourism, the characteristics of tourists and those of the destination areas, that tourism is a force which arises from and gives rise to geographical unevenness and social inequality.

The global significance of tourism is beyond doubt. It is now considered to be the most important single item in international trade, having recently toppled the oil industry from that poll position. How has it grown to be of such importance? Section 5.2 examines the development of contemporary tourism from its early origins in pilgrimages and the Grand Tour, through the rise of the nineteenth-century British seaside resorts to the development of mass international tourism since the 1950s, with the advent of cheap air travel and the package holiday. It asks why people travel, how they acquire the images they have of faraway places and the nature of the tourist 'gaze' itself. Following that, section 5.3 explores the rapid growth of international tourism in the post-war period and the ways in which a plethora of new – and ever more remote – destinations have been 'opened up' by the tourist industry. Section 5.4 shifts the focus on tourism to that of the less developed countries and to the costs and benefits which it may bring – economic, cultural as well as environmental. While tourism offers the promise of economic development, however, local benefits are often limited where the tourist industry and infrastructure is owned or controlled by western multinationals. Finally, section 5.5 takes up the question of tourism and the shrinking world and acts as a conclusion to the chapter. Let us start, then, with the nature of tourism.

5.2   From Mohammed to the mountains

Travel is a long-established tradition, dating back to the days of the Ancient Greeks, where tourism was not so much a voyage of adventure as a trip in accordance with tradition and ritual, allied to sport (the Olympic Games attracted visitors from abroad as well as thousands of domestic ones) and religion. Pilgrimage has played an important role since those days: people visited the Oracle at Delphi from far afield; Chaucer's 'Canterbury Tales' relates the adventures of a band of pilgrims to Canterbury in the late fourteenth century; the significance of the Holy Land to Christians, Mecca to Muslims, Varanasi to Hindus and Lumbini to Buddhists have all led to considerable international as well as domestic flows of tourists. The distances are thus shrunk as people seek to tighten and reinforce all-important social and cultural links. The same might be said of those renewing ties of family and friendship. As Andrew Leyshon remarks in Chapter 1, nowadays the relative ease of reciprocal visits means that the process of long-distance migration is a less daunting prospect than in the nineteenth century.

Over the centuries the picture was largely one of small-scale, individual travel, limited to the wealthy and privileged. How did this become transformed into the mass tourism of the present? The seeds for today's package tours, following a set itinerary, were, ironically, sown in the élitist Grand Tour of the seventeenth century. This was essentially an educational and political institution involving a three-year exploration of the capitals, politics, culture and society of Western Europe.

Travel did not cease to be the preserve of the wealthy until the coming of the Industrial Revolution. Murphy (1985) documents how this brought about major changes in the scale and type of tourism development. Increased productivity, regular employment and growing urbanization gave people the means and the motivation to go on holiday. Tourism began to embrace a broader social spectrum, but, as Murphy suggests, a class differentiation was still very evident. The emerging middle class were able to take annual holidays, 'seeking relaxation and restoration' in areas of natural beauty or in established prestigious resorts. The working class, with longer working hours and a lower disposable income, became involved more gradually, at first by taking day-trips visiting the working-class resorts, such as Blackpool or Morecambe, close to the major urban centres. It was not until the second half of the nineteenth century that week-long breaks were pioneered in the textile industry of the north of England, where 'wakes weeks' involved the total closure of a mill during the customary holiday period. Urry (1990) describes how major difference of social tone were established between otherwise similar places and how working-class resorts quickly developed as symbols of mass tourism.

Technological innovations were not, of course, confined to industrial production. The advent of the railways, the automobile and the aeroplane have all played an enormous role in improving accessibility and thus transferring tourism from a small business, catering for the élite, into a mass market.

The increased movements as a result of the opening of the railways indicated a need for professional travel organizers. The first and most famous of these was Thomas Cook whose first railway excursion in 1841 for 570 passengers spawned a multinational concern, including traveller cheque facilities, generating more than US$600 million in sales over 350 locations worldwide. Such has been the overall influence of this company in promoting inexpensive travel for the masses that the phrase 'Cook's Tour' – to mean an organized, albeit cursory, trip – has become part of the English language. The influence of Thomas Cook and of American Express (established in 1850) in shrinking the world in terms of ease of financial transactions for tourists should not be underestimated. A handwoven carpet bought in Kathmandu (which will be referred to again later) can grace a living-room back in Kew without a single rupee physically changing hands.

The years since the Second World War have witnessed a virtual exponential growth in tourism. As well as dramatic changes in mobility due to the development of jet aircraft, enabling large numbers of people to move great distances at high speeds, there were other notable forces at work permitting the growth of tourism. More people had the leisure time and disposable income which were the necessary prerequisites for vacations. Travel companies established tours and created familiar environments for the uninitiated traveller. Mass bookings brought prices down to affordable levels such that working-class people could afford to break with tradition and replace the local resort holiday with package vacations in more distant destinations. Such locations were initially the preserve of the privileged few but, in the search for new resorts, the ripples (or tidal waves!) of institutionalized tourism spread ever outwards. The prestige element has much to do with such pressures. It is no longer sufficient to get a sun-tan in Margate, Marbella or even Miami; Malaysia or the Maldives will do nicely. Tourism to the latter location grew from 17,000 in the late seventies to almost 200,000 in 1990. Urry (1990) refers to holiday destinations which are consumed not because they are intrinsically superior, but because they convey taste or superior status. The moment they become more popular, they cease to have 'direct social scarcity', in Hirsch's terms, and the élite move on.

The search for the out-of-the-ordinary experiences has led to a spectacular increase in adventure tourism. Estimated to be growing at between ten and fifteen per cent per annum, this market segment is growing at double the average growth rate of tourism as a whole. It is now even possible to spend a holiday climbing Mount Everest.

5.2.1 I am a traveller, you are a tourist

We all have our personal view of what is a tourist, from either home or abroad. Visit London in the summer months, and it is impossible not to be aware of groups of camera-toting Japanese, shepherded around the sights by flag-carrying couriers, or the lines of foreign coaches disgorging visitors at the main attractions. Over the years the term tourist has acquired a somewhat derogatory association, to the extent that tourists are treated almost as aliens: witness, for example, the term 'grockles' applied by residents of the south-west of England to the annual influx of tourists during the summer months. Everyone can slander tourists with impunity; even tourists hate tourists. Those who would claim to be more discerning, declare that they are travellers and not tourists (see **Massey, 1995**). Why tourists and tourism have earned an unenviable reputation will be examined presently, but let us first consider definitions of tourism before examining why people travel.

It is difficult to reach a consensus as to what constitutes tourism and who is a tourist. This is because tourists themselves are a very mixed bunch of people with different socio-economic backgrounds, demographic characteristics and aspirations. They have many different reasons for travelling: we have already seen that these will range from religious to recreational purposes.

To confuse matters, tourism statistics include not only those who travel for pleasure, but also those who travel for business. The reason is that the relevant decision-makers in tourism who use the statistics need to know the overall numbers involved. Transport-carriers and hoteliers are obviously interested in business travel as well, because it generates a sizeable proportion of their business. It does mean, however, that the aggregate statistics do not tell us enough about the behavioural patterns of tourists to different destinations. The annual flow of three million plus tourists to Belgium, comprising a fair proportion of Eurocrats, will have a very different set of implications to the almost equivalent flow to New Zealand (a large proportion of VFR traffic) or to Tunisia (largely package tours). Aggregate statistics mask the fact that not only is there a variety of tourist types, but also a variety of tourist experiences.

5.2.2 Why travel?

Modern tourists travel essentially for pleasure, the emphasis being on a break with routine. Urry (1990) introduces us to the concept of the *tourist gaze* where part of the holiday experience is 'to gaze upon or view a set of different scenes, of landscapes or townscapes which are out of the ordinary. When we "go away" we look at the environment with interest and curiosity ... In other words we gaze at what we encounter.' An important part of the holiday experience is the anticipation of that encounter. There are large profits to be made from creating 'the space of the dream', as described by Lefebvre (1991), where 'everyday life is put into brackets and temporarily replaced by a different life.' He suggests that regions then become exploited for the purpose of, and by means of, the consumption of space. This consumption of space results from people demanding a qualitative space: 'the qualities that they seek have names: sun, snow, sea. Whether these are natural or simulated matters little.'

tourist gaze

This last fact is particularly substantiated by the success of the Centre Parc concept. At the Centre Parc in the heart of Sherwood Forest, which receives approximately 300,000 visitors a year, an artificial environment is created all year round within a geometric dome. The dome encloses a 'subtropical swimming paradise in a balmy climate of 84°F, tropical vegetation flourishes, creating an exciting and exotic environment that is close to fantasy' (Centre Parc promotional literature, 1993). The Jungle Cruise attractions of the Disney theme parks and the artificially created environment of the island of Sentosa, off Singapore, are similar examples. Ironically, it can be argued that, by recreating idyllic but fragile environments, the pressures on the 'real thing' are reduced.

The search is not only for the extraordinary in terms of space but also in terms of time. Heritage tourism is growing in popularity, despite claims that it is 'bogus history', glossing over the gross social and spatial inequalities which occurred at the time. Heritage tourism 'presents' history in both senses of the word. One heritage location which has enjoyed increasing popularity over recent years is the Ironbridge Gorge Museum which attracted 305,000 visitors in 1993. Time–space compression can be viewed, therefore, not only in terms of reduction of the time-distances in the present, but also in the sense of bringing the past to the present, albeit in a superficial sense. An advertisement for the Indonesian national airline, Garuda, promotes the ancient Hindu temple of Borobudur on Java with the slogan – 'Closed from 800 AD to 1983 AD. Now open from 6.00 am to 6.00 pm.'

Essential to the anticipation of a holiday is the image that the tourist has of the potential destination. This is a composite impression formed from all the information received. How the tourists respond to the information will depend on their personality, personal values and attitudes which, of course, will also condition what they are looking for in their choice of destination.

How do tourists arrive at the images they have of destinations? There is a wealth of sources, informal (such as the recommendations of others) and formal, which contribute to the overall image of a destination. The most obvious example of the latter is the promotional literature of the tour operators and tourist boards. Other formal sources include advertisements on radio and television as well as in newspapers and magazines.

Activity 1 Examine some promotional literature for tourism – either advertisements or brochures from tour operators. What language is used to convey the images? What pictures accompany the words? Who and what are left out, both in terms of the tourists targeted and in terms of the image conveyed of the destination?

Such snapshot images may be augmented by more in-depth literature such as travel guides and travel articles, as examined in **Massey (1995)**, as well as by holiday programmes on the radio and television giving supposedly impartial information.

An increasingly important source of images and expectations is that of the travel documentary. To aspire to be a latter-day Attenborough would have been an unattainable dream twenty years ago, but now the prospect of seeing the orang-utans of Sepilok or the bird-nest gatherers of the Gomontong caves in Sabah in Malaysia is a reality.

The published travel guides have moved on a long way since the conservative days of Baedeker, Fodor and the Blue Guides. The Lonely Planet series and the Rough Guides now make it easy for the independent traveller to assemble their own itinerary, to use public transport and to find local accommodation and eating facilities at unfamiliar destinations. Indeed the influence of such guides in beating tracks to hitherto unvisited areas should not be underestimated. The Lonely Planet Guides, in particular, have become somewhat of a bible for the independent tourist, who may be frustrated to find that many other guide-toting travellers are following precisely the same itinerary. The world shrinks as the unfamiliar becomes familiar.

How real is the image of a destination that is gleaned by whatever means? In promotional literature it is undoubtedly superficial and idealized. The place has become a commodity to sell and so nothing to detract from the image and reduce its value will be presented. Visual impressions are particularly superficial: pictures of idyllic tropical locations do not convey the high temperature and humidity that drain the visitors of energy once they step outside air-conditioned buildings. Nor do they include the buzz of mosquitoes and insects waiting to make a meal of the unprotected traveller. More seriously and fundamentally, they do not convey an image of the abject poverty of a large proportion of the inhabitants in many such destinations, nor of the abysmal human rights records of many of their governments. So, what people internalize from these images are idealized representations. Urry (1990) suggests that, even when the object fails to live up to its representations, it will often be the idealized image that stays in the mind, as what the tourist has really seen.

Often the abstraction of reality through the tourists taking photographs will, ironically, complete the circle. Again, as Urry (1990) suggests, 'Our memories of places are largely structured through photographic images and the mainly verbal text we weave around images when they are on show to others. The tourist gaze, thus irreducibly involves the rapid circulation of photographic images.' He also suggests, however, that 'post-tourists', reacting against the characteristics of mass consumption implicit in mass tourism, will recognize the glossy brochure for what it is – no more than a 'piece of pop culture'.

Having formulated images of different destinations, the tourists will augment these with more detailed, practical considerations such as type of accommodation, availability of services and attractions, cost and length of stay. They will then attempt to match them with their own needs and aspirations. These will, of course, depend on lifestyle and household structure. The needs of a family with young children will differ very markedly from those of a single person or of a retired couple, for example.

We now move from the specific to the general. The sum of all these individual decisions, however they are arrived at, results in the gargantuan industry that is of such enormous significance in effectively shrinking the world.

5.3   Here, there and everywhere

5.3.1   Growth and change

Every day in 1992 there were 1.3 million people travelling outside their home country. This figure is set to almost double by the year 2010 to give a total of 937 million international tourist arrivals worldwide a year. The growth rate of the late 1990s of 4.4 per cent per annum is expected to stabilize by the year 2000, when it will fall to around 3.5 per cent (see Table 5.1).

Table 5.1   Growth in international tourism arrivals and receipts, 1950–2010

	Arrivals		Receipts	
	Total in thousands	Average annual percentage increase over previous 10 years	Total in $US millions	Average annual percentage increase over previous 10 years
1950	25,282	–	2,100	–
1960	69,296	10.6	6,867	12.6
1970	159,690	8.7	17,900	10.0
1980	284,841	6.0	102,372	19.1
1990	454,800	4.5	255,000	9.5
2000*	637,000	4.4	Not available	
2010*	937,000	3.5	Not available	

Note: * Predicted figures

Source: Adapted from World Tourism Organization

There are considerable problems in predicting tourist flows due to a number of variables which will have considerable bearing on future trends. The first of these is that of technological advance in transportation, particularly in aviation. The introduction of jet aircraft in the late 1950s, the 'jumbo' jets in the late 1960s and the longer-range aircraft of the mid to late 1980s have all had an enormous impact on ease of travel in terms of both time and cost. It is suggested that the next generation of aircraft, capable of taking 600 passengers, will soon be with us. Before they become operational, however, two issues need to be resolved: firstly, whether the design and capacity of current airports will be able to accommodate such mega-carriers; secondly, whether air traffic control (ATC) constraints can be surmounted. It is all very well to point to advances such as on-board satellite ATC links, but bottlenecks are bound to occur whilst the poor countries of the African and South Asian continents cannot afford their side of the satellite link.

It is possible to hypothesize, therefore, that certain routes – and therefore links between countries – are shrunk more than others. The globe, is thus effectively distorted away from its spherical shape in conceptual terms, much as we saw in Chapter 1. This is nothing new. Historically, those nations which have been convenient stop-over points on major long-haul routes, such as Singapore, Bangkok and Hong Kong, have seen a sustained growth in tourist arrivals. Remote island-states, off the international air routes, are a different story. If the airlines do not arrive, neither do the tourists. It is also interesting to note how past colonial links are perpetuated in terms of present-day airline route structures. British Airways has a marked presence in East, Southern and, to a lesser extent, West Africa whereas Air France concentrates on routes to North, Central and West African ex-colonies such as the Ivory Coast and Senegal. This, of course, has important socio-cultural and economic implications.

Despite this emphasis on air travel, it must be remembered that most tourism journeys are made by car. Continued advances in the safety, comfort and fuel efficiency of road transport will all have a rôle to play. Similarly, advances in rail transportation will be significant. The development of an integrated high-speed rail network throughout Europe, together with the opening of the Channel Tunnel, will have the effect of further concentrating economic activity in the so-called 'blue banana' stretching from the Midlands to Milan. What will the pressures of a population of around 150 million in that megalopolis be on the Alpine National Parks, for example? It can be seen, therefore, that distances are not shrunk evenly but differentially. This is true not just in terms of physical links, but also culturally, as will be seen presently.

How will cultural, political and economic factors shape the tourism patterns of tomorrow? How will fashion and taste change in the future? The 'in' destinations of the 1990s include Vietnam, Sarawak and Sabah, Bhutan and Patagonia. It is possible even to take a package tour to climb Mount Everest – if you have £22,000 to spare.

At the other end of the market, Spain, after a brief downturn in tourist arrivals partially attributable to a 'lager lout' image, receives over 35 million tourists, or almost eight per cent of the world total. How much this can be attributed to a revamping of the image of the Costas can only be guessed at, but it does suggest that notions of a *product cycle for tourism*, whereby tourist areas move through various stages of evolution from discovery to decline, is too simple. It is undeniable that resorts do experience cycles, for example the decline in popularity of bucket-and-spade resorts such as Weston-super-Mare. A simple cycle, however, tells us nothing of possible rejuvenation as a result of nostalgia. For example, Urry suggests how resorts might respond to falling demand:

tourism product cycle

Resorts will have to change quite dramatically if they are going to survive. Recent advertising by the Isle of Man on British TV indicates one possible way of responding. The advert states that 'You'll look forward to going back', to experiencing a seaside holiday as remembered from one's childhood. Time has supposedly stood still in the Isle of Man and the advert plays on our nostalgia for childhood, when pleasures were experienced more directly and were less contaminated by an apparent playful sophistication. Elsewhere I have argued that 'Resorts should not try to resist the trend to 'nostalgia' … Rather than trying to be modern and failing, they would do better to embrace it self-consciously … Soon there may be nothing in the Isle of Man to look forward to going back to.'

(Urry, 1990, pp. 102–3)

Diversification away from a single market sector is also another possibility; for example, many destinations promote conference tourism as a means of overcoming fluctuations due to seasonality as well as cycles in demand.

Changes in fashion and taste are only part of the picture. Political factors are also important influences on tourism patterns. What political changes will occur to influence these flows? How will the tremendously significant changes of the end of the twentieth century filter through the system? These types of changes are very difficult to predict or to incorporate. Who could have envisaged, for example, the opening up of the Soviet bloc, both in terms of tourist destinations and in terms of an enormous number of potential travellers? How could we have foreseen an integrated tourism circuit between Israel and Jordan? On the downside, it is difficult to anticipate the disruptive effects of military and civil disturbance, such as the Gulf war, the Tamil uprising in Sri Lanka and the fundamentalist Muslim bombing campaigns in Egypt and Algeria. While new destinations are opened up, others are closed down.

Political influences also include the decisions of governments to restrict entry – for example, Bhutan only admits 2500 visitors a year – or to open up hitherto closed areas to tourism, such as Mustang in Nepal and Arunachal Pradesh in north-east India. A resort hotel has been opened at Biak Beach on Irian Jaya, Indonesia (the western half of the island of Papua New Guinea), and the 'Longhouse Hilton' started operation in summer 1994 close to the Iban longhouses near Lubok Antu in Sarawak. The impact of such a development on a traditional indigenous society can be imagined. It is interesting to hypothesize that in the former case tourism is being used as a conscious measure by the Indonesian government to strengthen central control over outlying areas.

How will economic fortunes change to determine which countries of the world will become the prime tourist generators of the future? The number of Japanese international tourists is expected to rise through the 1990s to reach nearly twenty million by the year 2001, an average annual growth rate of ten per cent. The newly industrializing countries are also emerging as significant tourist generators; three of them – Mexico, South Korea and Singapore – figure in the top twenty nations in terms of tourism expenditure (see Table 5.2).

Table 5.2 The top twenty generating countries of international tourism in 1990, based on international tourism expenditures

		Tourism expenditure (US$ billion)	Rank 1980	Average annual growth rate 1980-90 (%)
1	USA	38.7	2	14.1
2	Germany	30.1	1	3.9
3	Japan	24.9	6	18.4
4	UK	19.8	3	11.1
5	Italy	13.8	13	21.9
6	France	13.5	4	8.4
7	Canada	8.4	9	10.4
8	Netherlands	7.4	5	4.7
9	Austria	6.3	10	8.2
10	Switzerland	6.0	11	9.9
11	Sweden	6.0	12	10.4
12	Belgium	5.7	8	5.6
13	Mexico*	5.4	7	2.6
14	Spain	4.3	18	13.2
15	Australia	4.1	15	8.9
16	Denmark	3.7	16	9.1
17	Norway	3.4	17	10.0
18	South Korea	3.2	28	24.6
19	Finland	2.8	22	17.7
20	Singapore	1.4	29	15.9

Note: * For Mexico, data are not strictly comparable due to change in methodology as from 1982.

Source: Cooper *et al.,* 1993; data from World Tourism Organization

It can be seen from this brief discussion of some of the factors determining the patterns of international tourism that the shrinking of the world in tourism terms has been uneven. In terms of who can travel and where the tourists go, the picture is also one of unevenness and inequality.

5.3.2 Where do the tourists come from?

The distribution of the world's tourists in terms of origin is very skewed, whether we think about it in spatial, economic, social or demographic terms. The industrialized nations account for the great bulk of the world's tourists. Four countries alone – the USA, West Germany, Japan and the UK – which account for only around ten per cent of the global population, generate almost half of the total international tourism expenditure. Table 5.2 shows the top twenty generating nations in 1990, compared with their 1980 ranking. Where the tourists come from has important repercussions for tourism destinations as it dictates their expectations, behaviour and consequent impact, as will be seen presently. Obviously those who travel will have higher disposable incomes than those who do not.

In addition to economic factors dictating who travels, and indeed allied to such factors, are considerations of gender. How free are women to travel, particularly on their own? Family responsibilities coupled with financial restrictions mean that freedom is often considerably curtailed. There is very little data on male:female participation rates in tourism, but one country where such participation rates were particularly transparent during the 1970s and early 1980s was that of Japan.

The dominance of Japanese male tourists was particularly evident to certain destinations in South East Asia, notably Taiwan, South Korea and latterly, Thailand, for sex tourism. Of half a million Japanese tourists who flocked to Seoul each year, 95 per cent were men. The pattern has changed somewhat more recently: the share of female to total Japanese tourists rose to 39 per cent by 1990 and the percentage of female independent Japanese tourists to 15 per cent. The OL (office lady [*sic*]) group, aged 20–40 with a higher proportion of disposable income is accounting for the highest rate of growth of Japanese tourists.

In addition to financial constraints, what are the constraints on the independent woman traveller in terms of perceived and actual threats to safety and security? It has been suggested that these have been exaggerated and, indeed, even exploited:

Our concerns about safety were exploited. While men operated on 'Orientalist' assumptions about lecherous Arab men who treated 'their' women 'like dogs', they failed to realize they were flexing their own patriarchal muscle. Since most women automatically weigh the potential danger in any public space, whether it's on a Birmingham street or in a Botswana village, we were already more sensitive to the different cultural expectations in the countries we were travelling through.

Yet until very recently women wishing to travel independently have been encouraged to equate venturing abroad with male conquest. European history is littered with examples of intrepid male explorers and only very recently have the chronicles of their female counterparts been unearthed.

(Wheelwright, 1993, pp. 26–7)

But the fact remains that such feelings may deter a woman from travelling on her own in the first place. There are also socio-cultural implications for both host and guest. Amongst traditional Islamic societies, for example, the very presence, let alone mode of dress, of female tourists automatically sets them apart from that society in terms of their apparent freedom. Advice in minimizing both risk and impact is given by a Bristol travel company in the form of seminars for women travellers and is incorporated in *The Handbook for Women Travellers* (Moss and Moss, 1991).

Tourism is also a selective process as far as age is concerned. This has an obvious bearing on stage in life-cycle, family structure and disposable income which in turn will affect the type of destination visited, distance travelled and frequency of holidaying. A recent survey found that the 45–64 age bracket was more likely than any other age group to have more than one holiday a year. In married middle age, in particular, holiday entitlement, income and mobility are often at a maximum, and this is reflected in the frequency of holiday-taking. This age group certainly dominates the more expensive, specialist type of holiday and is obviously a clear market segment for tour operators to target.

We move from those who can take more than one holiday a year to those who, for various reasons, cannot take even one. Significant sections of the population are marginalized. This may be due to the type of holiday on offer. Urry (1990) points out that certain social groups do not fit into the stereotypical characteristics of a 'family holiday', 'romantic' holiday' or 'fun holiday' and are consequently poorly served by the tourist industry. It may also be due to the fact that they are economically weak or otherwise disadvantaged (Murphy, 1985). This group will include low-income families (often lone-parent) as well as disabled people. Third-party intervention, in the form of social tourism, which involves the organization and provision of vacations for these groups in society, is often the only way of ensuring that such groups have a break.

5.3.3 Where do tourists go?

In the same way that they generate the bulk of the world's tourists, the higher levels of development of the industrialized nations means that they also attract the greatest proportion of the tourist arrivals. Europe alone accounts for around sixty per cent, the developing world for only around twenty per cent. What is significant, however, is that the developing countries are experiencing above-average rates of growth, of around six per cent a year on average, almost twice that of the developed nations. For certain individual countries these growth rates have been even more striking. International tourist arrivals to Nepal, for example, rose from only six thousand arrivals in 1962 to over a quarter of a million by the early 1990s. In 1990 China ranked eleventh in the world in terms of tourist arrivals (see Table 5.3). As increasingly remote destinations are brought into the locus of international tourism, we can again see how the world is shrinking. But political change can be rapid: between 1990 and 1995 Czechoslovakia split into two, the USSR ceased to exist and tourism to Yugoslavia virtually ceased because of the civil war.

Table 5.3 The top twenty destination countries for international tourism in 1990, based on numbers of international arrivals

		Tourist arrivals (million)	Rank in 1980	Average annual growth rate 1980–90 (%)
1	France	50.0	1	5.2
2	USA	39.8	3	5.9
3	Spain	34.3	2	3.9
4	Italy	26.7	4	1.9
5	Hungary	20.5	9	8.1
6	Austria	19.0	5	3.2
7	UK	18.0	7	3.8
8	Germany	17.0	8	4.4
9	Canada	15.3	6	1.7
10	Switzerland	13.0	10	3.9
11	China	*10.5	13	6.3
12	Greece	8.9	18	6.3
13	Czechoslovakia	*8.1	17	4.8
14	Portugal	8.0	21	11.5
15	Yugoslavia	7.9	12	2.1
16	USSR	7.2	15	2.6
17	Mexico	6.4	19	4.4
18	Hong Kong	5.9	27	13.0
19	Netherlands	5.8	20	7.6
20	Turkey	5.4	43	19.3

Notes: * Preliminary estimate. Since 1990, both the USSR and Czechoslovakia have split.

The top five destinations as measured by international tourism receipts in rank order are: the USA, France, Italy, Spain and the UK.

Source: Cooper *et al.*, 1993; data from World Tourism Organization

Why have certain countries experienced such rapid rates of growth but not others? Here we must consider a whole range of factors which constitute what might be loosely termed *tourism resources*. These include not just facilities in terms of infrastructure (roads, electricity, water supply etc.) and superstructure (airport buildings, hotels, restaurants etc.), but also natural attractions in terms of landforms, flora and fauna, climate and attractive beaches. Many 'third world' destinations, such as The Gambia, have a comparative advantage in attracting winter-sun tourists in the winter months as they are located largely within the tropical and sub-tropical latitudes. So-called *hospitality resources* refer to the cultural wealth of a country, such as arts, architecture, literature, music, dancing and the welcome extended to the tourists. Obviously, the marketing strategies of tourism firms and boards will also have a significant role to play. In terms of engendering a hospitable welcome, for example, the Wales Tourist Board is carrying out its 'Welcome Host' programme amongst the trade and public with the maxim 'You never get a second chance to make a first impression'. Conventionally, the marketing mix is thought of in terms of four Ps – product, price, promotion and place (Cooper *et al.*, 1993).

We must also consider flows of tourists within countries as well as between countries, whether of international or domestic tourists. Tourism is not spread evenly throughout a destination country in either time or space. Seasonality is usually the result of change in climate over the calendar year, a destination will experience peaks or troughs in tourist arrivals accordingly. Obvious examples are those of a ski resort or a beach destination.

tourism enclaves

In terms of spatial distribution, there will be inevitable concentrations of tourists at the main attractions and resort areas. These characteristics further illustrate the selectiveness of tourism as a process. There has been considerable debate about the role of *tourism enclaves* and resort areas such as the Nusa Dua area of Bali in Indonesia or Batu Ferringi, Penang Island in Malaysia. On the one hand they serve to concentrate the adverse impacts of tourism to clearly defined and confined areas but, on the other, any positive impacts which might have arisen locally will be likewise confined. Glaring examples of this are the Club Mediterranean resorts, the ultimate in holiday 'capsules' which operate as completely self-contained units. Similar examples are some of the resort islands in the Maldives where even money is dispensed with, having been exchanged for plastic beads.

In terms of the main attractions, there will inevitably be a limit, or carrying capacity which, if exceeded, will prejudice both the enjoyment of the visitor, and the maintenance of the attraction. The title of a report from the Federation of Nature and National Parks of Europe – 'Loving them to Death?' – indicates the likely effects of such popularity without proper management. In Box 5.1 John Anfield describes the problems of management in the Peak National Park, focusing specifically on Dovedale which was mentioned in the introduction; note that any development which is allowed must adhere to a strict set of conditions. In the UK National Parks in general, a prospective loss of environmental quality and, consequently, tourist attraction has been strong grounds for refusing applications. One such example is the refusal to allow Rio Tinto Zinc to undertake alluvial working in the Mawddach estuary, Snowdonia.

Whilst certain localities are suffering the effects of too many visitors, however, others are anxious to attract more. Many tourism authorities and boards, national and regional, are actively contributing towards the effective shrinking of distances by attempting to reduce the unevenness of development through the promotion of tourism. This is very evident in the case of several small developing nations, who, in the absence of any other significant resources, are anxious to capitalize on their tourism attractions to earn badly needed foreign exchange. Within the EU, An Bord Fàilte (the Irish Tourist Board) receives support from the European Regional Development Fund to implement its tourism policies. These aim to create employment, improve the balance of payments, increase Gross Domestic Product (GDP), generate extra tax revenue and contribute to regional development.

Activity 2 Now turn to Reading A, 'The longer-term effects of subsidized investment on tourism in the Republic of Ireland' by Kevin Hannigan. This article indicates that the economic, socio-cultural and environmental effects of tourism are very mixed. The economic benefits of tourism have tended to be over-stressed and, at the same time, the socio-cultural and environmental costs have been

down-played. When you are reading the extract, note these facts and answer the
following questions:

(a) What were the main attractions of increased tourism to the Irish government?

(b) Whilst the number of tourists has increased, what have been the characteristics
of this growth?

(c) What factors suggest that this growth might not be sustainable?

Box 5.1 Tourist pressure in the Peak National Park

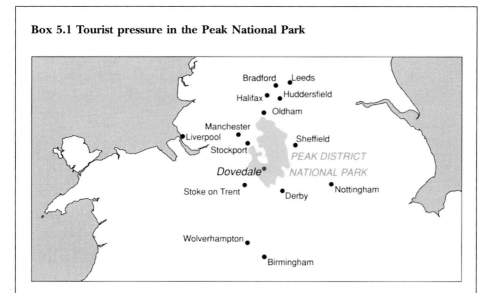

'The Peak National Park was established in 1951 with an area of 555 square
miles. It has 38,000 people living within its boundaries, and about 16 million
more live within one hour's travel time.

The result of its particular location in the north of England, particularly
between the conurbations and Manchester and Sheffield means that the Peak
National Park is under the greatest pressure. It has about 22 million visits per
year which makes it the most visited national park in Europe, and the second
most visited in the world. [...]

The national park is also under intense pressure for development of housing,
recreation developments, and even quarrying. The National Park Authority only
owns 4 per cent of the land. About 12 per cent is owned by the large national
conservation charity, the National Trust.

The Peak National Park has a board, with one-third appointed by the national
government and two-thirds by the local government in the area. It has a budget
of about £7 million per year (50 per cent central government, 25 per cent local
government and 25 per cent direct income) and has a staff of more than 200.
Apart from [the role of the board in providing] information, interpretation,
rangers, field staff, etc., the strongest powers are as a planning authority. Any
building in the park has to be authorised by the park authority and more than
1,000 applications a year are so received. More than 80 per cent of applications
are approved, but usually with tight conditions controlling materials, siting and
design. There is an appeal system against refusal. Normally, no compensation is
payable for a refusal. [...]

(*continued overleaf*)

(Box 5.1 continued)

Dovedale [in the south of the Peak National Park] first became famous 300 years ago after a well-known local figure described it in a book on fishing. The River Dove winds through a series of magnificent limestone dales and then into a deep gorge. [...]

Most visitors were arriving by car and parking in a very visible car park. They were causing traffic congestion and parking problems as well as eroding footpaths and valley sides – in a nationally important wildlife and geological site.

Visitors have been a mixed blessing for local people too. Owners of the car park and caravan site and those providing tourist accommodation earn money from them. However, farmers have suffered in their everyday work with problems from traffic jams, trespassers, disturbance to sheep and litter left by visitors.

Park managers could see that the carrying capacity of the valley was being exceeded and that action was needed. Although the national park owns no land in Dovedale, it is responsible for working with landowners and other organisations to make sure that the landscape beauty is conserved. A management plan was produced and was discussed with landowners, including the National Trust [...], as well as with visitors and local people. There was general agreement that action was needed to ease the problems, to improve visitor facilities, reduce pressure on the landscape and wildlife, enhance the dale and help the local community.

Elements of the plan have been implemented jointly by the national park, landowners and local councils. Car parking within the dale has been reduced from 750 to 400 spaces and new, smaller landscaped car parks have been built within three kilometres.

A ten-year scheme of footpath restoration was carried out. An all-weather path was created allowing visitors to enjoy the dale throughout the year without causing erosion. Only natural limestone has been used so that the path blends into the landscape. The work was carried out by local contractors and volunteers.

Traffic management was improved with a total ban on cars at the busiest times. Further improvements will be seen if current proposals are accepted to ban traffic on one stretch throughout the whole year. This will allow easy and safe year-round access for walkers, families (especially those with baby buggies) and people with disabilities. Other aspects of the project include improved ranger services, better public toilets and information for visitors, an environmental education service based at the nearby youth hostel and the restoration of eroded areas.

The scheme has been successful in reducing the number of visitors to the area and in increasing the capacity of the footpath for walkers in a way that is sensitive to the environment. Traffic congestion has been reduced, local peoples' needs have been taken into account, and the nature and landscape of Dovedale has benefited. The Dovedale project has also demonstrated the value of working in partnership, an approach that involves listening, understanding, discussion, negotiation and joint funding by all the partners concerned.'

Source: Anfield, 1994, pp. 90–4

Summary of section 5.3

o   Tourism discriminates. In terms of who can travel, the developing world contains three-quarters of the world's population and yet generates probably under ten per cent of the world's tourists. Within individual countries there are marked discrepancies between those who may manage two or more breaks a year and those who, for one reason or another, cannot get away at all.

o   In terms of where people go, there are obvious differences between destinations that are too popular for their own good and those which are anxious to attract the rounds of expenditure and investment that tourism can bring. What might appear a benefit at one level to one interest will often be a cost to another. Nowhere is this more evident than in the case of tourism development in the less developed world.

Let us examine this in more detail.

5.4   'Third world' involvement in tourism: incorporation or marginalization?

5.4.1   Calling the tune

Tourism offers an attractive prospect for 'third world' nations to enhance their foreign exchange earnings. Small states and island economies, in particular, view it as a welcome opportunity for *economic diversification* away from an over-reliance on primary products which are very vulnerable to the vagaries of the global economy. An example is the Caribbean island of Dominica where agricultural products account for 60 per cent of merchandise exports, and bananas alone for 90 per cent of those agricultural exports. The removal of protection for Windward Island fruits in the UK, as a consequence of the formation of the Single European Market, will have dire ramifications for the Dominican economy. The island is consequently promoting tourism based on its natural attractions as an attempt to diversify away from a virtual monoculture economy.

economic
diversification

Other economic benefits include the creation of jobs, as tourism is a labour intensive industry, and investment opportunities. Both of these have direct, indirect and induced effects. The direct results arise in those establishments which directly receive tourist expenditure, for example hotels. These establishments, however, buy in everything from food to electricity thus generating indirect employment and investment in those suppliers. Finally, induced effects arise through the spending in the local economy of money earned directly and indirectly. The higher the degree of local involvement in these three rounds of tourism expenditure, the greater the local tourism benefits, at least in theory. Unfortunately, the net benefits are substantially reduced by the significant foreign involvement in tourism to less developed countries.

What forms does this involvement take? As was described in section 5.3, the bulk of the world's tourists originate in the developed countries. Consequently their tour, travel and accommodation needs are largely co-ordinated by firms in those countries. It follows that such companies have become predominant in the control of international tourist movements. They can influence the volume of tourist flows to any one market, as they control the key link in the tourist flow chain – contact with the potential tourists. In addition, their expertise, marketing connections and capital resources give them an overwhelming competitive advantage over local tourism operators. Although the international tourism sector did not reach the mass production stage until quite recently, it is already dominated by transnational tourism corporations.

The three main organizational branches of the tourism industry are transport companies, the hotel sector and tour companies. They have all become increasingly transnational in their operations over the past two decades to the extent that their interests dominate the development of tourism in the 'third world'. The turnover of these large transnational groups will often approach the entire GDP of an individual country, so, not surprisingly, as Chapter 2 noted, they are powerful agents in further centralizing economic power.

An examination of each of these three major sectors reveals not only how each is dominated by interests in the developed countries, but also how the structure of the tourist industry at the international and destination levels leads towards monopolistic organization. The sectors themselves are not mutually exclusive. There is an increasing trend towards the vertical integration of the varied tourist services into larger corporate entities; Brittania Airways, for example is a subsidiary of Thomson Travel. Let us examine the market dominance by each sector in turn, beginning with transport companies.

Air transport is obviously one of the key operations in international tourism. In most less developed countries over 70 per cent of tourist arrivals are by air. Remote island locations, such as Hawaii or French Polynesia where 90 per cent of all tourists arrive by air, are even more dependent on airline operations.

Airlines based in the developed countries are by far and away the dominant carriers. Recent years have witnessed the emergence of the mega-carriers such as British Airways. They can influence the number of tourists arriving at specific destinations through marketing strategies such as discounting seats and changing seating allocations on specific flights. They also determine the viability of intermediate destinations as stop-over points. They have a strong competitive advantage over 'third world' airlines. It has been estimated, for example, that Kenya Airways carries less than ten per cent of holiday visitors arriving in Kenya. Not only do the companies of developing countries have little direct access to the tourist-generating markets located in the industrialized nations, but also it is estimated that their operating costs are 30 per cent higher. Fuel, servicing and training are purchased at high prices from countries in the industrialized nations. Air transport equipment (aircraft and ground equipment) is very expensive and is produced in a very small number of industrialized countries. The development of national carriers in these countries therefore requires heavy capital investment and very high foreign exchange costs. It is not surprising, therefore, that despite a few success stories amongst the national carriers of the newly industrialized countries (for example, Singapore Airlines), the national airlines of most 'third world' countries are little more than heavily subsidized flag-carriers.

Similar dominance by transnationals is found in other spheres of tourist transport such as sea cruises and car hire. Witness, for example, the pre-eminence of Hertz and Avis. The flows of tourism finance are also dominated by firms such as American Express and Thomas Cook.

The hotel industry shows a similar pattern of dominance by transnationals based in the developed world. Of the top fifty hotel chains in the world, thirty have their headquarters in the USA and account for more than half of the total rooms provided by that top fifty. As an estimated 100,000 hotel rooms are added every year to the total in hotels owned or managed by these major chains, their global significance is undeniable. The top chains have extensive interests in 'third world' locations. The repatriation of profits and of wages of managerial staff, together with import leakages resulting from the centralized purchasing policies of major chains, all considerably reduce the net earnings from tourism in the less developed world. The extent of these *foreign exchange leakages* is illustrated in Figure 5.1.

foreign exchange leakages

The final main organizational branch of the tourism industry is that of the *tour companies*. Half of UK tourists travelling overseas do so on inclusive tours. Tour operators have revolutionized international tourism since the 1960s through their successful packaging of transport, accommodation and additional services. This has raised the potential volume of sales far above that which can be expected from supplying a single service such as a ticket or hotel room on its own. The bargaining power of tour companies with the suppliers in the tourist industry has consequently been considerably enhanced. They can lower the costs by negotiating lower air fares and hotel accommodation prices through their ability to guarantee block bookings.

The past twenty years have witnessed the situation whereby a few tour operators have grown to the size of international companies, controlling large percentages of the market: in the UK, for example, the top three operators in 1993 – Thomson, Airtours and Owners Abroad – accounted for over 70 per cent of the UK inclusive tour market.

It is evident, therefore, that once again the developing nations are at a disadvantage. The actual location of these companies in the main markets places them at a strong initial advantage. Most holidays are bought 'sight unseen' by the tourist, so it follows that the image or perceived attractions of a destination are critical factors in directing tourist flows. Inevitably it is the larger tour operator companies based in the developed countries, with their direct sales and marketing links within these countries, which can successfully promote destinations through extensive advertising. Conversely, indigenous small-scale local operators within the developing world with their limited resources, limited experience and few connections within the industry, cannot hope to compete with the extensive image, power and resources of multinational companies.

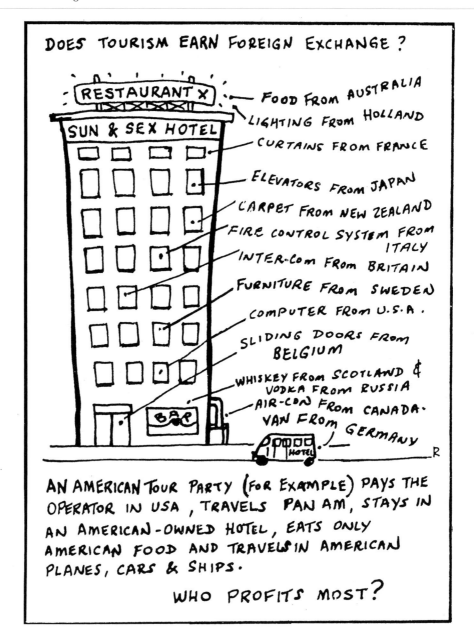

Figure 5.1 Foreign exchange leakages (Source: Bird, 1989)

There are two major implications of this pattern of dominance in the international organization of tourism. Firstly, the decisions affecting destinations are made from afar. They are more likely to be concerned with profits than with the impacts on host environments and populations. Secondly, as mentioned previously, the leakages consequent upon the location of headquarters of multinational tourism companies in the industrialized nations considerably reduce net tourism receipts in the less developed economies. Britton (1982) estimated these leakages to be of the order of 55 to 60 per cent of the inclusive tour retail price paid by tourists in their home country if a foreign airline is used. If both the airline and hotel used are foreign-owned, this figure rises to between 75 and 78 per cent.

It can be seen that the pattern of transnational involvement in tourism is a prime example of the global reach of such companies discussed in Chapter 2. These corporations have placed considerable investment into the establishment of computerized booking and reservation networks which serve to further concentrate their power and influence.

But what of the economic benefits that are generated locally? In a labour-plentiful, capital-scarce situation, surely the labour-intensity of tourism will result in gainful employment for a significant proportion of the local population? We must, however, look at the nature of that employment. Whilst tourism is a labour-intensive activity, most of the employment generated is low-paid, requiring low skill levels and with poor productivity. As many of the tasks involve housekeeping and food and beverage preparation, it is not surprising to find that women employees outnumber males. Urry (1990), for example, notes that the 'operative' positions (cooks, waiting and bar staff, kitchen hands, domestic staff and cleaners) are overwhelmingly filled by women. A qualification to this view must be made, however. In most 'third world' destinations we find that there is a further differentiation, with those service jobs with perceived extra benefits and greater prospects (notably waiting) being male-dominated; the more menial tasks, with little contact with the tourists and little prospects for extra reward and remuneration in the form of tips, are female-dominated. The jobs occupied by females are also frequently part-time positions with little opportunity to develop a wide range of skills and experience, or to become functionally flexible as full-time employees who are more likely to be male (Urry, 1990).

A further problem of tourism to 'third world' destinations is that of seasonality. It is commonplace to find staff taken on only for the peak months and dismissed in the off-season (for example, during the monsoon season in South Asia). If there was a degree of complementarity between different types of activity this would not be a problem, but often the period of maximum activity in agriculture coincides with the tourism peak. This highlights a further problem – the diversion of labour away from agriculture. Again, this would not be a problem if there were a surplus of agricultural labour, but there have been examples of where such diversion has led to a drop in agricultural production. There may be situations where tourism conflicts directly with other forms of economic activity. There are many such examples in National Parks and protected areas, where the local population may be denied access to their traditional practices of agriculture, nomadic pastoralism (for instance the Maasai of East Africa) and the gathering of fuel and building material. A graphic illustration of such a conflict between conservation and economic livelihood is that of the Taj Mahal in India where, in an attempt to reduce damage to the monument from industrial pollution, local factories are being threatened with closure and a consequent loss of thousands of jobs (see Figure 5.2).

Figure 5.2 *(Source: The Guardian, 15 November 1993)*

Taj Mahal stirs up anger after factories close

A jobs-versus-tourism row is dividing the people of Agra. Ajoy Bose reports

The Taj Mahal is at the centre of a fierce row after an order by India's Supreme Court closed more than 200 factories which pose a pollution hazard to the country's most cherished historic monument and biggest tourist draw.

Environmentalists and tourism officials are delighted that the monument's once glistening white marble will no longer be stained yellow by fumes from nearby factories.

But the court order spells disaster for more than 200,000 workers. With assembly elections scheduled later this week in Uttar Pradesh, the controversy over the Taj, in the heart of the northern state's industrial belt, has overtaken the region's traditional caste and communal politics.

Opinion is evenly divided in Agra, the industrial township where the Taj and other historic monuments stand near hundreds of iron foundries, chemical and rubber plants, and fertilizer units.

"The Taj is dying," Roshan Lal, a rickshaw-puller, said. "If the smoke from the factories is allowed to spoil the Taj for very much longer, tourists will stop coming here and we will all die."

But there is anger and resentment in the overcrowded and impoverished workers' colonies at what most consider an arbitrary move to push them towards starvation. "There is no justice in letting human beings starve to death just to save a stone monument," Babu Ram, an iron foundry worker, said.

Since the court order last August, workers backed by local industrialists have held demonstrations. In Ferozabad, an industrial town near Agra, the mood is even uglier. There is little tourism there and more than 100 factories have closed.

At first, defiant workers refused to implement the court order and the authorities had to send the fire brigade to douse factory fires.

In the meantime, political leaders and candidates in the elections are making promises to both the workers and the tourism industry.

One candidate has been known in the past two weeks to have assured industrial workers that his party would reopen the factories if voted to power. He has also promised rickshaw-pullers and tourist guides that Agra would be turned into the leading tourist city in the country.

More trouble is expected as the tourism department goes ahead with an ambitious plan to acquire hundreds of acres of land around the monument for a huge free national park.

This would mean not only the closure of many more factories, but the uprooting of several adjoining villages where angry residents have already filed court cases against the government to halt the park.

In a separate row, the city authorities decided two weeks ago to raise the entrance fee to the Taj from two rupees to 100 rupees. The move, aimed at helping foreign tourists to see the monument without being jostled by crowds, has aroused fierce protests from local tourists.

They are angry that the price rise has put the Taj out of their reach, and excluded them from visiting their own country's heritage.

Conflicting demands may also be seen in terms of pressures on an individual household, and in particular, upon the women within those households. Dankelman and Davidson (1988) identify three major types of work that women perform in rural areas of the less developed world. All are crucial in keeping the family and, indeed, the rural economy alive:

1   Survival tasks, such as the growing of food crops, the fetching of water and gathering of fuel. The latter, in particular, may occupy several hours a day. Biomass fuels (wood, charcoal, crop and animal residues) provide 75 per cent of the energy requirements of rural areas in developing countries. Collection of fuelwood has to be made from further and further afield.

2   Household tasks, such as food preparation and cooking which are also time-consuming, partly due to the inefficiency of the stoves.

3   Income generation, such as food processing and trading of agricultural products.

Trekking tourism fits into the last category but will probably conflict not only with the two previous tasks, but also with other opportunities for income generation. It will also place increased pressure on the resources of the household, notably fuel and water. Consequently there are greater and greater demands placed on the woman in a household involved in one way or another with tourism activity.

The situation of Janu Thapu at the Niceview Lodge outside Landruk in the Annapurna District of Nepal is typical (see photo). It is well before dawn, over an hour before the sun will touch the distant peaks of Annapurna and even longer before it penetrates the shade of this side valley. Janu has been quietly winnowing the beans that she shelled the previous evening. She is trying not to wake the five trekkers who arrived after nightfall needing an evening meal and accommodation. In addition to the survival and household tasks mentioned above, Janu will have to cater not only for the trekkers who stay

Niceview Lodge, Landruk, Nepal: trekking tourism is currently a growth area for tour operators

overnight but also for those who stop for refreshments during the day. The revenue Janu and husband Jahk receive for their efforts is very low: they charge only 5 Nepalese rupees a night per trekker (under 10p). Located on the outskirts of Landruk and just having started up, they are anxious to compete and attract custom. The profits from the meals quoted are even lower as the leakages are very considerable. Porters ply the trail, laden with crates of beer and mineral water, toilet rolls and trays of eggs, all to satisfy western tastes and needs. It has been estimated that only ten per cent of the revenue from trekking actually stays within the region. The menus offered to the trekkers are almost impossibly diverse, incorporating such dishes as rosti and pizza. Janu will have to juggle the different demands of the trekkers for such a variety of dishes, all to be cooked on a simple wood-fired range (see photo). The up-market lodges in the region even advertise hot showers. The pressures on the natural and cultural environment are very considerable, as described by Dankelman and Davidson:

Since Nepal opened its borders to foreign visitors in 1950, the dramatic increase in trekking has also damaged the natural and cultural environment. Ghorepani village, in the hills of Nepal, is a prime example. Tourists' demands for food and services have aggravated deforestation and had a major impact on the social and economic life of women. In addition to their traditional duties of fuel, fodder and water collection and agricultural labour, women and young girls perform many of the tasks involved in servicing the tourist industry, such as cooking and cleaning for trekkers. It is tourism (among other factors) that has discouraged girls from continuing education, as their labour is perceived to be of more value than that of boys. And some women have forgone marriage, since they feel a husband and children would only add to their existing work burden. Tourism has created some employment in tourist lodges, but the girls are rarely paid and earn only their keep.

(Dankelman and Davidson, 1988, pp. 60–1)

The kitchen at Niceview Lodge: typical cooking facilities in Nepal

The situation in the Annapurna Conservation Area is described in more detail by Gurung and de Coursey in Reading B.

Activity 3 Now turn to Reading B by C.P. Gurung and M. de Coursey, 'The Annapurna Conservation Area Project: a pioneering example of sustainable tourism?'. The Annapurna region, home to 40,000 mountain farmers, receives 40,000 mountain trekkers a year. It covers 7000 km^2 (2700 square miles). The Peak National Park looked at earlier, with a population of 38,000 receives 22 million visitors a year and extends over 1400 km^2 (555 square miles). Which area do you consider has the most problems of management, and why?

It can thus be seen that it is not sufficient just to look at the degree of foreign involvement in tourism in 'third world' destinations. It is also necessary to look more closely at local involvement, the form that it takes and the likely repercussions. It might be argued that inequalities are not only being perpetuated but also accentuated. Indeed, the situation is made even worse by the fact that not only does the host population not receive its just rewards, but their situation is worsened as they are marginalized in many ways; they are in an inferior position to counter the competing demands of tourism. In Goa, India, the illegal tapping of ground-water by the hotels has led to acute local water shortages. Locals also find themselves increasingly priced out of the market for land, and even basic foodstuffs, due to the inflationary effect of tourism. The relationship is therefore one of economic interdependency, but a markedly skewed one. Local people rarely have much influence or control over the scale or nature of tourism or over its effects.

5.4.2 My place or yours?

In summarizing the effects of tourism on societies in 'third world' destinations, we could draw an analogy with the characteristics of the visiting GI American soldiers during the Second World War. They were accused by the home population of being 'overpaid, oversexed and over here'. Let us examine these notions in turn.

In terms of being overpaid, relative to the absolute poverty of much of the local population in such destinations, the visitors indeed seem overpaid. The differences between host and guest are patently manifest in terms of the appearance and behaviour of the tourists. Clad in designer fashions, wearing expensive watches and jewellery and sporting the latest in hi-tech photographic equipment, they frequent luxury hotels and expensive restaurants. The price of even one meal in such establishments is likely to be more than a local will be paid in one month. It might be felt that the independent traveller who tries to use the local facilities will have a minimal impact in these terms, but the very presence of the traveller in the host country and not vice versa indicates the very unbalanced relationship that is at work. The vast majority of the indigenous population could never afford to be tourists themselves.

Writers have pointed to the working of the *demonstration effect* of tourism, whereby local inhabitants aspire to the seemingly superior consumption patterns flaunted before them. The demonstration effect is stronger the greater the gap between the two groups under consideration and the greater the awareness of that gap. Whilst tourism cannot, of course, be blamed for the existence of the gap, it is undoubtedly the most efficient agent communicating knowledge of it (others being the media, advertisement hoardings, cinema

demonstration effect

207

films and so on). It is the most immediate and the most tangible: the tourists are there in person. The situation was neatly summarized many years ago by the Prime Minister of Montserrat, when he accused tourism of 'promoting Cadillac tastes in bicycle societies'.

The 'McDonaldization' of the world has even witnessed the opening of a Kentucky Fried Chicken in Beijing (see **Allen, 1995**). The process is not one-way, however. Tourists are likely to return home more familiar with, and more receptive to, exotic fruits and vegetables and foreign dishes than before. The increasing array of weird and wonderful products in supermarkets such as Tesco and J.Sainsbury is due, in part, to this exposure. The role of travel in adding variety to our diet is evidenced when we think that thirty years ago avocados were a rarity, forty years ago yoghurt (whilst readily available just across the Channel) was virtually unknown. Five hundred years ago even the potato would have had us equally puzzled!

In terms of being oversexed, let us first of all examine the hedonistic lifestyles of the tourist on holiday before examining more closely the sexual dimension. As suggested in the introduction, one of the prime motivations behind the need to holiday is that of a break with routine. Tourists are consequently likely to behave in ways that would not be possible at home.

social distancing The *social distancing* which results from their journey releases them from the bounds of expected behavioural patterns. The positive side of this is that people oppressed by such expectations are freed from such constraints. It was notable, for example, that Thomas Cook's packages offered opportunities for women to travel unchaperoned around Europe and escape the restrictions of Victorian society. In fact, women outnumbered men on those early tours.

The negative side of this release is that not only might alternative behaviour be possible, but it might also be undesirable. Tourists feel freed from the restrictions and codes of normal living, anonymity is assured and they are likely to spend more freely. They are likely to eat more, drink more (hence the lager louts in Spain) and in general behave and act in manners they would not dream of doing back home. Topless sunbathing is an obvious case in point and a very real affront to many traditional societies. Much of this behaviour will offend the host population because it will quite often run counter to their cultural and religious beliefs. The consumption of alcohol is prohibited in Muslim societies. Strictly interpreted, this would pose difficulties of even handling alcohol for tourist consumption. On the Malaysian island of Langkawi, signs on the local beaches declare – not only in Bahasa Malay but also in English – that 'alcohol is the root of all evil' (see photo).

Of even more fundamental concern is the sexual behaviour of the visitors and consequent 'sexploitation' of the host population. Tourism alone cannot be blamed for the burgeoning sex industry in many 'third world' locations. In the notorious 'cages' area of Bombay, for example, a significant proportion of the clients are local cab-drivers. In the Mathare Valley of Nairobi, they are likely to be truck drivers plying the route from the Kenya coast through to Uganda. In Thailand, where prostitution is a home-grown and institutionalized industry, Thai males account for around three-quarters of all clients. There are two important facts to highlight, therefore: firstly, that prostitution is a reflection of the subordinate position of women and the young (there are an estimated two thousand boy prostitutes in Sri Lanka); secondly, that it is a reflection of the gross inequalities within and between societies. Again in Thailand, for example, it is a reflection of urban–rural

Sign at Tanjung Rhu beach, Langkawi, Malaysia: alcohol is often seen as an essential part of a holiday, but can pose problems for Muslim societies

inequalities: in the Chiang Mai area of North Thailand, sending girls to Bangkok has become an accepted family survival strategy. Williams (1988) suggests that many young women do not migrate to the city with the specific intention of working as 'service girls', but opportunities for the poorly educated are limited and even a moderately successful girl in a massage bar can earn ten times the wage of a waitress or building-site worker. This is not, of course, to absolve tourism from blame. The processes of tourism have undeniably created locations and environments which attract prostitutes and their clients. We find that there are certain 'areas' where the clientèle is almost solely foreign – for example, the debasing live shows in Patpong Street, Bangkok or the bars in Pattaya on the Thai coast.

The 'over-here' dimension of cultural impact is significant in terms of the demonstration effect discussed earlier, but is also important in terms of considering in what form the tourists are actually 'over here'. We examined the concept of tourism enclaves earlier, but in many other ways the tourist experience is packaged so that it becomes a 'bubble' wherein local traditions and practices, including the built form (such as the Longhouse Hilton in Sarawak), are tailored to suit the needs of the tourists.

This is particularly evident in the way that arts and crafts, dance, music and ceremonies are modified to suit the tourist itinerary: for example, the Toraja people on the Indonesian island of Sulawesi perform shortened versions of their burial practices for the tourists. They may also be literally encapsulated: for example, traditional Papua New Guinean carvings are reduced in size so that they fit into a suitcase, and Balinese dances are recorded onto tape-cassettes. The way that such practices are commodified has led to the accusation of tourism being culturally arrogant. The manipulation of traditions and customs to make them more interesting and satisfying to the tourist will inevitably result in inaccurate and romanticized images of destination areas and their populations. Urry (1990) cites the work of Boorstin (1964) who refers to such practice as 'staged authenticity'. To what extent such practices as the cultural and dance centres in Sarawak in Malaysia or the 'Aloha' and the 'lei' in Hawaii may lead to revitalization of traditional cultures, or whether they may be described as 'deep-frozen folklore' is also debateable.

environmental bubble The *environmental bubble* described by Boorstin also exists quite literally in terms of the physical space that tourists occupy as they are ferried between western-style hotels in air-conditioned tubes of aluminium (aircraft) and steel (buses and cars). The tourists could be anywhere in the world whilst they are hermetically sealed in such a way. One of the declared intentions of the Hilton chain of hotels was that each establishment should be, in essence, 'a little America' (further accentuating the import leakages discussed earlier as they strive for that standardized image). Urry describes the transformation of Singapore:

Singapore is nevertheless an extremely successful object of the tourist gaze but this has been achieved by playing down its exotic character. Much of the emphasis in the publicity material is on Singapore's attraction as a modern shopping centre, and there is indeed an extraordinary complex of shopping centres along the now wholly misnamed Orchard Road. Singapore has also transformed many of the old areas of Chinese shophouses into modern hotel complexes, including what is claimed to be the tallest hotel in the world. This has been built next to the world-famous Raffles Hotel, which has an impressive range of historical and literary connections as well as superb colonial atmosphere.

(Urry, 1990, p. 63)

The redevelopment of Raffles Hotel, Singapore in the early 1990s. The original hotel is in the foreground, to the right. The cleared area now contains a new extension. Note also the contrasts between the high-rise modern buildings to the left and the original structures to the right at the top

View of Singapore from the resort island of Sentosa, looking across to the skyscrapers of the modern business city

Raffles was closed for a period whilst it was completely refurbished and modernized, albeit retaining the original façade. It can be seen therefore that:

Singapore is 'in the east' but not really any more 'of the east'. It is almost the ultimate modern city and does not construct itself as 'exotic/erotic' for visitors.

(Urry, 1990, p. 63)

So we can see, as in Urry's terms '*in* the east' but not '*of* the east', the tourist might well be over here but not! This is a double-edged sword. Whilst the positive impacts of tourism might not be as great as they should be, the negative ones will in fact be minimized whilst the direct contact is deflected. If a multitude of interests are scattered at the local scale, they may penetrate the cultural and environmental fabric more deeply, and more enduringly, than conventional tourism to clearly defined and confined areas.

5.4.3   A break with nature?

There is a circular and cumulative relationship between tourism development and the environment. Most tourism development places additional pressures on the environmental resources upon which it is based, compromising the future prospects of the local population and, indeed, those of the tourists themselves. There is clearly a danger, therefore, that tourism development might not be sustainable. There are two issues here: the first is the wider one, that tourism activity will often result in different forms of environmental degradation; the second is that of an increasing awareness of the environment as a tourism resource. A clear indication of this is the way in which tourism based on natural attractions has now been identified as a market segment and is being promoted accordingly. Let us examine these issues in turn.

Whilst certain writers (Budowski, 1976) have suggested that there may be a symbiotic relationship between tourism and environmental conservation, this remains more of an ideal than a reality. The basic reason for this is that, as with all other forms of development, the environment has been treated as a free good and has not been allocated a cost in decision-making. The only time when it does figure in balance-sheets is when there is a commercial advantage to be gained from environmental protection measures. A classic example of this is the introduction of more fuel-efficient aircraft such as the Boeing 747–400. The reduction of eleven per cent in fuel consumption on a ten-hour flight over the previous model means not only a reduction in CO_2 emissions per passenger and tonne/kilometre, but obvious financial savings for the airline company. This we can describe as a win–win situation – win for the environment, win for other interests.

Such win–win situations are obviously more the exception rather than the rule. Amongst the adverse environmental impacts of tourism are the destruction of the protective vegetation cover and fringing coral reefs leading to problems of erosion, disruption of feeding and breeding patterns of wildlife, and over-use of local resources of fuelwood and water supply. There are also considerable problems of litter and pollution. It has been estimated in the Caribbean that the average tourist generates 1.68 kg of rubbish a day, three times the local household average. In 1990 alone, cruise passengers in the Caribbean generated 36 million pounds of solid waste. Special expeditions have been mounted to clean up Everest and remove the flotsam of decades of mountaineering expeditions (see Figure 5.3).

Tourism might also be described as an agent of transnational pollution as examined by Steven Yearley in Chapter 4. The consumption patterns of the tourists from the industrialized nations result in them simultaneously exporting their waste and importing the environmental carrying-capacity of the developing nations. We have already talked of CO_2 emissions and litter. Water pollution is also evident in the form of untreated sewage discharged into coastal waters and pollution by fuels used in boating activities. In the Kathmandu valley in Nepal, local river water is being polluted by chemical dyes from washing the carpets that have been woven for the tourists.

ecotourism　All these activities are likely to prejudice the integrity of the environment as a resource. This is particularly ironic because tourism based on natural resources – *ecotourism* – has become the fastest-growing market segment in tourism. In several small states and island economies ecotourism has been eagerly embraced as a way out of their classic impasse – the need to earn badly needed foreign exchange without at the same time destroying their natural resource base. How sustainable is ecotourism development in developing nations? Cater (1992) examines the case of the Central American state of Belize.

Activity 4　Now turn to Reading C by Erlet Cater, 'Profits from Paradise'. This article questions the assumption that ecotourism is automatically a sustainable option. As you read the article, attempt to list the ways in which sustainability may be compromised for each of the diffferent interests involved. You may add in others such as the national government and tourism firms.

High-altitude cleaners tackle Everest rubbish tip

By Christopher Thomas in Kathmandu

The world's highest rubbish tip is to be cleaned up — a tin, a bottle and an oxygen cylinder at a time. At 26,000ft, near the summit of Everest, it will be one of the most ponderous and bizarre environmental jobs ever tackled, and hardly anybody will ever see the difference.

Since Sir Edmund Hilary and Tenzing Norgay reached the summit in May 1953, nearly 150 expeditions have bivouacked at South Col, the last camp before the final ascent. On the way down, triumphant, tired and anxious to lighten their loads, they have all left rubbish. The Nepal Mountaineering Association says there are 17 tons of rubbish at South Col, with 23 bodies, some of which have been there fore years. Cold and lack of oxygen mean that nothing perishes or rusts.

Various devices are being worked on to clear the rubbish, including a system of winches to lower it far enough down the mountain for yaks to haul it away. Lightweight carbon-fibre sleds are being built in France to see if they can be shoved and pulled down the mountain, laden with the junk.

Everest is a crowded mountain. One day last year, 32 climbers reached the summit on the same day after queueing for up to an hour each, placing them in grave risk of frostbite. The Nepalese government, which is hungry for hard currency, gave climbing permits to an unprecedented 12 expeditions. The Everest base camp was packed with 268 climbers and back-up staff.

This year it will be worse: the government has permitted 19 expeditions, promising more chaos above the clouds and more rubbish.

The most common item of rubbish on Everest is the bright yellow oxygen cylinder. As many as 1,500 have been dumped, with tents, sleeping bags, ropes, medicines, food, binoculars, clothes, tin cans and cameras.

The mountaineering association, alarmed by the pollution, is trying to persuade everybody to bring down what they take up, and to start clearing what is already up there. Tek Chandra Pokharel, the former president of the association, said: "The problem is that the government is pushing up the price of climbing permits so high that nobody is in much of a mood to co-operate voluntarily."

A French–Nepalese team will begin the £520,000 attempt to clean the mountain in May. The improbable rubbish collectors will have only 15 to 18 days to work, when South Col is free of snow. It will be a Herculean task, because the body loses 80 per cent of its efficiency at that height.

The French–Nepalese team will send up 40 sherpas to collect rubbish with the aim of lowering it to a base camp at 17,550ft. From there it will be hauled by yaks to the nearest airfield, at Luckla, and on to Kathmandu for dumping.

The government has tightened rules, but rubbish still piles up. From this autumn only four expeditions a year will be allowed on Everest and only one team will be able to use the same climbing route at the same time.

That explains the rise in fees. The cut in the number of climbers should give the high-altitude rubbish collectors a chance to clear the existing build-up of rubbish.

Figure 5.3 (Source: The Times, *8 March 1993*)

Summary of section 5.4

o   It has been evident throughout this section that the shrinking of the world through tourism has both accentuated and highlighted the inequalities between and within nations. It is not surprising that, eventually, international tourism will engender hostility on the part of the host populations as they not only suffer the adverse effects, but at the same time receive less of the benefits.

o   It has been seen that in many ways the poorest are marginalized. The benefits that do accrue locally are likely to be reduced and inferior, resulting from the patterns and organization of international travel. They are also likely to accrue to a local élite whose interests are allied more to those of abroad than to the local community. The picture, once again, is of unevenness and inequality.

5.5   The future: tourism and a shrinking world

From much of the foregoing discussion, it might be construed that people and places would be better off without tourism. Certainly the picture is one of uneven interdependence, whether seen from an economic, cultural or environmental viewpoint. However, surely some narrowing of the gap between rich and poor nations is better than none at all. It must be remembered that many poor 'third world' destinations have little else to which they can turn in order to enhance their development prospects. Tourism earnings can be very significant to such economies: they form 43 per cent of the export earnings of Kenya, for example. To argue against tourism is to swim against the tide. It is here to stay and, as described in the introduction, is set to grow. It will also become increasingly significant for certain destinations. What we need to ask, however, is what form will it take in the future?

How far is there a swing away from conventional mass tourism? Certainly, there seems to be a trend towards what has been loosely termed 'alternative tourism' and, as one component of this, an increasing tendency towards individual travel. Small, specialist, tour operators note a continual upward trend in business and a growing popularity of more unusual destinations. Trailfinders, Britain's biggest specialist ticket agency which sells a quarter of a million air seats a year, declares its fastest-growing destination to be that of Vietnam.

alternative tourism   What is meant by the term *alternative tourism*? It is a term which has been heavily criticized for its lack of precision. Basically, there are two ways in which it might be viewed as alternative. First of all, it might be viewed as an alternative to institutionalized mass tourism and, indeed, with certain specialist forms of travel such as ecotourism being the fastest-growing market segments, it is an increasingly significant force to be reckoned with. It can never, however, replace mass tourism, the numbers game alone tells us that. Where would the European tourism industry be without Spain and that of Spain without the Costas? Secondly, it should be alternative in terms of its characteristics. Apart from the emphasis on greater local involvement at destination areas and all that implies, the emphasis should be on more responsible behaviour by tourism companies and the tourists themselves.

The search, however, is for the increasingly novel. Urry (1990) documents how the 'post(mass)-tourist' searches increasingly for the extraordinary. What used to be extraordinary is now ordinary and, inevitably, there will be problems as increasingly remote and undeveloped locations, with finely balanced cultural and environmental regimes, are drawn into the locus of international tourism.

We have examined how tourism has contributed to the shrinking of the world, but perhaps we ought to also ask the converse. How has the shrinking world contributed to tourism? We must remember that there is a circular process at work: as the unfamiliar becomes familiar, the flows of tourists are likely to increase to a particular destination. This is not only propagated by taste and fashion, as described in the introduction, whereby the élite open up a destination and then move on, driven by a desire for novelty and exclusivity, but also by the changing international scene. Political changes that have already been mentioned include places being taken off the circuit, for example, through the civil war in Yugoslavia; other examples would include the opening up of Vietnam and the changes in Central America, notably Nicaragua and El Salvador, as well as Cuba. From an economic viewpoint, the activities of the transnational corporations also generate a tremendous volume of business tourism, which in turn is the mainstay of much airline business.

So, tourism has undoubtedly contributed to the shrinking of the world (and vice versa) in a physical time–distance sense, in a cultural sense and in the ties of interdependence that bind locations around the globe. We have seen, however, how there are marked discontinuities between the various interests involved at different levels and at different points in time. Thus, those who suffer from the adverse impacts of tourism are not those who receive the benefits.

From the very moment a person is able to consider going on holiday (as opposed to not being able or to afford to do so), inequalities are manifest. The actual purchase of the holiday mobilizes a whole set of suppliers whose very foundations and operations are rooted in unsustainable relationships. As was suggested at the beginning of this chapter, tourism arises from, perpetuates and gives rise to unevenness and inequality. The overall picture, then, is a distorted one, where distances – whether physical or social – between places or peoples, are compacted unevenly. It might be a situation of being 'here, there and everywhere' for some, but for many it will be a case of getting nowhere.

References

ANFIELD, J. (1993) 'Sustainable tourism in the Nature and National Parks of Europe', *The George Wright Forum*, Vol. 10, No. 4.

BIRD, B. (1989) *Langkawi: From Mahsuri to Mahathir*, Selangor, Insan.

BOORSTIN, D. (1964) *The Image: A Guide to Pseudo Events in America*, New York, Harper.

BRITTON, S. (1982) 'International tourism and multinational corporations in the Pacific: the case of Fiji' in Taylor, M. and Thrift, N. J. (eds) *The Geography of Multinationals*, Croom Helm, London, pp. 252–74.

BUDOWSKI, G. (1976) 'Tourism and conservation: conflict, coexistence or symbiosis?', *Environmental Conservation*, Vol. 3, No. 1, pp. 27–31.

CATER, E. (1992) 'Profits from Paradise', *Geographical Magazine*, Vol. 64, No. 3.

COOPER, C., FLETCHER, J., GILBERT, D. and WANHILL, S. (1993) *Tourism Magazine: Principles and Practice*, London, Pitman.

DANKELMAN, I. and DAVIDSON, J. (1988) *Women and Environment in the Third World*, London, Earthscan.

GURUNG, C. P. and DE COURSEY, M. (1994) 'The Annapurna Conservation Area Project: a pioneering example of sustainable tourism?' in Cater, E. and Lowman, G., (eds) *Ecotourism: A Sustainable Option?*, Chichester, Wiley.

HANNIGAN, K. (1993) 'The longer-term effects of subsidized investment on Irish tourism', paper presented to the Conference on Sustainable Tourism in Islands and Small States, Foundation for International Studies, Valletta, University of Malta.

HIRSCH, F. (1978) *Social Limits to Growth*, London, Routledge and Kegan Paul.

LEFEBVRE, H. (1991) *The Production of Space* (English translation by Nicholsen Smith, D. (1991), Oxford, Blackwell).

MASSEY, D. (1995) ' in Allen, J. and Massey, D. (eds) *Geographical Worlds*, London, Oxford University Press/The Open University.

MOSS, M. and MOSS, G. (1991) *The Handbook for Women Travellers*, London, Piatkus.

MURPHY, P. (1985) *Tourism: A Community Approach*, London, Methuen (reprinted 1991 by Routledge).

URRY, J. (1990) *The Tourist Gaze*, London, Sage.

WHEELWRIGHT, J. (1993) 'Go on be a man!', *New Internationalist*, July.

WILLIAMS, P. (1988) 'Human toll of a red-light zone', *The Geographical Magazine*, March.

Reading A: K. Hannigan, 'The longer-term effects of subsidized investment on Irish tourism in the Republic of Ireland'

Tourism in the Irish Economy

The Irish tourist industry developed rapidly in the 1950s and 1960s boosted by strong ethnic ties with the US and UK and by the establishment of Bord Fáilte as the national tourism agency to promote and develop the industry. It concentrated on promotion partly because it was accepted that this was a public good but also because large-scale development was not thought compatible with the main attraction Ireland had to offer which was the unspoilt and undeveloped Irish countryside. [...]

Table A.1 shows the boom which has occurred in world tourism did not happen in Ireland up to the mid-1980s. Just as clear is the rapid growth of the past few years. Real revenue was static in the period up to 1987 although revenue in the OECD region grew by almost 350 per cent during this time. This boom was not confined to Mediterranean 'sun-lust' destinations with which Ireland could never hope to compete but was evident in many North European destinations offering similar types of holidays.

In the mid-1960s the Irish industry accounted for 1.1 per cent of worldwide arrivals and 1.4 per cent of receipts. Nationally it earned up to 20 per cent of Irish foreign exchange. By 1985 its share of exports was less than 5 per cent, while Ireland's share of European arrivals fell from 2.7 per cent in 1960 to under 1.3 per cent in 1987. This performance is reflected in the share of Ireland's main markets attracted each year. [...]

The many reasons put forward for this long period of poor growth fall into three broad categories:

1   Market conditions were unfavourable

It is true that a number of external factors such as decline in the importance of ethnic ties and a major move in the UK holiday market towards European and especially sun holidays were unfavourable to Ireland. However, until recently, little effective action was undertaken to counter this trend such as the development of package holidays to Ireland or investment in all-weather facilities.

2   Government policy was unfavourable

Tourism does not appear to have been afforded priority in economic planning for many years. The existence of Bord Fáilte meant that government policy amounted to little more than apportioning an annual budget to promote Ireland while from an industry operator's point of view the strong centralization meant there was little chance of an alternative channel emerging. This lack of an effective tourism policy was further compounded by the weak macroeconomic management which characterized the Irish economy for much of the period [...] Very high inflation rates partly as a result of large governments deficits funded by overseas borrowing were common. This was a somewhat misguided attempt to produce a high wage, high value-added economy built on encouraging inward investment by foreign multinationals which resulted in Ireland gaining a reputation as a high-cost destination. More accurately, Ireland offered poor value for money since the average tourist wishes to maximize utility over time rather than money and Ireland offered little to do other than admire the scenery. [...]

3   The political unrest in Northern Ireland

The impact of other factors may be small when compared with the effect of the outbreak of violence in 1969. Table A.2 shows the impact of the troubles on visitor arrivals.

Table A.1   Tourism receipts in OECD countries at constant prices, 1960=100

	France	Germany	Denmark	UK	Ireland	OECD
1960	100	100	100	100	100	100
1965	152	141	140	97	140	166
1970	161	196	176	151	123	213
1975	247	221	207	233	102	257
1980	304	304	222	290	104	338
1985	463	367	278	343	109	404
1990	623	429	336	406	153	541

Table A.2 Visitors to Ireland before and after the outbreak of political violence in Northern Ireland (thousands)

	British	Northern Irish	American	European
1968	1135	490	183	90
1970	1105	420	228	118
1972·	750	294	259	127
1974	820	363	252	165

Source: Bord Fáilte

[...]

Any attempt to describe Irish tourism over this period must take account of this situation. However by the late 1970s much of the tension had eased. By the mid-1980s, it was no longer feasible to blame inflation or world recession for the continuing low growth. Instead attention belatedly was focused on attempting to discover if anything could be done to obtain a share of what was obviously a booming market. By this time most European governments and even the European Commission had begun to realize the economic importance of tourism [...] Causing this interest is the fact that tourism is one of the few industries in Europe which manages to combine high labour intensity and regional diversity with high growth rates. This was recognized by the EC when reforming the structural funds. Tourism was recognized as a priority area (EC, 1990) and the first substantive steps towards formulating a European tourism policy were taken.

On the surface, a similar though more radical transformation took place in Ireland. But the background and thinking was quite different since in the mid-1980s Irish tourism was not a booming industry [...] The debt crisis prompted the realization that new initiatives based on indigenous strengths must be formulated. At the same time it became clear that the failure of tourism to grow was to a large extent due to internal failures [...] such as excessive seasonality, poor access and a lack of facilities [...] These resulted in low profitability and low investment as well as congestion in peak periods. [...]

Doubling the number of visitors was seen as a necessary prerequisite from which increased foreign exchange earnings and additional employment would result. Thus the policy adopted was aimed at developing mass as opposed to quality tourism [...] Promoting private sector investment by means of direct incentives was seen as the means to achieve this end. [...]

Initially the method used was tax breaks, given by expanding the existing Business Expansion Scheme (BES) to include hotels and certain other facilities. After 1989, funds from the reformed Community Structural Funds, particularly the European Regional Development Fund (ERDF), along with the International Fund for Ireland (IFI), which aimed specifically at overcoming the damage caused to economic activity by the troubles in Northern Ireland, meant that direct grants were given to prospective investors. The BES was curtailed in 1991 due to a perceived lack of targeting and certain abuses.

The job of distributing these funds to tourism was given to Bord Fáilte [...S]traightforward commercial criteria were applied with a role for government justified by the advantages bestowed on the economy from an increase in foreign tourism over and above those appropriated by firms.

A major programme of investment resulted. Investment in Irish tourism grew from £25 million per year in 1987 to over £200 million in 1992. An estimated £770 million will have been invested in the period 1989–1993 which is more than the total for the previous 20 years. There is little doubt therefore that the programme was successful in bringing forth investment.

The most obvious development in tourism in this period is the rapid growth which took place after 1987. World arrivals which grew by 26 per cent or 6 per cent per annum compounded from 1987–91 were outstripped by growth in arrivals in Ireland at 44 per cent or 10 per cent per annum compounded. Furthermore, revenue grew from IR£504 million in 1987 to IR£869 million in 1992, a cumulative growth of over 52 per cent in real terms for the period. This is in sharp contrast to the previous 20 years. Most of this growth was in the short-haul market and especially from Europe which accounted for 38 per cent of revenue in 1992 up from just 21 per cent in 1987. Initial figures for 1993 show this trend continuing but much lower growth overall. However, the rise in recent years has meant that visitor numbers approximately doubled in the period 1981–91 with Bord Fáilte forecasts showing 1997 figures at 34 per cent above 1991 levels.

This outcome has meant that the policy implemented is perceived as a success and it is expected that it will be continued into the new round of structural funds of which Ireland will be the largest recipient per head of population. A target of 35,000 new jobs from tourism in the next five years has been set with Bord Fáilte requesting £380m from the CSF. However, these figures hide a number of problems in the industry and ignore some less encouraging results now emerging.

Results of investment programme

While the beneficial results of subsidized investment are obvious in terms of increased business, employment, infrastructure and facilities, a number of problems still exist. In the longer term, problems of sustainability due to environmental and economic factors described below are likely to emerge. In the short term there are also a number of arguments against the notion that Irish tourism has embarked on a sustainable growth path which will relieve the country's economic problems. Three aspects are worth noting.

1 What has really changed?

A more in-depth examination of the industry shows that little progress has been made towards overcoming or solving the main problems identified in the mid-1980s as the causes for low growth. Among the most important of these were excessive seasonality, access difficulties and low expenditure per visitor. Regarding accessibility, some initial success was achieved in reducing fares to the UK by introducing competition and airline deregulation.

However, other regulations as a result of Irish regional development policy have meant that most American and many European visitors enter Ireland from the UK thus reducing time spent in the country. In addition, successive years of low investment and poor management in the state-owned national airline, Aer Lingus, have brought it to the verge of collapse. A major restructuring is taking place but a very clear and necessary role exists for government in ensuring easy access to the country before a strong tourism industry can be built. Congestion in peak periods has also caused problems on sea ferries and within the car hire business, and although some improvements have been made, the road infrastructure is still weak. Furthermore, the opening of the Channel Tunnel will make Ireland less accessible when compared to competing regions in Scotland, Wales and the North of England for the increasingly vital European markets. The problem of low expenditure per person has not been solved either. Euromonitor (1992) showed average expenditure in Ireland was second lowest in a broad range of European countries. [...]

Finally, there is little to suggest that any major or lasting advances in relieving the problem of seasonality have been achieved. Although highly peaked with over 50 per cent visitors arriving in the peak period from June to August, this is of course not unique to Ireland. However, the touring nature of the holidays offered has resulted in congestion at key points and sustained growth in the industry will require an improvement in this distribution. [...]

2 External factors are important

[...] Much of the growth was the result of an increase in the number taking second holidays or short breaks [...] Other factors such as the upsurge of interest in 'green' or natural products as well as scares about the damage done by sun holidays to health and environment, have also resulted in more favourable market conditions, a reversal of the process of twenty years earlier. As with economic boom, the danger is that such factors may be transient.

3 Aggregate figures can be misleading

Assessment of success or failure must depend on the number of jobs created and contribution to regional development before factors such as environmental and social costs are included. There is little to suggest that funds were allocated in a manner which took account of regional factors. The main regional division in Ireland is between the rural and largely undeveloped western region and the more prosperous eastern seaboard. In the period 1989–93 revenue from overseas tourists was split 45:55 between the east and west. The allocation of investment subsidies was in almost precisely this same ratio. [...]

Aggregate job creation figures have been used to show that 75 per cent of jobs created in the Irish economy in 1989–92 were in tourism-related activities (Tourism Task Force, 1993). However, a survey of grant-aided tourism projects conducted by this author suggests that figures such as this are of little value in evaluating the programme. Managers of tourism enterprises indicated that they believed about 50 per cent of these jobs could still have been created in the absence of the subsidy. Of greater importance are the types of jobs being created. Only 48 per cent of those created were full-time and permanent compared to 60 per cent of all jobs in these projects, and managers believed that although the total created would have been less without the subsidy, a higher proportion of those created would have been full-time [...] Many such atypical jobs are filled by people from outside the labour force thus greatly reducing the impact on unemployment (Ball, 1988) [...] Low value jobs were concentrated in the poorer western region. About 60 per cent of jobs created in the west were seasonal with a further 17 per cent part-time while only 16 per cent of jobs in the east were seasonal with 67 per cent full-time and permanent (Cousins, 1992). Thus it is wrong to assume that jobs created by tourism are equivalent to jobs created in manufacturing in previous decades but true that a job created in tourism in the western region is less valuable than one in the east. This outcome underlines the failure of tourism development to redistribute income to poorer regions and is very much at odds with policies being pursued which aim to create a high value-added economy utilizing what is a highly educated workforce.

In the longer term there are indications that two major characteristics of Irish tourism may inhibit its chances of sustaining recent developments. A contradiction in the policies pursued [...] exists between developing mass tourism and the natural environment on which the Irish industry depends (Deegan and Dineen, 1993) [...] In framing the original objectives for Bord Fáilte it was explicitly recognized that as a state-sponsored agency its aims were not just to increase tourism but to do so in a manner compatible with the Irish heritage [...] By the mid-1980s, successive corporate plans made it clear that Bord Fáilte saw its role as maximizing foreign revenue from tourism and that other objectives would be pursued only if they made a direct contribution to revenue in the short or long term. Thus the role of the government in protecting the cultural and social environment was made secondary to developing tourism [...] In its most recent five-year plan, Bord Fáilte sets out its priorities as to create employment, improve the balance of payments, increase GDP, generate extra tax revenue and contribute to regional development. It is very noticeable that maximizing social and economic benefits has been replaced by simple measures of tourism's contribution to broad economic variables as the aim of the board. This is quite an important shift in direction and means that the main tool of government policy in the tourism sector does not consider that protecting the environment or cultural heritage is a priority.

This situation exists although it has been argued that aims such as environmental protection or providing infrastructure are within the capabilities of government intervention, while goals set in terms of job creation and revenue targets result in government action distorting the market [...] As in most destinations, once the cost of travel is excluded the four main items of tourist expenditure are accommodation, food and drink, attractions and retail items. Government subsidies have been concentrated on improving accommodation and attractions except for that part of food and drink supplied by hotels. However, 80 per cent of the jobs created in Ireland in tourist-related businesses between 1988 and 1992 were in licensed premises which were not grant-aided. Assuming that domestic demand was roughly constant over this short period and that productivity changes are small, due to the nature of the business, this would indicate that this sector has managed to gain much of the increased demand from tourists. In this period, employment in restaurants was static while hotels and attractions showed modest increases. Much of this increase in employment in pubs was the result of massive investment in catering facilities for food as distinct from alcohol sales. […]

Conclusion

This paper reviews recent developments in Irish tourism against the general economic background of the huge national debt and high unemployment rates which beset the Irish economy. Just as the Irish electorate tend to view the EC as essential to recovery although twenty years of membership have not brought the promised rewards, a coincidence of political and economic factors in the late 1980s put the tourism industry at the centre of plans to resolve these problems although it had performed poorly previously. A major programme of subsidized investment has coincided with strong growth since 1987 but many of the underlying problems which previously inhibited growth are still present. Seasonality remains a major problem resulting in low profit rates and congestion in peak periods. Many of the jobs created are seasonal and as such are not a solution to unemployment. Access transport remains a problem in urgent need of action and expenditure per head remains well below European levels. This is not surprising given the emphasis in

the development programme in increasing visitor numbers rather than revenue per person and this policy carries many dangers regarding the sustainability of the developments taking place. The situation is made worse by the apparent abandonment by Bord Fáilte of its role in protecting the natural and cultural heritage of Ireland where such a role may clash with the attainment of short-term economic targets.

Despite this subjugation of other considerations to economic objectives and the money poured into the industry, the very organization of Irish tourism with a highly protected sector able to gain much of the profit opportunities created may mean that the intervention will fail to create the conditions necessary for the private sector to continue to invest in development. In such a situation the industry will return to the lower growth path previously observed.

References

BALL, R. M. (1988) 'Seasonality: a problem for workers in the tourism labour market?', *The Service Industries Journal,*, Vol. 8, No. 4, pp. 501–13.

COUSINS, M. (1992) 'Social security and atypical workers in Ireland', *International Labour Review*, Vol. 131, No. 6, pp. 647–60.

DEEGAN, J. and DINEEN, D. (1993) 'Irish tourism policy: targets, outcomes and environmental considerations' in O'Connor, B. and Cronin, M. (eds) *Tourism in Ireland: A Critical Analysis*, pp. 115–37, Cork University Press.

EUROMONITOR (1992) *European Travel and Tourism Marketing Directory*, Euromonitor Publications, London.

EUROPEAN COMMISSION (1990) *Annual Report on the Implementation of the Reform of the Structural Funds 1989*, Brussels.

TOURISM TASK FORCE (1993) *Report to the Minister for Tourism, Transport and Communications*, Stationery Office, Dublin.

Reading B: C. P. Gurung and M. de Coursey, 'The Annapurna Consevation Area Project: a pioneering example of sustainable tourism' _____

The Annapurna region: mountain agriculture and trekking tourism

The area surrounding the Annapurna mountain range in western Nepal has long been recognized, both nationally and internationally, as one of the world's most spectacular landscapes. Over 7,000 square kilometres in size, this region harbours an outstanding array of both biological and cultural diversity […] The world's deepest river valley, the Kali Gandaki, cuts a thin, 1,824-metre chasm between the lofty summits of Annapurna 1 (8,091m) and Dhaulagiri (8,151m), two of the world's highest mountains. Extreme climate and topography create excellent habitats for a wide variety of flora and fauna, including the endangered snow-leopard, over 100 varieties of orchids and expansive stands of rhododendron, bamboo and pine forests.

The majority of Annapurna's residents live at subsistence level or below, primarily as farmers, labourers, herders or traders. While some inhabitants are able to meet their daily requirements fairly comfortably, many in the more remote regions still suffer from food deficits. However, they are all dependent on the natural resources as over 90 per cent of local energy needs are met by forest. Forests also provide a host of other essential products such as fodder, building materials, medicines, game, wild food stuffs and raw materials for domestic purposes.

Unlike the tropical lowlands to the south, the Annapurna region never experienced the acute population pressures that contributed to massive deforestation and environmental degradation in those areas. The harsh and unforgiving terrain kept most outsiders away, allowing residents to use and manage their nearby resources as they saw fit. While local populations have grown significantly over the years (2.6 per cent annually), basic needs remained at a level readily accommodated by the existing resource base. To sustain local livelihoods, numerous indigenous systems evolved to manage natural resources. While not perfect, these systems have helped to maintain the quality of Annapurna's environment.

Over the last two decades, the explosion in trekking tourism has upset this delicate ecological balance and contributed significantly to a loss of cultural integrity in the Annapurna region. Its unparalleled attributes and the relative ease by which one could reach the heart of the Himalaya have made the Annapurna region the number one trekking destination in all of Nepal. In 1991, a total of 270,000 tourists visited Nepal. Seventy thousand of these visitors were trekkers, out of which 38,500 (55 per cent) headed for some part of the Annapurna region (see Table B.1)

Table B.1 Growth in number of trekkers in Nepal, 1980–92

	Everest	Langtang	Annapurna	Other	Total	% +/-
1980	5,836	4,113	14,332	3,179	27,460	–
1981	5,804	4,488	17,053	2,155	29,500	+7.4
1982	6,240	4,535	19,702	1,855	32,332	+9.6
1983	6,732	4,030	21,119	417	32,298	-0.1
1984	7,724	4,792	25,422	3,268	41,206	+27.6
1985	8,347	4,610	18,960	813	32,730	-20.6
1986	9,900	5,250	33,620	805	49,575	+51.5
1987	8,998	6,107	30,914	1,256	47,275	-4.6
1988	11,366	8,423	37,902	3,582	61,273	+29.6
1990	11,314	7,826	36,361	7,497	62,998	+2.8
1991*	–	–	38,447	–	–	–
1992*	–	–	44,417	–	–	–

Note: * Based on ACAP records

It is estimated that for every trekker there is at least one outside support staff, pushing the annual number of visitors to well over 77,000, almost twice the local population. A standard commercial trek around the Annapurna Circuit (22–25 days) for 12 clients sets off with a support staff of approximately 50 members. The situation is further exacerbated by the fact that the majority of trekkers tend to bottle-neck in three areas: the Annapurna Sanctuary, the base of the 6,000 metre Thorong Pass (Thorong Phedi) and Ghorepani village, a major trail intersection. The trekkers are also seasonally concentrated: owing to the prevailing weather pattern, over 60 per cent of the trekkers come in four months of the year – October, November, March and April. These high-impact areas, and to a lesser extent along the rest of the main trekking routes, have suffered tremendously from *laissez-faire* tourist development. Over 700 tea shops and lodges have been built that cater to a tourist population whose needs are much greater than local standards. Localized deforestation from spiralling fuelwood and construction demands has led to a decrease in forest habitats – including Nepal's showcase rhododendron forests – and further destabilization of surrounding hillsides. Virtually all food and housekeeping items have to be imported from Kathmandu and Pokhara, inflating local economies and introducing non-nutritious diets. Inadequate sanitation facilities and indiscriminate practices by tourists and trekking groups have left virtual 'minefields' of human excreta and toilet paper. Toilets, if they exist at all, are often dangerously close to water sources. Non-biodegradable litter such as plastics, tins and bottles, used primarily by tourists, are disposed of in nearby streams or strewn in piles at the edge of the settlements. Tourism, as a messenger of outside values and behaviours, has also affected local cultures. Village youths are easy prey to the seductiveness of western consumer culture as tourists are laden with expensive trappings such as hi-tech hiking gear, flashy clothes, cameras and a variety of electronic gadgetry.

The need for a new concept in protected area management: the creation of the Annapurna Conservation Area Project (ACAP)

[...]

In the Annapurna region, environmental problems are multifaceted. Hence, instead of prescribing one single mitigative measure, the problems have been addressed holistically. Integrated strategies have been devised that will incorporate all the relevant issues. In order to avoid resistance from the people by designating the area as the National Park for the Annapurna region, a new designation was needed which addressed the needs of the local people, of *human development*, as well as the need for *nature conservation* and the need for *tourism management*.

As a result of the Annapurna region's unique socio-economic, cultural and environmental factors, a new designation was called for which encompassed the three main components discussed above. Thus, Conservation Area designation means slightly less restrictive management policies than those of Nepal's National Parks, but is broader in scope and coverage. With the assignment of a large degree of management responsibility to local populations, Conservation Area status is designed to avoid excessive bureaucracy (Sherpa, Coburn and Gurung, 1986).

With the approval of His Majesty's Government of Nepal, the operational plan was implemented by the King Mahendra Trust for Nature Conservation (KMTNC) in 1986, establishing the Annapurna Conservation Area Project (ACAP) (see Figure B.1).

The study had found that virtually 40,000 people were living within the Annapurna region, dependent upon local natural resources for their livelihood. Owing to its large size, the region encompasses a variety of cultures and microclimates, which have given rise to many indigenous management schemes. These traditional practices were much more effective than those of projects initiated and implemented by government agencies with much larger foreign assistance. Consequently the study team felt strongly that, unless the local people

223

were brought into the mainstream of conservation, measures taken to conserve the natural and cultural heritage of the region may not be successful. Hence, a new approach was necessary to allow the local residents to remain within and around the conservation area, and permit them to use the resources in a sustainable manner. In essence, the local people would be the custodians of the resources.

An applied experiment in integrated conservation and development: essential elements of the Annapurna Conservation Area Project

Guiding Principles

The main guiding principles of ACAP are:

o Sustainability
o People's participation
o Catalyst (or Lami/a match-maker)

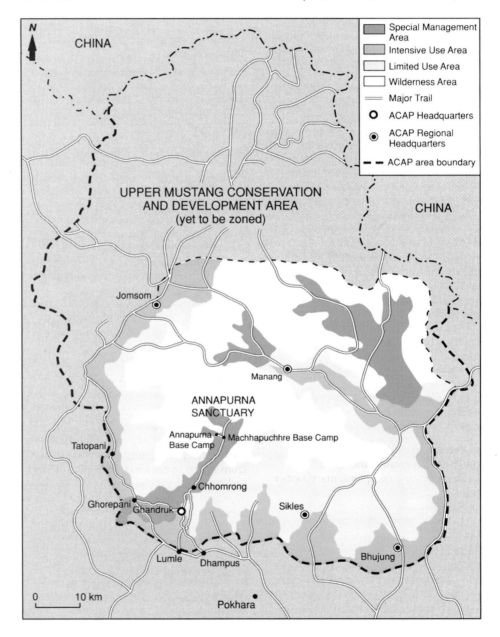

Figure B.1 Area covered by the Annapurna Conservation Area Project

o   Conservation for development

o   Grassroots methods

o   Multiple-use

o   Implementation of programmes by stages

Sustainability in this context does not only mean financial sustenance. It also refers to the availability of trained personnel in and from the region, utilizing both formal and informal expertise. Both of these aspects are incorporated in any community development and conservation projects implemented by ACAP through the local people.

Peoples's participation The sustainability of conservation and development projects depends upon the participation and motivation of the local people. Fundamentally motivation comes from a realization that it is their own project [...] Thus, the sharing of both successes and failures is part of the development process. The involvement of local people is also a necessity in tourism management. Hence training is given to trekking lodge-owners and lodge management committees are formed [...]

Catalyst or Lami approach Various development and conservation projects have been implemented by both national and international agencies in the region [...] Since the majority of the population is deprived of basic facilities such as drinking water, health care and education, ACAP plays the role of facilitator by bringing in outside resources to fulfil the needs of the local residents.

Conservation for development ACAP contends that conservation and development are complementary rather than opposing forces. Development programmes, if incorporated within the conservation aspects, will be more sustainable [...]

Grass-roots methods With a long-term view in mind, ACAP adopts a more decentralized, bottom-up approach to revive conservation. Local people are actively encouraged to take a leading role in conservation and development activities, expressing their needs and concerns in open forums [...]

The multiple-use concept Tourism, farming, forestry and biodiversity conservation are carried out jointly in the Annapurna Conservation Area. To avoid possible conflicts, as an initial step ACAP was zoned according to various levels of use, both by tourists and villagers [...]

Implementation of programmes by stages Owing to its large size, existing administrative structure (5 Districts, 70 village Development Committees) and the varying levels of impact, ACAP is designed to be implemented in stages. The areas hardest hit by trekking were addressed first [...]

Major programmes

Alternative energy Deforestation is a major issue in the Annapurna region. Certain localized areas have been devastated by the sudden influx of trekking tourism. Forests are depleted in order to fulfil energy and construction requirements to meet the needs of tourists and the fodder requirement of the local residents. Thus the problem of deforestation is tackled from many different angles, including alternative energy sources, energy-saving technologies, reforestation and community forest management schemes. ACAP has been promoting several alternative sources of energy and fuelwood saving devices in the conservation area in order to reduce the pressure on forests. [These include back-boiler water heaters, solar-water heaters and micro-hydro projects ...] In part of the area of most acute fuelwood shortage ACAP has implemented a kerosene-only policy [...]

Two new technologies have [also] been introduced which store energy produced from micro hydro-electricity. Both these technological developments are produced in Nepal, and can be easily repaired and maintained by the Nepali technicians. [These are a low wattage cooker and heat storage cooker.]

Tree nurseries and reforestation [...] In addition to the introduction of alternative cooking technologies, over ten tree nurseries have been established in various places [...]

Community forest management In order to protect the existing forest, local-level

Conservation and Development Committees and Forest Management Committees are formed [...]

Community development programmes
Through the project, ACAP has been helping various community development projects to fulfil their basic needs. Thus, health posts have been established; maternal and child-health clinics have been set up; and mothers groups have been formed to carry out the various community development and conservation projects [...]

Conservation education and extension [...]
Unless awareness is raised among the users of the resources, both locals and outsiders, sustainable development cannot be achieved. As a result, ACAP has identified three target groups: the children in the village, the adult population and the international visitors [...] In order to motivate the international tourist, information centres have been set up and the ACAP has developed a *minimum impact code* which is incorporated in a brochure distributed to all trekkers going into the Annapurna region.

Research and training One of the main aims of the project is to develop locally-trained labour, ensuring that the project should become sustainable in terms of employment [...]

At present, there are several research programmes underway, e.g. a floristic survey of the Annapurna region and the Biodiversity Conservation Data Project. These programmes are compiling an inventory of the flora, fauna and non-timber forest products. The information collected will be very useful in updating the management plans of the conservation area.

Financial sustainability Once the basic infrastructuré is established with financial assistance from donors, ACAP will have its own financial base to cover the operating costs of the project, relieving the government from an additional burden.

[...]

Conclusion

The ACAP believes that tourism, properly managed, can bring great benefits to the land and the people of the Annapurna region. Rather than a necessary evil, tourists are regarded as partners in fulfilling the goals of biodiversity conservation, cultural revitalization and sustainable economic development. In the Annapurna region, nature and culture share the tourist spotlight. Trekking is a unique form of recreation that allows tourists to enjoy these features in an interactive, challenging and educational manner. In return, they can supply the region with much-needed capital to carry out conservation and local development programmes. The challenge remains to develop pro-active policies and practical methods to mitigate the negative effects of tourism and highlight the positive. [...]

References

BJONNESS, I. M. (1980) 'Ecological conflicts and economic dependency on tourist trekking in Sagarmatha (Mt Everest) National Park, Nepal: an alternative approach to park planning', *Norsk Geogrrafisk Tidsskrift*, no.3, pp.119–38.

BOO, E. (1990) *Ecotourism: The Potentials and Pitfalls*, USA, World Wildlife Fund.

BOO, E. (1992) 'The ecotourism boom: planning for development and management. Wildlands and human needs: a program of the world Wildlife Fund', WHN Technical Paper Series, Paper No. 2.

SHERPA, M. N., COBURN, B. and GURUNG, C. P. (1986) *Annapurna Conservation Area, Nepal: Operational Plan*, Nepal, King Mahendra Trust for Nature Conservation.

THOMPSON, S. (1992) 'Trekking to save the tree line', *Geographical Magazine*, August, pp. 30–33.

WHELAN, T. (ed.) (1991) *Nature Tourism: Managing for the Environment*, Washington, DC, Island Press.

Within the tourism industry the fastest-growing sector is that of ecotourism, which has consequently generated unprecedented interest in the travel trade. The first Caribbean Conference on Ecotourism, held in 1991 in the small Central American state of Belize, attracted 350 delegates from the Caribbean, Central and South America and the USA.

Ecotourism has been variously defined. Interpreted loosely it can be used to describe any form of tourism which is based on the natural ecological attractions of a country, ranging from snorkelling off coral reefs to game viewing in savanna grasslands. A more rigorous definition, used by the recently formed Ecotourism Society, stresses the need to conserve natural environments and the well-being of local people through responsible travel. It therefore appears to offer developing countries the opportunity to capitalize on their natural attractions without incurring the adverse effects, now widely recognized, of conventional tourism.

Some important questions need to be asked, however. Does ecotourism really offer a sustainable option whether it is from the viewpoint of host nations, tourist guests or the environment? Is it a significantly different departure or is it just a more acceptably dressed-up version? There is a real danger that ecotourism may merely replicate the economic, social and physical problems already associated with conventional tourism. The only difference, and herein lies perhaps the greatest threat, is that often previously undeveloped areas, with delicately balanced physical and cultural environments, are being brought into the locus of international tourism.

What, then, are the major flaws in the argument that ecotourism is a substantially different hybrid from conventional tourism? In order to be truly sustainable, any form of tourism development should:

(a) Meet the needs of the host population in terms of improved living standards in both the short and long term.

(b) Satisfy the demands of a growing number of tourists and continue to attract them in order to meet this first aim.

(c) Safeguard the natural environment in order to achieve both of the preceding aims.

To examine the extent to which ecotourism meets these requirements of sustainability it is relevant to examine the recent experience of Belize. As a relative newcomer to the international tourism circuit, Belize is anxious to avoid the pitfalls of uncontrolled mass tourism. Within its small land area of 23,000 square kilometres, Belize has a wide variety of vegetation types ranging from mangrove swamps and wetland savanna to mountain pine forests and tropical rain forest. This range of habitats hosts such fauna as the manatee, jaguar, tapir, and howler monkey. In addition, Belize's spectacular barrier reef is the longest in the Western hemisphere and the second longest in the world. Added to these natural attractions are several notable archaeological sites of the Mayan civilization which are open to the public. The headquarters of the Mundo Maya organization, founded to promote the cultural, historical and environmental heritage of the ancient Maya in Central America, is located in Belize.

Using World Bank criteria, Belize rates only as a lower middle income country, with a per capita GNP in 1991 of US $2010. Ecotourism, therefore, based on bountiful natural attractions, appears to offer a welcome opportunity to augment considerably their foreign exchange earnings. International tourism receipts rose from US$7 million in 1980 to US $91 million in 1990 (see Table C.1)

The government has declared its commitment to balanced and environmentally sound tourism development by promoting ecotourism. As a destination Belize is being actively promoted as 'Belize so natural', 'friendly and unspoilt' and 'naturally yours'. How far this emphasis on ecotourism will constitute sustainable tourism development is questionable. Early signs

Table C.1 Belize: international tourist arrivals and receipts

	International tourist arrivals (thousands)		Percentage rate of change (ave. annual)	International tourism receipts (millions US$)		Percentage rate of change (ave. annual)
1980	64			7		
		'80–'85	9		'80–'85	14
1985	93			12		
		'85–'90	28		'85–'90	15
1990	222			91		

Source: World Tourism Organization, *Yearbook of Tourism Statistics,* Vol. 1, 1982, Vol. 1, 1992

suggest that there will be similar problems to those faced by conventional tourism development.

Common to most developing countries, Belize is subject to domination by the more developed countries (MDCs) as far as the patterns and organization of international tourism are concerned. Although most visitors do not arrive on mass market package tours, their tour, travel and accommodation needs are largely co-ordinated by firms based in their country of origin. When import leakages – resulting from the need to import significant amounts to support

the tourist industry – are added into the picture, net tourism receipts for Belize are substantially reduced. Until recently the tourist accommodation in Belize consisted almost solely of small-scale, family-run hotels, but the opening of two large international hotels in 1991 signifies change. Ecotourism has become big business.

An examination of the list of delegates to the ecotourism conference reveals that almost 70 per cent were representatives from travel agencies, tour operators, transport companies, hotels and resort developers (see Figure C.1). Only 15 per

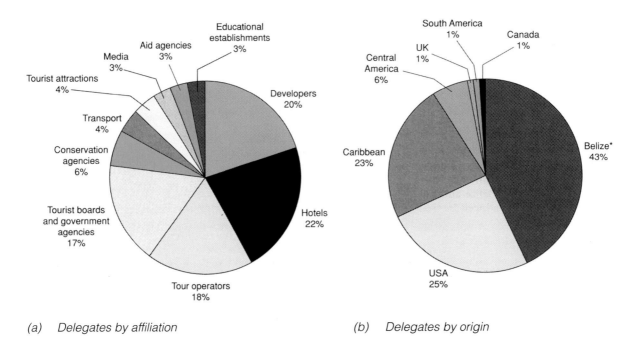

(a)   Delegates by affiliation

(b)   Delegates by origin

Figure C.1 Caribbean ecotourism conference

Note: *A significant proportion of delegates registering from Belize were expatriate Americans.

cent could be said to have no declared financial interest in the development of ecotourism, coming from conservation groups, educational institutions, aid agencies and the media. The remaining delegates were primarily from tourist boards within the wider Caribbean. Furthermore, a high proportion of the commercial interests represented were North American. A quarter of the delegates came from the USA and a significant number of those registered from Belize were American expatriates. Belize is only two hours' flying time from Miami, Houston and New Orleans. The environmentally insensitive development of resorts in Mexico such as Cancun has led to a scramble towards relatively unspoilt destinations in Belize, Honduras and Costa Rica.

Belize has a declared intention of promoting small as opposed to large-scale development, which would appear to be a more sustainable option. The amount of land held by a foreign individual in Belize is restricted by law. In practice, however, numerous small-scale foreign developments add up to the same thing as a few large-scale foreign developments, notably permanent alienation of land from Belizean ownership and control. In some ways such development is more detrimental. The level of demand is such that not only have land prices become inflated, often beyond the reach of Belizean nationals, but also estimates suggest that 90 per cent of all coastal development is now under foreign ownership. The Minister of Social Services and Community Development of Belize admits that there are no plans to restrict this foreign land ownership – typical of so many developing countries, Belize needs foreign investment. Not only are the benefits to Belize and her nationals considerably reduced by the degree of foreign involvement in the tourism industry, but also the local population can rarely afford to enjoy their own natural tourism resources.

How sustainable is the development of ecotourism in Belize from the point of view of the tourists themselves? While the present tourist arrivals (around 200,000 per annum) may be sufficiently low to guarantee individual satisfaction, the rapid rate of growth (28 per cent per annum, 1985–90) and the concentration of visitors in relatively few locations will prejudice that guarantee. Already the Hol Chan Marine reserve is showing signs of black band disease, a killer algae which attacks corals that have been knocked and broken. Researchers have also found a marked decline in the population of commercial species such as conch and lobster due to overfishing in Belize, partly to satisfy tourist demands. Furthermore the protagonists of ecotourism assume that ecotourists will be automatically enviromnentally sensitive. While well-briefed specialist tours conducted in small groups meet this criterion, the increasing tendency towards day-trips to nature reserves on an ad hoc basis refutes this assumption. A recent guided tour in Guanacaste National Park, Belize, promoted the wry observation from a Guatemalan ecologist that a length of sloughed snakeskin on the path had been trampled underfoot, unnoticed, by the rest of the large group. Unless careful attention is paid to the carrying capacity of localities, dictated not only by their characteristics but also by the numbers and behavioural characteristics of the tourists themselves, ecotourism will not be a sustainable venture.

The concept of carrying capacity prompts a query about the extent to which the environment is being safeguarded to ensure sustainability for both hosts and guests. The crucial issue here is that while the designation of National Parks and reserves may meet the needs of conservationists and, if properly managed, those of present and future tourists, the prospects for sustainable development of the host population may be compromised. The Belizean government has designated 16 large tracts of pristine rain forest, comprising 30 per cent of the entire land area, as national reserves. Land has also been set aside for National Parks such as at Guanacaste, Cockscomb and Crooked Tree (see Figure C.2). Farming has been banned in the reserves, placing a check on the traditional slash-and-burn style of agriculture. Such cultivators along the Hummingbird Highway were pointed out by a tour leader this summer as posing a threat to the interests of ecotourism. No

Figure C.2 Location of protected areas in Belize

concern was shown for the basic survival needs of these subsistence farmers.

There are, however, two more positive examples in Belize of where the local population has become actively incorporated into tourism development, thus ensuring long-term sustainability. The first is the Community Baboon Sanctuary at Bermudian Landing. This sanctuary is a completely voluntary conservation programme based on the co-operation of local private landowners who have agreed to confine their slash-and-burn practices to protect the habitat of the black howler monkey. In return they benefit from the increased revenue that tourism has brought to the area. The second is the Sandy Beach Lodge cultural centre and hotel built by the Sandy Beach Women's Co-operative at Hopkins village, south of Dangriga, in 1988. The co-operative offers local Garifuna cultural attractions including dances, handicraft, art and cuisine. They also offer trips to the nearby cayes (low islands) so that the natural attractions of this coastal area may be appreciated. Members of the co-operative are paid according to the services they render, so this is a truly locally based enterprise.

Ecotourism may aim to be more environmentally sensitive but, as numbers of tourists increase, it will inevitably generate similar infrastructural demands to traditional tourism. New coastal development in Belize involves clearing the mangrove swamps and then infilling the low-lying land. Mangroves perform three vital functions: they act as a filter for off-land sediment, as rich feeding-grounds for fish and as a protection against coastal erosion. The infill comes from the wetland savanna a few miles inland where the topsoil is literally shaved off, leaving large scars devoid of vegetation. Ironically the Biltmore Plaza, which was the venue for the ecotourism conference, has itself been built on land which has involved the destruction of two distinct ecosystems. Even small-scale developments are no guarantee against environmental degradation. The island of Caye Caulker with its small guest houses has for several years been regarded as a refreshingly low-key alternative to the prime tourist resort of San Pedro on Ambergris Caye. [In 1991] the government carved an airstrip across the island, ignoring the wishes of the local population, who regarded fresh water supply and adequate sewage disposal as higher priorities. The land excavated nearby to backfill the site has not only destroyed nesting sites but has also created a lake of stagnant water which will undoubtedly furnish a breeding ground for mosquitoes. This is hardly a sustainable solution for the local population, the tourists or the environment.

To conclude, there is a great danger that the sophisticated marketing and promotional strategies of travel and tour operators based in the MDCs will lead to the false belief that ecotourism is a panacea for all tourism's ills. It is not even guaranteed to be ecologically sensitive, let alone sustainable as far as host populations, tourists and the environment itself are concerned. Yet to argue against ecotourism is to swim against the tide. In an increasingly environmentally conscious world the search for unspoiled nature will remain high on the tourist agenda. Ecotourism, despite its faults, is a lesser evil than uncontrolled mass tourism. Tour companies have eagerly jumped on this highly profitable bandwagon. At the same time they are able to promote a seemingly more conscientious image which may or may not go beyond shrewd marketing tactics. The inevitable outcome is that the main beneficiaries of ecotourism, as with tourism in general in the developing world, are tourism enterprises, all too often located in the MDCs. A more complete understanding of the issues involves the recognition that tourism of whatever type is but a process cast in a markedly unequal context, whether within or between countries. Unless the basic issues are addressed, ecotourism may well be regarded as a form of eco-colonialism.

Source: Cater, 1992

Uneven worlds

Chapter 6

by John Allen and Chris Hamnett

6.1 Introduction

If the world does appear to you to be a smaller place and the distances between places seem to be that much less, you share this experience with many a well-to-do European traveller making their way around their respective Empires at the end of the eighteenth and nineteenth centuries. From the preceding chapters it should be apparent that the notion that the world is shrinking in distance terms is far from a new idea. Although the phenomena of footloose multinationals, transnational pollution, accelerated financial markets and the ever-increasing spread of tourists across the globe are fairly recent developments, they may be every bit as global in scope as, say, the colonial ties laid down in the eighteenth century or the dense web of economic transactions that made up the world economy at the end of the nineteenth century. The different ties, the different lines of connection between places, represent successive phases of globalization (see **Allen, 1995**). So when, today, we speak about a world that is shrinking in size, it is not the novelty of the movement which should hold our attention, but rather the qualitative shift in our experience of space and time brought about by the latest wave of global processes. If the present era is one of great spatial upheaval then, arguably, it is the immediacy and intensity with which we experience 'elsewhere' which distinguishes it – whether it be through a series of networked media images, high-speed travel, eating out in a global city, or by suddenly finding ourselves working for a foreign multinational on a subcontract basis.

The main purpose of this chapter is to stand back from the detail of global issues and to take a closer look at the nature of this experience, in particular at its profoundly uneven and unequal character. The latest wave of globalization may appear to be lowering social and spatial barriers and, according to some, dissolving the different and distinctive characters of places, but as we have seen in each of the preceding chapters there are a number of ways in which general acceptance of this view would not only be premature, it would also be misplaced.

It would be misplaced for at least three broad reasons, each of which is the focus of a subsequent section of the chapter.

In the *first* place, the experience of the world getting smaller or shrinking in distance terms has not been happening evenly across the globe. Some parts of the world have literally been missed out by the types of developments discussed in Chapters 1 and 2, for example. They are either not part of the network of telecommunications or they remain largely untouched by the movement of goods and money that criss-cross the globe. And in other parts of the world, where places have been brought together through revolutions in transport and communications technologies, some people find themselves by-passed or constrained by the self-same developments. More generally, the lowering of spatial barriers, such as the relaxation of controls erected by national governments to the flow of multinational investments or the decrease in telecommunications and transport costs, have not resulted in an indifference to places now that they appear to be more within our reach.

In fact, it is precisely through such differences that global processes work. Put another way, global processes of the kind that we have been considering in this book work themselves out unevenly and, in turn, are shaped by the pattern of uneven development previously laid down. We will consider this view at some length in section 6.2.

A *second* reason for adopting a rather cautious stance to an all-embracing view of globalization is that, even if places are tied in globally, it does not follow that everywhere is moving in the same direction, along the same path of development, with the same prospects and converging cultural lifestyles. The various ways in which nations and peoples have been drawn together into a tighter, more interdependent world through closer economic, political and cultural ties have produced a profoundly unequal world. We look briefly at these issues in section 6.3 by taking a broad historical view of some of the social ties that have shaped relationships between countries.

And a *third* reason to qualify the speed at which social and spatial barriers are dropping is that it is not only the ties between places which are structured unequally. Within cities and towns, we find groups of people linked into the global system in different and unequal ways; ways that, despite the compression of space by time, may leave groups more remote from one another in the same location than if they were at opposite corners of the globe. The contact with other parts of the world may have rendered the experience of previously isolated cultures more immediate, but the remoteness of everyday life in the global cities is not reducible to physical distance. It is this particular form of unevenness that we explore in section 6.4.

6.2 The end of geography?

This was the rhetorical question posed at the end of Chapter 1 and answered in a rather sceptical manner. In a world of spatial upheaval, where people and places come closer together as distances recede, the idea that geographical location is no longer as significant as it once was is compelling. Certainly for O'Brien (1991), who forcefully posed the question, our sense of geography has been redefined by dramatic economic, political and technological developments in the past few decades. According to him, many of these developments 'defy' geography: they challenge conventional notions of distance, boundaries and movement. And in one sense, as we have seen in this book, they clearly do challenge such notions. They are also said, however, to defy the difference and diversity of locations that is a crucial part of geography. It is the latter view which, for us, needs to be placed on one side and reconsidered. For the networks of social relationships stretched across space are not simply uneven in their global reach, they also work through *geographical difference and diversity*. Geography matters in this instance, precisely because global relations construct unevenness in their wake *and* operate through the pattern of uneven development laid down.

geographical difference and diversity

6.2.1 Uneven global relations

Cast your mind back to the discussion of transport and communications networks in Chapter 1 and the fact that they have produced a dense web of connections across the globe since the middle of the nineteenth century. Recall the submarine cable, railways and McLuhan's electronic communications media and how they tied more and more people and places together. Remember also, the flows of money that today move across the globe at the speed of light as photons along fibre-optic cables. Now pause for a moment and consider the vast areas of the globe with virtually no links of any kind going to them. Take the example of money first.

Clearly, distances have shrunk the world of finance, but the majority of places are not on the maps of finance. Much of the 'third world', for example, is excluded from the global financial system and, if anything, it is further away from the developed world in the 1990s than it was a decade earlier, as Chapter 1 pointed out. The flows of finance are geographically selective, as they are for all forms of communication. Fibre-optic cables and satellite link-ups may bring the likes of New York, Tokyo and London together, and even Baghdad and Singapore, but in Niger or Cambodia a telephone is still a rare sight.

The idea that there has been an acceleration in the pace of life, a speed-up, as it were, in the almost intangible flows of communication and information has its tangible counterpart in the form of factories and workplaces. At one extreme, there is the playful image conjured up by Gordon (1988), 'of capital as the roadrunner, whizzing around the globe, honking every time it escapes the grasp of local labour and pausing to rest, only for a moment, when profit conditions seem perfectly ripe.' But this notion of firms as footloose, capable of sweeping across the globe at will is, as we have seen, something of a caricature. Multinationals today certainly possess the potential to open and close plants with surprising speed, certainly greater than the mobility of their workforces, yet equally surprising is the vast majority of multinationals which stay put. The costs of investment in plant and equipment and the location of markets have both served to limit not only capital mobility but also the global scope of investments. From Chapter 2, for example, we have learnt that far from more and more of the world being drawn into the net of multinational investment, foreign direct investment is concentrated in relatively few locations; Figure 6.1 illustrates the extent.

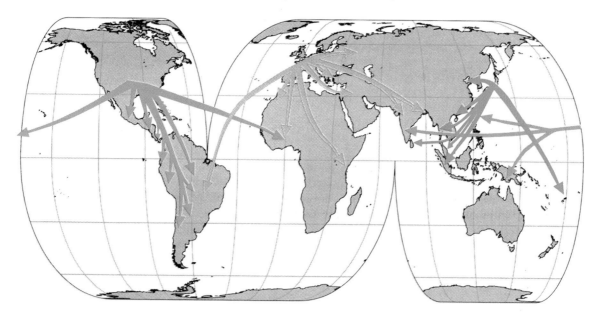

Figure 6.1 Foreign direct investment clusters (economies in which the US, Europe and Japan dominate inward FDI stocks and/or flows) (Source: United Nations, 1993)

Apart from historical ties connected to past colonial practices, the pattern of investment is broadly one of three clusters of countries – or *global region* – each dominated by a powerful neighbour. In the case of Western Europe, countries principally invest in one another, as well as in Eastern Europe. In South and East Asia, the dominant investor is Japan, and the investment reach of US firms, apart from Canada, is principally to central and southern America. All in all, the markets of the rich, industrialized world – North America, Europe and Japan – take over three-quarters of overseas investment, with a handful of industrializing countries in Latin America and Asia taking the the remainder. Sub-Saharan Africa – 'the third world's third world' – is virtually missed out, for instance. In population terms, with North America, Europe and Japan accounting for only fourteen per cent of the world's population in the early 1990s, it takes little more than a back of an envelope calculation to realize that, like finance, the vast majority of the world is off the map of multinational investment in so far as technology and jobs are concerned.

global region

What is also interesting to note about the overall pattern of investment is its gendered character. As indicated in Chapter 2, when multinational investment in the form of 'global factories' went to the industrializing countries of Latin America and South East Asia from the 1960s on, many of the firms sought explicitly to employ women on a low-wage basis. As Haraway (1990) and others have pointed out, however, it is not simply that women represented the preferred labour force in the export-processing sectors of the less developed economies, whilst men monopolized job opportunities in the first world. That may have been true of certain developments in the 1960s, but it does not capture the situation today. Within the economies of the developed world, especially those of North America and parts of Europe, women would appear to be the preferred labour force for many of the jobs coming on stream in both manufacturing and services, leaving men, especially those without skills and qualifications, in a position of job loss and insecurity.

The broad increase in job insecurity in the older industrialized economies has not, however, led to a stemming of the flows of migrants from less developed to developed economies, regardless of gender. At the very moment when the 'West' is experiencing an inability to create sufficient jobs, the poorer peoples of the world appear to be moving in greater numbers to its global cities. Attracted by the prospects of a better lifestyle, economic migrants have headed for the big cities of Western Europe and North America, precisely to be 'on the map' – to be at those points on the globe where the lines of investment and prosperity intersect. Indeed, as Chapter 3 pointed out, one of the reasons behind the flow of migrants to cities such as New York, Los Angeles and London, as well as Paris, Milan and Berlin, is because they are perceived to be tied in more closely to the workings of the global economy than are many other locations. Such cities are not simply 'on the map', their institutions are regarded by many to be primarily responsible for the economic map; that is, the networks of social relationships that lie behind a global economy characterized by geographical unevenness and inequality.

Activity 1 Think about the *cartography* of the lines of communication, finance, investment, migration and the like that we have considered here. We have spoken about some places as 'on the map' and of other places as 'off the map', implying that certain parts of the world are tied in to the processes of globalization, whereas others are missed out by them. From this it should be possible to gain a sense of the uneven geography laid down by these particular global processes. If you were to map this pattern, what kind of geographical image comes to mind? Use Figure 6.2 to map the connections based on what you have learned from the previous chapters. The principal telecommunications flows have been mapped to start you off.

One aspect that struck us was that if you were to superimpose the different lines of telecommunications, trade, monetary flows and overseas investments by multinationals, one on top of the other so to speak, the image produced would be one that is characterized by a density of ties across the developed world, becoming sparser the further one reached into the less developed world. In the southern half of the globe, for example, there would be significant areas with few lines of any kind going to them. As noted in the introduction, parts of the world – sub-Saharan Africa, for instance – would be unlikely to figure on a whole range of economic and social maps.

What is also striking about this image of global unevenness is that the lines of interdependence and interconnection are *centred* in the developed North. Centred in the sense that, although the networks stretch well beyond the developed countries, the global economic relationships are held in place and largely reshaped by forces in the rich, developed nations and, to a lesser extent, some rapidly developing nations. In that sense, much of what happens to the geographical spread of communication lines or, for that matter, industrial production, is still likely to be driven by institutions embedded within the three global regions of North America, Europe and East Asia.

Also centred in the industrialized world in this way is a rather different kind of global flow from those discussed above, one which indeed all countries would wish to see pass by them: namely, transnational pollution. From Chapter 4, we have seen how pollution has increased in both its impact and global spread. The spread, however, varies depending upon the source of pollution with, for example, the discharge of unwanted wastes by ship and carbon dioxide emissions from the burning of fossil fuels posing a threat to the global commons, whereas much land pollution tends to be local in character. Local pollution, however, may spill over into adjoining countries, as in the case of industrial sewage from US-owned plants in the maquiladora zones in Mexico rebounding on the US through water pollution in California.

Those who cause the pollution in one part of the world are not necessarily those who suffer its consequences, however. The rich, industrialized nations may export their pollution in a variety of ways, thus compounding environmental differences between places. Invariably it is the poorer countries in pursuit of foreign exchange which are on the receiving end of such export flows, giving rise to what some have called 'garbage imperialism'. The example outlined in Chapter 4 of the North exporting hazardous wastes to countries in the South is an illustration of this point. As with the global flows of finance and investment, pollution has an uneven geography with certain places in control of the flows, whilst others are passed by or, even worse, experience the negative outcomes.

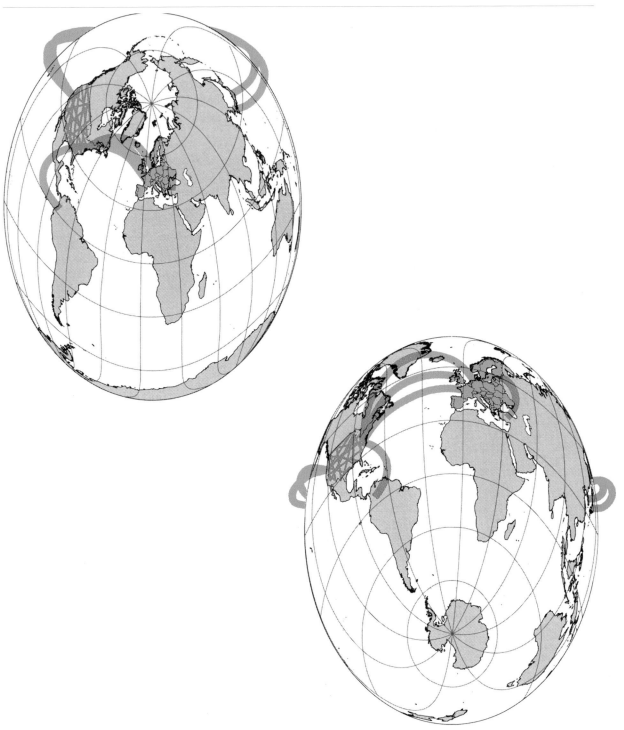

Figure 6.2   On and off the map of globalization: a diagrammatic representation

In sum, therefore, the web of interrelationships and ties stretched out across the globe – whether they involve communications networks, financial ties or pollutant trade relationships – work themselves out in an uneven geographical manner between and indeed across countries. Such processes lay down patterns of uneven development. They also, as we are about to see, work through the differences constructed between places.

6.2.2   Distance and location

It is perhaps something of a paradox that as distance in terms of miles and kilometres is overcome, so the difference between locations tends to become more not less significant. The 'annihilation of space' that has come about through developments in transport and communications technologies has in one sense not only made the far-off seem less distant, it has for many people raised their awareness of the diversity of peoples and places.

Activity 2   Travel is one of the most obvious ways in which places are, as it were, much nearer than they were before. Spatial proximity through travel, whether through tourism or through the simulated kind that can be called up on our television screens, has brought us into contact with other parts of the world. People from many parts of the globe are able to draw contrasts between locations and to recognize their distinctive characteristics. Consider, then, the kind of heightened sensitivity to the difference between places displayed by tourists from the first world and by economic migrants trying to move there. What characteristics of places are the two groups likely to foreground?

For tourists, the sensitivity to the difference between tourist destinations is likely to vary along cultural and class lines. Following Bourdieu (1986) and Urry (1990), the differences between places add up to a kind of symbolic system in which locations come to embody particular class 'tastes'. Distinctions are drawn between places: some resorts are tacky, others dull, whilst still others are exotic and refined, and so forth. And the distinctions may change, as places that were once thought of as remote and exotic, become routine and commonplace. Much of this should be familiar from Chapter 5, where specialist forms of tourism such as ecotourism have taken on a certain distinction in comparison with, say, mass tourism in Spain. In this context, it is not simply that a desire to see ecological attractions in far-off destinations conveys a sense of superior status; rather, it is the actual ability to appreciate ecology which indicates cultural competence. Not everyone is assumed to be able to 'appreciate' the social significance of natural ecological attractions such as the richness of a tropical rainforest or a mangrove swamp and this in itself serves to distinguish between people and where they choose to holiday. Thus, as the possibility of long-distance movements increase, minute judgements of taste may be made between a greater range of tourist destinations spread out across the globe. Access for the wealthier tourists is not, of course, likely to be an issue.

In contrast, it is precisely the question of access which will figure prominently in the minds of economic migrants. Nations differ in the barriers to entry and residence that they put up to immigrants. Some countries lay stress upon family connections as a condition of entry, others upon 'special relationships' (usually of a historical kind), and others like Germany at present have no immigration laws to speak of, only a system of regulations that denies citizenship to virtually all incomers. Somewhat ironically in a world that is said to be getting smaller, the barriers to migrant entry erected by the rich industrialized nations are probably greater today than they were a hundred years ago. The attempts by migrants from poor countries to get 'on the map' of prosperity is one fraught with difficulty, as life on the borders of any affluent nation will testify. The persistent rush of illegal immigration across the Californian US/Mexico border is perhaps one of the best-known examples of this state of affairs. It is not all about spatial proximity, however. In an era when you can be transported faster and further than ever before, the immigration authorities at international airports can give you a different experience of *time–space compression* if you are unaware of the restrictive policies laid down by a particular country.

time–space
compression

Political and cultural differences between places are also likely to figure prominently in the investment plans of global firms. While many firms are capable of a global reach, most governments have regulatory barriers of one kind or another to the free flow of capital, goods and services. On the latter, it is only recently that a number of countries have opened up their service sectors to foreign investment, in particular those of banking, insurance and telecommunications. Even then, however, the conditions of entry and establishment are likely to specify requirements on the nature of the operation, the transfer of technologies (know-how as well as the 'hard' variety) or the repatriation of profits. On top of which, national governments will frequently discriminate against multinationals on the grounds of their nationality, for political and historical reasons such as those of military occupation. Having said that, most governments actually encourage overseas investment within their borders, offering a range of measures from tax incentives to subsidies or labour options in order to attract certain kinds of multinationals.

Contrary, therefore, to the impression that such terms as a 'borderless world' may convey of a world in which geographical difference and unevenness is

Mexicans wait to cross the US/Mexico border

on the demise, it is the very fact of difference between places that motivates the global corporations to be in some countries and not others. Even Ohmae (1990) is fully aware of this when he argues that the big corporations have to be inside the rich markets of the first world if they are to compete and survive at the global level. More than that, such firms will make use of the differences between places within the world's regional markets to meet their *particular* locational requirements.

We can see this in the example of the big US and European electronics multinationals back in the 1960s choosing to locate their routine assembly operations in places like Singapore, Hong Kong and Taiwan primarily for cost reasons, notwithstanding issues of political stability, taxes and the like. Now, however, such multinationals have a presence in the East Asia region not only because their labour requirements may still be met (with the low-cost operations shifted to, for example, Malaysia, Indonesia, Thailand or China), but also because the region is one of the world's fastest-growing markets. It is not only tourists and migrants, therefore, who have a heightened sensitivity to the difference between places.

Summary of section 6.2

In the wake of the latest wave of globalization, statements which herald the end of geography may provoke misunderstanding as to what a 'shrinking world' entails:

o   Distances have shrunk on the maps of finance, communications, investment and tourism, but in an uneven and unequal manner, leaving large tracts of the globe barely touched by global networks.

o   Although the lines of interconnection and interdependence reach out well beyond the developed nations, the processes are centred in the industrialized world, especially in the global cities.

o   Paradoxically, as the barriers of physical distance have been lowered or, in some cases, collapsed, bringing everywhere closer as it were, the distinctiveness of places has become all the more important.

6.3   An interdependent world

uneven development

In the previous section, it was mentioned in passing that *uneven development* is not just about taking note of difference and diversity, it is about geographical inequality too. So far, we have touched mainly on the inequalities produced where places are 'off the map' of global connections and ties. *An unequal global geography, however, is as much the product of the ties that bind places, as it is about those that are not tied in at all.* Being 'on the map' may result in a variety of outcomes, not least of which is that some places may benefit at the expense of others. Whilst true for transnational pollution, this has also been

unequal exchange

true historically, from the forms of *unequal exchange* in the trading links and cultural ties between western Imperial powers and their Empires – both formal and informal – up to the present day and contemporary forms of unequal economic exchange and cultural negotiation.

6.3.1 Unequal global relations

We have only to look back as far as the nineteenth century to observe the creation of an international economy. Although, as Chapter 2 pointed out, its emergence dates back to an earlier period of trade and colonization, it is the 'age of Empire' which witnessed an increase in the scope of global relations, as well as in the sheer volume of transactions (Hobsbawm, 1987).

A number of ties across the globe arose from the burgeoning demands of the industrialized and industrializing economies of Europe and America. To satisfy the new industries and their appetite for raw materials – tin, copper, rubber, oil being among the most important – ever more remote locations were opened up. Rubber, for example, initially came from the tropical rainforests of Amazonia, moving (via the 'colonial botanical gardens' at Kew in London) in the late nineteenth century to Malaysia, Indonesia and Sri Lanka in response to the growing demand from vehicle production in the industrialized economies. Similarly, as the consumption demands of the metropolitan populations approached that of mass standards, the search for foodstuffs – in particular, grain, meat, tea, coffee, sugar and various tropical products – was largely satisfied from the colonial and semi-colonial territories. Significant quantities of grain and meat came from the European settler colonies in the Americas, sugar from the plantation economies of the Caribbean, tea from India, Sri Lanka and East Africa, coffee from Brazil and Kenya, and so forth. And moving in the other direction, laying down different kinds of ties, was the export of manufactured goods and capital from a handful of developed economies to the rest of the world. In the case of Britain, the largest of the Imperial powers at the time, much of the capital investment went to the settler colonies and to places like Argentina and Uruguay to finance infrastructural developments and the furtherance of trade (Kenwood and Lougheed, 1992).

Activity 3 Think about the nature of the ties involved above; in particular consider the different economic roles performed by countries at either end of the economic ties. What kind of inequalities, if any, may arise from the nature of these exchanges? Bear in mind that many of the countries supplying raw materials and foodstuffs to the industrialized world specialized in one or two products.

Trade appears to be a central feature of the ties between countries, with each side dependent on the other for the exchange. The form of economic interdependence between the two sides, with one side exporting manufactured goods and capital and the other exporting foodstuffs and raw materials as a basis for the former's manufacture, was frequently of an unequal nature, however. Countries in South America or sub-Saharan Africa, for example, which were virtually dependent on the export of primary products such as copper or tin, saw the fortunes of their economies rest on the price for metals determined at world level by the developed economies. If a particular metal such as copper could be sourced from any number of countries, the relationship between the two sides of the exchange was, as Hobsbawm has pointed out, a profoundly unequal one.

It was not only the international economy at that time which was characterized by *relations of inequality*, however; the cultural relations between Imperial powers and their dependencies were also ones characterized by a form of unequal exchange. Perhaps the most significant illustration of this is

relations of inequality

243

the way in which a particular kind of 'Englishness' was constructed through the web of relationships that made up the British Empire in the nineteenth century. To be 'English' at that time was to be located in a *particular geography*: one which gave the English not only a sense of superiority in relation to others, but also an ability to speak on their behalf – be they in India, Egypt, Sudan, British East Africa or parts of the Far East coloured a reddish pink on the map.

As Hall (1991) has remarked of the 'English' identity,

It is located in a place, in a specific history. It could not speak except out of a place, out of those histories. It is located in relation to a whole set of notions about territory, about where is home and where is overseas, what is close to us and what is far away. It is mapped out in all the terms in which we can understand what ethnicity is. It is unfortunately, for a time, the ethnicity which places all the other ethnicities, but nevertheless, it is one in its own terms.

(Hall, 1991, pp. 21–2)

To be placed by this particular English identity, as indeed were those in the colonial territories, was to experience a one-sided form of cultural exchange. 'Englishness' as a way of life, a set of values, a specific way of doing things, was not represented as a way of being, but as *the* way of presenting one's self. It involved a set of attitudes which took for granted not only that distant territories and peoples had a need for some kind of civilizing values, it also comprised a vocabulary which spoke about the worthiness and suitability of particular peoples in far-off places (Said, 1994). As such, it spoke *as if* it were culturally all-embracing. To pick tea on an English plantation in India, therefore, was not simply an act of profit and accumulation; it was to find oneself within a colonizing project. Moreover, such a project entailed a geography which for the English abroad helped to maintain a particular lifestyle 'back home' and produced a vision of what life 'overseas' should be like. No matter that few of the English sent to India to become part of the Indian civil service learnt the local language, whereas the local clerks were quick to learn English; the *imaginary geography* of Empire was sufficient to legitimize this form of unequal cultural exchange (see **Massey, 1995**).

imaginary geography

What, then, is so different about the cultural and economic impact of globalization a century or so later? Clearly the *depth* of global relations was keenly felt under colonial and Imperial rule. But, as noted in the introduction to the chapter, the experience of space and time was qualitatively different. Communication by telegraph or travel by ship between the various outposts of the old Empires does not equate to the immediacy that modern transport and communication systems allow. The world may have shrunk considerably in the nineteenth century, but the new interdependencies that have sprung up in the latter half of the twentieth century are negotiated at a different *pace*.

More than that, the density of interrelationships that criss-cross the globe is greater than before, although here we need to remind ourselves of the distinction between those relationships which connect places together in a more immediate fashion, such as electronic mail or satellite links, and those that represent some form of *interdependence*. The latter relationships, as noted in Chapter 2, carry a certain vulnerability to the ties involved, which may be more important to one end of the relationship than to the other. This was

interdependence

English identity was inseparable from 'its' far-flung geography

certainly the case for the primary product producers in the nineteenth century and its contemporary equivalent may well be those countries who have enticed multinationals across their borders only to see them leave at short notice for more profitable locations.

According to Cardoso (1993), however, that is not the main concern of the less developed countries. Rather it is that they will no longer be able to attract overseas investment and foreign involvement, as the comparative advantages of cheap labour and resources lose their significance in a more capital-intensive, information-based global economy. This may be somewhat exaggerated, but it does point to the importance of being *on* the global economic map, especially when the flows of money and capital are unevenly concentrated in the three 'global regions'. Indeed, the example of the recent growth of the East Asian economies – Hong Kong, Singapore, South Korea and Taiwan – *within* a complex set of global interdependencies is perhaps a better indication of the mutual vulnerabilities that come from being part of today's global economy. Countries such as Singapore, for example, may have acted as cheap labour locations for western multinationals in the early post-war period to become part of the flows of finance and industry, but at the turn of the millennium, as noted earlier, MNCs remain in Singapore because it is an integral part of one of the three global regions. While South and East Asia remain economically dynamic, the relationship between MNCs and Singapore will become many-sided, in contrast to the one-sided form of dependence of earlier years.

Culturally, there is a similar form of complexity at work between countries. At one level, an unequal cultural exchange may appear to persist in the export of western lifestyles to countries aspiring to emulate the trappings of an industrialized culture. The ubiquitous trainers and jeans, for example, are valued in many poorer countries not simply for their material content, but for the identity that they convey about their owners. Cultural identities, however, are not reducible to such superficial images; rather the languages, traditions and histories which make up peoples are the product of more complicated encounters than that of simply western consumption styles. Indeed, the very fact of movement and mobility amongst the world's populations has produced a cultural unevenness and mix within the global cities of the first world as much as elsewhere. 'Englishness' today, for example, is not the overbearing, class-saturated culture of the nineteenth century; it is no longer primarily located in the 'blank spaces' of a particular Imperial geography; rather it is part of a complex geography of different ties and connections which are in the process of translating the old cultural interdependencies (see **Hall, 1995**).

6.3.2   Distance and proximity

Living in an interdependent world characterized by movement, mobility and rapid forms of communication does not only conjure an image of the world as shrinking in size, then, it also implies that what happens elsewhere may well affect your life-chances and lifestyles. From newspapers, television and the radio, we know what is happening half-way across the globe shortly after it has happened – and what, if any, consequences it holds for us. With proximity, therefore, comes a certain vulnerability which may not have been there before. The experience of being tied in to global relationships in various ways, especially if they are of an immediate or intense nature, heightens our sense of their uneven nature and impact.

In the case of transnational pollution, for example, such events generate anxiety and opposition. Every day, according to estimates, tons of hazardous waste leave the port of Los Angeles destined for recycling plants in the less developed world. Awareness of this trade in places where the waste ends up – in the Philippines, for example – has been sufficient to generate outright opposition to such dumping. It is not only the wealth of the first world which is around the corner, therefore; as Chapter 4 pointed out, so too is their garbage. Environmentalists are also keen to point out the proximity of environmental threats in what is, after all, *one* interconnected world. The loss of tropical rainforests, in Amazonia, for instance, is represented not only as a cultural and economic loss to local peoples, but also as an ecological disaster that touches us all. Such rainforests may not exactly be around the corner, but what happens to them is a source of anxiety and resistance.

The same is perhaps true for a variety of global connections and ties. The reverse side of the increasingly concentrated patterns of global investment and trade, for example, is a greater awareness of who is missing out – and perhaps why. It may well be the World Bank that informs us that it is likely to be forty years before sub-Saharan Africa returns to the level of wealth it had twenty years ago in the mid-1970s, but the post-colonial writers of the 'third world', from first world platforms, are able to spell out both the impact that earlier forms of globalization had upon their countries and reinterpret what the latest wave of globalization should, as opposed to might, have in store for them. Whilst it would be wrong to talk about such a consciousness as a recent phenomenon, it is tempting to suggest that the shifts in movement, mobility and communications discussed in this book have empowered those who are on the sidelines of globalization to register their demands within a *global* context.

Activity 4 This is not so much an activity as an opportunity to reflect upon what views of globalization you might find were you to place yourself in Gabon or Cameroon, or in the Philippines or Cambodia. Imagine yourself writing a geography of the ties and connection that entangle or by-pass you *back to* the first world. In what ways would the compression of space by time have altered your *experience* of globalization?

Summary of section 6.3

o   Uneven development, therefore, is not simply about the difference between places and peoples, but rather about how the differences are produced and reproduced through ties of interdependence.

o   An interdependent world is one characterized by relationships stretched across the globe which link peoples of unequal power in complex, vulnerable ways.

o   A further characteristic of an interdependent world is that the experience of being near to everywhere may generate resistance to and anxiety about what is happening elsewhere and, indeed, globally.

6.4   Worlds apart

So far, we have spoken largely about distance and proximity in relation to the spatial barriers and horizons which have altered in response to global shifts. Drawing people closer together across space is not the same thing, however, as social proximity. People may occupy the same workplace, for example, or live in the same street, yet be part of quite different networks of global relations. Movement and mobility is central here, as different groups of people are to be found side-by-side with other groups, yet the social spaces they occupy may be as remote from one another as if the distance was measured in hundreds or even thousands of miles. In this section, we look at two forms of movement that are in part responsible for the kinds of social juxtapositions that are a key element of everyday life in global cities today: namely, migration and tourism.

6.4.1   Social distance

As we saw in Chapter 3, global cities are characterized by a high concentration of economic and financial control and co-ordination functions. As a consequence, the social structure of these cities is distinct from that of other cities. They have a high proportion of highly skilled and highly paid professional and managerial workers who staff the company headquarters, banks and commercial services they contain. Global cities also contain a marked concentration of highly paid personnel in the cultural industries and the mass media. But while highly skilled workers are significant in the occupational structure of global cities, they are not the only groups, nor even numerically the most important. In addition to the army of administrators and secretarial workers, there is also a large and generally low-skilled and low-paid group of service workers employed as chambermaids, waiters, security guards, cleaners and the like.

What is interesting about the latter group of workers, however, is that they may be every bit as global as the professional workers in the financial and commercial sectors of such cities; they are simply part of different *networks of global relations*. These relations overlap in locations like global cities, yet are lived in ways that reveal much about the manner in which they are connected across space through their networks.

networks of global relations

If we take each group in turn, on the one side there is a large and growing volume of skilled international migration of professionals, managers and other specialists. Some of these migrants, such as film producers, actors and technicians moving to Los Angeles, do so in order to be where the work is. Many of them move because they are needed to staff the large numbers of companies and banks in global cities. The American and Japanese banks in London, for example, contain many UK workers, but they also have a high proportion of foreign nationals in key positions. Similarly, UK companies and banks abroad will have a strong proportion of UK managers and skilled workers. As the global economic and financial system becomes more integrated, so the level of skilled international migration increases. Some skilled international migration is permanent, but most is temporary. The migrants work for only a few years abroad before returning home. In the case of corporate migrants, it is often company policy to rotate staff in order to give them experience of operations in different countries or to work on specific projects.

Skilled international migration is a relatively recent phenomenon, however. The dominant flow of migrants to global cities in the post-war period has been quite different in nature and has involved migration from ex-colonies and the 'third world' to the metropolitan centres. This migration, which is predominantly of less skilled or unskilled workers, represents an interesting reversal of the migrant flows prior to the Second World War. In the colonial period, the major flows of migrants were generally from the western metropolitan core outwards to the periphery: from the 'West' to the rest. In addition to military postings, tens of thousands of planters, traders and colonial administrators went out to the far corners of the Empire to seek their fortune or to build a career. But the past thirty to forty years have seen a reversal of this pattern of migrant flows. Today, the dominant migration flows are from the rest to the 'West', particularly to the major cities where the employment opportunities are greatest – a movement which is effectively captured in the title of the book *The Empire Strikes Back* (CCCS, 1982).

In Britain migration has been primarily from the Caribbean, India and Pakistan, Hong Kong, Uganda and Cyprus. In France migration has come from Algeria and from their other former African and Caribbean colonies. In the Netherlands the migration is from Indonesia, Surinam and the Moluccas (the heart of the colonial Dutch spice trade) to the port cities of Amsterdam and Rotterdam. In the United States the migration has generally been from Mexico and Puerto Rico, and more recently Vietnam, Korea and India; it is estimated that about a million Mexicans emigrate (either legally or illegally) to the USA each year. In recent years many Western European cities have experienced migration from Eastern and Southern Europe. In Germany the migration has commonly come from Turkey and the former Yugoslavia, but the pattern is changing: the migrations are becoming more global in character. The major Italian cities are attracting Yugoslavs, Senegalese and Filipinos; many of the latter are women, coming to work as maids and domestic servants, channelled through the Catholic institutional links between the two countries (Pugliese, 1993). In New York, Washington or Los Angeles, the cab-driver may be from Eritrea, Vietnam or Russia.

The flows of these two quite distinct groups of migrants to the major cities of the western world have resulted in the juxtaposition of migrants from different backgrounds and different cultures who perform very different roles. On the one hand, the large-scale 'third world' migration to global cities provides a classic example of what has been termed the *peripheralization of the core*. Migrant groups have brought their own cultures and languages with them, and live in what are, to all intents and purposes, their own cultural networks, many of which stretch across the globe. Hannertz (1990) argues that some ordinary labour migrants are unlikely to integrate. Drawing on Theroux's suggestion that travel for some constitutes 'home plus'(1986, p. 133), Hannertz suggests that for skilled migrants:

peripheralization of the core

> *For them going away may be, ideally, home plus higher income; often the involvement with another culture is not a fringe benefit but a necessary cost, to be kept as low as possible. A surrogate home is … created with the help of compatriots, in whose circle one becomes encapsulated.*
>
> (Hannertz, 1990, p. 243)

This is particularly marked in some American cities: Los Angeles, for example, not only contains a highly diverse population, drawn from a wide variety of Latin American and South East Asian as well as European countries, it is also the second-largest Spanish-speaking city in the world after Mexico City, and well ahead of Madrid. It is this combination of global city characteristics and a predominantly 'third world' population which leads Soja (1987) to characterize LA as 'the capital of the third world'. The new arrivals may be *in* the world city, but not socially part *of* it; effectively, they bring their own geographies and social networks with them or attempt to recreate them in situ in often novel and mixed ways.

In contrast, skilled international migrants are highly unlikely to be isolated by language. If they are coming to work in a professional or managerial capacity, they will be working alongside others from the host society and will require a command of the destination country's language. They are also likely to share strong elements of international middle-class culture or an occupational culture which transcends national boundaries just as the job market does. They will thus be more socially integrated into a *transnational culture*: 'Wherever they go, they find others who will interact with them in terms of specialized but collectively held understandings' (Hannertz, 1990, p. 244).

transnational culture

What is significant about these developments is that, although both groups co-exist within the same city, they occupy radically different positions and perform quite different functions. They overlap within the same space, but their social relations are different and unequal. Whereas the international business élite constitutes part of what has been termed the 'service class' (they service the needs of capital), personal service workers are part of what can be termed the 'servicing class': their job is to service the service class, often quite literally.

You will recall from Chapter 3 that Friedmann and Sassen argue that both groups – the international business élite and unskilled migrant labour – are part and parcel of the processes of economic restructuring which are reshaping global cities. According to Sassen (1991), the processes which are generating more professional and managerial jobs are also generating more personal service jobs. In this view the groups are also mutually interdependent in that each requires the existence of the other. But, while they may inhabit the same place, they inhabit very different social spaces within the city, and even if they work in the same place, they work in different parts of it, and/or at different times. The cleaners in the City of London's banks and office blocks, for example, may work in the same offices as the transnational élite but they rarely see one another and their social interaction is minimal. As the Industrial Strategy of the Labour-controlled Greater London Council commented in 1985:

London is not a single labour market, but a set of overlapping ones: wider in range for the better paid, for men and those without domestic responsibilities, narrow for manual workers, particularly women, and many of London's 314,000 black workers. There is no clearer example of the distance between them than in Tower Hamlets. There, council tower blocks stand facing the commercial skyscrapers of the City: the one representing one of the most depressed areas of Britain, the other sited in one of the richest square miles in the world. It is a contrast which has been seen before in London's past. It is also well known in the Third World. But lacking a modern Mayhew or a Charles Booth, it still today awaits some wider recognition.

(GLC, 1985, p. 8)

Yet, although different social groups inhabit different social worlds in major cities, these worlds are not isolated from one another and they may come into disruptive and often violent contact. Despite the efforts of some wealthy residents to segregate themselves in high-security residential compounds (in Los Angeles) or high-rise blocks (in New York), it is impossible to avoid all contact and the tensions implicit within overlapping social relations are ever-present. Nor will the attempt to raise the immigration drawbridge, and create what some observers have termed a 'fortress Europe' to keep out foreign migrants, necessarily solve the tensions within. Immigrants living in many major European cities in the 1980s and early 1990s have been subject to frequent racist attacks, fire-bombs and the like.

If immigration into global cities provides an example of peripheralization of the core, certain types of tourism provide an example of western dominance at the periphery. As Chapter 5 showed, the last twenty-five years have seen an enormous growth in international tourism. The development of cheap long-haul flights has reduced the time and money costs of long-distance travel and brought more and more of the world into the tourist net. In the process, mass tourism has pushed further afield and the frontier of European tourism has been rolled back into ever more remote areas: the Costa Brava to the Costa del Sol to Greece and Turkey, to California and Florida, Australia, Thailand, Malaysia and Hong Kong. Notions of near and far begin to break down when much of the 'Far East' is only 12–14 hours' flying-time from Western Europe. The world may well shrink as the unfamiliar becomes familiar, but, it has to be said, in rather odd ways. Mass tourism is an important aspect of globalization in its own right. But what is important in the context of unequal global integration is that most tourist destinations are characterized by a mix of affluent visitors from the major industrial economies and low-wage service labour. Paradoxically, in cities such as London, Paris, New York and Amsterdam, the tourist may also find themselves served by staff from less developed nations who have migrated to escape poverty at home. This disturbs any simple notions of what is near and what is far.

The role of the affluent tourist in global tourism is totally different from that of the low-paid worker, however. As Chapter 5 pointed out, the USA, West Germany, Japan and the UK currently generate almost half of total international tourist expenditure. This is changing as increasing numbers of tourists now come from the rapidly developing East Asian countries of Hong Kong, South Korea, Singapore and Taiwan. As these countries continue to develop, so their share of international tourism will increase. But the point remains that international tourism is an activity almost entirely dominated by the affluent, while the tourist industry is overwhelmingly serviced by low-waged workers.

The parallels with mass immigration from the poorer parts of the world to western cities are striking. Whereas immigration can be seen as the margins moving centre-stage, mass international tourism is an example of the centre colonizing the margins. Although the 'third world' accounts for only twenty per cent of tourist arrivals compared to sixty per cent in Europe, some less developed countries are experiencing rates of growth double those of industrial nations. The growth of tourism in South East Asia, where a 'service culture' exists, is particularly rapid.

In both cases, however, 'third world' labour ends up with the dirty work. The main difference between cleaning or washing-up in London or New York rather than in Hong Kong or Malaysia is that the relative level of pay is higher in the former than in the latter; the work, of course, is much the same. Again, however, the tourists and the room-cleaners and waitresses inhabit different worlds. There is little interaction between the tourists and the local population except in very restricted service roles. The locals are, to all intents and purposes, out of sight except where, in the case of markets and similar activities, they provide a colourful, local back-drop for the tourist, the raw material for holiday photographs. As Paul Theroux has suggested, many tourists do not want to get involved with local people and local life, except in a controlled way as participants in 'Greek evenings' and the like. They travel, as noted earlier, for the purpose of 'home plus' – Spain is home plus sunshine, Malaysia is home plus palm trees, and Africa is home plus elephants and lions. What is important is that they should have all the comforts of western life plus a degree of local exoticism (but not too much). If 'third world' immigrants bring their own cultural worlds with them to global cities, so western tourists often take theirs on holiday. Distances may have shrunk for tourists, but the social gap between tourists in their luxury enclaves and general living conditions for the local population is as great as ever.

Activity 5 If you have ever had a holiday abroad, try to list the different types of social interactions you had with local people. Were any of your interactions with local people outside their service role to you as a tourist?

Although tourism is actively encouraged in many developing countries as a source of foreign exchange and as a way of promoting economic growth and diversification, the domination of the tourist industry by western-owned airlines and hotel chains means that a large proportion of tourist revenues finds its way back to the developed nations. Although almost all the labour is local, except for hotel managers, wage-levels are generally low and prospects for career advancement are limited. Local people are faced by lifestyles and living standards which they may aspire to, but can rarely hope to emulate: as Chapter 5 noted, tourism can be said to promote 'Cadillac tastes in bicycle societies'. It can be argued, then, that just as some 'third world' countries have thrown off the yoke of colonialism, they have taken up the yoke of tourism.

Until recently western tourists seemed largely immune from the social problems which characterize both global cities and less developed countries. Generally, they live in privileged, almost hermetically sealed, environments. But the contrast between tourists, the western wealth and values which they represent, and the social and political conditions of tourist destinations is beginning to manifest itself in a number of threatening ways. Overseas tourists in Florida have been robbed and murdered in a number of attacks; tourists in Egypt have been subject to bomb attacks by Islamic fundamentalists as a way of putting pressure on the government; Kurds in Turkey have kidnapped foreign tourists. In other countries there are criticisms of the environmental damage and changes in local cultures wrought by tourism. As a consequence, the globalization of tourism is not one of unproblematic extension. As new areas are opened up for tourism, others are being closed down. Overseas tourism is no longer, if it ever was, socially innocent.

Summary of section 6.4

o   Spatial proximity is not the same as social proximity. People may work in the same place or live in the same area, yet be part of very different networks of global relations.

o   Global cities clearly exemplify this. They attract both large numbers of unskilled workers from former colonies and the 'third world' and a growing number of skilled international migrants. Their salaries and lifestyles are often worlds apart.

o   International tourism brings affluent visitors and service-workers into close contact, extending particular sets of social relations across the globe and creating new forms of social distance, despite the effective collapse of physical distance.

6.5   Conclusion

This chapter – and indeed much of this book – has been concerned with a world that in a broad sense is said to be shrinking in distance terms. It has also been concerned to show how the world has shrunk for some people more than others and that some places are perhaps further apart than hitherto. Put another way, the global processes that reach out across the world, drawing together distant locations in a network of social relationships, have *unevenness* built into them.

Parts of the world, we have suggested, are barely touched by the latest wave of global processes. Others are simply 'off the map' of globalization, missed out by the developments in telecommunications or transport or multinational investment. And for those places that are tied in, for many the experience of being 'on the map' of, say, global investment or tourism is to experience the inequality of global connections. Development in such instances is not solely to the benefit of one side and to the detriment of the other, however; the economic and cultural relationships stretched across the globe often involve both ends in complex, vulnerable relationships, where the outcome is the product of their respective powers. This is the stuff of uneven development.

Rather than a world in which everyone is moving in the same economic and cultural direction, that is, a world characterized by similarity rather than difference, we find unevenness, diversity and difference reproduced through global relationships. Perhaps the most telling example of this is the one you have just considered, of global cities and ever more remote tourist destinations, where the global relations lived by different groups of people cross one another in the same place, yet to all intents and purposes barely touch. In a profound sense this does not herald the end of geography, but rather its increased salience and complexity.

References

ALLEN, J. (1995) 'Global worlds' in Allen, J. and Massey, D. (eds).

ALLEN, J. and MASSEY, D. (eds) (1995) *Geographical Worlds*, London, Oxford University Press/The Open University (Volume 1 in this series).

BOURDIEU, P. (1986) *Distinction: A Social Critique of the Judgement of Taste*, London and New York, Routledge.

CARDOSO, E. H. (1993) 'North–South relations in the present context: a new dependency?' in Carnoy, M., Castells, M., Cohen, S. S. and Cardoso, E. H. (eds) *The Global Economy in the Information Age*, University Park, PA, The Pennsylvania State University Press.

CENTRE FOR CONTEMPORARY CULTURAL STUDIES (1982) *The Empire Strikes Back: Race and Racism in 70s Britain*, Centre for Contemporary Cultural Studies, University of Birmingham, London, Hutchinson.

GORDON, D. M. (1988) 'The global economy: new edifice or crumbling foundation?' in *New Left Review*, No. 168, pp. 24-64.

GREATER LONDON COUNCIL (1985) *London Industrial Strategy*, London, GLC.

HALL, S. (1991) 'The local and the global: globalization and ethnicity' in King, A. D. (ed.) *Culture, Globalization and the World System*, Basingstoke and London, Macmillan.

HALL, S. (1995) 'New cultures for old' in Massey, D. and Jess, P. (eds) *A Place in the World? Places, Culture and Globalization*, London, Oxford University Press/The Open University (Volume 4 in this series).

HANNERTZ, (1990) 'Cosmopolitans and locals in world culture', *Theory, Culture and Society*, Vol. 7, No. 2–3, pp. 237–51.

HARAWAY, D. (1990) 'A manifesto for Cyborgs: science, technology, and socialist feminism in the 1980s' in Nicholson, L. J. (ed.) *Feminism/Postmodernism*, New York and London, Routledge.

HOBSBAWM, E. J. (1987) *The Age of Empire 1875-1914*, London, Weidenfeld and Nicolson.

KENWOOD, A. and LOUGHEED, A. L. (1992) *The Growth of the International Economy 1820–1990*, London and New York, Routledge.

MASSEY, D. (1995) 'Imagining the world' in Allen, J. and Massey, D. (eds).

O'BRIEN, R. (1991) *Global Financial Integration: The End of Geography*, London, Pinter.

OHMAE, K. (1990) *The Borderless World: Power and Strategy in the Interlinked Economy*, London, Fontana.

PUGLIESE, E. C. (1993) 'Restructuring of the labour market and the role of Third World migration', *Society and Space*, Vol. 22, No. 5, pp. 513–22.

SAID, E. W. (1994) *Culture and Imperialism*, London, Vintage.

SASSEN, S. (1991) *The Global City: New York, London, Tokyo*, Princeton, NJ, Princeton University Press.

SOJA, E. (1987) *Postmodern Geographies*, London, Verso.

THEROUX, P. (1986) *Sunrise with Seamonsters*, Harmondsworth, Penguin.

UNITED NATIONS (1993) *World Investment Report*, New York, United Nations.

URRY, J. (1990) *The Tourist Gaze: Leisure and Travel in Contemporary Societies*, London, Sage.

Acknowledgements

Grateful acknowledgement is made to the following sources for permission to reproduce material in this volume:

Text

Chapter 1: *Reading A*: Harvey, D. (1989) 'The passage from modernity to postmodernity in contemporary culture', *The Condition of Postmodernity*, Basil Blackwell Ltd, Copyright © David Harvey 1989; *Reading B*: Reprinted from *Nature's Metropolis: Chicago and the Great West*, by William Cronon, by permission of the author and W. W. Norton & Company, Inc. Copyright © 1991 by William Cronon; **Chapter 2**: *Box 2.1*: Donaghu, M. T. and Barff, R. (1990) 'Nike just did it: international subcontracting and flexibility in athletic footwear production', *Regional Studies*, Vol. 24, No. 6, pp. 537–52, Regional Studies Association; *Box 2.2*: Beneria L. (1989) 'Subcontracting and employment dynamics in Mexico City', in Portes, A., Castells, M. and Benton, L. A. (eds) *The Informal Economy: Studies in Advanced and Less Developed Countries*, © 1989 The Johns Hopkins University Press. All rights reserved; *Reading A*: Pearson, R. and Mitter, S. (1993) 'Employment and working conditions of low-skilled information-processing workers in less developed countries', *International Labour Review*, Vol. 132, No. 1, © International Labour Organization 1993; *Reading B*: Lall, S. (1983) 'The rise of multinationals from the third world', *Third World Quarterly*, July 1983, © Third World Quarterly 1983; Hall, P. (1966) 'The metropolitan explosion', *The World Cities*, Weidenfeld and Nicolson, also reprinted by permission of the Peters Fraser & Dunlop Group Ltd, © Peter Hall 1966; **Chapter 3**: *Reading A*: Sassen, Saskia (1991), 'Overview', *The Global City*, Copyright © 1991 by Princeton University Press. Reprinted by permission of Princeton University Press; *Reading B*: Cross, M. and Waldinger, R. (1992) 'Migrants, minorities and the ethnic division of labor', in Fainstein, S. S., Gordon, I. and Harloe, M. (eds) *Divided Cities: New York and London in the Contemporary World*, Basil Blackwell Ltd, Copyright © Malcolm Cross and Roger Waldinger; *Reading C*: Davis, M. (1990) 'Fortress LA', from *City of Quartz: Excavating the Future in Los Angeles*, Verso/New Left Books, © Verso 1990; **Chapter 4**: Summers, L. (1992) 'Why the rich should pollute the poor', *The Guardian*, Friday 14 February 1992; *Reading A*: Jacobs, M. (1991) *The Green Economy: Environment, Sustainable Development and the Politics of the Future*, Pluto Press, Copyright © Michael Jacobs 1991; *Reading B*: Michalowski, R. J. and Kramer, R. C. (1987) 'The space between laws: the problem of corporate crime in a transnational context', *Social Problems*, Vol. 34, No. 1, pp. 34–53. Copyright © 1987 by the Society for the Study of Social Problems. Reprinted by permission; *Reading C*: Leonard, H. J. (1988) *Pollution and the Struggle for World Product: Multinational Corporations, Environment, and International Comparative Advantage*, Cambridge University Press; *Reading D*: George, S. (1992) *The Debt Boomerang: How Third World Debt Harms Us All*, Pluto Press, Copyright © 1992 Susan George; *Reading E*: Weale, A. (1992) *The New Politics of Pollution*, Manchester University Press, Copyright © Albert Weale 1992; **Chapter 5**: *Box 5.1*: Anfield, J.R. (1994) 'Sustainable tourism in the nature and national parks of Europe', *George Wright Forum*, Vol. II, No. 1, The George Wright Society; *Reading A*: Hannigan, K. (1993) *The Longer Term Effects of Subsidised Investment On Irish Tourism*, Conference Paper presented to the Islands and Small States Institute of the Foundation for International Studies, Malta, 18–20 November 1993;

Tables

Figures

Photographs

pp. 13, 245: Mansell Collection; *p. 31*: Copyright © Sky News 1992; *p. 57*: Courtesy NYLERIN; *p. 89*: Hyundai Corporation; *p. 105*: J. Allan Cash Ltd; *p. 120*: Courtesy S.G. Warburg Group plc: *p. 124*: © Gideon Mandel/Network Photographers; *pp. 144, 148*: Friends of the Earth; *p. 151*: Associated Press; *p. 169*: Julio Etchart/Reportage; *pp. 205, 206, 209*: Erlet Cater; *p. 210*: John Cater; *p. 211*: B. Chesser; *p. 241*: © A. Webb/Magnum.

Index

acceleration
  in the pace of life 20, 44, 236
  in production and
    consumption 46–7
acid rain 152, 181
Africa
  and foreign direct investment
    68, 89, 237
  and tourism 7
Afro-Caribbeans, in London 137,
  138
agglomeration, in global cities
  117, 120, 129
agriculture
  and the development of the
    railways 28–9
  and pollution 149, 156–7
  and tourism 203, 229–30
air pollution 6, 147, 149, 151–2,
  163
air transport
  airline route structures 190
  developments in 1, 21
  and environmental
    conservation 212
  and the growth in tourism 190
  shrinking costs and distances
    184
  to the United States 13
  and tourism in Ireland 219
  and tourism in less developed
    countries 200–1
Argentina
  industrialization 97
  overseas investments 98, 99,
    100
Asia
  immigrants to Britain from
    137, 138
  offshore data processing 93, 95
  US immigrants from 134,
    135–6
  see also East/South East Asia;
    individual countries
balance of world power, and the
  transport revolution 27
banks
  central banks 38
  employment of foreign
    nationals in 248
  and foreign exchange 39
  international debt and

transnational pollution 166–8,
  178–9
  merchant banks 37
  transnational 128, 130–1, 133
  and US dollars 39
barter economy 37, 49
Belize, and ecotourism 212,
  227–31
borderless world 61–2, 241–2
Brazil
  overseas investments 98, 99
  pollution 149
Britain
  financial markets and the
    telegraph 24–5
  location of nuclear industry
    163
  migration to 248
  see also London; United
    Kingdom
British Empire 12, 13, 30
  and 'English identity' 244, 245
  telegraph system 25–6
capital
  'footloose' 73
  turnover time of 20, 23, 35
capitalism
  and the development of the
    railways 28–9
  and industrial pollution 161–2
  and time–space compression
    20
car ownership 21
Caribbean
  immigrants from 134, 135, 136,
    137
  offshore data processing 93–4,
    95, 96
Central America *see* Latin America
Centre Parc concept 187–8
CFCs (chlorofluorocarbons)
  144–5, 147, 152–3, 158, 160
Channel Tunnel 191, 219
Chernobyl nuclear power plant,
  impact of explosion in
  Britain/Europe 155–6
cities
  decline of industrial 115
  film and television images of
    and geographical knowledge
    16–17

medieval 129
  and time–space convergence
    17–19
  United States social and racial
    divisions 43
  world's largest 108–9
  see also global cities
City of London, merchant banks
  36
class differentiation, and tourism
  185–6, 240
'Columbian Age' 27
communications technology
  equal access to 34
  and global cities 120
  and the global financial system
    36
  revolution 1, 3, 12, 16, 22–34
  satellite 32, 35, 39, 48–9
  see also telecommunications
    technology
conservation
  Annapurna Conservation Area
    Project 207, 222–6
  see also environment; pollution
corporate services, global cities as
  concentration of 114–15
cultural convergence 8
cultural relations, inequality of
  243–4, 245–6
culture, transnational 249
data processing, offshore 88, 93–6
debt boomerang, in less
  developed countries 168–9, 170,
  178–80
demonstration effect of tourism
  207–8
detraditionalization 32–3, 34
developing countries *see* less
  developed countries (LDCs)
differential shrinking 34
distanciated managerial
  organization 29
division of labour
  international 80
  spatial 29
Dromocratic Revolution 22–3
East/South East Asia
  and overseas investment 68, 69,
    237, 242, 245
  women workers in 86, 237
  see also individual countries